Tourism Social Science Series
Volume 14

Modern Mass Tourism

Tourism Social Science Series

Series Editor: **Jafar Jafari**
University of Wisconsin-Stout, USA, University of Algarve, Portugal
Tel (715) 232-2339; Fax (715) 232-3200; Email: jafari@uwstout.edu

Associate Editor (this volume): Graham Dann
Finnmark University College, Alta, Norway.

The books in this Tourism Social Science Series (TSSSeries) are intended to systematically and cumulatively contribute to the formation, embodiment, and advancement of knowledge in the field of tourism.

The TSSSeries' multidisciplinary framework and treatment of tourism includes application of theoretical, methodological, and substantive contributions from such fields as anthropology, business administration, ecology, economics, geography, history, hospitality, leisure, planning, political science, psychology, recreation, religion, sociology, transportation, etc., but it significantly favors state-of-the-art presentations, works featuring new directions, and especially the cross-fertilization of perspectives beyond each of these singular fields. While the development and production of this book series is fashioned after the successful model of *Annals of Tourism Research*, the TSSSeries further aspires to assure each theme a comprehensiveness possible only in book-length academic treatment. Each volume in the series is intended to deal with a particular aspect of this increasingly important subject, thus to play a definitive role in the enlarging and strengthening of the foundation of knowledge in the field of tourism, and consequently to expand the frontiers of knowledge into the new research and scholarship horizons ahead.

Published TSSSeries titles:

Tourism Social Science Series
Volume 14

Modern Mass Tourism

JULIO ARAMBERRI
Hoa Sen University, Vietnam

United Kingdom • North America • Japan
India • Malaysia • China

Emerald Group Publishing Limited
Howard House, Wagon Lane, Bingley BD16 1WA, UK

First edition 2010

British Library Cataloguing in Publication Data
A catalogue record for this book is available from the British Library

ISBN: 978-1-84855-238-8
ISSN: 1571-5043 (Series)

Emerald Group Publishing
Limited, Howard House,
Environmental Management
System has been certified by
ISOQAR to ISO 14001:2004
standards

Awarded in recognition of
Emerald's production
department's adherence to
quality systems and processes
when preparing scholarly
journals for print

INVESTOR IN PEOPLE

For Esperanza Saguar

Contents

Acknowledgments

I believe in intellectual craftsmanship and I try to practice it. Craftsmanship means high-quality work. I would not be the best judge of my own labor; therefore, I refrain from passing a verdict on whether this book passes muster. However, I would appreciate to be taken to the most demanding standards by others.

High-quality work means both solid knowledge of the basics and independent thinking. I say "solid knowledge of the basics" because it is often sorely missing in the specialized literature that comes to my attention. Our field brims with borrowed arguments that one suspects many authors would be unable to reproduce independently. They just accept at face value what some "reputable" lenders have concocted. Additionally, among tourism researchers, "independent thinking" often means reciting a few politically correct mantras they learned in kindergarten. I have strived to debunk some of them in the pages that follow.

Therefore, I do not have too many people to acknowledge. Most of the time, I just read, think, and write, refraining from participation in conferences and other public forums, or in cozier environments like academic clubs. I have not obtained—nor applied for—financial help from any institution to write this book.

Having a rather dyspeptic distance from the ambiguous comforts of academic life does not mean that I do not count some good friends or that I have not benefited from the help of some colleagues who contributed their valuable efforts to my own.

This book would not have seen the light of day without the encouragement and support of Jafar Jafari. Since we first met in 1983 at Nieborow Castle (Poland), he has showered me with undeserved attention and invaluable advice. Jafar warmly supported this book project from its inception and has waited for it over the long years I took to complete it. His patience at moments when I was about to throw in the towel proved decisive, especially at the time when I had to face that my backpack had been stolen with everything inside, including the computer where I had an advanced draft of the book as well as the backup drive. I do not know if Jafar has done himself a great favor with his support, but I am deeply indebted to him.

The thankless task of editing my drafts came to Graham Dann. It will be obvious to any reader that our idea of tourism puts us in opposite camps. Some of my differences with him are told aloud in one of the chapters. I know that he will reply forcefully and in kind in future "elsewhere" as it may be his wont and his right. No matter our conceptual distance, I could not have dreamed of a better editor. Graham excels at details as much as he does at the whole picture. He has made my non-native English sound not too disruptive; so if, in spite of having done his best to make me abide by the rules of style, flaws still exist, the buck stops solely with me. Even more important, Graham never tried to prompt me away from my path or to impose his own views in any way. Some will think that he just allowed me the length of rope I needed to hang myself. On my side, I rate his job as a paragon of intellectual honesty that is not easy to match.

In writing this book I have been rewarded with respectful deference on the part of Phil Handel, my department head at Drexel University. Some times I had the impression that Phil saw the repeated appearance of my protracted labors in my yearly performance reviews as a cover for other, less deserving tasks and that it might never reach safe harbor. If he thought so, he never showed it by action. On the other hand, he always accommodated my needs as much as Drexel University bylaws would allow. Other colleagues at Drexel were also extremely supportive and helpful.

The final stage of the book was reached while I was acting as dean at Hoa Sen University in Saigon (Vietnam). It was a challenging time in my old age. Let me thank Dr. Bui Trang Phuong, its president, for her unstinting support and her gentle understanding when I had to spare some measure of my managerial efforts to complete my manuscript. I also want to mention here Prof. Xie Yanjun, dean of the School of Tourism and Hospitality at DUFE (Dongbei University of Finance and Economics) in Dalian (China) and to Dr. Liang Chunmei, a DUFE lecturer. Over the last few years I have taught a number of courses at DUFE, and they both enriched my views with long discussions, eventual joint ventures, and extensive mahjong games.

Saigon, August 2010

Introduction

EXPLORING THE CONTINENT

Modern mass tourism (MMT)—such is the object of our quest. At first sight it might seem an incongruous quest. Today's travel and tourism come out as downright linked with modern times and mass societies. Why should it be necessary to highlight their obvious connection?

Often, though, face value does not provide a satisfactory grasp of facts. In this research, MMT stands as a name for just a historically specific set of phenomena that will be examined in detail later. For now, the moniker will be used in order to set it apart from other series of facts equally travel-related, but different in purpose and carried out by divergent means. Some of them can still be found today and can even be practiced by many people, but they are not MMT.

The obvious antonym for MMT is elite travel. It has been practiced in most societies for which there are historical records. The powerful, the rich, and the famous in many premodern societies had one or more of what are today known as second residences where they would travel in summer or occasionally at other times. Quite often they would engage in visiting friends and relatives (VFR) traveling to palaces and mansions of other nobility or gentry to pay visits, court patronage, or show respect. Hangzhou, as described by Marco Polo (IMS 2005), the Western Hills of Beijing (Headland 1909), and Pompeii (Steele 1994) are but some names of the many upscale resorts that flourished in the most powerful empires of ancient times. The Grand Tour, that rite of passage for the scions of the British gentry in the 17th–18th centuries, can also be included in this entry (Black 1992; Brodsky-Porges 1981; Towner 1985). Presently, elite tourism, of which celebrity travel is but its most public display, means travel to exclusive resorts, yachts, ranches, and villas. Definitely it is not the type of tourism undertaken by millions.

Mass travel itself is nothing new. As a matter of fact, humans have spent most of their time traveling since *homo sapiens* started roaming the face of the earth about half a million years ago. Most hunters and gatherers were nomads constantly on the move looking for resources or safe shelters. Relative to their numbers, those nomadic communities were definitely engaged in mass travel. However, there is common agreement that they cannot be considered tourists in the modern sense of the word. Moving around was a way of life, not a sporadic occurrence.

Mass travel indeed has taken place in many premodern historical contexts. Its best known modalities are pilgrimages to religious sites or to participate in religious festivals (Vukonić 1996; Rinschede 1992; Swatos and Tomasi 2002), but business travel, VFR, and sightseeing were also common. In India,

> vernacular forms of traveling (*Yatra*) and touring (*Ghumna*) had a vivid and vigorous presence in the country [...] whether it be in the form of religious tourism, namely *Tirtha* (pilgrimage), or secular travels such as *Milna* (visiting people) and *Dekhna* (sightseeing) (Singh 2004:35).

In Christian Europe, the Middle Ages saw Rome and Santiago de Compostela in Spain become focal centers for pilgrims, attracting endless flows that came from as far away as Russia. Along the way, they dynamized trade and disseminated religious art and secular culture. Many other Christian destinations drew considerable numbers of visitors, as Chaucer's Canterbury Tales attest. In the Islamic world, the *Hajj* (one of the Five Pillars of Islam) refers to the pilgrimage to Mecca, which adult Muslims, men and women, have to complete at least once in their lifetimes. Pilgrims have come to the holy sites of Islam for ages from the furthest limits of the Muslim world with economic and cultural effects similar to those in the Christian countries (Peters 1994; Wolfe 2001). Other Muslim sanctuaries and shrines also generated significant travel flows.

Mass religious travel was close to MMT in many respects. It mobilized large numbers of people, and requested a non-negligible amount of infrastructure (roads, inns, stables, caravans). Not all participants were equally moved by piety—in fact, shopping in markets and bazaars, buying relics (forerunners of souvenirs), and even finding some love for sale as today's sex tourists do, all motivated them. Areas around main temples (such as Senso-ji in Tokyo's Asakusa district) were the equivalent of malls and offered many kinds of services to the demanding tourist. However, religious tourism lacked most of the institutional infrastructure requested by

MMT. Furthermore, in spite of the great number of participants, it was usually assumed that it was an once-in-a-lifetime undertaking—not a cyclical pattern.

Closer to today, there have been other types of mass tourism. The totalitarian regimes of the 20th century found that travel smoothed and solidified the dictatorial rule they imposed on their subjects. Paid vacation time was indeed introduced by the freely elected French Popular Front government of 1936, but the Nazis in Germany and their Fascist counterparts in Italy and in Spain also knew how to offer the travel carrot to the masses. Organizations such as *Kraft durch Freude* (KdF, Strength through Joy) (Baranowski 2004, 2005; Spode 2009), *Dopolavoro* (After Work) (Liebscher 2005; Sgrazzutti and Beltrán 2005), and *Educación y Descanso* (Education and Rest) provided, among other things, recreation, cultural programs, and vacation colonies for the deserving laborer. "In 1933, only 18% of German industrial workers took a holiday at all; in 1934, 2.1 million took trips of a week or more to German destinations; in 1938, 7 million" (Overy 2004:323). KdF even initiated the production of the people's cars, known in Germany as *Volkswagen*. Stalin's USSR Constitution of 1936 proclaimed that

> [c]itizens of the U.S.S.R. have the right to rest and leisure. The right to rest and leisure is ensured by the reduction of the working day to seven hours for the overwhelming majority of the workers, the institution of annual vacations with full pay for workers and employees and the provision of a wide network of sanatoria, rest homes and clubs for the accommodation of the working people (article 119).

Like the Moscow metro, this proclamation was mostly a showcase for the regime, but good Stakhanovite workers and their families were presented with vacations usually organized by the trade unions or the *Komsomol*, the league of the communist youth. With the necessary adaptations, similar systems were introduced in the socialist bloc after World War Two (Allcock and Przecławski 1990).

In the 19th and 20th centuries, in nontotalitarian societies some types of vacation packages were provided to working families or to working class children by voluntary organizations, such as trade unions, political parties, and churches. Before the Nazi takeover, the German Social-Democratic Party had created its own civil society within the larger society through a network of self-help associations and clubs that provided rest and recreation to their members, from chorales to low-cost vacation packages. This type of mass tourism was called social tourism (Lanquar and Raynouard 1995; Lengkeek 2009; Minnaert et al 2009), and was a major form of vacation making in Europe until the 1960s.

Mass tourism clearly has an age-old genealogy. Therefore, if we want to refer to today's mass tourism and to understand why it is different from similar phenomena, we need to qualify it somehow. In my opinion, to distinguish between today's mass tourism as shaped since the 1950s and previous forms of mass travel, it is mandatory to prefix it with the adjective *modern*. Today's mass tourism is closely intertwined with *modernity*.

What do we understand by *modern* and *modernity*? In their most general meaning, Merriam-Webster (2002) defines them in a chronological way (something that extends from the past to recent times or something characteristic of the present). Both are thus rather blurry notions. In everyday parlance, though, these two words mean different things such as trendy, fashionable, well designed, and so on. In social research, when talking about modernity, one brings into play a more concrete value. Usually modernity is seen as a social form that organizes the production and distribution of goods and services, the creation and diffusion of knowledge, and the political decision-making through the combined agency of markets, science/technology (also known as R&D), and the rule of law. Basically, those institutions lean on individual decisions to buy, to research, or to vote. With a more conflicting name, modernity can also be called capitalism.

Modernity is a recent episode in human history. Although many aspects of this social compound (commerce, rational thinking, and local democracies) can be found here and there in the distant past, only recently did they coalesce to form a specific ensemble. The industrial revolution and the colonial expansion that followed the Napoleonic wars in Europe at the beginning of the 19th century are customarily seen as its initial landmarks. We can call this period classical capitalism, industry-based capitalism, Fordism, or Modernity 1.0 with a fashionable software-like moniker. In this first stage, modernity only developed in a limited number of countries on the North Atlantic rim, but capitalism extended to many regions of the globe often in a forcible and lopsided way through imperial expansion. Modernity 1.0 ended around World War Two and the subsequent process of decolonization with the expansion of mass production and consumption. One might call this stage with many different names such as late/post-/ mature/contemporary/whatever modernity. Modernity 2.0 is used here, although not exclusively, because univocal labels tend to be misleading.

At any rate, what we mean is that markets were—and remain—the key institution for the production and exchange of commodities (including labor) all along these two periods. Modernity 1.0 fell victim to its own crises as epitomized by the Big Depression after 1929 and its exclusionary dynamics—relatively low living standards, rigid class distinctions, and limited franchises at home; poverty and discrimination for the native colonial populations; and exclusion of some powerful nations (Germany and Japan) from the colonial windfall.

While the drama unfolded in Europe, Asia, and Africa, a second wave of modernity was in the offing. It involved the emergence of mass societies and can be called mature capitalism or Modernity 2.0. Modernity 2.0 is more inclusive than its older sister. Mass societies brought for a majority a consumption norm beyond strict reproduction (i.e., beyond the bare essentials of life—housing, food, clothing, energy, transportation); the emergence of the market as the central agency for the allocation of resources; an expansion of the middle classes; and the political franchise for most citizens.

The first modern market-based mass society or Modernity 2.0 appeared in the United States in the first two decades of the 20th century (Aramberri 1999). The United States enthusiastically pursued innovation in science and technology. After the 1929 economic crisis, it found in increasing mass consumption a counterweight to the overproduction drifts of classical capitalism. In spite of slavery and the later apartheid imposed on black Americans, the polity opened its borders to successive waves of migrants, above all Europeans fleeing from poverty and oppression in their native soil. By the end of the 19th century, the country was the world's rising star. From the 1950s onward, the American success story generated a second wave of capitalism (lately called globalization) that is still unfolding with different versions (Modernity 2.1, 2.2, 2.3, and even some Beta ones as one could name the successive economic "miracles" that took place in the second half of the 20th century).

Modernity 2.0 did not assert itself without much meandering. After 1917, Soviet Russia challenged the first wave of globalization with the creation of a centrally planned economy, state control of foreign trade, and abolition of most private property. After World War Two this model was forcibly imposed on the Soviet zone of influence in Eastern Europe, but also elicited genuine followers (China, Cuba, Vietnam). The model was supposed to challenge first, and substitute later the market-based mass societies, portrayed as the capitalist enemy. Most developing countries adopted some of its features—the public sector as growth engine, deep limits to private ownership, and import substitution to favor fast local industrialization.

The collapse of the Soviet Empire in the 1990s showed that this alternative model, to put it in today's fashionable lingo, was not sustainable. Most Eastern European nations abandoned it as soon as they obtained real independence after 1989. Russia and the new countries of central Asia are still coping with a legacy of backwardness. Other developing states, like China, India, and Vietnam, have started to dismantle their public sectors little by little and to expand property rights, allowing the market to become the key mechanism for the allocation of resources in spite of official claims to socialism and a still sizable public sector. Finally, those developing countries that copied some of the Soviet features in Latin America, Africa, the Middle East, and South Asia, and still remain faithful to them were left in a limbo of slow, if not negative, economic growth that they are painstakingly trying to leave behind.

Nazi Germany was another challenge to the expansion of market-based mass societies or Modernity 2.0. Its economic model took into consideration the strength of the German private sector and did not attempt to completely replace the market. However, with the acquiescence of the top echelons of the capitalist class and of many Germans, the Nazis subjected the economy to the needs of the war machine they built to alter the international scene to Germany's advantage (Overy 2004). The short duration of the regime does not allow picturing what its eventual evolution would have meant. However, its main goal was to alter the prewar international order and have Germany replace the old colonial empires. Germany's treatment of the occupied countries of Europe (not to mention the attempted total extermination of Jews, Gypsies, gays, and disabled people there and at home) leaves few doubts about how benign her behavior would have been had this goal been reached. Mass societies based on free markets and the rule of law were not exactly a priority for the aspiring German overlords. The Greater Asia Co-Prosperity Zone imposed by Japan on the Asian nations it occupied during World War Two veered in the same direction.

At the beginning of the 21st century, in spite of many political and cultural differences, becoming market-based economies and mass societies still seems the most attractive goal for most countries, perhaps the only possible one between development and backwardness, even in spite of the new economic crisis that started in 2008. With different institutional molds, varied degrees of growth and affluence, and different policies, many countries the world over have strived to create them. The mirroring of the American model started in Western Europe, Canada, Australia, New Zealand, and Japan in the immediate aftermath of World War Two. It was relayed by the transition to affluence in some countries of Europe

(Spain, Portugal, Ireland, Greece) and of East and Southeast Asia (South Korea, Taiwan, Singapore, Hong Kong, Thailand), Oceania (Australia and New Zealand), and even Latin America (Chile). As previously noted, China, Vietnam, and lately India have been converging toward the same pattern. Initially born in the West, the league of effective and aspiring mass societies includes nowadays many non-Western countries and cultures.

Why did the model become so successful? The short answer is that market-based mass societies deliver their promise and include more than any other known models (Micklethwait and Wooldridge 2000). They deliver economic growth, reducing poverty and increasing consumption for most social groups in the countries that adopt them. They deliver social diversification with an expansion of the middle classes and growing options in education, health, and leisure for most of their members. Some also have gradually included formerly excluded groups (women) and minorities (ethnic, regional, linguistic, disabled people) in the social contract and in the political franchise. All this comes, indeed, with many national and regional variations that adapt the expansion of mass societies to local needs and cultures. The revolution in information technologies (IT) of the last 20 years has globalized their appeal, at the same time that it has glocalized many of their features. Global media and the Internet have extended their allure to the whole world, thus contributing to what is the second greatest change in human history—the Neolithic Revolution of some 12,000 years ago being the first.

MMT has been a significant, though limited part, of this process. Market-based mass societies have dramatically increased leisure for their members, offering them, above all, paid vacation time. In spite of the neo-romantic view that hunters and gatherers had a more leisurely life (Fernández-Armesto 2001; Harlan 1992, 1998), the truth is that mass societies have extended life expectancy well beyond that of their forerunners thus giving a bigger chunk of leisure to their members, not to mention the much richer options the latter have when deciding how to use it. Additionally, they have increased disposable income (that part of earnings that remains after paying for basic living expenses). Indeed, if people do not have the money, chances are that they will not travel; but mass societies have generally put more cash in their members' pockets, henceforth creating, among other things, an impressive growth in MMT. Finally, they have created a global travel and tourism (T&T) industry that caters to increasingly diversified travel requests on a market base. Therefore, MMT is the specific way in which mass societies organize the travel behavior of their members. In relative and absolute terms, both domestic and international travel have grown exponentially since their inception. Over the last 60 years, T&T has become part and parcel of the lives of millions of consumers the world over.

At this point one cannot escape the ritual invocation of some macrodata. The World Travel and Tourism Council (WTTC), an umbrella agency for some of the major T&T firms in the world, estimated that in 2010 the T&T economy would account, directly and indirectly, for 9.2% of the world's gross domestic product (GDP) to a total of US$5.7 trillion (WTTC 2010). In 2009 the World Tourism Organization (UNWTO), an agency of the United Nations (UN), gave 880 million as the number of international arrivals throughout the world (UNWTO 2010a).

For the purposes of this introduction, the most significant figure, however, is that the volume of international arrivals has grown more than 30 times since 1950. Even more fitting, the estimation is that MMT will still double until 2020 (UNWTO 2005) when it will reach 1.6 billion. This impressive growth is noteworthy on three counts. First, it is contemporaneous with the expansion of mass societies. Second, it has grown at a very high speed, outpacing the growth rate of the world economy. Third, we have a statistic record of the whole past and foreseeable future of its international dimensions, which seldom happens with other subjects for social research.

Issues unfortunately are not so clear when it comes to the largest part of MMT—domestic tourism. Often neglected in scholarly research, domestic tourism accounts for, roughly, 81% of all tourist consumption (WTTC 2005:12), leaving only about one-fifth to international tourism. Unfortunately, information about domestic tourism is very limited, so the academic gaze mainly focuses on the international part. This view is so ingrained among scholars that the Research Committee of the International Sociological Association that deals with tourism (RC50) still calls itself Committee on International Tourism (ISA 2005). However, to possibly mark the change of times, ISA's RC50 devoted one of its recent sessions to domestic tourism (Jaipur 2009). As we will argue, this neglect affects the picture of MMT development in a way that shrinks our field of vision and blurs a comprehensive understanding of the subject.

Is it not a trifle flippant to identify the limited UNWTO statistical data on international tourism with MMT? In fact, international arrivals include travelers from countries that cannot be identified as mass societies. Furthermore, statistics lump leisure tourism with other categories that have existed in premodern times—for instance, business and deferential travel ("deferential" here means traveling with the goal to defer to human or divine instances. Among the former, VFR—visiting friends and relatives—is the most common, but one should include travel to comply with administrative or political duties as well. The latter includes religious tourism).

There is not much that can be done right now to improve the statistical dearth. Generalizations always need to be qualified, but in the field of tourism, at present, this task cannot be easily carried out given the fragmented and incomplete status of the main statistical databases. However, mining other sources such as Eurostat or the limited data accessible in some private sources provides a richer view of the phenomenon, in the expectation that one day it will be possible to count with better information. For the time being, however, one has to make do with what is available. Additionally, one can point to the fact that business and most deferential travel nowadays rely on the collaboration of the T&T industry and use services that are bought in the same markets as leisure travel. In this way, they share with the latter many features that allow one to call them MMT, even though they are not completely identical.

A final precision is necessary at this juncture. In addition to the foregoing qualification, the general discussion of MMT in this book, following the tacit assumption of most researchers, will have vacationing and leisure travel at the top of its interests. In fact, what definitely created MMT, turning it into a major social phenomenon and setting it apart from previous forms of travel in the historical record, is, above all, the extension of leisure to many millions of people made possible by the growth of market-based mass societies.

WHAT KIND OF SOCIOLOGY?

A sociological approach—such will be the main disciplinary thrust. With a twist to be explained momentarily, though. In this sense we will stray from the present mainstream of theoretical research. As will be argued in greater detail, current tourism research finds itself in a scissors crisis. "Scissors crisis" is used here as an analogy to what Trotsky underscored in Russia during the 1920s. Agrarian and industrial prices were running at such varying speeds that they threatened to inevitably pit the two pillars of Soviet power—the industrial proletariat and the peasantry (Carr 1958)—against each other. Likewise for tourism research. On one hand, most research deals with techniques to improve revenue management. Researchers that follow this path take for granted the existence of the market as the key agency in MMT and do not bother to ask any questions about its overall performance, legitimacy, social dynamics, and other theoretical frills.

On the other hand, a numerous cluster of people who discuss MMT usually accept a postmodern (*pomo*) paradigm to make sense of it. Often the notion is that *pomo* is just a sequential name for something that came after modernity so that it may be better defined or complemented. This would be a serious mistake (see Chapter 3). *Pomos* put forward a thorough critique of modernity and of MMT, though usually by stealth. It is intended to be a radical theory without seemingly radical consequences. Its followers seem quite content to point out the flaws of modernity stating that they should be righted without bothering to show how this can be done. Additionally, best practices, some privileged forms of tourism, definitions of "the tourist," or preferred sustainability policies are proposed regardless of their costs or of their eventual consumers—in fact, often *pomo* views would request the withering away of markets, though not spelling these consequences openly.

The first research strategy does not feel the need to investigate when and why MMT came about, and abstains from any discussion of its role in today's world and from its relations with other societal spheres. Its followers discuss subjects like the Chinese tourists' meal experience in Australia and its contribution to tourist satisfaction, or the creation of the original program for chicken grilling in a combi steamer, or determinants of solitary mature customers' dining out tendencies, or a feasibility study toward the inclusion of "White Coffee" in protected food appellation schemes (all of them subjects of papers presented at a conference attended by this author), though one can find similar examples in most conferences the world over. References to their authors are withdrawn so as not to single them out as though they were the sole perpetrators. All these issues may perhaps help economic efficiency, but they do not tell us much about how MMT exists and what is its true shape.

The second research strategy relinquishes analyzing the way in which markets behave and the manifold interactions of consumers and providers. What interests its devotees is how the latter should behave. Discussions of sustainability, for instance, often lead us to think that sustainable tourism can only be achieved by backpacking, community-based tourism (CBT), or propoor tourism. Or tourism development is discussed without a single reference to the avatars of the airline industry or to cruises. If one is consistent with this logic, one has to think that, in fact, places like Las Vegas, Orlando, Majorca, Venice, Macao, Hong Kong, and Bali, that is, the places where MMT really happens, are unsustainable even though, as of today, this would be difficult to substantiate. On the other hand, one can make a case that backpacking, CBT, or propoor tourism are but a marginal part of the global tourism system. For all their importance, those market segments only include a few million practitioners in the vast world of MMT. Do their fans really think that sustainability can only be achieved in this way? When one thinks that sustainability, more or less, means that stakeholders should have the last word on how a destination or a resort is managed (Sofield 2003), one should not be surprised that stockholders will think twice about investing their money there. However, one seldom finds such issues addressed.

The quick growth of tourism research that has been with us since the 1990s remains unabated, with these two traditions veering toward a rising mutual disinterest and an increasing divergence in methods and outlook. Sometimes, one wonders whether Dann (1996c) and Mackay (2005), writing on the semiotics of tourism, are in fact talking about the same thing, or whether MacCannell's (1992a, 1999a, 2001b) tourist and Plog's (2003) tourists happen to be the same entity, or whether that *perpetuum mobile* of a world where Urry (2000, 2003) and other mobilizers dwell has any resemblance with the mostly stable markets that populate many management papers published in some of the best known journals (two instances among hundreds being Papatheodorou 2001; Yang 2004). For this writer, both sides thus coincide in their lack of interest for the basic issues created by the ways of the world and of the markets. While the former veer toward pointless pragmatism, the latter glide into unbridled prescriptivism. Between business administration and *pomo* cultural studies, MMT's key issues get lost.

One should not be surprised that tourism research cannot find a shared paradigm, that is, a framework underlying most theories and the methodology accepted by a majority of researchers. Sociology could not dodge the predicament of most social research. With the exception of economics, where the market paradigm is accepted by most practitioners and the discussion revolves around which factors are responsible for the varying growth rates among different areas of the system (Aghion and Howitt 1998; Rodrik 1999; Romer 1989), or the different globalization strategies (Bhagwati 2004; Stiglitz 2002), or the future prospects of capitalism (Krugman 1994; Mankiw 2002), the situation is similar in other social sciences. In fact, it reveals the many difficulties the latter face in keeping apart facts and values, which is why they are often rightly labeled as "the weak social sciences." Unlike economics, which cannot escape some simple theorems imposed by scarcity, such as "you cannot forever consume more than you produce," its own brand of a Newtonian gravity law, most social sciences are not subject to similar strictures.

The surprise, though, lies elsewhere—in the happy state that accompanies the Mutually Accepted Disinterest (MAD) policies on each side. Economists listen to the tirades against consumerism or commoditization—which are indeed their own bread and butter—with the same interest that one hears the rainfall or the grass grow. Perhaps they know that, no matter how much their critics wail, consumerism and commoditization are here to stay and that their demise does not seem likely. They are paid back in their own tender when *pomo* cultural scholars ignore that tourism cannot be severed from the industry that makes it possible, thinking markets can be replaced at will—or at least ignored.

Was this not a sociological quest? Why pay so much attention to economics? At the risk of disappointing those who believe in strict boundaries to knowledge, sociology here is used to keep a distance not from this or that other social science; the word targets a methodological distinction. It looks for an inspiration alien to the pointillism of much of what today passes for economic research in the business schools tradition, *and* to the *emic* blindness of much anthropology, social psychology, and sociology. It harks back to the intuition of some Enlightenment masters (Hume, Smith, and, qualifiedly, Kant) that humans produce their lives under the constraints of scarcity imposed by their environments, both natural and social, and their previous reactions to them. One should add that they do so surrounded by the uncertainties of the future and the unforeseeable intrusions of randomness. Multidisciplinarity, unfortunately, is no answer to this predicament. If the sciences one turns to suffer from similar pointillism and *emic*-ness, we will only compound the problem. What is proposed here is not anything new, though, just a rejection of those two dead ends.

One cannot avoid feeling that—as the Rolling Stones put it—when too many colleagues are "tellin' me more and more/about some useless information/supposed to fire my imagination/[...] I can't get no satisfaction." On one side, one has little patience for our engineers. They indeed have a place in the food chain, but nothing appears less intellectually challenging than the new techniques to save five minutes in emplaning a load of air travelers, or the training models used in airline call centers, or the influence of ethnicity on evaluative criteria used when selecting a Japanese restaurant in the United States (again from the proceedings of the conference mentioned above), important as those issues may be. On the other hand, *pomo* researchers have fallen into unbridled generalities and a subsequent moralism where reiteration has replaced creativity.

What this book will strive to is a change in the conversation. Theoretical tourism research is dominated by various strands of thought with something in common—they loath modernity or think with varying degrees of intensity that it is expendable. This mind-frame leads them to propose explanatory models of the tourist system that are wanting in empirical research, preordained in their goals, and normative. I have already mentioned the last quality. Let's now turn to the other two.

The dominant cultural model of the tourist system offers an inverted vision of reality. Based on the statistics of international arrivals it ignores domestic tourism and its dynamics, neglects interregional tourism (taking place in the same continent), and highlights the importance of long haul, intercontinental or cross-cultural tourism. As will be argued, this is the polar opposite of what happens in the real world. The model also maintains that tourism is but another effect of the economic imbalance between the rich North and the poor South and that it produces and reproduces the cultural hegemony of the West over the rest of the world. It is the tourism-as-infection model.

However, the little that we know about tourist flows points to the opposite direction. Tourism started mostly within national frontiers, spilled over to the nearest borders and cultures, and has become cross-cultural in a very limited way. The development of MMT looks like a patchwork of oil stains growing around their outer limits and occasionally converging here and there. From a national inside it radiates toward the near outside and, much more limitedly, it touches the farthest reaches of its perimeter. In this way, one can better understand why tourism grows fast in some regions and why it lags behind in others. One can understand why it does not only travel—in relatively paltry amounts, by the way—from the rich North to the poor South. One can understand why East and Southeast Asia are growing—thanks mostly to Asian travel—or why sub-Saharan Africa and Latin America, lacking any regional growth engines (Lew 2000), are not moving. Following this template, the book will attempt to draft a different form of understanding the development of MMT and criticize most of the assumptions based on ignoring its economic dimensions. While culture is endlessly elastic, economics is not.

The lack of attention to facts in the prevailing mainstream explanations of MMT is not just an accident. It is preordained by their methodology. The diffusion of mass societies has coincided with an onslaught of critical views usually referred to as deconstructionism or postmodernism (*pomo*). This movement created a theoretical matrix based on the idea that our world—any world—is a cultural or social construction that reflects different power situations. In this way, achieving some degree of objectivity is an impossible dream. Objectivity only means self-legitimizing fact selection to reproduce the established social order and benefit its rulers whoever they may be—the West in the international arena, white men, males in the household, straights in the gender sphere, tourists in the pleasure periphery, and so on in many other power situations whose listing would be nearly endless.

Indeed, objectivity cannot be complete within the human purview. However, instead of devising ways to reduce value judgments to a marginal function and make room for facts, which is the goal of the modern scientific method, the *pomo* matrix maintains that it is possible to dispense with them—they have to be deconstructed as any other power relation. The deconstruction frenzy has affected everything. One can remember here Alan Sokal's hoax, when the author facetiously sent an article to *Social Text* concluding that "the content and methodology of postmodern science provide powerful intellectual support for the progressive political project," after stating a number of blatantly half-baked hypotheses of physics to this effect and saw the paper reach publication (Sokal 1996a, 1996b).

That everything reflects a power relation is a risky proposal. If taken seriously, deconstructionism could not avoid circularity. How can we state that all facts reflect power relations and, at the same time, maintain that some are exempt from this norm? In real life, however, *pomos* forget about this article of their faith, and accept that in fact some exceptions to the rule do exist as some facts (those that confirm their theoretical framework) accurately reflect the world, viz., are objective. Tourist behavior, for instance, is said to be a social construct made of unequal power situations; however, some forms of tourism (ecotourism, sustainable tourism, CBT, backpacking, in general everything that somehow seems to contradict the ways of the market or favor small developments) help to debunk the prevailing power structure, thus being more objective than others. The initial rejection of objectivity thus turns out into a convenience to select facts by researcher fiat. MMT is a contraption to reproduce the Western social order, we are told, so they feel entitled to forget the 1.1 billion Chinese domestic tourists counted in 2004 (CNTO 2005) who would do an awkward job as imperialist agents; or one can maintain against all evidence that today's prostitution in Southeast Asia is mainly a creation of Western sex tourists and/or that it is the World Bank's chosen development strategy for the zone (Bystrzanowski and Aramberri 2003).

Pomo fondness for probing the endless layers of meaning any phenomenon can yield comes at a steep price—naïve moralizing replaces facts. How this came about in the social sciences, including tourism research, can be deconstructed following how the *pomo* matrix went from a cavalier rejection of the scientific method (Lévi-Strauss) to the confusion between nonlegitimate power forms and legitimate rule (Foucault). Even though one is usually advised to kowtow to those and other grandees, no research can be taken seriously that does not question conventional wisdom. In this way we will have to stray from tourism research proper to roam into theoretical sociology. Taking this bend in the road seems mandatory if we want to understand where many conundrums of today's tourism research originate.

Calling upon sociology, broadly defined as above, to help us will no doubt seem somehow old fashioned. Social research is not immune to fashions. So, when one heard the Parisian *soixante-huitards* proclaim that liberation would come the day the last bureaucrat would be hanged with the last sociologist's guts, one could realize that the guild certainly had overstepped its limits. Like today's tourism engineers, many of its members had for too long celebrated the prevailing order of the world. This was not, however, the mind of its founders. As Talcott Parsons showed in his most interesting book (1937), sociology has since its inception been closely related to classical economics and to politics, trying to explain why and how the myriad of often conflicting individual decisions and interests generates some legitimate social order. Insofar as tourism research tries to understand the part of T&T in this process, it cannot do without the ambitions—and the strictures—provided by sociology in combination with economics and history, that is, by the sciences usually frowned upon by *pomo* cultural studies. Underlying the MAD policies, the real scissors crisis in tourism research (as in other weak social sciences) reflects the ongoing clash of methodologies—between sociology-*cum*-political-economy on one side and cultural studies on the other.

Accepting that tourism research is a battleground of paradigms is unsettling; therefore, people refrain from accepting the notion. Would not there be a way to escape it? Usually when it comes to the divergence of paradigms, multidisciplinarity is summoned to do the task. Jafari's rose-compass of disciplines in tourism research (2001) or the more recent attempts to introduce *mobilities* in this field (Coles et al 2005) are only provisory expedients to displace the conflict of views and disciplines, putting it back for a later time. Jafari's idea gives equal validity to any gaze on tourism. Religion and agriculture, for instance, should contribute to its study on an equal footing with economics or sociology. Coles, Duval, and Hall believe to have found a postdisciplinary way to shatter interparadigmatic conflicts by proposing to understand tourism as a continuum that would go from short shopping trips on one end to migrations on the other. However, neither solution really confronts the issue of which should be the relative weight of the different methods of study.

Our idea boils down to what might be seen as a loaded dice. Indeed, tourism research stands to benefit from many contributions from different fields or objects, cultural anthropology included. However, we cannot escape the final decision on whether our methodology has to be based on facts or on interpretation. At this juncture, this book decidedly veers toward the first. Instead of a house made with many different cards, it looks for structural firmness. It may veer in many directions; it may accept many sorts of contributions. However, when it comes to theory, it follows the rather deterministic approach based on the triad of sociology, economics, and history. Only they provide us with serious reasons why some given phenomena, T&T in our case, appeared at a given juncture in time and not at another and why we can understand their evolution—an asymmetry of the time vector usually unexplained by conventional wisdom in present-day cultural studies. Sociology thus understood seems the best antidote for the liberties that the *pomo* matrix takes with facts.

A PERSONAL JOURNEY

Introductions usually suffer our talking in the first person singular. Even though it will not add to or detract from the merits of the following argument, readers expect to have some inkling as why one has decided to stake a claim on their attention. *Noblesse oblige*. Therefore, I will explain the reasons that led me to write this book, using personal information only here, where it matters for a better understanding of the argument. Otherwise I would mislead the readers who have paid for something else than a book of memoirs.

T&T has had a substantial influence on my personal and intellectual evolution. Coming of age in Madrid, Spain, in the 1950s was not exactly coming of age in Samoa. General Franco's dictatorship cast a long authoritarian shadow in most areas of our lives with the solicitous help of the Roman Catholic Church. Among other forbidden fruits, sexual education was nonexistent. If, like me, you happened to come from a traditional family, had no sisters or other close female next of kin (other than mother), and attended a boys-only religious school, there was no easy way to make sense of the changes in your body and their accompanying drives, except for the conventional clerical wisdom that they were evil. The will to know was boundless, but the means to deflect it were unlimited—or nearly. Fellow students who spent their vacations on the Costa del Sol, one of the areas of the then bourgeoning tourist traffic to Spain, reported unexpected news. They had met The Swedish Girl. Tall, blonde, and seemingly impervious to guilt, The Swedish Girl had taught them a few things that steadied their teenager's restlessness and that they would quite gladly share with the rest of us. Unlike we were told, sex and happiness need not be mutually exclusive.

Beyond her easygoing sexual mores, many Spaniards also learned other lessons from The Swedish Girl and sundry fellow tourists (Pack 2004). In spite of the dictatorship's claims ("Spain is different" was the payoff in some of the regime's tourism promotion), freedom did not seem to be at the root of all social evils. In fact, far from creating havoc in their places of origin, the freer lifestyles of the foreigners seemed more cohesive and appealing than the ways of our parents. When our turn to go abroad finally came, this conclusion became obvious. France effectively became the nearest destination where one could buy any book, read papers of all kinds, meet with new people, and discuss new ideas. Whenever we had money, we would escape to Paris for a daily diet of two, three, even four movies that would never make it to Spain, spending the rest of our riches in the bookshops of the *Quartier Latin* and in some of the good nearby restaurants when there was some change left.

Other Spaniards were also traveling at this time. They were not tourists, but they were leaving the country in droves. They were migrating to France, Germany, Switzerland, the Netherlands, and Scandinavia—anywhere they could find a better future. They were Spanish, just like me, but, unlike me, luck had not smiled on them. They had been born to peasant families, mostly landless, and tilling the fields did not provide many opportunities for advancement. Most only had access to a modicum of formal education, not enough for skilled employment. Indeed, Spain was in the middle of an urbanization process that would have dislocated them no matter what, and Europe needed this infusion of labor for the postwar economic miracle. But, at the time, their tough fate seemed another reason to rebel. And rebel I did, parting ways with the faith of my forefathers. Another faith would replace it, though.

Marxism seemed to be the natural destination for those whose scorn for the dictatorship left no room for nuances—intellectuals though we were. Some of us chose a less traveled path and found in the far-left a new track— we naïvely then believed—untainted by Stalinist crimes and the treacherous compromises of the social democrats and the trade union bureaucracies. In the end, however, the world was more unyielding to our illusions than we ever expected. In June 1977, Spain had her first free elections since February

1936, and I was a candidate for a far-left grouping of sundry anti-Stalinist revolutionaries. Electoral campaigns are great teachers. Even more than in factories and campuses, you learned a lot in working-class shopping malls. Among the cacophony of the *Internationale* blaring from a screechy loudspeaker, one could see that even though sharing the same mother tongue, working-class women lived in a world different from our own. They did not talk about the impending revolution—they worried about paying their mortgages, getting contraceptives from social security, buying a dishwasher that would save time from their house chores, or about where to go for a vacation that would get them some deserved rest.

As soon as the election was over, I quit politics for good. One thing, though, I learned after those years—not to blame the world for the frustration of my overdone expectations. If reality followed lines that did not coincide with my own prescriptions, it were the latter, not the former, that had to be challenged. After all, those housewives were just taking a trail already blazed by many other people in mass societies, and for good reason. I promised to myself never to give in to new faiths.

My years with the Spanish National Tourist Agency (1984–96) would also help me to reorder my intellectual priorities. It was difficult to accept, for instance, that tourism was another form of imperialism (Nash 1996; Nash and Smith 1991) and/or a new kind of colonialism (Crick 1996; Karch and Dann 1981; Turner and Ash 1975)—the trendiest explanations at the time. Spain's main foreign markets were the United Kingdom and Germany. Great numbers of incoming tourists from those countries originated in working-class areas (the Midlands, the Ruhr Gebiet) and were industrial workers. How could it be maintained with a straight face that they were doing the work of Sir Cecil Rhodes, Sir Thomas Raffles, or Mr. Georges Clemenceau? In fact, the more this theoretical current tried to mirror the tenets of the dependency school, the shakier it looked.

Maybe with this in mind, the later postcolonial (*poco*) persuasion did not excite my imagination either. It abandoned the pretense that economic connections are the fabric that bonds tourism and imperialism. *Pocos* tread other paths. They translate the postulate of Western domination into a more ethereal notion of cultural hegemony. Tourism contributes to the reproduction of Western values, and therefore tourism reproduces Western imperialism. In fact, however, there is no logical sequence here. Western cultural hegemony is defined in such broad terms that it can catch anything in its fuzzy net. No attempt is usually made to define through reliable indicators what is meant by it. Unlike Western colonialism that had some, Western cultural hegemony has no defining features or boundaries.

Now and then, it is surmised that it is co-equal with something called the Judeo-Christian tradition. However, this sweeping social construct of Western hegemony as a single Judeo-Christian cultural universe is to be found nowhere. It ignores the many polytheistic beliefs in the West—Greek philosophy and classical Roman jurisprudence to start with; and it ignores the Enlightenment that grew in confrontation with the theocratic cosmos of Judaism and Christianity. Additionally, it forgets that within the framework of those two religions there were many subcultures that did not and still do not coincide in their tenets, even to the point of having provoked much effusion of blood in their wake. Judaism has been a fertile soil for contradictory theological schools, as Haskala, Kabala, Hasidism, and other names make us recall. In Christianity, if one has not enough with the Reformation, the disputes between Judaizers and Hellenists in the primitive Church, or between the adherents to the homoousios or the homoiousios schools on the doctrine of the Trinity (the former believed that Jesus of Nazareth was God; the latter thought that he just had the same nature as God), or the multiple theological persuasions that contested dogma until the Council of Nicea, all this should give us some pause. Often the only link that unites the Jewish and Christian cultural worlds and their subcultures is monotheism. But if this is what one wants to stress, why not include Islam in the package even at the risk of being charged with the unmentionable sin of Orientalism that Said (1979) leveled against all Western culture.

Other times the notion of the West covers an even wider ground. It stands for anything abhorred by the *poco* consensus. It may be the practice of slavery, even though it predates by far the very emergence of Western, that is, European nations; or that of patriarchy, though it surely existed much before Judaism or Christianity appeared on the face of the earth; or male supremacy, likewise. Were the *pocos* Procrustes himself and could they stretch his bed to the maximum, yet all of those theories and institutions would not find it possible to make space in it at the same time. In modern times, what we call Western tradition has been nothing else than at times a veritable battlefield of opposing intellectual and moral options (Buruma and Margalit 2004).

One wishes that *pocos* were more precise. What they fire at is, indeed, modernity itself. Unlike the Western tradition, modernity has a definite profile, and it is this profile that has been subject to attack by their peers over the last three decades. They often claim that sciences and technologies threaten sustainable development, that consumerism and markets commoditize human relations, and that the rule of law has been used to discriminate against some social categories such as women or minorities. Even though many such instances can be verified, the truth would be better served if they mentioned in the same breath that modernity has been able to address many of those problems with an alacrity not found in other social forms.

These critiques usually come from some groups, mostly academics, within the same societies where modernity has been widely accepted, and are mirrored with varying intensity in some areas of the world left behind by its deployment. For a great majority of people in actual and aspiring mass societies, however, Modernity 2.0 with all its paraphernalia, including MMT, retains its glitter and not by accident or wicked plot. It fires their imagination and their desire to attain a better life where they have increasing options—among other things about where to spend their vacations. It is surprising that so many academics find in it evidence of their submission to a foreign cultural yoke. Deep down, this viewpoint is a crooked reflection of the colonial purview. In the past, non-Western people were seen as children unable to organize themselves, wherefrom sprang the need to control, exploit, and govern them. Today, they seem equally childish, for they accept Western models and behavior without the glimmer of a doubt, wherefrom they need the right advice to exorcize their inner demons. Such crafty explanations could not prove their mettle in the past. They cannot do it today either. Underscoring the limits of our mainstream theories about tourism seems required to leave the room in which we are enclosed with one single toy. Perhaps a more accurate paradigm will emerge.

A TICKET TO RIDE

Let us quickly recap the structure of the book. Our starting point (Chapter 1) will be the scissors gap in today's tourism research and its already mentioned MAD conclusion—a majority of researchers occupy themselves with revenue management, taking for granted the modernity paradigm without further ado; a *pomo* minority considers it the root of all the problems that afflict today's societies. In between there is no space for fact-based general hypotheses. Such a predicament surely leads to a more disquieting condition—an increasing chasm between the ways in which MMT really develops and the academic schools that see it as "the enemy" (Harrison 2002:205). The outcome can be summarized in a quick conclusion: most tourism research has fallen prey to a sort of mannerism that lacks intellectual ambition and repeats by rote a few mantras that conform its conventional wisdom. The following chapters will discuss some of them.

So that we can understand how this state of affairs has come about, we need to approach the subject so widely attacked—modernity—as MMT is one of its scions. Does the structure of MMT warrant the unrelenting critiques it receives (Chapter 2)? In the negative, what is the intellectual matrix that inspires the critics and which are the reasons it proffers? An analysis of the postmodern matrix (a matrix is not a paradigm; it is at the same time more encompassing and less stringent) and of its downright rebuttal of modernity follows in Chapter 3.

In tourism research the *pomo* matrix has triggered many contributions. The best known, often quoted and seldom rightly understood, is the work of Dean MacCannell. His accidental approach to tourism (for him the tourist is but a metaphor for modern man [*sic*] in general, not a specific subject for analysis) concludes with a call to arms against every display of modernity and for a return to an idyllic Never-Never Land where corporations, industrialization, and even the division of labor will not exist (Chapter 4). Another group of theoreticians has proposed what here we call Liberation Theologies. These contributions do not have much in common with theology except the shared ambition of making sense of something that, by definition, human minds cannot grasp (the *Deus Absconditus* or Hidden God of Thomas Aquinas). However, they express a common hope (or despair, as in the case of Erik Cohen) that tourism may contribute to free humans from an essentially alienated condition. They find their reasons in the dissociation between the ordinary and the extraordinary modes of social life inspired by Victor Turner's work. From this starting point they delineate a gamut that runs from commonsensical functionalist explanations to others that are openly senseless (Chapter 5).

In the *pomo* vulgate Western cultural hegemony wreaks havoc everywhere it lands. Nothing could be more obvious and, at the same time, sickening than the vagaries of Western sex tourism. Along a line that seldom makes a difference between consensual prostitution and sex trafficking or child prostitution, some authors have discovered the Iron Laws of Sex Tourism. Chapter 6 deals with this outlandish discovery. Taking its cue from tourism and society in Japan, Chapter 7 examines a more ambitious challenge to Western cultural hegemony—the struggle of identities to affirm themselves.

Over the years Graham Dann has made a number of well-informed and interesting contributions to what he calls the "language of tourism." Chapter 8 recalls them and critically discusses some of his tenets pressing the need to travel from a uniform definition of the language of tourism to the recognition that there are different "languages of tourism" and that not all of them are equally contriving and/or misleading.

While Chapter 1 focused on the scissors crisis in tourism research, Chapter 9 draws on the strange league of interests elicited by some theoretical alternatives to MMT. This is the area where engineers in the business schools tradition, open critics of modernity, and international bureaucrats have sealed an ongoing peace treaty. When the wise people of the tribe reach such a wide compromise, sheep have reasons to worry. One or more will be sacrificed in the following banquet. The chapter raises some claims that will not be universally liked. Will the financial expenses that those wise people consider absolutely necessary to mitigate global warming be worth as much? On a more general note, the chapter also strays from conventional wisdom. Often critics of MMT surmise that they have found a cure for its alleged excesses in different forms called alternative tourism (backpacking, ecotourism, CBT, volunteer, propoor tourism, etc.), that is, in small development. Small may be beautiful. Will small development tourism be as profitable for its providers as MMT has been for many other destinations?

Is this all there is to a theoretical discussion of MMT? With more than 70 English-language journals (and counting), such a claim would be preposterous. If only 15 years ago one could follow (increasing hardship notwithstanding) most academic production in the field of tourism, today this would be a superhuman chore. The book thus discusses a selection of just some authors that, according to the writer, have made the most interesting contributions to the theory of tourism. A few others may have been involuntarily omitted. Others, finally, have been left aside on purpose. This applies to Urry's work that, in spite of its popularity, cannot stake a claim to much originality.

Urry's often-quoted *The Tourist Gaze* (1990) provided a timely Foucauldian promptuary for tourism academics in search of new horizons beyond—or complementary to—those opened by MacCannell and the contributors to Valene Smith's *Hosts and Guests* (1977). Other than the modifications to adapt tourism to the requirements of the new *episteme* (scientific field in Foucauldian lingo), Urry did not enrich much his master's voice. Tourists gaze at their objects in a socially constructed way. Their construed world reflects the views of the dominant or hegemonic groups in their societies. As tourists are mostly international and as affluent societies are the main generating markets, the tourist gaze is a synonym for the imposition of Western values and norms. Through this prism—allegedly objective, but in fact subservient to the needs of the dominant strata—tourists see what they want to see or, better, what they are told to look at.

Tourism is thus but another manifestation of the modern mythology that hides its rampant drive to domination in "objective" language, also known as scientific. From there, with some extra help from Bourdieu, Urry deconstructs this wily myth in many, often surprising ways. Among the latter, the reader discovers that the sense of sight has been unduly lionized by Western and bourgeois modernity. Evolutionary psychologists (Crawford and Krebs 2008), though, have made a convincing case that the primacy of sight was an excrescence of the evolutionary drive to adapt to environmental pressures, shared by humans and other predators such as lynxes or eagles (maybe the latter belong to the zoological bourgeoisie) and not so much by other animals (bats mostly rely on hearing; dogs on smell). This and other similar discoveries helped Urry to find the correct approach to modern gazers in a quote of Nancy Mitford placed at the frontispiece of his book: "The Barbarian of yesterday is the Tourist of today."

Urry, though, reserved a surprise to his followers. A few years later (2000), his social world became less constructed and more structured. "Structured" in this case is a malapropism, for this brand new world has no structure—it is endlessly mobile. One needs it, though, to stress that Urry's new world has an objective reality of its own and does not need the help of the former constructivist paraphernalia. The science of society formerly known as sociology has now become the science of mobilities—kinesiology one dared say except for fear of brand piracy. In unison with Zygmunt Bauman (2000, 2010), Urry claims that nothing ever stays equal to itself in this modern world of ours. Modernity is liquid; one thought to have heard similar themes in Heraclitus in ancient Greece and in Lady Murasaki's *Tale of Genji* written in 11th-century Japan, even though modernity had not been adumbrated yet. This oldest of notions, however, has recently created a feeding frenzy among academics in search of a comparative edge and, in keeping with our mobile times, has already spawned a number of books (Cwerner et al 2009; Lash and Urry 1987; Urry 2003, 2007), and at least one academic journal, appropriately christened as *Mobilities*. Time will say whether this restless kinesiology has a longer staying power than other fleeting fads.

The book ends with a short coda on the future of MMT. The conclusion follows from what has been previously maintained. There are no reasons to announce its demise as long as modernity continues to keep its promise to a growing number of people. The problem at the time of writing this introduction is that the former bright lights have dimmed, and the proviso might not work in the future. The ongoing economic crisis that started at the end of 2007 remains open-ended and will follow a still unwritten scenario. When Schumpeter completed his most popular work (1942), he was not overly optimistic about the future of capitalism and modernity. Far from being the product of divine Reason, modernity is but a social arrangement reached through much toil and many errors. It has improved the lives of countless people and still remains an aspiration for many more. MMT has been a modest contributor to these benefits. However, both of them may be but a fleeting moment in the long history of humankind. The Roman, the Spanish, the British, and the Soviet empires, the Tang and the Song dynasties, and many others have disappeared from history even though nobody would have bet on their demise at the times of their splendor. Modernity and MMT might not be spared a similar horizon.

A few final words of dubious comfort for those who will continue reading this book: When its concept was initially proposed for this book series, it went through the customary single blind review by two colleagues whose identity I ignore. One of them was openly bellicose, for the proposed book did not pay due respect to Bacon's *idola tribus* (the venerables of the academic tribe). S/he was not amused. How would the author dare? Off with his head. The other ardently supported a most creative contribution (his/her words) to shake tourism theory out of its slumber. I understand the rage that my contrarian, and often outspoken style aroused in the former, and I still blush when I recall the eulogy of the latter. It is not my task to award the Golden Apple that Eris, the Greek Goddess of Discord, threw on my path. I can only hope that readers will feel equally irked or gratified. One should always prefer a tryst with Eris to one with Indifference.

Chapter 1

The Scissors Crisis in Tourism Research

BETWEEN ENGINEERS AND GURUS

When it comes to discussing tourism, the prevailing mood is celebratory and clichéd. Usually, one provides mantra-like statistics that show how this modern social phenomenon has become the biggest temporary population movement of people in history. The World Tourism Organization (UNWTO) customarily reports yearly increases in the number of international arrivals all over the world and in the amount of money spent. Occasionally, clouds appear in the horizon. Since the turn of the 21st century, we have witnessed, among other things, global terrorist attacks (September 11, Bali, and others), two main international wars (Afghanistan and Iraq), two epidemic scares (SARS and swine flu), the big tsunami of 2004, and other minor events that created a less favorable environment for the development of travel and tourism. However, even such a difficult turn of the century only deterred tourism for short periods of time or otherwise redirected flows from some areas to others. Tourists are always ready to start a new journey, either at home or abroad. As *The Economist* summed it up at the beginning of 2003,

> [f]or wealthy Westerners, travel is now an addiction. […]
> Neither economic nor security threats can get them to kick
> the habit for anything but a very short period—especially if
> there are bargains to be had. [As soon as threats are over, JA]
> it will be time to pack a suitcase and be off again. Almost
> anywhere (2003).

Both the social habit of tourism and the industry that caters to it have proven to be quite resilient (Aramberri and Butler 2005).

Perhaps, the future will not be as rosy as UNWTO or WTTC (World Travel & Tourism Council, an umbrella institution for the biggest world tourism corporations) expect. Since 2007–2008 the economic crisis that impacted most economies and is still deeply felt has dented the apparently unrelenting ascent of tourism, domestic and international. *Coeteris paribus*, though, one can reasonably expect a still extended period of upswing, boosted by demographic colossi such as China and India joining the trend and developing their own demand for travel. There are undoubtedly many reasons to celebrate a growth that has significantly enhanced the options of tourists, and the income and living standards of service providers in many parts of the world.

When it comes to theoretical explanations and diagnoses, though, we leave Mardi Gras and enter Ash Wednesday. Let us state our views from the word "go". The present state of theory in tourism research is dismaying. Broadly speaking, academic production comes in two main shapes: *why* and *how to* research. At face value, one might think that this distribution overlaps the now classic post-Kuhnian division between basic and everyday science (Lakatos 1970). The first provides paradigms or solid theoretical constructions that shape a given field of knowledge for a long period of time—epoch-making discoveries that provide a general problematic and sharpen research hypotheses. Everyday science, on its side, gladly accepts the paradigm, works within its framework, and solves tiny or sizable problems, following a methodology of research programs (Kuhn 1996; Lakatos 1970) that strengthens the accepted theoretical framework. It formulates research goals and designs experiments. Everyday science is not a *why* type of knowledge, but it is not *how to* either. Genuine *how to* or applied science is better known under the name of engineering or technology.

The contention is that, on the one hand, contemporary tourism research contains plenty of engineering geared, in the tradition of business administration, to tinker with the tourism industry (including transportation, hospitality, food and beverages, entertainment, shopping, and other aspects of supply) and to improve its effectiveness, as well as much social engineering, following the tradition of international bureaucracies, in search of best practices to make the former friendlier and fairer to local providers. These two ways of approaching tourism usually work within the paradigm of modernity, or the present global capitalist economy (and its social and political formulas) stressing different ways to organize it better, either through more proficient technological or marketing mechanisms or through increased regulation of its workings. Most *how to* analyses belong to this category.

On the other hand, a significant amount of literature prefers to address *why* issues. It starts with a kind of Husserlian *epoché* (a purported technique that allows to reach the innermost substance or essence of things beyond their observable properties) that allows its practitioners to bracket the experiential world and then continues proffering generalities on the tourist, authenticity and the like, while getting away with it under general acclaim. Countless case studies and a few openly theoretical works are designed in such a way that things such as tour packages, airports, beaches, and sundry other attractions and facilities fade away from the horizon. Often times, the research concentrates again on a Husserlian eidetic unity of essences, claiming that the paradigm of modernity should be cast aside on account of its many theoretical shortcomings and its rather unpalatable practical consequences. Tourism is but another instance of the twisted arrangements created by a societal model that produces, reproduces, and sanctions the inequalities that lie at modernity's core between the haves and have-nots in the national and international arenas, between genders and between races, among ethnic groups and cultures. The postmodern (*pomo*) matrix contends that another world is possible or, at least, that consistent evidence shows that the paradigm of modernity does not live up to the standards proposed by its fans. Whether aware of their role or not, tourists and the industry play a major role in the extended reproduction of domination of the South by the North, or of the powerful over the power deprived.

In this way, the *why* approaches reflect only one of the possible ways of theorizing about modernity. The *why* mainstream thinks that the conjunction of science/technology, markets, and open societies that is usually known as modernity can certainly be exposed as a sham. This is nothing new. With a genealogy traceable to the origins of the developed societies of the North (which incidentally today also include Japan, South Korea, Taiwan, Australia, and New Zealand plus some other aspiring countries like Thailand or Chile), similar things have been maintained since the romantic critique of modernity at the beginning of the 19th century (Berlin 1999). The conflict between these two opposing views of our world has become sharper since industrialized societies took a new bend in the road to emerge as mass societies at the end of World War One and to undergo increasing globalization since the end of World War Two. This is the contemporary scissors crisis in tourism research (and in many other social sciences).

It is not surprising for tourism research to reproduce a conflict that has run through the social sciences for over two centuries, as it is a branch of them. The vexing part, though, is that in tourism research the pro-modernity tradition has vacated the field. While the *how tos* devote their energies to the improvement of known management techniques or to the formulation of endless lists of best practices for the industry and the markets, the *whys* have occupied the hegemonic position. As in Cold War times, both sides seem quite happy with an arrangement based on MAD or Mutually Accepted Disinterest, acknowledged and practiced by all parties. In this way, the *how to* tinkerers can proceed with their problem solving without feeling the need to justify their key assumptions and their actions. Models and equations are all they care about. One can read, for instance, a cavalier *how to* dismissal of Cohen's typologies of tourists (1972, 1979) because they are not based on empirical research (Sharpley 1994) and, at the same time, attempts at building a notion of the global tourist by means of psychographic categories with a dubious empirical base (Swarbrooke and Horner 1999:221–222). A genuine illustration of those standpoints may be found in the position of most contributors to the two best encyclopedias dealing with travel and tourism (Jafari 2000; Pizam 2005)

For their part, the cultural critics are allowed to occupy the heights of theory *tout court* (Eagleton 2003) and, with them, the higher moral ground without having to bother with the burden of proof. MacCannell (2001b), for instance, announced recently the incoming demise of tourism as we know it without showing any evidence other than his own expert opinion, that is, what wine tasters know as the nose. The majority, on their side, tries to haphazardly reconcile both. Even some of those one considers the most interesting authors in our field light, as the Spanish saying goes, a candle to God and another to the Devil. On weekdays, they observe the strictures of *The Cornell Hotel and Restaurant Administration Quarterly*; on holy days, they lament the ways of the world after the latest homily in any of the widely read professional journals. If readers happen to feel somehow skeptical of both, they will have to put up with both the churlish moral superiority of the *pomos* and the unbearable conceptual lightness of the engineering crowd.

Most non-*pomo* colleagues prefer to forget about the issue and so avoid the funky feeling I am expressing. Others think that the conflict of paradigms is but a transient phase that will be overcome as the discipline becomes a real science. Jafari, either alone (1987, 1990, 1994, 1997, 1998, 2001) or in good company (Jafari and Aaser 1988; Jafari and Ritchie 1981; Jafari and Pizam 1996), has proposed on different occasions an interesting and creative solution out of the quagmire. In his formulation, tourism research has grown through the successive cross-pollination of a number of hypotheses or "platforms," as he prefers to call them, which paved the way for the scientification of tourism research.

First was the Advocacy Platform. Advocates of tourism (mostly private corporations, public agencies, and industry associations) explained that mass tourism, above all in its economic dimensions, was an unqualified blessing for practitioners and providers. It was followed by its Hegelian antithesis—the

Cautionary Platform. Its followers indeed cautioned that, far from a blessing, tourism might be a curse. Not only did it not keep its promise of sustainable economic growth, but it also created a great number of additional social, cultural, and environmental problems that showed it as a not-so-palatable road to the well-being of provider communities (Hall 2007b).

Time, however, smoothed the rougher ends of these two initial platforms. Both in practice and in theory, tourism followed more meandering courses. Beyond mass tourism and its critics, it developed new alternative forms (baptized with many and quickly forgotten names such as controlled tourism, alternative tourism, community-centered tourism, nature-friendly tourism, ecotourism, and so on) and more precise theoretical discussions. This was the Adaptancy Platform.

Further down the road, and coinciding with increasing academic interest in the subject, the discussion of tourism has shown a more scientific approach—the Knowledge-Based Platform. In it, tourism is seen more as a system of structures and functions whose complexity exceeds the initial limited notions of good and bad impacts, with research leading us to a holistic treatment whose main goal is the formation of a scientific body of knowledge in tourism. This holistic dimension is captured in Jafari's encompassing definition of tourism research as "the study of man [*sic*] away from his/her usual habitat, of the touristic apparatus and networks, and of the ordinary (home) and nonordinary (touristic) worlds and their dialectic relationship" (Jafari 2001:32).

Recently, Jafari (2005) has added a fifth platform—the Public Interest Platform. More than a stage in theory, this latest remodeling reflects that the increasing pervasiveness of the Knowledge-Based Platform reverberates in many different social quarters increasing the interest of the public in matters touristic. For Jafari, crises such as terrorist actions and the effects of unexpected epidemics like SARS or the 2004 tsunami with their toll on the expansion of tourism have turned it into a subject of attention and public debate, which bodes well for a future of sustainable development.

On top of an analytical cluster, Jafari's idea of Platforms hints at some historical clues to the development of tourism. It somehow reads as a tourism research version of Moore's Law of computing power. Every 10 years or so, theories of tourism go through inner rearrangements that improve on the past, thus providing quick scientific growth. The Advocacy Platform developed in the 1960s, the Cautionary Platform in the 1970s; the adaptation of theory to the new forms of tourism happened in the 1980s, and the 1990s saw the growth of its scientification. The first decade of the 21st century has brought an upswing of public interest that, together with a better knowledge of the phenomenon, may provide more thorough theoretical discussions complete with a new positioning of tourism in the social pageantry. Tourism research—so runs the implied conclusion—is on its way to purge the conflicting and limited paradigms of the past, reaching a more harmonious state where scientific discussion will make them obsolete.

Suggestive as it is, Jafari's plastic notion of a succession of platforms in tourism research cannot dispel a few strange things that happened on the way to scientification. For instance, the date of the new research field provides it with an unexpected but welcome rejuvenation. It is not so sure, for instance, that academic reflection on tourism started in the 1960s. By that time, the *École Hôtelière de Lausanne* (Lausanne Hotel School) in Switzerland (founded in 1893) and Cornell's Hotel Department (founded in 1922 to evolve later into today's School of Hotel Administration) had been in business for a long period and were imitated the world over. Indeed, since their early days these two institutions were mostly examples of the *how to* approach, with their educational and research programs closely linked to the needs and avatars of the hospitality sector. Their outlook was defined rather narrowly and shunned other dimensions of tourism and its social dynamics (dynamics will be used here in preference to dialectics, as the latter is too loaded a concept). However, those are not compelling reasons to expunge them from the historical record. Delaying the birth of academic tourism research until it became adopted by a group of English-speaking anthropologists (Cohen 2004a; MacCannell 1999a; Smith 1989) years later only gives a plus of legitimacy to the claim so often touted by the *why* side that tourism can only be roundly understood ignoring or downgrading its economic and managerial aspects. Additionally, it has been argued lately that sociology and anthropology of tourism have a lengthier but mainly unrecorded, non-Anglophone tradition in Continental Europe (Dann and Parrinello 2009).

One can also take issue with Jafari's model at a second level. It is true that tourism research has become more complex and more detailed as mass tourism has followed a path of increasing fragmentation. In this sense, it seems accurate to talk of a growing conceptual sophistication and better understanding of many new trends beyond the mass model that lay at the base of the Advocacy Platform. However, that today we may know more about other dimensions of tourism does not mean that, at the same time, we may have reached a point where alternative paradigms are redundant. In this vein, the postulation that tourism research had already reached a Knowledge-Based Platform in the 1990s may be too optimistic, when one considers the fact that their tension has gone underground or remains ignored for a definitive solution to the conflict. It seems that our engineers, following a time-honored tradition of business schools, shirk from every possible theoretical confrontation, preferring to go about their day-to-day business and defer paradigmatic issues to other branches of economics. But one should not conclude that they might live within the *pomo* paradigm. Even if they tried hard, our *how to* pacifists would find impossible to honestly cohabit, for instance, with all the *pomo* white noise against commoditization. Without commodities, there is no market; without markets, those who ponder how to improve them would soon find themselves unemployed.

The hostilities between paradigms of modernity and postmodernity may be carried out in stealth, but they remain unabated nonetheless and no advantage will accrue from hiding them under the guise that both contribute to growth in knowledge. Growth in knowledge, whatever this may mean, is not a checking account whose increase will always remain unabated. This cunning device—that a given paper under review does not contribute to the growth of knowledge—may come in handy in double-blind reviews when one feels in sheer want of arguments for rejecting a manuscript when one does not like it, but in itself the concept does not mean much, especially in the social sciences. No device has been found yet that permits the measurement of this dimension. Additional data, however, do not build a science, in the same way as a pile of bricks is not a house. Sciences require hypotheses, theories, and paradigms, and these are much more difficult to come by and be shared in what is known as social and behavioral sciences than in the physical and biological ones. Precisely for this reason the former are more likely to become a battlefield of ongoing conflicts between two or more paradigms, and find themselves in the ongoing condition of warring states.

The conflict about fundamentals, as already noted, has been with us for a long while and will not go away just because we choose not to confront it. This predicament, though, should only discourage the fainthearted. What is really dismaying in the present state of the art is the phony pacific coexistence of paradigms. If the *pomos* have declared victory, it is not because of their merits; it is just because our engineers have as haughtily as willingly refrained from picking a fight. It is therefore not out of sympathy with the latter that this book has been written. If they are unwilling or unable to defend their claims to legitimacy, they deserve being looked down upon. Why should one put up with their many inconsistencies and their unwarranted self-righteousness? We need to go beyond the limitations of our contemporary engineers and gurus.

RULES OF ENGAGEMENT

Before starting the game, it seems proper to refer to some rules of engagement. Right after their first movement, *pomo*s usually pull a gambit, a dramatic move to disconcert their opponents. They like to remind us that anything we say or do is a social practice or a social construct. In this there is not much to object at face value. However, on closer inspection it is evident that the statement is a tautology. If, by definition, language and institutions have been created by human interaction, they must have been socially constructed somehow. Nevertheless, there is more in the *pomo* notion of constructivism than meets the eye. According to it, social constructs mirror and at the same time conceal power struggles. According to the definition of struggle one adopts, this may be right. Then we are told that those power struggles coalesce in the social sciences as universally valid statements while in reality they are nothing else than the reified version of the winning side. Though not so easy to concede, one might make a case for this. From there, however, the rest follows downhill. The winners, usually called modernity or the West or the North, are dangerous company never ready to relinquish their power. Fortunately for the downtrodden majority, *pomo*s have put together a morally superior cause. Those of us in the skeptical mode, however, would like some more consistency. If every theory is a social construct that mirrors and conceals power, there cannot be any special cases or cultural exceptions. *Pomo* notions are as socially constructed as any other and should give up preaching to the choir and provide more legitimate grounds for their claims than just an assertion of self-righteousness. We are thus thrown back to an age-old issue—value judgments. Can the social sciences live without them? We already know the *pomo* position—by no means. The issue, however, is a bit more complicated.

   The initial response of social scientists to the relations between facts and ethics surmised something similar. At the end of his Introduction to the *Catéchisme Positiviste* (Positivist Catechism), Comte's Priest answered a question posed by the Woman in the following way:

> [P]ositivist religion embraces in one stretch our three major ongoing constructions—philosophy, poetics and politics. But morals always impose their will, be it upon the development of our knowledge, the rise of our feelings or the course of our actions. Morals relentlessly lead our three-pronged search for Truth, Beauty and Goodness (1874:71). (Own translation here and elsewhere).

A few years later, in a discussion with other members of the *Société Française de Philosophie* (French Society of Philosophy) published in 1906, Durkheim maintained that morals "far from preventing us from evaluating reality give us the means by which we arrive at *reasoned* [italics in the original] evaluations" (1970:62). He would defend a similar viewpoint to the end of his life, the rather more cautious note sounded in his 1911 communication (on value judgments and judgments of reality) to that year's World Congress of Philosophy notwithstanding.

In Germany, against the grain, some social scientists defended a different position. Max Weber made the best and most painstakingly developed case. In 1904, the incoming editors (Werner Sombart, Edgar Jaffé, and Weber himself) of the *Archiv für Sozialwissenschaft und Sozialpolitik* (Archive for Social Science and Sociopolitics) opened the new period with an editorial written by him that squarely rejected the notion that empirical science should be subject to moral considerations or might supply them. "In our opinion, it can never be the task of an empirical science to provide binding norms and ideals from which directions for immediate practical activity can be derived" (1973:197). In spite of the lively resistance from other German academics, the so-called *Werturteilsstreit* (Value Judgment Dispute) that raged in the years before World War One wound up with a victory of the Weberian position. Social sciences, if they want to deserve their name, have to maintain scrupulous axiological neutrality. Values are for the politician, facts for the scientist. Social scientists do not have to decide between conflicting values. Their job is to elaborate a kind of cost–benefit analysis between conflicting courses of action. Additionally, they can warn decision makers of the foreseeable consequences of their choices, but nothing else. This is the stand Weber also took in his vulgarization of the issue in the lecture on *Wissenschaft als Beruf*, or Politics as Vocation (1973).

Unfortunately, even for Weber, the distinction is not so clear-cut. When he deals with how to construct a social science fit for an object that does not have the stability and regularity of natural phenomena, he has to eat some humble pie. Human action cannot be understood without taking into consideration meaning or the cultural significance of individual events. Analysis of causes can be appropriate for the physical sciences, but social action, in addition, has to be comprehended. Causality and meaning-accounting or *Verstehen* (comprehension) are equally necessary. Thus, when we deal with history, the expectation that it can be spontaneously described as it really happened (*wie es eigentlich gewesen ist* in Ranke's formulation) leaves us on the verge of a nervous breakdown for it is an impossible dream. In order to understand history and culture, the scientist must make an initial decision about which point of view will be used to comprehend them and will have to stick to it later. It is not possible to skip the selection of a vantage point that will make the explanation convincing.

How did Weber reconcile this *Verstehen* principle with his advocacy of value-free science; how unfettered subjectivity in the choice of vantage points to construct ideal types (1973:190) might serve as firm ground for the objectivity of the social sciences is still a matter for discussion. Here, however, we are not so much interested in the solution to the riddle as in pointing out the difficulties of discarding value judgments from the start. The attempts of the logical positivists to create a clear distinction between the context of discovery and the context of justification (Salmon 1970) have not fulfilled their initial promise. To some extent, both Popper's notion of objectivity as intersubjectivity (1980) and, even more, Kuhn's idea of scientific revolutions as paradigmatic changes within the scientific community (2001) cannot do away with the human factor. Kuhn especially veers toward a notion of science as sociology of the research community. Quite possibly the human mind cannot aspire to a vision of history and culture free of decisionism, thus becoming open to bias and value judgments. It has been argued that this predicament is also valid for the physical and biological sciences inasmuch as they are formulated by humans (Ziman 2000). *Pomos*, therefore, seem to have carried the day in this discussion. Or have they?

Once one has acknowledged the impossibility of completely objective knowledge, we still have crossroads ahead. One can concede defeat, even celebrate it. Or go across the difficulty. *Pomos* eagerly claim that there is a plurality of means to account for social reality, of which the intellect's logic is but one. This page, perhaps unbeknown to them, had already been written by Hegel in his critique of Kant. Logical or scientific reasoning provides only limited knowledge; it is reason, defined in many different ways after Hegel (national spirit, local culture, history, and so on), that offers vaster and more promising vistas. If we could only forget about the illusions of the limited scientific mind, a new world of meaning and actions would open before our eyes—a view one finds repeatedly expressed in today's tourism research.

Embodiment devotees, for instance, find that so far the tourist has lacked a body (Byrne Swain and Mommsen 2001a). It is not that tourists have a preternatural quality—it is only that researchers have chosen to depresentify them to concentrate on macrostructural dynamics. For researchers,

> [o]nly the pure mind, free from bodily and social subjectivity, is presented as having been at work when analyzing field experiences, which has taken place from the distance required

by the so-called scientific objectivity, from the position-in-general (Veijola and Jokinen 1994:149).

This distance ignores that every configuration is a local relationship of time, space, and power that manifests itself through the bodies of the people in the relation. As bodies are sexed, it also ignores that

> the economy of the male imaginary supports the Western symbolic order: scientific theories, among other visible works of imagination, are based on images, fantasies and identifications whose roots in male experience remain unconscious (Jokinen and Veijola 1997).

Reflecting on her own work among the Sani Yi in China, Swain stresses that

> [w]hile I did not use the rhetoric of "embodiment" at the time, I was acutely aware that my body and theirs made an enormous difference in how I conducted my research, what I was able to learn about Sani women tourism entrepreneurs, and how I might affect their live (2005).

It is not easy to understand how the economy of the male imaginary, which in the previous quote of Jokinen and Veijola seems valid for all men at all times, can solely be defined by the historically bounded Western symbolic order, but this is not the main point here. The new rhetoric of embodiment comes across as a dark looking glass. It is not easy to see what it is all about. One possibility is that our writings might read like this:

> the notion that if S then P was first put forward by Peregrine Testadiferro, a single, middle aged, metrosexual male, stocky and balding, beer guzzler, red meat lover, heavy smoker, Nascar fan, baseball expert. This notion obviously runs counter to the richer view proposed by Prof. Sally Mindtwister, a young, up-and-coming, lesbian teacher of mixed Anglo-Thai-Caribbean ancestry that loves vegetarian food, romantic evenings, jazz, long strolls on the beach and conference hopping.

According to the tastes of the reader, Testadiferro may be more of an attractive personality than Mindtwister—or the other way around. However, all this prattle would not easily add anything new to the arguments put forward by each party, though it would unnecessarily increase the number of words in our texts. Environmentalists could reasonably complain that this would be an invitation to increase woodcutting.

Let us take another example. In her otherwise hagiographic biography of Max Weber, Marianne Weber, his wife, makes a surprising revelation—that they had an unconsummated marriage (Weber 1975). If the fact were correct, would such an embodied information contribute anything to the understanding of his thesis on the Protestant ethic and capitalism; would his writings on the 1905 Russian Revolution or the methodology of the social sciences or the role of religion in social life have a different meaning under this light? No doubt some people will answer in the affirmative, but it is difficult to see the connection. Even if it existed, one would have to explain how those theses were adopted without loss of meaning by other people that followed on cue, though they possibly had a different approach to married sexuality than Max Weber apparently had.

There is another way to read the embodiment proposal that in fact seems closer to what their proponents intend. It is a new development of the slogan "the personal is the politic," to mean that any hypothesis or theorem that comes from the nonmale imaginary deserves a plus of credibility. In this way, not only are value judgments welcome in the formulation of theories—we can also know which ones deserve more kudos than others according to the bodies that voice them. That approach, however, takes the slippery slope, and one should not be surprised when it misfires, as it so often does.

Let us take an example outside the world of tourism research. It is because this type of embodiment that Justice Clarence Thomas could take over Thurgood Marshall's post in the US Supreme Court. Thomas had a short but well-documented record of conservative positions clearly beyond the mainstream of American society when President Bush Sr. picked him for the Supreme Court. However, being a black man who had pulled himself out of poverty drawing on his bootstraps, as his fans liked to say, moderates and liberals were clearly reluctant to challenge him. Finally, he was subject to an attack by another embodied person, Anita Hill, a black female professor of law who accused him of sexual harassment. The outcome of the episode is well known, and it is not my intention to discuss the story here. Let us, however, propose a counterfactual. Imagine that Thomas had been effectively derailed in his nomination because of the accusation and that the president had selected another body with the same characteristics of being black, self-made, and a paragon of ultraconservatism. Should he or she have gotten a pass? Should his/her ultraism be silenced as it effectively was all along the protracted and complex process of Thomas's confirmation? Sparing Thomas from the treatment meted out to Robert Bork a few years before just because of his body helped to secure his nomination under the pretense that it was a progress for African-Americans and, therefore, all Americans.

METAPHORS

Something similar can be said of the metaphor-as-theory crowd. Metaphors, Dann reminds us, are ubiquitous. "All sciences, both hard and soft, depend on arbitrary constructs" (2002:2) like absolute zero, perfect elasticity, perfect competition, Protestant ethics and so on. Furthermore, as our knowledge is always relative, metaphors "supply an understanding that goes beyond the literal (2002:2)". They allow us to compare two different things on the basis of some shared characteristics. If both the speaker and the listener understand the comparison, metaphors are the most powerful device to change attitudes, even though comparisons are not always easy, given the polysemic character of many metaphors. Under the paradigm of modernity, "the world was very much an ordered universe of rational decision taking, of equivalence and literal truth" (2002:5). However, because postmodernity dissolves divisions and clear-cut profiles, metaphors are needed more than ever to cope with a blurry reality that changes more quickly than ever before. If *the traveler* was the metaphor of modernity, conveying the sense of travel as education, of a path to moral growth, of the scientific and imperialist exploitation of unknown territories; *the tourist*, as defined by MacCannell and Urry, has become the paramount metaphor of the changing human condition in *pomo* times. If those two early formulations can be criticized, says Dann, it is only because they partially failed to see the warp speed of social change. The metaphor of the tourist also helps us to understand why research should

> yield to more flexible models that questioned the scientific and positivistic assumptions of the past. These new forms of theorizing were instead much looser, more relative and less deterministic in nature (2002:5).

Part of present-day research agrees with Dann's idea that, *pace* Husserl, our human minds cannot reach the deep nature of the *ding an sich* (the thing itself). This could be expected only from a divine mind that some people postulate exists out there. Our human mind, the one we are really conversant with, is limited by our senses and mental hardware and seems unable to grasp reality without the aid of practical tools, such as sensory data, metaphors, images, concepts or stereotypes—much maligned as the latter have recently been—and logical reasoning. All of them contribute to knowledge and, what is more important, to the survival of the species (Pinker 1997).

However, the assertion that they are all equally important for research does not necessarily follow. In fact, we apply them following a ranking that varies with the type of language or rhetoric we use in each case. When it comes to the sciences, hard or soft, the convention, the social construct, the protocol, or however we want to call it is that logical reasoning, controlled experiments, and repeated observations, together with critical probes of the mindframes or paradigms that help us to order and classify them, are a better way of knowing and changing the world out there than examples, parables, allegories, or, well, metaphors, no matter how useful the latter may be. The speed of social change may make it more difficult to achieve scientific evidence, but it does not alter the convention, the social construct, the protocol, or however we want to call it of scientific knowledge. In the same way, when making love, most of us will prefer the sensory experience of kissing the warm lips of our lover instead of a gem, even though on some occasions we may compare them to rubies.

To substitute metaphor for logical reasoning allows, no doubt, for more subjectivity, but it is difficult to understand how academic discussion, not to talk about everyday life, would be improved by this change. Discussing whether the tourist is a pilgrim, a flâneur, a homeless drunk, a prostitute, or any other of the metaphors collected by Dann (2002:5–6) may be an appropriate proposal to alleviate the boredom of faculty clubs with witty conversation, but not all metaphors are equally innocuous. When the Hutu media in Rwanda described the Tutsis as cockroaches or the Nazis portrayed the Jews as vermin, genocide followed suit at an even higher speed than social changes occur in our postmodern world. Indeed, one can say that under normal circumstances, metaphors will be used responsibly and that self-censorship will police their "good" and "bad" uses. Try, however, to tell politically correct bedtime stories to the *jihadis* that, like the Cabots of Massachusetts, speak only to God and receive from Allah itself (no disrespect meant; theologians will tell that God is beyond gender) direct orders to kill, among other infidels, those new crusaders that parade as tourists, or to President Bush Jr. when he pondered whether Jesus would go to war with Axis-of-Evil countries and, obviously, found a ready answer.

Let us confine metaphors, as much as possible, where they belong, that is, in religious, artistic, and esoteric languages. The wisdom of the centuries has often accepted it, for instance, talking through the voice of Kukai, the founder of the Japanese branch of Shingon Zen. "The Esoteric scriptures are so abstruse that their meaning cannot be conveyed except through art" (quoted in Bary et al 2002:172). Additionally, esoterism requires a higher authority than the normal person's mind, be it God itself or a qualified prophet, to interpret the scriptures—just the opposite of free thinking traditionally associated with the sciences. This runs counter to time-honored scientific traditions. Some metaphors are highly flammable, and there is long evidence that, even though the outcome will sometimes deceive our legitimate expectations, logical reasoning, not other well-meaning images, is still the best help to defuse them.

Granted, subjectivity or personal decisions about where and how to start our research projects, that is, value judgments, continually get in the way of objective knowledge and, whether we like it or not, will always accompany our inquiries. Granted, this is what makes our social constructs so prone to bias, manipulation, wishful thinking, or self-delusion. Granted, paradigms will always be in perpetual collision. All those, however, are so many reasons to make the life of metaphors miserable—not the other way around. What would one think if policemen decided to give free rein to felons because even their best efforts will never and for good stamp out crime? There is an additional reason to keep metaphors at arm's length. They easily pave the way for political pet causes to invade the domain of knowledge, and even the most *enragés* of our academic subjectivists bristle when told that their work is no better than promotional speech. We can do better. We can acknowledge the persistence of subjectivity and, at the same time, look for ways to defuse its less palatable aspects. In fact, that is what scientists have tried for ages.

The idea sounds encouraging. Does it have any truth value? Well, perhaps a quick metaphor—real-life courtroom dramas—may come in handy. It is difficult to be more biased than a prosecutor or a defense lawyer. Both are paid to prove that defendants are either crooked beyond repair or as pure as on the day they had left their mothers' womb. To this end, they will turn any number of gambits and innuendos, untold chicanery, and as many tricks as they may find in their books. Few things are so subjective, emotional, passionate, and what not as closing arguments are. Yes, but lawyers are not allowed to change statutory rules; judges conduct the trials, and accept or discard evidence according to established protocols; and the jury has to be convinced beyond a reasonable doubt. Do such dramatic performances find the truth? That is not the way to formulate the question, as it has no answer. Sometimes the final verdict will be shown to have been biased or wrong in the light of new evidence; the losing party will most of the time be persuaded of his/her innocence. However, society will usually be ready to live with the provisory security verdicts provide. Justice is messy, but we are ready to accept its messiness for it looks better than tossing a coin, reading tealeaves, tormenting the defendants for confession, or any other similar arrangement.

Academic or scientific research would be well served if it could count with similar tools to reduce uncertainty. It does. No long lists will be provided here. They have been elaborated with greater patience and more authority than I will ever wield (Ziman 2000). A few can be called back to mind though. First and foremost, scientific reasoning must be based on facts. Facts, indeed, are not easy to construct, and one could be accused of circularity in calling them up. However, there is a lot of compelling evidence in the social sciences (let alone the physical and biological ones where researchers have a more comfortable position) about many facts. One can document beyond reasonable doubt that Columbus took his first trip to America in 1492 CE. A number of independent sources will attest to it. It may be difficult to ascertain the causes that moved the Queen of Castile to support him. Even more difficult would be to probe into the private motives of the Admiral for even though we have letters and personal documents, we cannot be sure that they accurately reflect his meaning, his real feelings, or the world outside his mind. Historians, however, have developed over the centuries an arsenal of tools to probe the authenticity of some sources and discard others. Logicians have put forward a panoply of good defenses to avoid arbitrariness. The same can be said for most social sciences. Would one be better off if facts and protocols of evidence were cast aside and replaced by a number of deft metaphors?

Second, hypotheses have to be formulated at the proper level of generality. Attributing some features of a phenomenon to all possible subjects tends to be tricky. Labeling, for instance, as patriarchal all relations where men are in a position of supremacy over women has been shown to be a bad research strategy. Additionally, those general hypotheses should be enunciated in a way that is open to falsification, according to the Popperian canon. If one believes that colonialism is the cause of all evil in subject societies, one has to explain how this dependence came about with a less fuzzy concept than, for instance, Western cultural hegemony—a category usually applied to such different things as open or covered interventions in the affairs of some non-Western societies, as well as to the free options for Western consumer goods and lifestyles made by many non-Westerners. Such a formulation is not general. It is vague and cannot be disproved. Much as we may dislike Western cultural hegemony, as scientists and researchers we should avoid intruding in fields better covered by those professionals who have made preaching their call in life.

Third, established protocols of evidence should be respected in their integrity and special cases only sparingly accepted. Requesting cultural exceptions for some categories of individuals or facts just because they are said to be exceptional under some aspect, or because they are differently gendered or embodied or acculturated, cannot be granted—precisely on the argument that, barring some exceptional cases, all human beings have similar logical capacities. Indeed, their reasoning abilities can be perfected by formal education, and one can discuss why this latter good is so unequally distributed and/or propose measures to change the situation. But as a matter of principle, special cases have no merits in the logic of scientific discovery.

Finally, we have to be true to our own premises. We can discard our previous paradigms if we find them useless, but, as long as we accept them, we have to put up with their logical strictures. If one adopts a Marxian point of view, one cannot forget about the existence of social classes and their alleged struggle when facts do not fit in the template. Scientific research, including tourism research, is a special kind of rhetoric (Chapter 8); therefore, it counts with procedures to regulate its specific language and its inner conventions. Those rules of engagement should be made clear from the very beginning and should ideally be shared by all—otherwise we will be deafened by the noise. But once we have agreed on the rules of engagement, the legitimate thing to do is use them to disprove rival explanations, fighting to our wit's end while we are at it.

A FEW HEURISTIC GUIDELINES

Let us start with a modicum of determinism. My knowledge of the physical and biological worlds is even more limited than my acquaintance with that of human societies. Even so, one gathers that the world of living things, including humankind, seems to be dominated by evolution or, what amounts to the same, survival. The environment in which different types of organisms live sets specific boundaries to their probabilities of surviving as species. So species develop a number of strategies to cope with this unwelcome predicament. If not unlimited, those strategies show a surprising variety. Humans are not an exception in this panorama. As a species, they have been provided by evolution—that blind watchmaker, as Dawkins calls it (1987)—with a drive to copy ourselves, that is, to reproduce as much as the rest of living beings. Furthermore, it is not possible to say that their strategies for survival are better or more successful than those of other species. Most insects were thriving on planet Earth many eons before the appearance of hominids, and it is impossible to guess which species will survive longer in the many eons still to come. As of today, we have been unable to decipher in detail the strategies for survival adopted by many other species; therefore, we provisionally assume that ours are more sophisticated than theirs, but nobody can say so for sure.

At least, one can state that humans have been quite successful in their efforts to reproduce, being able to thrive in the most difficult environments of the planet and to grow to the, give or take, 9 billion people expected to occupy it around 2050. Their capacity, as a species, to match means and ends in an intelligent way, and to communicate and transfer findings to other fellow humans through evolving software and media, seems to have been quite instrumental to this end. Nevertheless, those skills have not dissolved the links to the rest of the biosphere. Human needs are still quite similar to those of other living beings, and no matter how successful the species, as individuals, we have a limited span of life that develops within predictable rhythms of birth, growth, and death. In the end, after a much longer life span, one can surmise that the species itself will suffer similar fortunes. In this evolutionary sense, the expectations of sustainable development will some time be defeated, though it is not easy to say when or how.

The management of scarce goods is key to human survival strategies. Humans or, more specifically, the many societies known to us have lived up to this day subject to some degree of scarcity that, even more ominously, has been unequally distributed over time. In our very special farm, some animals have been and still are more equal than others, irrespective of our comparable genetic endowment and skills for survival. Even those who entertain the notion that hunting and gathering were happy states from where the species was regrettably expelled by the Neolithic Revolution, industrialization, and, generally speaking, productivism (Clark 2007; Fernández-Armesto 2001, 2002; Harlan 1998) do not deny the deep differences existent even within primitive societies as to the production and enjoyment of resources. Be that as it may, production and distribution of goods has been and still is the main occupation of humans, and the rest of their endeavors revolve around them. Marx's formulation that "[i]t is not the consciousness of men that determines their existence, but their social existence that determines their consciousness" (Marx 1904:27) stresses this human predicament. It is, however, one of those tricky formulas that beguile with their apparent clarity.

Gripping and successful as the rule has been, its genealogy can be traced to an earlier generation of British philosophers, including Hume and Adam Smith, and is not particularly Marxist, inasmuch as it does not include any reference to the idea of class struggle. Most liberal economists did and still do subscribe to it. In this version, managing scarcity has given rise to a number of complex strategies—some of them easily traceable to their economic source; some others increasingly disconnected from it—called cultures and subcultures. Economic determinism, however, should not be construed as anything else than a heuristic principle or a guide to understanding—not as a universally valid solution. Accounting for its manifestations is no easy task—in fact, for some things such as artistic and literary works as well as some other events, often times it sounds like mission impossible. Take the example of Heian society in Japan. How, in the middle of an economy that can easily be defined as faintly developed (Sansom 1999), a court culture, admittedly limited to the tiniest upper crust of society—one-tenth of 1% of the 5 million Japanese people at the time (Morris 1994) seems a good estimate—did appear, where noble women enjoyed private property and a high degree of sexual freedom, while providing a number of gifted authors (Murasaki Shikibu and Sei Shonagon are but the two best known among a good dozen others) to the universal literary canon, remains for most of us a cipher still to be decoded.

Indeed the Marxian vulgate turned the subordination of the mind to the strictures of the environment into a couple of clusters of infra- and superstructures to which one could readily relate any and all social phenomena. Bourdieu for one did not hesitate in ascribing all symptoms of distinction (cultural capital and habitus) to the superstructure, and through this ruse assigned them to the class fractions and subfractions that populated his mindscape (1979). From a theoretical perspective, one would reasonably wish that things were so easy; when it comes to the actual enjoyment of life; however, one feels thankful that they are not.

However, the intricacies of applying the rule to real events should not encourage us to disregard the accent on focus. The *cui prodest* principle remains worthy both in thrillers and in social life. At least, it works better in its presence than in its absence. Cultural anthropology has often tried to reverse the order of explanation, as though food's only reason of being were to unleash thought. It wants to take us from the evolutionary zoo to the analyst's couch. From Douglas (2003), and even before, since Boas himself (1962), to Lévi-Strauss and Geertz (1973, 2000), and a long etcetera, it has become trendy to deny any meaningful role to economics in the deployment of human behavior. Cultural anthropologists have reminded us of the many uncharted areas in the deterministic position, often at the price of creating many more on their own. As we will attempt to show when analyzing some of their contributions to the study of tourism, cultural anthropologists have created huge amounts of delusion.

Similar reasons should help avoid the eclectic inducement. Eclectics have a serious problem—they make awful chefs. As even amateur Epicureans know, delicious food requires not only a number of right ingredients but also an order or protocol, that is, recipes and techniques that discriminate between flavors and textures. Eclecticism, however, acts as fusion cuisine at its worst, unable to tell the raw from the cooked, mixing honey with ashes in happy oblivion of proportions and with a slapdash concept of zest and zen. From the fact that ingredients have all a savor of their own, it does not follow that any mix of good flavors will be pleasant to the palate. This latter proviso seems more urgent as it has become a fad to insist that in pursuing any scientific endeavor, multidisciplinarity should be the rule. Not here. Following the deterministic standard, the science of managing scarcity, that is, economics, with the help of social history will govern much of what we have to say on tourism research. Cultural anthropology will be welcome but just as a sometimes-useful addition.

Accepting a modicum of modesty should be the second heuristic principle. Determinism requires a strong will not to delude ourselves. The subordination of culture to the way societies earn their own lives works in many unexpected ways. In fact, no human footprint can have complete control of its environment. There are always many forces, natural and social, with an impolite penchant to wreak havoc with our expectations. As mutual fund marketers ritually tell, past performance does not determine future profitability. Randomness often confounds our best expectations. Sometimes our own acts, in modifying the environment, contribute to change the ways in which it has been operated until now. Most of our actions have unexpected consequences. Sometimes, there are forces whose effect we cannot even notice at the time they appear. When this happens, our analytical tools go blunt, and retooling becomes mandatory.

Nowadays randomness is readily highlighted. Insisting on the futility of the best-planned human actions, Gray, for instance, strives to send us back to the evolutionary zoo from the analyst's couch (2002). One appreciates his reminder that it is difficult to discern any sense in human history and that, in the end, it may have none. However, precisely because humans participate in the blind evolutionary game as individuals and as species, they must infuse some sense to their actions and act with some consistency. When we express this idea in a stilted way, we usually say that our actions make history meaningful. It is but rhetoric posing as truth. Our actions are often contradictory and unleash a cascade of unexpected consequences. However, both in everyday life and when coping with changes in the environment, we usually follow rules to avoid the undesirable consequences that might stem from the lack of them.

Randomness always lies out there. Acknowledging its existence and untimely sallies serves as a cure to the thought that human history has been somehow preordained after some intelligent design, be it God's, reason's, history's, the Zeitgeist's (spirit of the times), the nation's, or any other of the myriad illusions that continually haunt us. No single strategy for survival, no single culture can boast of being the chosen one. Diamond (1997) has made a convincing case of the role of chance in the rise of Western culture in modern times. It just so happened that some disparate trends that had started to operate in unexpected ways in olden times all of a sudden came together, in response to changes in the environment of Western European societies, and provided an ensemble of techniques (science and technology, market economy, and the rule of law and democracy) that have proved quite powerful once adopted (Landes 1998). It might have happened elsewhere and in other times. For many centuries, China, because of her technological advances and her mastery of social organization, seemed poised for the role, and she might have become a model for all and sundry under the Tang or Ming dynasties (Ebrey 1999; Fernández-Armesto 2001; Gascoigne 2003). She did not.

Chance, however, does not mean that anything may happen. When new techniques and strategies increase our survival chances, we tend to stick with them. After they modify our environment, they cannot easily be dispensed with. One may lament that they once started their journeys, but Columbus and Vasco da Gama cannot be undone. The ensemble of techniques that we call modernity may one day run its course and be replaced by other, more efficient ones. Greening some of Marx's ideas, Desai has made a vibrant case for the demise of capitalism, though he readily admits the difficulty of foreseeing the precise way the process may follow (Desai 2002). Many of the main features of our present-day societies will surely wane the same as they waxed. In the meantime, however, acting consistently on the premise that tomorrow will probably be similar to today still seems a sensible strategy for survival.

Let us complete the holy heuristic Trimurti (Hindu Trinity of Brahma, the creator; Vishnu, the preserver; and Shiva, the destroyer). From what has been said, any judicious reader might quickly infer the next step—not much credit given here to multiculturalism. For those who bristle at the slightest hint that not all survival strategies or cultures are equally effective—they are not. As has been suggested, for many centuries China had an advantage over most other cultures. Leaving aside preferences about future lives and about definitions of happiness, if we confine ourselves to life in this sublunary world, even though we lack precise statistics, people in China seemed to live longer and in better conditions than their counterparts elsewhere, including those in the Mediterranean basin (Mote 2003). Ibn Battuta praised Chinese silk and pottery and remarked that hens in China were bigger than geese at home (1929). Whether Polo actually reached Cathay or just voiced hearsay, paper money, the Grand Canal between Beijing and Hangzhou, the use of coal or the efficiency of the imperial post that he so admired were not just figments of his imagination. Had they been members of a jury, most humans at the time would have chosen Chinese culture as clearly superior to any other.

Something similar happens with that complex social formation that we call modernity—that peculiar mixture of science/technology, markets, and the rule of law. Some may think that in thus defining modernity we lionize Western culture by stealth. That is their privilege. However, they will not find easy to show that Western culture and modernity are the same thing, nor that the former is something else than a geographical accident west of China and Asia. Some do think of Western culture as the Judeo-Christian continuum. However, the modern notion of science, usually called Western science, harks back to the new reading of Aristotle by Abu al-Walid ibn Ahmad ibn Rushd, known in Europe as Averroes, an Arab and a Muslim. Additionally, it does not easily tolerate religious guidance. The sweeping social construct of the Judeo-Christian culture also ignores the many nonmonotheist subcultures produced in the West or that the Enlightenment's notion of reason as nothing else than the individual's mind dispensed with divine intervention in human affairs as much as it had got rid of it in the cosmos at large. The biblical critique started by Renan, Loisy, and others is as much of a Western product as the religions themselves. It is difficult to see how all those things might belong to the same intellectual matrix. What about the rule of law and democracy? A sizeable chunk of the culture of the West or, better, some of its subcultures and political traditions has been sworn enemies of those two things. Hitler and Stalin were part of the West as much as Churchill and his fabled British milkman. In modern times, what we call Western tradition has been nothing else than, at times quite literally, a battlefield of opposing intellectual and moral options.

Unlike the Western tradition, modernity has a definite profile. It is this profile that has been subject to attack by *pomo* critics over the last three decades. They often see modern science and technology as threats to sustainable development, consumerism and markets commoditizing human relations, and the rule of law and democracy as often used to discriminate against social categories such as women or minorities. In the international arena, modernity helped to legitimize all types of imperialist enterprises and still does.

Curiously, these critiques usually come from some groups within the same societies where modernity has been taken for granted for over two centuries, not from the allegedly subject societies. Gray (2002, 2003), among many others, maintains that the present globalization wave creates all types of threats. With the help of the World Bank and the International Monetary Fund, the United States is trying to create one single type of capitalism the world over. This, he says, composes the illusions of the 19th century with that peculiar American idea that the United States has a universal mission. He even goes further back in time. This attempt to impose globalization is but another monotheistic illusion. Even science and technology, he maintains, contribute to this ill-conceived task. They are highly efficient, but there is an ongoing risk that their creations might be used lethally, for in the end nobody can control them. In fact, monotheistic globalization only deepens the crisis humankind faces.

Like the Marx Brothers going West, Gray throws more and more wood at the locomotive to keep it running—nostalgia for those wonderful times of hunters and gatherers living in harmony with nature, vanishing species because of the human footprint, catastrophic climate changes, new lethal epidemics, and increasingly cruel wars. He may be right, but there is no need to take him at face value. Malthus and his followers have spent the last 200 years arguing that none of the good things that have occurred since were possible. Some day they will be right, as indeed this world of ours will come to pass. However, when they try to precisely date the event, they have been as successful as Marxists were in predicting the downfall of capitalism or any of the some three thousand and four score prophecies that announced the end of the world for last year, or the year before, or the year before the year before (Daniels 1999; McIver 1999).

Modernity still goes on and not by accident or wicked plot. It still fires the imagination and desires of many people. When Chinese students started a number of protests in Tiananmen Square on April 1989, they did not seem so weary of Western-style freedom and their Goddess of Democracy suspiciously looked like the Statue of Liberty. Freedom knows no geographical boundaries and can be assimilated by most people under most circumstances. When the Soviet Empire collapsed, people in Eastern Europe showed a deeply felt penchant for implementing market reforms. When youngsters in South-East Asia spend their money, they want to buy brand commodities. Markets are the least bad method known to this day to distribute scarce goods and services; brands help customers to orient themselves in the market. Allow me some embodiment for once. Even though I am a senior citizen now, I have still spent the longest part of my life under a dictatorship. General Franco had won the Spanish civil war a couple of years before I was born and did not die until I was 34. During those years, increasing numbers of Spaniards longed for the day when we would have a modern economy and a Western-style pluralistic regime. Even those who, like me, were on the Marxist far left and longed for socialism would define it in very similar terms to Jeffersonian democracy perfected by the magic wand of equality. All of the above, and many others, thought that modernity offers more options to more people than any other cultural combination known until now. Were they—were we—so wrong? I still cannot respond in the affirmative.

One understands that some colleagues may share in what Swain has called "Group Colonalization Guilt." In fact, lots of crimes have been committed under the banner of modernity. She blames herself for "what I looked, sounded and acted like. I embody many signs of imperialism I could not conceal: I'm White for a start" (2005:33). Everybody is entitled to his/her feelings. Only when those feelings are turned into public policy does the issue become foggy. There are no compelling reasons to adopt this new form of guilt by association. That somebody may be branded as an imperialist just because he or she is white, just because he or she is heterosexual, or just because he or she was conceived in the wrong geographical area defies all logic—it is biology as destiny, mirroring word by word what authentic imperialists had to say in favor of their domination. Dominated peoples were also collectively disparaged by association. This reasoning also went hand in glove with the practices of Nazism, Stalinism, Maoism, and Pol Potism, all of them sworn enemies of modernity. A mere look at some recent fiction (Gao 2002; Ha 2004) and nonfiction (Chang 1991; Overy 2004) written about these regimes shows how this is one of their main crimes. Fortunately, guilt by association has not easily entered democratic traditions, this being one of the reasons why so many people that do not enjoy their benefits dream of them.

*Pomo*s prefer to side with the angels (Marwick 1998). They do not condone any of the above, they say, but immediately add that there is a better world between those totalitarian societies and a modernity based on repressive normalization. As Kant would say, their 20 thalers look exactly like legal tender but in existence. One is never told where that *pomo* region lies or how we can reach it. However, our modern polities have shown surprising adaptive skills to integrate most of the claims put forward by social groups that were, in an uneven way, left out of the mainstream. There is no reason to think that those skills have been already exhausted. Such are the intellectual bearings that will help in constructing and explaining the ideal types of modernity and modern mass tourism.

A final proviso to go back to tourism research. For all the previous reasons, we should be very modest about our own field. Whether it is or is not the main industry on the face of the Earth, tourism does not have any cathartic features. It is an important part of life in mass societies and in the present capitalist system. Just that. It offers to more and more people some options to enjoy themselves, thus helping them to pursue "constructed" happiness. For many of the providers for whom the pursuit of happiness is also an important goal, it offers new venues for improvement. Many other local providers, and to some extent their societies, also benefit from tourism, though in varying, unequal, and disputed ways.

Being international, one element of tourism creates interactions between members of different cultures. Even at home, domestic tourists, usually more urbanized and affluent than local providers, often contrast with the latter's ways of life. Undoubtedly, in all its forms, tourism increases cultural exchanges. For better or worse, however, those are not the only ones, nor the most decisive. Globalization, for instance, is not mainly due to tourism. It travels at a quicker speed and with its own means. Economic forces, political processes, the mass media, and modern forms of communication (from pictures to TV to the Internet) all contribute much more to the well-being or to the poverty of nations. Even where international tourism is nearly nonexistent, radios, satellite television, and even the Internet accessed in communal computers act in many unforeseeable ways on the lives of people. The proverbial grain of salt about our own importance shows once more its need, in tourism research as in most other environments.

Chapter 2

The Global Tourism System

INTRODUCTION

It is surprising how little we know about the real structure of the global tourism system. Usually, we accept that there is out there something like a system. We also take for granted that this something is quite large. To show how large, we usually point to the UNWTO databases. Given the dearth of other sources, its statistics, which record an already long time series of international arrivals and receipts, incline us to make the error of taking these parts for the whole. Parsed in detail, however, those numbers of international tourists do not offer much to support long-winded claims that the tourism industry is *the* global industry *par excellence* and that MMT is one of the main engines of globalization.

Neither the flows of international tourists nor the amount of international receipts allows us to draw such a conclusion. International arrivals in 2009 were 880 million. With the world population at 6.7 billion, about one person in eight (12% of the total) took an international trip. If one reckons that some of those persons did travel more than once that year, and that many of them crossed different borders in one single trip, the proportion ratchets an additional notch down. If the expectation of nearly doubling this number by 2020 is fulfilled—which seems likely—the percentage of international tourists will still reach around 20% of a 7 billion world population or one person in five. In 2008 international tourism receipts reached US$944 billion, less than 2% of that year's world GDP. With such foundations, it is difficult to argue that international tourism is indeed "the" global industry if it can ever be deemed to be just one (Leiper 2007).

Intuitively we know that the total number is much higher once we add domestic tourism, and that the money generated by both international and domestic trips well exceeds the foregoing amount. However, it has become an ingrained habit to consider international tourism as a synonym for the whole. There would be no space in one book to quote all the instances when this trope has been used. Just one example. As previously mentioned, the

International Sociological Association has only one research committee dealing with tourism, and it appears under the label *International Tourism* (ISA 2006). The committee that occupies itself with it has only recently (Jaipur 2009) started to delve into domestic tourism. Until then it seemed that such tourism was bereft of interest, or did not unleash any significant dynamics. Tourism research pays a high price for this metonymic illusion.

Some of its consequences are just trivial; others quite serious. Let us look at some of the former. As soon as one talks about international tourism, nation-states become the key players, and their place in the ranking of international destinations becomes an arena for the passions of national prestige measured by the number of international arrivals. The efforts of some countries to inflate the numbers of their arrivals are well known. In the 1960s and 1970s, Spain, then under General Franco's dictatorship, openly paraded the number of foreign arrivals as a proxy for the political legitimacy it was lacking (Pack 2004). After the country found a new democratic structure, international tourists were displayed like so many approval ratings for the new course, and the desire to inflate the numbers lingered on. France is another case in point. Around 1989, in a tribute to the bicentennial of its revolution, it decided to refurbish its tourism statistics, and, all of a sudden, the formerly sagging numbers surpassed those of its competitors in one fell swoop. Once France got a 30% head start over the next runner, it became the number one destination in the world. It has remained there ever since.

It does not matter that prestigious numbers of international arrivals are often accompanied by a relative decline in receipts. According to UNWTO (2006b), in 2004 France reached 71.4 million international arrivals and earned $40.8 billion in receipts, with an average expenditure of $543 per tourist. For Spain, the respective amounts were 52.4 million international arrivals, $45.2 billion in receipts, and $863 in expenditure per tourist. When compared with the rest of the top 10 tourism money earners (Table 1), France was the destination that made less money per head of tourist. Spain ranked number 7.

Therefore, if instead of ranking international arrivals, one orders destinations by their economic returns (defined in terms of dollars spent by head of tourist), the two most successful countries in terms of arrivals are easily surpassed by destinations as varied as the United States, Australia, Italy, Cambodia, Denmark, Panama, India, and many other supposedly lesser powers. Although they are the most salient examples of the comedy, Spain and France are not the only instances of such behavior.

Other aspects of the metonymic illusion are less satisfying. Focusing on international data to define global tourism often leads to view it as one of the

Table 1. Expenditures per Arrival: Top Destinations (2004)

	Receipts (US$ Billion)	Arrivals (Million)	US$ Per Arrival
Australia	13.6	4.7	2,894
USA	74.5	46.1	1,616
Germany	27.7	20.1	1,378
UK	28.2	27.8	1,014
Italy	35.7	37.1	962
Turkey	15.9	16.8	946
Spain	45.2	52.4	863
Austria	15.3	19.4	789
China	25.7	41.8	615
France	40.8	75.1	543

Source: Author's elaboration of UNWTO (2006d).

forces, perhaps the main one, behind globalization, only to charge it with all the latter's allegedly noxious effects. Most current tourism literature views globalization along the template found in the best-known encyclopedia on the subject (Jafari 2000). Globalization, one is told there, marks a new stage in the development of capitalism, later identified with neoliberalism. This process affects every component of economic activity and rests on the diminished economic power of nation-states and on the ascent of the multinational firm. Globalization has influenced tourism deeply. While travel has for a long time seen global demand (people have crisscrossed the Earth since time immemorial), new developments have recently unleashed a global supply of tourism services provided by multinational firms, from airlines and tour operators to hotel chains and fast food companies. Together with the liberalization of economic policies and loose controls on foreign exchange, the new supply chain wrests most economic benefits from local communities through high leakages and low multipliers. For their part, entrepreneurs in developing countries lack the wherewithal to afford the industry's high entry costs and avoid such unseemly consequences (Wilkinson 2000). This narrative has met with wide uncritical acceptance in our field (Boniface and Cooper 2005; Hall 2006; Harrison 2001; Nash 1996; Oakes 1995, 1996).

The storyline is not easily sustainable, though. There may be a number of multinational firms in the world of tourism, but small and medium enterprises outrank them by far (Smith 2005), which shows that the former do not hold sway over the system and that entry costs may not be as prohibitive for locals as so many evidence-challenged researchers anticipate. More importantly, competition among multinationals is fierce—it is difficult, for instance, to see how the 600 odd scheduled airlines with an IATA (International Air Transport Association) code (Travel Images 2009) and the big numbers of hotel chains would not compete with each other. Leakages do not only or mostly affect countries in the so-called pleasure periphery (Aramberri 2005). Thus, globalization is not a one-way street that prevents changes in the international structure of the capitalist system, as attested by the economic ascent of many Asian countries, with China on top of the list (Bhagwati 2004). Neither does it increase world poverty; rather the other way around (Barro and Sala i Martín 1995).

The interesting questions lie elsewhere. Which is the place in this jigsaw of domestic tourism where, by definition, there are no international transactions among parts? What about international exchanges of tourists among countries that are more or less equal in power and share a substantially common cultural background? For instance, one of the most salient recent developments in this industry has been the growth of tourism in East Asia. Page (2001:87) has shown how the old West–East air travel alignment between Southeast Asia and Europe has recently been replaced by a North–South axis, as a consequence of the growing numbers of intraregional tourists from Japan, Korea, Taiwan, and, more recently, China that have transformed the tourism landscape of the region. This reality has been acknowledged in the change of promotional priorities operated by many national tourist offices of the area. While in the past, Europe and the United States were their main targets, today many put Japan, Australia, New Zealand, Hong Kong, and Taiwan at the top of their list (Hall and Page 2000:24). Raguraman hints that India's lagging performance in international tourism may be due to a wrong distribution of promotional priorities (1998). Similar reflections can also be made in the case of many Eastern European countries that have found in domestic and intraregional traffic a mainstay for the nascent tourism industries. But these questions are not usually asked.

The post-Romantic imagination can thus run wild when unburdened from economic restraints, and this is the precise effect of the metonymic mirage of reducing the tourism system to its international component. Since the totemic book of the 1970s (Smith 1977) on the anthropology of tourism, it has become conventional mainstream wisdom that tourism dynamics lead to commodification (Berghoff 2002; Shaw and Williams 2002; Turner and Ash 1975), loss of identity in local cultures (Burns 2006), threats to indigenous rights (Butler and Hinch 2007; Higgins-Desbiolles 2007;

Johnston 2006), abetting Western hegemony (Pussard 2005) increasing the negative aspects of globalization (Richter 2007), and being an irresistible globalizing force (Morgan and Pritchard 1998). MMT has thus become a usual suspect for every conceivable crime and misdemeanor with the sole exception of patricide and good taste.

One wonders, however, how all this can be taken as legal tender without supporting evidence. Can tourism sustain so many arguments? Can it be the cause of so many ills? In fact, if one takes the time to inquire about its inner structure, most of those flights of the imagination vanish into thin air.

SHAKY GROUNDS

Most of our understanding of the global tourism system relies on the information contained in the two databases maintained by UNWTO, especially the one on international arrivals. This database has a number of weaknesses of which we should be aware. To start with, it relies on data collected by its member governments, and often their collection techniques are questionable. More importantly, it comprises only international travel, that is, border crossings, and this is far from the real number of people who travel away from their usual place of residence for a period of over 24 hours and less than 1 year (the accepted statistical definition of tourism). Eventually, in so doing, the UNWTO database sidelines travel by residents in their own country, also known as domestic tourism. This would not necessarily matter were it not for the fact that data on domestic tourism are sketchy, and as a consequence, researchers tend to ignore them. In this way, as mentioned, international trips become shorthand for tourism as such.

Additionally, it stands to reason that the number of international arrivals will be higher in those areas of the world that are densely populated and, at the same time, count a great number of mid- and small-sized states. Even if its dwellers did not have their present high level of disposable income, Europe would still flood the international tourism statistics, as is actually the case. A car traveler from Manhattan spending a weekend in Washington, DC, does not register as a tourist. The same person going by car for the weekend from The Hague in the Netherlands to Paris in France, roughly the same distance, would be counted as four arrivals—twice in Belgium, once in France, and once in the Netherlands. If the tourist goes with a family of three additional siblings, there will be 16 arrivals in the roster against none in the first. No surprise that Europe's share of the global tourism market has hovered above 50% over the years.

A quick thought experiment illustrates the point further. Sometime in the not-so-distant future, the European Union may become one single political entity, and its citizens would not have to cross national borders when they travel from, say, Germany to Greece or Sweden to France. If it were so, tourism statistics would experience a dramatic downturn. Had it been the case in 2009, the number of international arrivals would have been more than halved. Should we then conclude that the global tourism system would find itself in decline? Would the industry have been dealt a mortal blow? The answer—*of course, not*—is a foregone conclusion.

The point, however, is not trivial. The habit of identifying tourism with long-haul international tourism has become so ingrained that it narrows our theoretical views down to some deeply flawed hypotheses, some of which have been already mentioned. If one focuses on Americans going to Polynesia or on Europeans going to South Africa, that is, long-haul tourism to some scarcely developed areas of the world, one might find some shred of evidence for the so much hyped uneven cultural exchanges that apparently are the essence of tourism. However, those are not the places where the overwhelming majority of tourists are to be found.

Following this trail, the relatively few millions that go continent-hopping are deemed to be more significant for the study of tourism than the 1.7 billion domestic tourists China generated in 2007 (CNTO 2010), or the 2 billion leisure trips that Americans took inside the United States in 2006 (US Census Bureau 2010). Any of those two flows fuels much higher numbers of people than their international counterparts, but theoretical research on tourism's complex dynamics remains firmly anchored in the latter, and most of the time ignores them. In assessing the contribution of tourism to globalization, similar assumptions will not help much, not just because they are too general, but because they are not general enough. In fact, the global tourism system has a different and more intricate structure than is usually granted.

If we want to forecast the development of MMT today or over the next few years in relation to the trend toward globalization, it seems mandatory to redimension the whole phenomenon. To this end, therefore, topics of classifying the present global tourism system, discussing its inner structure or shape, and hinting at its foreseeable contribution to the general globalization process should be considered.

CLASSIFYING THE GLOBAL TOURISM SYSTEM

Globalization is a fuzzy concept and, with its unrestrained use, becomes more so by the day. In what follows, it is defined in a stricter way. In economic terms, one should describe globalization as a movement in the direction of increasing international economic integration through the reduction of natural and human-made barriers to exchange and increased international flows of capital and labor (Wolf 2006:15). This drift toward integration will never be complete, that is, reach a stage in which transaction costs will come to zero, as economic activities are deployed in space. However, globalization progressively thwarts those barriers, makes people and countries more interdependent, and reduces the possibility of unilateral or autarkic growth. What started many centuries ago with the first traders has thus become a general arrangement in which an increasing world division of labor grows together with the international production of goods and services.

Therefore, globalization will be quicker—a point one should stress firmly— wherever international flows promote exchanges of progressively intangible goods, with information coming topmost. On the other hand, whenever, as in the case of tourism, globalization requires physical displacements as one of its components, it will trail behind the standards of other globalizing sectors. Important as the dynamics, economic and otherwise, unleashed by tourism are, their integrationist contribution and speed cannot compare with those of finance, banking, movies, television, or the Internet.

Here we will thus challenge the view that tourism has reached a high level of globalization. While it is an activity practiced all over the world, it is scarcely global. The Tourism Satellite Accounts (TSA) provided by the WTTC offer significant support to this view (2006a). They are not widely used among tourism researchers, maybe because they have not reached the high level of accuracy required by statisticians. Indeed, WTTC data sometimes surprise us. Take the lionized role accorded to Burma/Myanmar in the MMT system. In 2004, WTTC ranked the country as number 11 out of 174 in expenditures on personal travel (the part of residents' tourism that is not business travel or governmental expenditures for the upkeep of tourist attractions), number 19 in total demand, and number 12 in the size of its tourism industry, all of which seem highly unlikely.

However, such flaws do not necessarily discredit the overall TSA picture, which seems more reliable. Therefore, the low level of attention paid to it by tourism researchers remains surprising when one thinks that the institution counts as its members many big corporate actors in the world of tourism (airlines, hotel chains, tour operators, financial services, think tanks, etc.). Indeed, WTTC is an advocacy group; however, those companies make multibillion-dollar decisions each year, and one would think that their joint TSA research helps them in this task. This should appear as a good reason to use them in academic research. If trustworthy, WTTC-TSA may help broaden our scope beyond the pale of international tourism, and avoid its metonymic entrapments, thus improving our insight into the workings of the global tourism system.

TSA do not focus on individual international travel, but measure the financial contribution of tourism to the world economy or to that of given countries or regions. Discussions of TSA research methodology can be found on the WTTC website (WTTC/OEF 2006), so we will not follow this trail here. In what follows, TSA will be adopted with the same leap of faith that one accords to the UNWTO database and will be used as a valid tool that has been improved significantly since it was introduced.

In 2004, WTTC-TSA offered data for tourism economic activities for 174 countries and territories. Obviously, tourism has spread all over the globe. However, by itself this may not translate into a global activity in the sense just mentioned—greater integration of the world economy. Many inhabitants of the planet might practice tourism without it becoming global if national residents of a country would mostly stay within their borders, or if the industry would mostly be local, or if most capital investment or labor were not foreign. This is exactly what happens in present-day tourism—that global components in the tourism system are rather limited. At least, they are if we consider the relation between total GDP and the part of it that is attributable to the tourism economy.

We can find it by crossing WTTC and World Bank data. This can be done in two different ways, either by measuring what WTTC calls "T&T [travel and tourism] Demand," that is, the aggregate of all tourism nominal expenses, direct and indirect, in the resident economy and comparing them with its GDP, or by using so-called T&T Consumption—including only those expenditures made by and on behalf of tourists, domestic or international, in the resident economy. In short, T&T Consumption considers only the direct economic dynamics of tourism in a given economy, while "T&T Demand" includes both direct and indirect impacts. Both show rather similar results in percentage terms, but we will use the more limited measure, because it is closer to the real movement of people and sidetracks other components such as investments in infrastructures, marketing, and related exports that, significant as they indeed are, mark some degree of conceptual distance from actual tourism behavior.

In 2004, the GDP of the 155 countries and territories for which one could find data in both WTTC and the World Bank (World Bank 2006) reached $40.7 trillion at current prices. World T&T Consumption that year came up to $3.9 trillion, that is, around 10% of it. The average tourism contribution to different national GDPs was 12.5%. It seems a rather high ratio, and it should be noted so, but those are the data one can retrieve from the TSA research. Even if it is in fact lower, taken together, the data do anyway display some interesting features, and one can attempt an initial classification of the different components that form the global tourism system, combining their economic development stage (developed, developing, or least developed countries or LDCs) with tourism impact in their GDP (Table 2). Three main clusters can be noted.

The first group we call "Top producers." It comprises a total of 26 countries where tourism makes a very high GDP contribution. After that, the rest can be divided in two additional categories. The second (successful developers) is made up of 67 countries, and runs between the first developed nation to appear in the ranking (Austria with number 27 and a tourism contribution to its GDP of 18%) and Japan (with number 94 and a tourism contribution to its GDP of 8%). The third (laggards) includes countries with a contribution below 8% of GDP. In total, there are 62 countries in this last category, and the ratio for the great majority of them (47 countries) is equal to or below 6.5%.

Some trends can be noticed in this classification. Let us start with the 26 top producers (Table 3), just before the first developed country is found. Once again, one should point out some oddities in this group—Myanmar/Burma, Jordan, and Syria—that intuitively should not be there. The case of Bahrain, on the other hand, is not surprising for the island has experienced rapid growth over the last few years.

Table 2. Classifying the Global Tourism System

Countries	Number	Remarks
Top producers	26	18 at the top have T&T Consumption >25% GDP
Successful developers	67	T&T Consumption between 18% and 8% GDP
a. Developed countries	37	High GDP; highly diversified economies
b. Rising stars	11	Quickly developing economies
c. No clear trend	25	Varied economies
Laggards	62	T&T <8% GDP (for 47 countries <6.5% GDP)

Source: Author's Elaboration of WTTC (2006c).

Table 3. The World Tourism System (2006)

Top Producers		Successful Developers						Laggards			
		Developed Countries		Rising Stars		No Clear Trend		8–6.6%		<6.5%	
Countries	%	Countries	%	Countries	%	Countries	%	Countries	%	Countries	%
Maldives	62.1	Austria	18.2	Tunisia	15.4	Papua-New Guinea	15.8	El Salvador	8.0	South Africa	6.5
Antigua and Barbuda	55.3	Estonia	17.1	Thailand	14.2	Kiribati	15.7	Trinidad & Tobago	7.9	Congo, Republic	6.4
Seychelles	53.8	Iceland	17.0	Morocco	13.6	Lebanon	15.7	Nicaragua	7.8	Benin	6.4
Bahamas	50.2	Portugal	16.9	Costa Rica	12.5	Albania	14.4	Philippines	7.8	Oman	6.3
Saint Lucia	42.6	Switzerland	16.0	Malaysia	12.1	Ukraine	14.3	Belarus	7.8	Guatemala	6.3
Vanuatu	41.2	Spain	15.6	Egypt	11.1	Guyana	14.0	Malawi	7.7	Ecuador	6.1
Barbados	40.7	Greece	14.4	Kenya	10.4	Comoros	12.0	Ethiopia	7.7	Iran	6.1
Saint Vincent and the Grenadines	30.7	Hong Kong	13.5	Turkey	9.1	Ghana	12.0	Russian Federation	7.7	China	5.9
Grenada	30.5	Belgium	12.7	Senegal	8.9	Suriname	12.0	Rwanda	7.6	Korea, Republic	5.7
Burma	28.7	New Zealand	12.6	Cambodia	8.8	Uganda	11.9	Botswana	7.5	Argentina	5.7
Jamaica	28.0	UK	12.3	Indonesia	8.0	Qatar	11.6	Vietnam	7.5	Niger	5.6
Cape Verde	27.8	France	12.1			Solomon Islands	11.3	Lesotho	7.3	Colombia	5.6
Zimbabwe	27.7	Italy	12.1			Honduras	10.8	Central African Republic	7.2	Haiti	5.5
Cyprus	27.4	Slovenia	11.7			Gabon	10.7	Peru	7.2	Paraguay	5.3
Malta	27.1	Denmark	11.5			Tonga	10.4	Slovak Republic	7.1	Brazil	5.3
Fiji	26.4	Singapore	11.4			Sri Lanka	10.3	Burundi	7.1	Zambia	5.1

Country	%	Country	%	Country	%	Country	%	Country	%
Saint Kitts and Nevis	25.9	The Netherlands	11.3	Namibia	10.3	Sao Tome & Principe	7.1	Chile	5.1
Gambia, The	25.4	Australia	11.2	Tanzania	10.2	Latvia	6.8	Congo, Democratic Rep	5.0
Dominica	22.7	Hungary	10.9	Panama	10.1	Mali	6.8	Togo	4.9
Croatia	22.5	Luxembourg	10.7	Kuwait	9.8	Cote d'Ivoire	6.7	Venezuela	4.9
Dominican Republic	21.9	Finland	10.6	Nepal	8.9	Macedonia FYR	6.7	Guinea	4.9
Belize	20.3	Sweden	10.5	Laos	8.8	Bolivia	6.7	Sierra Leone	4.8
Bahrain	19.7	Czech Republic	10.3	Madagascar	8.7	Swaziland	6.7	Cameroon	4.7
Jordan	19.6	Germany	10.2	Uruguay	8.6	Mexico	6.6	Burkina Faso	4.6
Bulgaria	19.2	Canada	10.1	United Arab Emirates	8.0			Yugoslavia FR	4.3
Syria	18.9	Norway	9.4					Yemen	4.3
		USA	9.4					Romania	4.2
		Israel	9.3					Pakistan	4.1
		Ireland	8.8					Bosnia & Herzegovina	4.0
		Lithuania	8.2					India	3.8
		Poland	8.1					Saudi Arabia	3.4
		Japan	8.0					Libya	3.4
								Bangladesh	3.3
								Nigeria	3.3
								Chad	3.0
								Algeria	2.7
								Sudan	2.4
								Angola	2.2

Source: Author's elaboration of WTTC (2006c) and World Bank (2006).
Percentages have been obtained dividing what WTTC/OEF (2006) calls T&T Consumption 2004 (including Personal and Business T&T and Visitor Exports) by World Bank GDP Data 2004. WTTC/OEF categories include items such as transportation, accommodation, food and beverage, etc. For a more detailed methodological explanation, one should go to the referred paper.

Most of the countries in this group share some features:

- They are small islands, archipelagos, or territories.
- They are considered "less developed countries."
- Their GDP is quite low in absolute terms.
- Their economies do not have a high degree of diversification.
- Internal demand is weak.
- They are close to some big generating markets or have become quite popular in some of them (like the Maldives in Germany and France).

The second group is made of what we call "successful developers." It includes, among others, all developed countries, with the only exception of South Korea, whose tourism contribution to GDP remains below 6%. This second group is far less homogeneous than the top producers. Three main clusters can be found: 32 developed countries (Table 3), plus another 5 European Union members that can be seen on their way to become fully developed; 11 rising stars that have already become top international destinations; and a remainder of 25 countries where no clear trend is easily detectable.

The main common features of the developed subgroup are as follows:

- They are large or mid-sized continental countries (with some exceptions like Hong Kong and Singapore).
- They are developed or nearly developed countries.
- They have highly diversified economies compatible with a high degree of tourism development.
- Their internal demand is thriving.
- In most cases, their tourism consumption exceeds 10% of GDP. Only seven are below this mark.
- They are both the main generators and the main destinations of the world with great number of mutual exchanges.

The members of the second subgroup or "rising stars" (Table 3) also have some features in common:

- They are continental countries.
- They are quickly developing countries.
- They have increasingly diversified economies where tourism has become a key ingredient.
- They have become well-known tourism destinations over the last 20 years.
- Most are close to key generating markets (Tunisia, Morocco, Egypt, and Turkey to Europe; Costa Rica to the United States and Canada; Thailand,

Malaysia, Cambodia, and Indonesia to Northeast Asia and Australia), Kenya and Senegal being the only exceptions.

The remaining subgroup of 25 countries where there is no clear trend (Table 3) has features akin to those of the three previous groups and subgroups. Some are small islands or archipelagos or territories with nondiversified economies (Kiribati, Tonga, Solomon Islands, Comoros, Qatar, Kuwait, United Arab Emirates); some are more developed or find themselves in the vicinity of important generating markets (Ukraine, Uruguay); some are rising stars that have either established or are in the way to establish a good record as tourism destinations (Namibia, Papua-New Guinea, Tanzania, Nepal, Laos, Madagascar). Their fluid state might be an opportunity to consolidate an ascending trend or, perhaps, to join the last group of the packet—"the laggards."

This last group (Table 2) is made up of 62 countries that are not counted as developed economies and have a tourism impact of less than 8% of GDP. Once again, there are some surprises here that have no easy explanation. Mexico, widely considered as one of the top tourism markets in the Americas, apparently has a very low penetration of tourism in its GDP (6.6%), the same as China (5.9%) in Asia. Many countries in this category have some similarities:

- Located in slow developing areas of the world (Africa, Latin America, Middle East, and South Asia).
- Mostly less developed countries.
- Low GDP.
- Scarcely diversified economies.
- Far from key generating markets.

If these data are accurate, one can make, above all, a case for the relation between development and tourism. In fact, all the 37 developed or near-developed countries, except South Korea, have a sizeable tourism sector, with a much-diversified supply of tourism products, and an active foreign-oriented area. Tourism is an important complement for other zones of their economies and finds a thriving internal and external demand. On the other hand, most of the laggards are less developed countries. The second decisive factor in having an active or globalized tourism economy harks back to local policies. All 11 rising stars have consistently implemented good developmental and promotional policies over time. Most of them are geared toward the foreign sector, but in some cases (Thailand, Malaysia, and Turkey), a growing part of their tourism facilities caters to the needs of domestic tourism. Finally, closeness to the key generating markets (Europe, North America, and Northeast Asia) accounts for much of an active tourism economy. Caribbean islands are one of the best examples of this trend.

Therefore, for all the success stories found in some areas of the world in developing a tourism industry, one has to bear in mind that most countries have a low tourism input in their economies. Even though many would definitely profit from the development of tourism, for the time being, globalization has not reached their gates.

THE UNBELIEVABLY SHRINKING GLOBAL TOURISM SYSTEM

For all countries, in general, together with their development stage and tourism impact on GDP, a third element has been creeping its way into this classification—location relative to the main generating markets. Let us try to shed some light on this last aspect. UNWTO offers a highly structured picture of the world market share for international arrivals in 2005 (Figure 1).

Europe comes on top with over 54% of world arrivals, followed by the Americas and Asia-Pacific, both with a similar size (17% and 19%, respectively). Africa and the Middle East fill the bottom of the table with 5% each. Noting once more that TSA do not address the movement of persons, WTTC reaches a dissimilar picture in dealing with the way tourism is

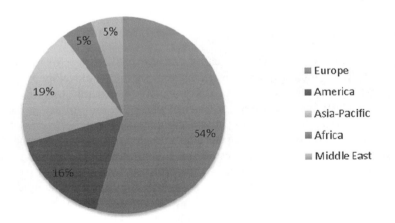

Figure 1 International Arrivals per Region (%). *Source*: UNWTO (2006b).

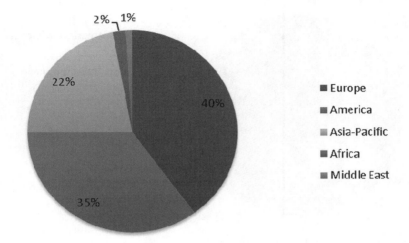

Figure 2 World Market Share (2006). *Source*: WTTC (2006c).

produced by different world regions (Figure 2). Tourism generation is at its top in the Americas (40% of the world) followed by Europe (35%) and Asia-Pacific (22%). Africa (2%) and the Middle East (1%) remain far behind those three regions.

Bearing in mind that the methodologies of these two charts differ, and that they compare different items, one can find some interesting pointers. The most salient, no matter how well expected, is the exaggerated importance of Europe in the UNWTO database, already explained. On the other hand, however, from our vantage point, it is even more important that two main geographic and economic regions (Africa and the Middle East) have a very low level both of international arrivals and of tourism impact. This allows us to conclude that tourism (both international and domestic) only gathers in bulk around some areas of the world. But this is only the beginning. If one breaks the five regions just looked at into more detailed areas or subregions, this lopsided picture becomes even more unbalanced (Figure 3).

Together, North America (33%), the European Union (31%), and Northeast Asia (15%) account for 79% of total tourism world production. If one adds their adjacent areas in the rest of Europe, Southeast Asia, North Africa, and the Caribbean, the total scores an additional 10% to reach 90% of world production. On the other hand, Latin America, the Middle East, South Asia, and sub-Saharan Africa produce only a trifling 7%. Oceania (3%) seems a somewhat similar case (see below).

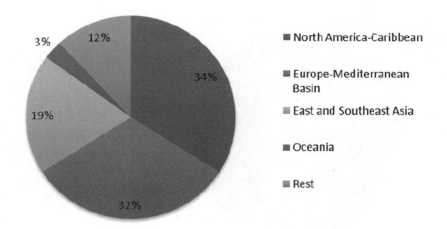

Figure 3 World Tourism Market Share by Subregion (2006). *Source*:
Authors elaboration on WTTC (2006c).

This regional distribution supports the hypothesis of a very limited
globalization of the world tourism system. Far from a generalization of the
trend to all its components, it appears that tourism becomes more and more
integrated in some areas, of which the three main ones are Europe plus
the African Southern Mediterranean, North America and the Caribbean,
and East and Southeast Asia. The case of Oceania where Australia and
New Zealand act as the anchors of a regional subsystem that includes the
rest of the islands of the South Seas seems like a miniature of the bigger
picture and its inner trends (Figure 4).

The global tourism system thus appears to be structured around three
main regions, each one of them with its hinterland. In each one of these areas,
a core of well-developed and quickly developing countries both have an
impressive tourism production within their own borders and generate major
tourist flows to the rest of their vicinity, whether LDCs, developing countries,
or developed countries. Regions need to have one or more growth engines to
secure tourism development. In plain English, these growth engines mean the
existence of one or more nuclei with a big population that enjoys high
disposable income. Where, as in Latin America, Africa, or the Middle East,
this core does not exist or is quite remote, tourism remains sluggish. If Brazil,
with its 190 million population, had a per capita income close to the median
of the European Union, quite surely the outlook for tourism in Latin
America would be more encouraging than it has been up to now.

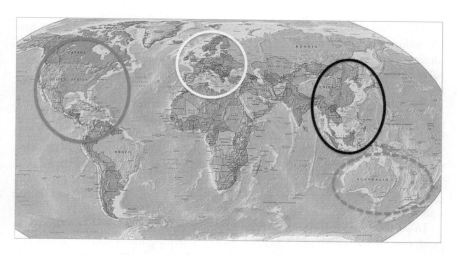

Figure 4 The Global Tourism System: Main Clusters. *Source*: Author's elaboration (Map from http://en.wikipedia.org/wiki/File:Worldmap_Land AndPolitical.jpg).

From an economic point of view, both the core developed countries and their immediate peripheries have increasingly close relations and benefit from those tourist exchanges. The rest are mostly excluded. Whether these groupings create uneven exchanges, as per the neocolonial analysis, or reflect a central or hegemonic relation between the main partners in each one of the regions and their "pleasure periphery" (Turner and Ash 1975) as per the postcolonial hypotheses is not a key question to be treated in this chapter. Just a word of caution—a pleasure periphery is an expression that has no other economic sense than naming one or more areas that provide a high number of leisure and/or tourism services, in the same way as one could speak of the oil periphery, the steel periphery, or the whatever periphery to convey the meaning that some goods or services are the main products of that given area. The pejorative innuendo against pleasure only reveals the basic puritanical approach of many users of the expression (Butcher 2002; Turner and Ash 1975) as though some zones in the Maslovian pyramid of needs were more legitimate than others. The expression, therefore, should be used with restraint if it has to keep some meaning. Otherwise, one can see pleasure peripheries in any sunny beach or pleasant coastline in Taiwan (Lin 2004), in the outer islands of the Netherlands (Ashworth 2007), or in any other destination where people enjoy themselves.

At any rate, the discussion would be more focused if we knew more about the relation between domestic and international tourism in its double dimension of intraregional and long-haul travel. Unfortunately, this issue is surrounded by darkness. Let us, instead, try some probing where there is a modicum of light. The majority of international arrivals, as measured by UNWTO (2006c), happens overwhelmingly in the same continent where it originates or, in its jargon, is made up of intraregional arrivals while long-haul ones (jargon again for continent-hopping) are the minor part. Most African tourists remain in Africa, most Asians in Asia, and so on. According to UNWTO (Table 4), in all five regions of the world, over 70% of tourists stay within their continent of origin. As could be expected, this is especially true in Europe, given the special features (population density and mid-sized national units) already mentioned.

In its forecast of tourism development until 2020, UNWTO (2006a) also points out a similar share. The split between intraregional and long haul has been changing to make the latter somehow bigger. However, if in 1995 the ratio between the two was 80:20, it will still remain close in 2020 with a 75:25 share.

How international and domestic tourism are related is a thornier question. In fact, there is no known satisfactory calculation of their relative weight. WTTC-TSA, however, offers some pointers to educated guesses. Tourism expenditures closer to physical travel, whether domestic or international, are "Personal and Business Travel" and "Visitor Exports" (WTTC/OEF 2006). Although at the level of individual countries, they do not exactly match, when it comes to world estimations, the sum of the first two categories comes close to expenditures on domestic travel, while the third one would be money spent by international tourists.

Table 4. Intraregional Arrivals (2004)

Region	%
Africa	71.4
Americas	71.3
Asia-Pacific	78.4
Europe	86.1
Middle East	77.3

Source: UNWTO (2006c).

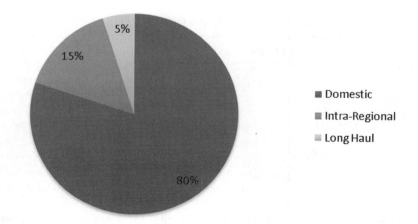

Figure 5 The Global Tourism System (2006). *Source*: Author's elaboration of WTTC (2006c).

WTTC estimates that in 2006, the total amount of money spent for "Personal T&T" and "Business Travel" reached $3.51 trillion, while tourism exports topped $896 billion. Total expenditures for individual T&T would thus be in the region of $4.4 trillion. This would roughly suggest (Figure 5) that tourism exports, closely related to international travel, constitute just one-fifth of total travel.

If we divide exports between intraregional and long haul according to the UNWTO ratio of 75:25, this would mean that domestic tourism accounts for 80% of total T&T, while intraregional travel (international travel within the same continent) would reach 15% and long-haul travel only about 5% of the total.

If this is the shape of the world T&T system, then it is much less global an activity than usually claimed. Accordingly, we should also reassess what these economic considerations mean for the unceasing talk about social and cultural gaps between tourists and providers of tourism goods and services. In fact, the vaunted cultural gap would be at its most dramatic in just 5% of cases. Intraregional contacts would be much more common (and thus cultural distance minimized), covering about 15% of total T&T communication. Domestic tourism would have the lion's share, therefore reducing even more the opportunities for cultural dissonance between tourists and locals.

UNWTO data on international arrivals support a similar conclusion. Long-haul travel reaches 139.5 million trips, not exactly a trivial number.

Table 5. Long-Haul Tourists (2004)

Continent of Origin	Millions
World	139.5
Africa	5.3
Americas	37.5
Asia-Pacific	31.7
Europe	60.4
Middle East	4.6

Source: UNWTO (2006d).

But if one looks closely into the figures, the picture of international tourism as a whirlwind of exchanges between alien cultures or "close encounters of the third phase" becomes highly unlikely (Table 5).

Table 5 has been calculated according to the UNWTO breakdown between intraregional and long-haulers for 2004—79.8% of world tourism happened within the same continent, while the residual 20% was either long haul (18.3%) or of unspecified origin (1.9%). In this way, the total long-haul travel in 2004 reached 139.5 million. Excluding the 10 million tourists generated in Africa and the Middle East, the remaining 130 million—over 90% of all long-haul tourists—originated in the Americas, Europe, and Asia-Pacific. The exchanges between the Americas and Europe, not exactly the most culturally distant of places, reached a total of 47.5 million (25.8 million tourists went to Europe from the Americas and 21.7 million Europeans took the opposite route), leaving a total 82.5 million long-haul tourists among whom one could eventually find the type of cultural dynamics that neo- and postcolonialist thinkers have in mind. One should discount as well the 24.6 million tourists from Asia-Pacific to the Americas and Europe, plus the 7.1 million Asia-Pacific flows to Africa and the Middle East—not exactly the usual suspects of cultural misdemeanors—and then the numbers go down to a total of 47 million.

Therefore, well-developed countries account for the overwhelming majority of long-haul travel, but most of it takes place between them. Long-haul travel from them to the rest of the world, though not negligible, accounts for just 6–7% of total international travel, if these calculations are accurate. It does not mean that there will not be cross-cultural encounters among tourists and locals within the three main tourism areas, but one should use a lot of caution before claiming that all tourism is a form of colonialism (Gmelch 2003; Nash 1996), that it is one of the main means by which the West imposes its hegemony over the rest of the world (Burns 2001a; Hall 2007a), or that it is one of the most powerful sources of globalization (Mowforth 1997; Mowforth and Munt 2003; Weaver 2005). Most of the world lies beyond the pale of international tourism.

If we look at tourism categories as used by UNWTO, the picture seems remarkably similar. Business people usually travel to meet colleagues in their same trades, and most of the time they do not participate in other tourism activities. Those who visit friends and relatives tend to move within a well-known cultural environment where they are part of the local society. Health and religious tourists are mostly interested in pursuing those interests, not in mingling with the local culture. Therefore, it is up to leisure tourists to take most of the brunt of cultural dynamics. In 2004, 50% of international tourists were for leisure; 15.6% for business; 26% for visiting friends and relatives, health, religion, and others; and 8.4% were unspecified. If they followed the mentioned 80/20 distribution between intraregional and long haul, out of 150 million total long-haulers, only 76.6 million would have been leisure tourists (Table 6).

WHAT ABOUT THE FUTURE?

Hypotheses about tourist behavior should take into consideration the real structure of world tourism. Getting a better picture of it was the task attempted in the previous sections. Now it is time to see whether available evidence validates the expectation that, barring serious and unexpected crises, in the mid-run T&T will probably remain the same as it is today.

Table 6. Long-Haul Tourists by Travel Motivation (2004) (Millions)

	Total	Leisure	Business	VFR and Others	NA
World	152.8	76.6	23.9	39.5	12.7
Africa	6.7	3.7	1.0	1.6	0.4
Americas	25.1	11.2	2.9	4.0	7.0
Asia-Pacific	29.1	13.4	4.3	6.1	5.3
Europe	84.6	43.9	14.7	26.0	0.0
Middle East	7.3	4.5	0.9	1.8	0.0

VFR, visiting friends and relatives. *Source*: Author's elaboration of UNWTO (2006d).

The answer should be a qualified "yes." Qualified not so much by doubts about its development, but because the future will hopefully bring along a better knowledge of its structure, and thus force a change in our description.

The first hint refers to international arrivals. Unless the European Union becomes a single political entity, the UNWTO estimate that they will double their present dimension to reach 1.6 billion tourists in 2020 seems possible (UNWTO 2006a), in spite of the ongoing economic crisis. WTTC reaches a similar conclusion. In current monetary terms, the world T&T demand will nearly double from 2006 to 2016, passing from $6.5 trillion to $12.1 trillion. Will it also become more global in the sense we have just discussed?

Let us repeat it once again: there is not much solid evidence to rely on. However, WTTC data offer a not-so-unexpected surprise. Within the next few years, the T&T market share by continents (Figure 6) will bring about a loss in the Americas (3%) and a quicker one in Europe (6%), while Asia and the Pacific will surge eight points (from 22% to 30%). Africa and the Middle East will remain at the very bottom of the table (2% each).

By subregion (Table 7), the highest percentage growth will be reached in Asia, where the three regions of the Northeast, Southeast, and South will double the amount of current dollars they made in 2006.

The Middle East, sub-Saharan Africa, and the Caribbean will also keep the expectation of a doubling in T&T production. The rest of the world will

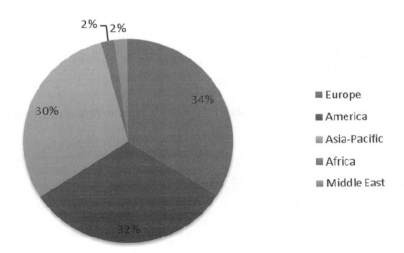

Figure 6 World Market Share (2016). *Source*: WTTC (2006c).

Table 7. Regional Change 2006–2016 (US$ Billions)

Region	T&T Industry (2006)	T&T Industry (2016)	Growth (%)	Difference
North America	601.8	964.5	1.6	362.7
European Union	437.5	676.4	1.5	238.9
Northeast Asia	260.7	577.4	2.2	316.7
Southeast Asia	75.4	151.6	2.0	76.2
Other Western Europe	56.6	87.3	1.5	30.7
Central and Eastern Europe	38.2	74.1	1.9	35.9
Oceania	50.9	73.3	1.4	22.4
Latin America	48.1	72.7	1.5	24.6
Middle East	27.3	58.9	2.2	31.6
South Asia	22.0	42.0	1.9	20.0
North Africa	19.4	35.9	1.9	16.5
Sub-Saharan Africa	16.9	33.1	2.0	16.2
Caribbean	11.6	23.7	2.0	12.1

Source: Author's elaboration of WTTC (2006c).

lose speed by comparison, with sluggish growth in North and Latin America, Europe, and Oceania. Figure 7 shows the new distribution for 2016.

However, there will be no big changes in the broader picture by 2016. The three big areas of North America and the Caribbean, Europe and the Mediterranean, and Northeast/Southeast Asia will still account for 90% of the entire world tourism, Oceania for 3%, and the rest will come up with just 7%, exactly as though the passing time was of no consequence (Table 8).

Finally, the whole tourism global system will remain structured in the same way as it is now (Figure 8). Domestic tourism will lose a couple of percentage points to intraregional tourism, while long haul will stay put in the 5% it had in 2006.

Tourism will indeed be one of the ways in which globalization will proceed in the near future. However, it will not be its mainstay. People movements will not easily go beyond their national borders; when they do, tourists will remain in their original continent, and only a tiny minority will venture to faraway regions. Furthermore, this last group will not only go to the most exotic destinations. A sizeable share of long haul will still be made

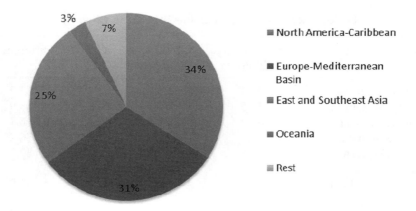

- North America-Caribbean
- Europe-Mediterranean Basin
- East and Southeast Asia
- Oceania
- Rest

Figure 7 World Tourism Market Share by Subregion (2016). *Source*: Author's elaboration of WTTC (2006c).

Table 8. Arrivals by Continent of Origin and Destination (2004) (%)

Destination	Origin						
	World	Africa	Americas	Asia-Pacific	Europe	Middle East	Unspecified
World	100	100	100	100	100	100	100
Africa	4.4	71.4	0.8	0.7	2.7	8.3	33.1
Americas	16.5	2.1	71.3	5.7	5.0	1.0	14.9
Asia-Pacific	19.0	4.5	7.3	78.4	4.0	4.3	14.8
Europe	55.4	13.9	19.8	11.1	86.1	9.2	23.9
Mid-East	4.7	8.1	0.8	4.2	2.2	77.3	13.4

Source: UNWTO (2005).

by business people shuttling among Europe, North America, and East Asia to tend to their trades. Long-haulers will probably grow, as higher numbers of people increase their disposable income, but it will still mostly happen among those three regions. In this way, the perception that tourism is wholeheartedly global and that it mainly connects the richer parts of the world with the poorest pleasure peripheries is but a figment of the

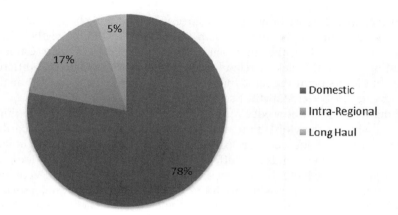

Figure 8 The Global Tourism System (2016). *Source*: Author's Elaboration of WTTC (2006c).

post-Romantic collective imaginary, so dominant of late in tourism research in spite of being largely unwarranted.

If for the time being it is not possible to tread firmer ground, one can add some pointers for future research. Better statistics are a must if we want to grasp how "the biggest industry on Earth" works. This is easier said than done, as UNWTO efforts to set up a TSA system show. But there is much more statistical production than meets the eye. The issue is often one of better dissemination. Beyond the general or systemic databases, a number of countries provide reasonable amounts of information. However, it is not easily found except after an often-frustrating expedition into their websites. If they could find a way to offer their data in some centralized way, this would be a great plus. UNWTO also has a wealth of analyses that would help researchers. But in spite of being a public sector organization amply funded by taxpayers' money, it insists in making users pay for access, thus limiting its usefulness.

Better knowledge usually means better policymaking. So the second pointer looks in another direction. A significant part of present tourism research revolves around so-called experiences or the self-styled encounters between hosts and guests. Policies based on such flimsy foundations, when taken seriously, usually miss their goals, because they ignore the ways the tourism system works. Better statistical sources accurately tracking market trends and the thrust toward consolidation in the industry (noticeably hotel mergers and acquisitions, or the outcome of recurring crises in the airline industry) would assist policymakers, investors, and stakeholders in acting more wisely and would, indeed, help researchers to discharge their tasks more efficiently. For the time being, though, we remain in a Catch-22 situation, where the lack of reliable databases pushes the latter to different areas of discussion at the same time as their attention deficit disorder makes the absence of better statistical sources palatable.

Finally, a better knowledge of the subject will help us in discussing things such as whether the global tourism system will collectively evolve according to the pattern of lifecycles or, perhaps, follow a world-systems template. While the former tends to offer a closed evolutionary outlook on development, the latter is more open to the interplay of broad economic and social factors that might enrich our view of the dynamics unleashed by MMT. These and other similar issues would highly benefit from a better understanding of the tourism system and its place in the process of globalization.

Unfortunately, one does not see much interest in basing tourism research on a more accurate knowledge of the global tourism system. When engineering pointillism and its usual companions (case studies and best practices) get sidelined, it is in order to let the researcher's imagination fly around a region of "constructed" theories with their backs to the real world. This is the basic predicament of the *pomo* matrix (Chapter 3) and its main ramifications in tourism research paradigms (Chapters 4 and 5).

Chapter 3

The Postmodern Matrix

POSTMODERNISM

The divorce between the shape of the global tourism system, and the views of it offered by many researchers, is not just the creation of some people working in isolation from the rest of the social sciences. It traces its roots to the cultural revolution that coalesced around the 1960s. It was the triumph of a new matrix or framework for the social sciences based on the nearly exclusive explanatory value of cultural factors. The new matrix promoted a wide-ranging turn of mind, and affected a vast swath of social research. We will call it the postmodern or *pomo* matrix.

Nowadays postmodernism has become a familiar word in everyday life. Indeed, with increased popularity, it has lost some of its precision. Most of the time, it means lifestyles that frown on domineering persuasions; ironic in their distant contemplation of the world; and open to fusion, to cross-breeding or to ongoing transactions. In general, this mindscape coincides with what Susan Sontag once called *camp*—a dandy's proper deportment in times of mass culture (2001a, 2001b). In this way, we speak of *pomo* aesthetics, love, architecture, music, travel, cooking, and just about everything else. The *pomo* outlook is pervasive in most self-respecting pursuits of one's own place in the social pecking order—a birthmark of present-day distinction.

Pomo also has other meanings when used in the social sciences. Its mindset is the mass-produced, mass-consumed offshoot of a number of theories about life, world, society, ethics—that is, a collection of philosophical statements. As the word indicates, *pomo* is a way of looking that has risen after modernity, sometimes meant as a correction, though mostly as a denial of it. This sequential/antagonistic character requests a definition of modernity. As has been said, *pomo* matches modernity with the theories and practices epitomized by the ascent of mass societies. In a nutshell it describes them as a world outlook with the wrong notions of the way the human mind operates, a historicist bias, a twisted set of theoretical priorities, and thus the wrong ethical approach. So, *pomo* carries forth a methodological overhaul, at the same time as it seeks a new texture of the social world and a fresh look at the moral tasks that humankind faces.

It should be noted that, not being a paradigm, the *pomo* matrix flows in different and occasionally disparate currents. Its origins are usually seen in the productions of a group of post-World War Two French thinkers who share a common corpus of theorems in spite of their different intellectual backgrounds and diverging scholarly interests. Names such as Lacan, Lévi-Strauss, Barthes, Althusser, Foucault, Baudrillard, Deleuze, and Derrida come to mind, among others. *Pomos*, though, cross-pollinate their views with ideas from the Frankfurt School, Norbert Elias, Boasian cultural relativism or historical particularism (Harris 1968), and symbolic inter-actionism. These seem to be the main streams that coalesced into what Eagleton refers to as just The Theory (2003), with a capital T. Apparently, after *pomo*, if not history, philosophy has come to an end.

The so-called softer social sciences, that is, all except economics have felt the heavy weight of *pomo*. In some of those fields of scholarly interest that have been institutionalized in academia just recently, such as public relations, advertising, sociology of consumption and leisure, and, indeed, tourism research, the *pomo* mindset has become the persuasion of choice crowding out any alternative approaches. If we want to understand the themes and the professional jargon of today's tourism research, we have to examine the theoretical roots of postmodernity. This is attempted in the next paragraphs, followed by other chapters which offer examples of how the postmodern matrix was imported into various areas of tourism research.

HOW THE MIND WORKS

Going back in time, perhaps the initial formulation of the new views should be credited to Claude Lévi-Strauss. At the start of his work on the savage mind, he compares the logic of modernity, also known as scientific logic, and that of the savage mind.

> Neolithic, or early historical, man was [because of his capacity to reach goals in a systematic way JA] the heir of a long scientific tradition. [...] [The savage mind and modern science JA] are two distinct modes of scientific thought. These are certainly not a function of different stages of development of the human mind but rather of two strategic levels at which

nature is accessible to scientific enquiry: one roughly adapted to that of perception and the imagination; the other at a remove from it. It is as if the necessary connections which are the object of all science, Neolithic or modern, could be arrived at by two different routes, one very close to, and the other more remote from, sensible intuition (1966a:15).

If science is defined as any arrangement of means and ends, the savage mind was producing science many centuries before moderns thought it might have been possible. To further make his point, Lévi-Strauss reminds us that even in the modern world scientific logic cohabits with that of *bricolage*, a French word not readily translatable into English that conveys the sense of creating artifacts out of bits and pieces.

The "bricoleur" is adept at performing a large number of diverse tasks; but, unlike the engineer, he does not subordinate each of them to the availability of raw materials and tools conceived and procured for the purpose of the project. The set of the "bricoleur's" means cannot therefore be defined in terms of a project [...] It is to be defined only by its potential use or, putting this another way and in the language of the "bricoleur" himself [*sic*], because the elements are collected or retained on the principle that "they may always come in handy" (1966a:17–18).

Science and *bricolage* are but two possible ways of the mind whose relation cannot be grasped in terms of a gradient of development.

With this blunt remark, however, Lévi-Strauss not only threatens to do away with the modern notion of science, but also with the difference between δόξα (perception and imagination) and επιστήμη (rigorous knowledge) already known in Greece. When most philosophers and historians of science are of one mind in claiming that there is a basic difference between ideas based on necessary or solid principles, and those just grounded on opinion or whim, one should proffer some compelling reasons for the need to break with it.

Expecting them from Lévi-Strauss is a vain hope. Instead, he veers into a completely different argument to contend that both science and the savage mind represent instances of reasoning. From there he easily reaches the conclusion.

> Mythical thought, that "bricoleur", builds up structures by fitting together events, or rather the remains of events, while science, "in operation" simply by virtue of coming into being, creates its means and results in the form of events, thanks to the structures which it is constantly elaborating and which are its hypotheses and theories. But it is important not to make the mistake of thinking that these are two stages or phases in the evolution of knowledge. Both approaches are equally valid (1966a:22).

Evolution or not, one should be legitimately wary of an ophthalmologist that proposed to perform eye surgery with the help of a Paleolithic ax instead of a laser beam because they are both cutting tools, but Lévi-Strauss' logic would not see any difference between them. They would be but two instances of the many possible shapes of the mind in action. For Lévi-Strauss, who since the beginning of his career waxed as a sworn enemy of any kind of historicism and evolutionism in the social sciences, biological evolution seems to be a highly probable hypothesis, but cultural evolution is just a metaphor (1956:131). Far from developing along a single axis, human life makes no progress. If at all, it is made up of discontinuities and breaks—nothing else.

Was this not the unremitting refrain of the functionalist school as well? Yes and no. In fact, Lévi-Strauss appropriates their notion of *context*, but uses it with a different meaning than Malinowski and his followers. Functionalists see cultures as heaps of facts that should be analyzed with the empiricist's tools (ethnographic description, participant observation, statistical techniques, and so on). For Lévi-Strauss, this was "a preliminary form of structuralism" (1948:357), but its very reliance on empirical methods left it wanting. Functionalism prized ethnography when what we need is a structural anthropology (1958:19–25). Facts are chance-ridden. Nothing is gained from describing a system of kinship, a ritual or a myth if we ignore the overall logic of the mind that structures them. In the end facts are signs and, like signs, they need interpretation, which in its turn requires a code or grammar that precedes, illuminates, and makes them intelligible. Anthropology and the rest of the social sciences need a retooling similar to that already undergone by linguistics.

Words seemed to be the realm of the capricious until Saussure, Jakobson, and the Prague Circle found an exit towards rationalism. For Saussure, the old discrepancy between the signifier and the signified, between sounds and meaning, could be bridged through the right interplay and combination of syllables within the area defined by a language. Anthropology should undergo a similar change. "*At another level of reality* [Lévi-Strauss' italics], kinship phenomena are phenomena of the *same type* as linguistic ones" (1958:41). Ethnographic facts should be equally understood as so many signs operating within a system or a universal semiology. This is the crucial difference with the logical atomism that had Functionalism in its grasp. Grammar takes precedence over facts; reason will finally keep history in check. This is what Barthes had rendered as the apparently banal difference between the French *le structural* and *le structurel* (1957:119ff). For Lévi-Strauss, this new semiology that had already turned linguistics into the only social science capable of matching the exact and natural sciences (1973:344) can accomplish the same task in the rest of the social sciences.

So, social facts are signs, but signs of what? Lévi-Strauss has a ready answer—signs of the Unconscious. Freud thus makes an appearance at this juncture. Indeed, did not Lévi-Strauss refer (1968a) to psychoanalysis, Marxism, and geology as his three intellectual mistresses? His Unconscious, though, like Bachelard's (1972, 1973), only has a nominal resemblance with Freud's. It is not the Id, that unrelenting pleasure seeker prey to the Oedipus predicament. It has nothing to do with real sexual drives felt by men and women and the history of their repression. Neither is it the ensemble of unwilling relations of subjection people contract in their social life, highlighted by Marx in his famous scrutiny of merchandise fetishism. Nor is it the Hegelian Spirit, the self-quest of which is the real substance of all history. It is rather the logical fabric of the Mind, understood not as an attribute of individual human beings, but as a system of logical variations and subsystems of combinations. Any cultural event or artifact is but a particular symbol of that potentially endless combinatory. "We will not attempt to show how men think through myths, but how myths think themselves through men, even without their knowing it" (1964:20).

Foucault has become more popular than Lévi-Strauss in the last 30 years. With an extended cult following, his philosophical works attempt to show that if major shifts in theory can be explained fully, one has to forget about their historical genealogy and concentrate in the logical conditions that made them possible at a given point in time. Here he is of one mind with Lévi-Strauss.

Since the opening sequences of his *leçon inaugurale* (inaugural lecture or maiden class) as reader in the *Collège de France* (College of France, perhaps the most distinguished institution of higher education in that country) on December 2, 1970, Foucault (1971) shows his opposition to 19th-century thinkers that believed time was an open vector of cumulative change. The historicist tradition took a number of oppositions (reason/madness;

true/false; normal/pathological) for granted while excluding some supposedly well-defined practices (researchers have to cast aside politics, value judgments, and moral issues). It is precisely when discourses are said to flow freely for the first time in history that they seem to resemble the modern human individual's condition according to Rousseau—"everywhere in chains"—as free discourse has become a ritual of the word (1971:47).

Conversely, though, the analysis of discourse should cast doubts over this idyllic panorama to introduce, "at thought's own roots, randomness, discontinuity and materiality" (1971:61) lest it falls for "[either] the endless generosity of sense, [or] the monarchy of the signifier" (1971:72). This summarizes the program he called an archeology of knowledge (1972).

The name refers to the need for researchers to overcome the limits of the materials they usually work—documents whose meaning can be interpreted. To his end, though, they should be treated as monuments, that is, discourses made of discontinuous and, to some extent, unpredictable elements. And he concludes: "What, in short, we wish to do is to dispense with 'things'. To 'depresentify' them" (1972:47). It is the dispersion of logical possibilities, as opposed to empirical facts or historical events, what for him represents randomness, discontinuity, and materiality.

This bow to randomness, discontinuity, or materiality, however, has a fleeting duration. Foucault just tips his hat to them in passing in order to immediately concentrate on the logical relations between signs while their invariant structuring takes precedence over the rest. Indeed, discourses or collections of logical conditions of possibility vary over time, but once they crystallize they become invariant—or with the rather gauche name he bestows on them, become historical *a priori*, positivities or epistemes. Ephemeral as they may be, those historically *a priori* formations are instances of what he calls the Archive (an equivalent of Lévi-Strauss' Unconscious) or "the law of what can be said, the system that governs the appearance of statements as unique events" (1972:129), the whole of *a priori* formations, positivities, and epistemes. In an earlier work, Foucault (1970) attempted to exemplify this view. After having dealt in other works with the formation of discourses in medicine (1973) or in psychiatry (1965), he endeavored to show that what is commonly seen as the history of sciences is but the display of different rational positivities at work in linguistics, biology, and economics, and their horizontal discontinuities.

This is a difficult posture. We are told to focus on how logical formations follow each other, and that this is a sequential, not a causal order. But in so doing, Foucault has to pay the toll of renouncing to explain how epistemic changes come about. For him, they just lie there. The mind, the unconscious, however we call his, and Lévi-Strauss' demiurge has no real mover. Why does the metaphor, or the archive, or the Mind express itself through varying metonyms? Why does it not remain always equal to itself, as Parmenides wanted? How is change possible? Can it be understood without a proper reckoning of the impact of time, history, and human material interests? To speak plain English, can we characterize, for instance, the trend to globalization without referring to the technological changes that have made it possible? When they face these problems, structuralists claim that, like a kaleidoscope, the Mind creates different, though symmetrical and ordered, combinations by rearranging its basic elements. However, kaleidoscopes would not change shapes unless externally propelled either on purpose or just by accident. Left to their own devices, they would never depart from the previous state.

It is often suggested that the lack of explanation for change finally requires glorifying the heretofore forgotten reality as the design of a superior mind, either with a pre-ordained plan in the Hegelian version, or with no plan whatsoever as in the Mind's endless *a priori* combinations. However, this is not exact. We will see that the Theory has a rather nonconformist, even radical face. What is really worrying is that the deconstructionist methodology that comes after this ontological stage lends itself to all kinds of manipulations.

THE SOUNDS OF SILENCE

Lévi-Strauss is also the source of the new methodology. He did not call it *deconstructionism* at the time, but he provided the kernel for what would come later. The new methodology sees the creation of a grammar of discovery as the prerequisite for ordering the usually chaotic world of cultural objects, showing how each of them has a place in a preexistent logical order, often called a discourse or, more recently, a narrative. The grammar will fill in the blanks that facts are so often careless enough to elide or silence themselves.

The origins of the new method can be found in two of Lévi-Strauss' best-known works: the already cited study of the savage mind and another, more technical work on totemism published in the same year (1962). In both one can see the lengths he will go to in order to reintegrate every single event or artifact or sememe in the order of discourse. Imagine, Lévi-Strauss says, a tribe (let's call it Tribe A) that was once structured into three clans, each one of them named by an animal symbolizing a natural element. We could represent this as in Figure 1.

However, anthropologists usually do not find ancient societies in their original state. Often, it happens that, because of demographic changes, the Bear clan might have disappeared, while the Turtle clan was so successful that two new subclans—Yellow Turtle and Grey Turtle—stemmed from it and over time became two independent units or proper clans. It also might have also happened that those changes occurred in such a distant time that even the own tribe members couldn't remember them. An anthropologist doing fieldwork among them would see that their present social structure was organized as in Figure 2.

How can the anthropologist re- or deconstruct the forgotten process whose outcome has been the present situation?

> Now, on the theoretical as well as the practical plane, the existence of differentiating features is of much greater importance than their content. Once in evidence, they form a system that can be employed as a grid is used to decipher a text, whose original unintelligibility gives it the appearance of an uninterrupted flow. The grid makes it possible to introduce divisions and contrasts, in other words the formal conditions necessary for a significant message to be conveyed (Lévi-Strauss 1966a:75).

With the aid of grid-reading, that is, selecting the relevant evidence beyond its immediate, historical appearance, one can prevail over any anthropological riddles or silences in the material in the same way as binary oppositions of

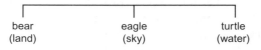

Figure 1 Original Structure of Tribe A.

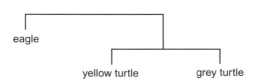

Figure 2 Present Structure of Tribe A.

signifiers led Saussure—at least he believed they did—to fill the chasm between the sound of words and their meaning within a given language.

How can we then listen to the sounds of the silence—the title of Simon and Garfunkel's song comes in so handy—that shrouds many anthropological facts? Just look at Figure 3.

Following some rules of binary oppositions—that is, following the unlimited divisions and contrasts of the material to be studied, not its content—we can follow the leads and grasp not only that their initial position has gone through a number of changes, but also what they are. If the first conclusion seems knotty enough—how do we reckon how many, how intensive, or how protracted those changes were?— the second is mission impossible. There was no merit to reach the outcome in Figure 3; in fact, we had been told beforehand what the changes between Time 1 and Time 2 were, and we knew their direction. It is highly improbable, though, that other anthropologists or observers might retrace the particular sequence of this change in exactly the same way, merely based on oppositions as

(yellow : grey) :: (day : night) :: (water : air)

that contradict/affirm, first, the two sub-Turtle clans and, then, their relation with the Eagle clan while letting us know that a third element related to earth (the Bear clan) is no longer there. If this is so in a system that has known only one change within a rather limited four-variable structure (bear/eagle/yellow turtle/grey turtle), one can easily imagine what would happen in a universe of unlimited oppositions along a temporal chain of unknown duration. Duplication and replicability, usually considered basic features of scientific method, would have all but vanished into thin air.

This is exactly what happens in his masterwork on myths. Let us select one of the 385 myths Lévi-Strauss examines in *L'Homme Nu* (The Naked Man), the fourth volume of his *Mythologiques* (1964, 1966b, 1968b, 1971),

Time 1	Bear	Eagle	Turtle	
Time 2		Eagle	Yellow Turtle	Grey Turtle

Figure 3 Grid-Reading Tribe A.

and let us do it at random. One just opens the French version of the book about its middle, and one finds the nearest myth on pages 322 and 323. That happens to be M#661a and #661b—the myth of the two brothers retrieved from the Nez Percé tribe. The story involves a mythical character that ascends into the sky propelled by the sudden growth of a plant or a tree.

Lévi-Strauss develops a protracted exegesis of the myth (1971:304–314) that we will spare readers. In a nutshell, he concludes that it is a regulating cell (1971:313) that teaches the different peoples of the area how to avoid war in pursuit of more peaceful endeavors. All's well that ends well. However, one counts at least 16 symmetries/discontinuities among the different sequences of the story with Lévi-Strauss jumping from one to the other without warning. In fact, the probability that another researcher unaware of Lévi-Strauss' analysis reaches the same conclusions starting with the same materials must be close to nil.

Foucault readily joins him, though not in the details of ethnographic description. He just shares in the main vision, which is not surprising. After all, both Lévi-Strauss and he are part of the same intellectual milieu, and have common relations in scholarly heritage and similar mind frames. Foucault, though, shines as the more straightforward; he just takes a few shortcuts. In structuralist lingo, one could say that he favors symptomal over expressive reading (Althusser and Balibar 1970:22), though with a twist. He is all in favor of grid-reading, but has no appetite for the dance/contra-dance of binary oppositions we witness *chez* Lévi-Strauss. Just say no. No to the meaning that given documents or texts seemingly convey to their positive meaning; read rather what they do not say. Silence (Simon and Garfunkel's song plays again) is indeed more telling for it illuminates any text even to the point of contradicting it if hermeneutics so requires. One only has to put the text on to the grid of its logical preconditions. The technique has become the method of choice for *pomo* analysis in nearly every semiotic field, from literary criticism to fashion analysis. One cannot be so sure, though, about its reliability. Grid-reading either leads to indefinite regression or becomes amenable to any passing whim.

The text, the finite and positive communication pack, has to be interpreted by silence, that is, by all that it is not. Take the fashionable view, obviously inspired by grid-reading, of the US Declaration of Independence, written by Thomas Jefferson and approved by Congress on July 4, 1776 when it says that:

> [w]e hold these truths to be self-evident, that all men are created equal, that they are endowed by their Creator with certain unalienable Rights, that among these are Life, Liberty

and the pursuit of Happiness. That to secure these rights, Governments are instituted among Men, deriving their just powers from the consent of the governed,–That whenever any Form of Government becomes destructive of these ends, it is the Right of the People to alter or to abolish it, and to institute new Government, laying its foundation on such principles and organizing its powers in such form, as to them shall seem most likely to affect their Safety and Happiness (USA 2003).

In an expressive reading, this is a revolutionary document that bases its indictment of the British Crown and the subsequent need to create an independent and free nation on a set of philosophical axioms that anyone can understand. The text seems to have been dictated by universal reason. However, one can also read it in a symptomal way.

With this tool in hand, the Declaration is said to be surrounded by a couple of telling silences. It addresses men, not women, so, even after independence the latter were still counted as second class citizens, deprived of the full enjoyment of those inalienable rights. Additionally, Congress was made up of many gentlemen farmers that could not accept the possibility that slaves might enjoy the said rights. The Declaration, thus, may appear as a universal, humanistic document; however, in grid-reading, it reveals itself as an act of exclusion. The universality of rights proclaimed by the Declaration is, in fact, a warrant for particular interests.

But those are not the only silences in the Declaration. It also overlooks the rights of future generations of immigrants; or how gays and lesbians might pursue their happiness; or the treatment of people with disabilities; or the right to abort or to same-sex marriage. To think about it, it does not say anything of the reasons George III adduced in defense of the *status quo*, effectively depriving him of his right to defense; or of the opinion of its signatories on Newtonian physics; or of why it chose to ignore the beliefs of those in the 13 colonies who did not agree with creationism; or how the weather report for Philadelphia on that July 4 might have influenced the mood of the Founding Fathers; or many other, infinite possibilities equally silenced. Why should grid-reading select but two of them?

Had we attempted this task, though, we could not have avoided being bombarded with similar enquiries as to any of those eventual silences, thus causing an infinite regression. Unless we become enticed by the promise ("Thou shalt be like God") of being able to perceive everything plus all its endless ramifications (what medieval scholastics used to call *futuribiles*, that is, all the things that may be imagined as possible in the future) in real time, the proposed task exceeds human reason (Saint-Victor 1961). This may be within the purview of the structuralist Mind, but it is by no means within that of the humans it speaks through. Humans will still have to put up with the broken language of content discontinuities or, in plain English, the specificity of discourses. Exactly what the symptomal or grid-reading techniques are so eager to avoid. But why should we accept any Foucauldian claim to be the prophet of the new revelation?

Infinite regression, though, would at any rate be the lesser of two evils triggered by this treacherous way of reading. The other, the deadlier one, is the use of it as a James Bond-like license to kill anything not easily conforming to what the researcher's agenda defines as correct. This has become the road more traveled by *pomos*. A case in point, among the myriad we might bring about, is Derrida's exegesis of the Marxian narrative of the fetishism of merchandises (1994:110ff). All of a sudden, Marx does not talk about the different modes of production, or *Das Kapital* does not portend to show the process that will cause the end of capitalism. The fetishism of merchandises is a ghost story. According to Derrida's abstruse rhetoric:

> this woody and headstrong denseness [Derrida is referring to a table JA] is metamorphosed into a supernatural thing, a *sensuous non-sensuous* thing, sensuous but non-sensuous, sensuously supersensible"), merchandises are brought about by Marx to illustrate the role of ideology in general, not as social relations contracted through work. The question of fetishism "deserves perhaps to be put the other way [...] [T]hey are always *there*, specters, even if they do not exist, even if they are no longer, even if they are not yet (1994:104).

The conclusion could not veer further away from Marx's positive meaning. Instead of social forms that will disappear some day with the end of capitalism, ideologies are here to stay; we even can learn from them, Derrida says. He may be right, but what we want to stress is that his grid-reading, avidly listening to the sound of silence, allows him to say that what Marx really said was what Marx really did not say—or the other way around (Marx here refers to Karl, not to Groucho, who, as Otis B. Driftwood in *A Night at the Opera*, might have said the same and even more).

Grid-reading brings to mind memories of another technique of finding out lost evidence—the so-called regression therapy or recovered memory syndrome (Hunter 2000; Tebbetts 1987). The technique allegedly made people fill in the missing boxes of their memory, that is, remember, often through hypnosis, deleted episodes of their infancy or early adolescence. It was quite widespread in the 1990s, and was used in legal cases involving sexual abuse or incest in the United States (Prendergast 1996:283–321), the United Kingdom, and Canada, creating a feeding frenzy in the media. It was soon the object of severe scrutiny by different scientific institutions that led to its discrediting, as the consequences of this so-called syndrome were quite serious for the legal protection of the defendants (Brandon et al 1998; Loftus and Ketchum 1996). Grid-reading, indeed, has not undergone similar probing, but its peculiar and unchecked way of filling in the blanks of documents should not find the approval of researchers who think skepticism is a healthy turn of mind in scientific ventures. Grid-reading looks suspiciously like a license to overkill. A further step and *pomo*s will start shooting.

ENTER DECONSTRUCTIONISM

It is highly doubtful that, by themselves, structuralism and grid-reading with its bizarre ways of listening to the sounds of silence might have propelled this theoretical matrix to mass recognition. An additional block in the grid had to be filled before that happened, viz., the formulation of a number of social and ethical theorems that were initially of interest to just a few intellectual elites, but finally drew a mass following. It was deconstruction-ism. Deconstructionism integrates a number of elements of different origin. French structuralism was at the top, but it fitted handily with certain variants of American symbolic interactionism, especially as represented by Erving Goffman. It also coincided in part with the findings of Norbert Elias.

From his *Madness and Civilization* (2001) to the later volumes of the *History of Sexuality* (1978, 1985, 1986), Foucault endeavored to read and explain the varied intellectual genealogy of all kinds of repression in modernity. One could ask why his silence about other historical epochs or world regions, but this question will be momentarily cast aside. *Madness and Civilization* discusses how modernity constructed the notion of folly in successive stages. The Renaissance (15th–16th centuries) had a rather benevolent view of folly as a will to attain (false) wisdom. The artistic *Narrenschiff* [Ship of Fools] genre of the times shows a delicious landscape where desire reigns supreme. On the other side, though, the Renaissance ranks folly uppermost among human vices. It is its peculiar way of making madness comprehensible.

In the 17th century, the Salpêtrière General Hospital was founded. In Foucault's view the new institution did not answer any medical need.

It was but an instance of the order the monarchy and the bourgeoisie introduced in France around the same period. From then on, fools were subject to confinement, which is the real reason for the creation of the said hospital and many similar ones in the rest of Europe. Fools were thus separated from the sane world with a double effect—absorb unemployment or, at least, blur its more visible social consequences. The new morality not only imprisoned deviants (fools but also paupers, prostitutes, petty criminals, and other lower orders); it made them responsible for their own deviation. Madness became the scarlet letter for moral failure.

With the alliance/dispute of psychology and morals, 19th-century "scientific psychiatry" entered the stage. It demanded a stricter definition of madness. Many economists in the 18th century maintained that a sizable and active population would increase the wealth of nations. Confinement had therefore to be abandoned for it limited the growth of the labor force. On the other hand, charitable foundations that had traditionally been assigned to deal with poverty tied a sizable amount of capital that might be mobilized to create additional growth. The poor, especially the deserving poor, had to be separated from other deviants. But liberating a part of the population previously under surveillance requested new types of control. The new asylums, such as Tuke's *The Retreat*, did not rely on physical violence; they preferred to turn fools into minors. Minors needed parents, and the new asylums got ready to play the part of the patriarch within the bourgeois family. Madness used to be an individual fault; now decadent families, unable to rise to the standards of bourgeois morality, favored the reversed order of mad behavior. This, in Foucault's view, sealed the final reconciliation between the critical and the medical notions of madness that would be epitomized by Freud. With him, madness flows unfettered from confinement and violence, though at the price of empowering doctors with a quasi-divine status. It also shows the peculiar definition of madness as the lack of adjustment to socially constructed normalcy.

Erving Goffman was making similar remarks around the same time (1961). In reviewing the moral careers of mental patients, he announced a comparable finding:

> The student of mental hospitals can discover that the craziness or "sick behavior" claimed for the mental patient is by and large a product of the claimant's social distance from the situation that the patient is in, and is not primarily a product of mental illness (1961:130).

Mental institutions operate as a "ward" system whose main goal is to show that "everything a patient does on his own can be defined as symptomatic of his disorder or of his convalescence" (1961:206). He somehow anticipated Randle Patrick McMurphy's ordeal (Kesey 1973) in *One Flew over the Cuckoo's Nest*. Catch 22—if one submits to the psychiatric establishment, one confirms the need to be cured, and proves them right; if one resists, then one needs further treatment.

Goffman would later extend a similar methodology to broader social issues and institutions in his discussion of stigma. Societies classify people through attributes expected to be possessed by members of each category. When we meet strangers, we anticipate that they may be classified in the same way. If this expectation is not fulfilled, we tend to think that this person bears a stigma, an undesired difference.

> By definition, of course, we believe that the person with a stigma is not quite human [...] We construct a stigma-theory, an ideology to explain his inferiority and account for the danger he represents, sometimes rationalizing an animosity based on other differences, such as those of social class (1963:5).

Stigmas are ways of coping with what veers away from societal notions of normalcy, and are thus the concrete product of dysfunctional cognitive interaction. Hence, they are not marks deserved or determined by the nature of individuals or groups; just demeaning marks other groups or communities make them wear.

Goffman, however, is quite cautious when dealing with mental illness and stigma. He does not see them exclusively in terms of distorted social practices arbitrarily constructed. All social bonds carry restrictions usually based on nonexplicit assumptions (1961:174) that unleash sanctions when they are overstepped, ignored, or unrecognized. Although he does not venture explanations, he acknowledges that stigma has accompanied human life for many centuries. He seems thus skeptical at the possibility of ever doing away with it. However, he leaves unresolved the issue whether there is in fact anything like mental illness beyond its social component. One dares say that effective disruptions in communication between human beings appear regularly, and that many of them seem to be beyond repair (schizophrenia, Down, and Alzheimer syndromes, some types of autism, etc.). Even if we were able to prove beyond any reasonable doubt that they are but social constructs, and that nuclear families or societies at large are to be blamed for the outcome, individuals thus labeled would still need some kind of special attention, that is, psychiatric treatment. Their wounds, perhaps inflicted by others, linger on and impair their social skills.

These ideas would take a drastic turn in Laing's antipsychiatry and his insistence that all mental illness, even the deepest cases of communicative disruption, schizophrenia for instance, are socially constructed (1998a). Their causes will not be found in the patients, but in the institutions that shape their reactions like the (bourgeois nuclear) family and (modern) society at large (1998c, 1998d). Ken Loach gave a vivid illustration of this approach in his film *Family Life*.

For Laing, the only sensible way to deal with people with mental disorders is to acknowledge their inner sanity and even let them leave the mental institutions where their conditions worsen (1998b). Indeed, modern psychiatry has made exorbitant claims to diagnose and cure madness with some techniques that may include drastic interventions (from physical violence to the use of psychotropic drugs to electroshocks to lobotomies). Many of those procedures have been debased and discredited, but it is difficult to conclude from their use that psychiatry is a sort of quackery better proscribed altogether. One might say that better theories should be proffered instead of exorcisms. Overall advocacy of antipsychiatric practices may create more problems than it solves. For instance, it became an additional alibi for the massive cuts in federal aid to municipal governments sponsored by Ronald Reagan. "In 1980 federal dollars accounted for 22% of big city budgets. By the end of Reagan's second term, federal aid was only 6%" (Dreier 2004). Such precipitous drop wreaked havoc with schools, libraries, fire departments, and other municipal facilities. The subsequent closure of many public hospitals and clinics contributed to a noticeable increase in urban homelessness, but did not diminish the number of people in need of psychiatric assistance. It just deprived them of it.

Foucault's interests are more encompassing than a critique of psychiatry. What started as an appraisal of mental illness finally became an overall indictment of modernity. His critique of madness is a call for a sweeping societal overhaul. The rest of his story is well known. Narratives of domination can be found in all fields of social life. *Discipline and Punish* (1995) argues that the modern penitentiary system has its roots in the previous practices of social retribution by way of torture and executions (Hay et al 1977). It is a softer way of making deviants accept social order, but it does not diminish repression. In fact, for Foucault, this new way of punishment has become the norm for all modern forms of social control.

Bentham's *Panopticon* goal of prison stability through vigilance at a distance today pervades most social activities and ensures the dominance of the powers that are, making them unseen, even palatable.

There may be a way out of this trap, he says. In the history of folly, a different kind of madness emerged in the 19th century—derangement as lucidity. The new mad lucidity can allow humans to reach the deepest limits of their self-estrangement from themselves in Western societies. For the first time in history, madness forces the world to take the stand as the defendant, not as the prosecutor. Through those new types of folly, mankind may devise, often as through a dark glass, ways to overcome previous narrowly defined norms always in need of increasing repression. Foucault not only provides an analysis of the causes—he also supplies a textbook for liberation from them.

The first part of his argument deserves further probing for it is counterintuitive. One would readily say that there is some degree of difference between the gory descriptions of executions and torture that Foucault uses as an overture to *Discipline and Punish*, and modern punitive systems. Modern European societies, for instance, show their pride at having proscribed the death penalty from their legal codes. Foucault does not ignore it, but notes that the vivid images of punishment meant to provoke awe and fear among the viewers of the classic age (exemplary representations, he calls them, as in the procession of convicts from Newgate prison to the Tyburn scaffold in London; Linebaugh 1977), have been replaced by a new punitive order that rests on the modification of behavior. "Rather than on an art of representations, this punitive intervention must rest on a studied manipulation of the individual" (Focault 1995:128).

Why? The disciplinary mechanism seeks to punish within a system of norms, usually known as the rule of law. Individuals or bodies hence have to become standardized, that is, normalized. In societies that treat them so, individuals lose their *raison d'être*. This creates a continuum of discipline that has, at one end, the enclosed confinement institutions and, at the other, functional mechanisms to make power lighter, subtler, gentler, and therefore more effective (Allen 2004). Domination through the use of scientific techniques has also become the purview of sexual control and of the disciplining of bodies, narrated in his *History of Sexuality*. A final stage of power is reached when, as is the case in most social activities, the subversive impetus, either of sexuality or of alternative ways of life is tamed through the diffusion of so-called new social sciences (psychoanalysis, sexology, marketing, advertising, and so on). Similar opinions have been echoed by other French authors in Foucault's wake (Bourdieu 1984; Derrida 1994, 2002; Deleuze and Guattari 1977, 1987).

Still a doubt lingers in the reader. Is it possible that there are no real differences between domination by imposition or repression, as in the classic age, and the willful acceptance of the rule of law, no matter how passive this acceptance may be, in democratic societies? There is a long tradition in Western thought, going from Hobbes to Locke to Mill to Max Weber to Nye's (2004) idea of soft power that maintains there is a distinction between both. Weber explains in various places of his work the conflict of *Macht* (Power) and *Herrschaft* (Domination), or illegitimate and legitimate domination (1971:16, 122–176, 541–550). The main feature of the latter is the consent to power on the part of the citizenry. Lately, Tilly has stressed how the breach of this belief contributes to social turmoil (1978), while its maintenance makes domination stable and sustainable (2001). Another tradition initiated with Constant (1980) and De Tocqueville (1866) has precisely considered the rule of law or normative systems to be the fundamental difference between the *Ancien Régime* (Old Regime) and modern democracy, between old and modern freedom. Foucault, however, would not recognize himself in either one of them. Legitimate or not, domination is domination; power is power. Even when the public choice is expressed in free elections? Even then.

This encompassing approach to power and modernity leaves a serious problem unresolved. If we follow Foucault's logic of power, the difference between democracy and authoritarianism has no sense. Both exercise power; both equally impose themselves on their subjects. Reading Foucault one can hardly avoid the feeling of being confronted with an anacoluthon. There is an unresolved tension in his work between, on the one hand, the inevitability of power struggles which are the essence of any discourse and of all social practices, and, on the other, the need to assert their asymmetry. If we accept the first part of the dilemma, Foucault cannot avoid the *reductio ad Hitlerum*. Papering over the differences among political regimes leads to the blind alley of seeing Hitler as legitimate (or illegitimate) as any other ruler. He exercised power, just as any other leader does. Broadly speaking, he sought power as much as the next participant in any social interaction does, though more successfully.

In the field of punishment, one reaches a similar blind alley. It is not possible to tell torture from imprisonment, as both are but diverse modes of repression. In practice, following his logic of repression, one has to suspend judgment on the abuses of power in Abu Ghraib and Guantanamo under George W. Bush's watch. How would they be different from the judicial review of a crime following the rules of due process and of trial by jury, if the latter is also a blatant expression of repression? Foucault thus takes the reader back to something like the Hobbesian state of nature, a perpetual confrontation of powers, of action and resistance, and of opposed cultures and countercultures with no room for moral judgment.

Foucault knows that the equivalence principle can debunk his critique of modernity. Why criticize the subjection of the bodies, or the alleged disciplining of sexuality or of folly when power is symmetrical, that is, can be equally found in all social practices? How can we exonerate the Other of this heavy and inescapable burden? If any identity or position or discourse or narrative or any similar code for power is as good as the next, why demand changes in the current state of affairs? Perhaps all reason is repression; but, then, why should we believe Foucault's pledge that liberating madness will not be, as in the Spanish expression, the same dogs with changing collars. Perhaps everything has failed, but it does not follow that his promise will be necessarily kept. The skeptic has a right to be wary of Foucault's brave new world. Bouvard and Pécuchet's incessantly started new projects, each one of them more calamitous than the previous one. Foucault's sympathy for Khomeini's revolution in Iran did not bode well for his political wisdom (Afary and Anderson 2005).

Deep down, he can only proceed by fiat, that is, substituting moralizing for reasoning. He is not interested in explaining how things happened, only how they should be. At times, Foucault takes some leaves from Marx's book, but he is only laterally interested in economics. He bundles people targeted by the successive Poor Laws in Britain with the population considered to be mad. He does not present serious data on the size of the workforce provided by fools. In 1685, England's population was an estimated 5 million; within this total about 3,250,000 were farmers, laborers, servants, and poor. The number of vagrants, among whom one should look for the majority of fools, was 30,000 (Trevelyan 2000), that is, less than 1% the amount of the working and poor population—rather small to be considered a significant economic force. He explains the beginning of the repressive treatment of madness by an undefined alliance of the monarchy and the bourgeoisie, even though it is difficult to say that this social group was hegemonic in 17th-century France. He avoids assessing the merits of the classical economists in identifying charitable foundations, monasteries, non-alienable property rights on land as major fetters on economic development. Of course, Foucault does not show interest in probing the nooks and crannies of the capitalist mode of production. He is not interested in the details of class stratification and political game theories. Factual questions do not move him—no big surprise after the painstaking extremes he went to in his epistemological writings to erase them from the structuralist field of vision. This may also explain his silence towards the history of repression in nonmodern or non-Western societies. For all his scorn towards the evolutionary view of history, it seems that Foucault believes in the existence of a red thread in the development of power—it is a race to the bottom whose nadir was finally reached with the birth of Western modernity. Why bother with anything else than the biography of this mishap?

There are many coincidences in this narrative with other contemporary currents. Foucault and the French deconstructionists were not alone in singling out modernity. Indeed, this was also the Frankfurt School's top prized sport. Though they located the blight of Western culture in other areas of human intercourse, their conclusions were similar to Foucault's. Horkheimer and Adorno blamed technology and the will to overpower nature as modernity's capital sin (1972), next being the manufacturing of authoritarian personalities (Adorno et al 1964). The denial of Eros (1955) and the subsequent one-dimensionality of human life (1966) under advanced capitalism entertained Marcuse's musings on civilization (1955, 1966). With capitalism, mass societies, and liberal culture, the West apparently reached the highest possible levels of misery.

Norbert Elias is perhaps the one closest to Foucault's logic. *Zivilization* (Civilization), that is, the process that brought about our modern, bourgeois societies, triggered a complete overhaul of the economy of affections and emotions. In Europe, from the Early Middle Ages to the Renaissance to the absolutist era to the bourgeois 19th and 20th centuries, civilization came along with an extensive repression of natural drives through new forms of control.

> Today the circle of standards and rules weighs so heavily over men; the control and the pressure of social intercourse involved in their customs is so unbending that there is only one alternative [...]: either submit to the socially expected rules of conduct or be placed out of the realm of civilized life (1997:I, 283).

The new subsystems of behavioral control usually started among the upper rungs of the social ladder to be later internalized by the lower orders. Elias offers a wide range of examples in fields usually excluded from scholarly research such as meat consumption, diets, table manners, home privacy, erotic mores, tolerance of public nudity, and so forth (1997:II, 379–392).

Changes follow an increasing gradient of more or less automatic self-control; they demand the subjection of impulsive emotions to the mechanical norm of delayed satisfaction; and they prompt to acquire a Super-Ego paraphernalia ever more profuse and rigid. Modern "civilized" society, finally, has increased exponentially the role of insecurity and shame in the control of individuals. Elias' conclusion comes unfettered from those premises. The scholarly opposition of "natural" and "civilized" life with its inherent belief in the superiority of the latter holds no water. If at all, humans were in better terms with their own selves in the societies that preceded modernity.

Or were they? Duerr has noted that the evidence Elias offers in support of his thesis is flimsy, to say the least. Most uncivilized societies use a machinery of shame, embarrassment, lost face, and so on, quite similar to the one favored in civilized ones to control public shows of emotion. Even in those groups where nudity or near nudity is widespread, there are clear limits to the way their members can look at each other (Duerr 1992). Additionally, Elias' epiphany of an increasing repression of nudity and of sexual activities within the Western affective economy has not aged graciously. Spring breaks, Mardi Gras, *Fasching*, and other similar occasions aside, topless female sun worshippers and nudist areas have become so common on most European beaches that they no longer attract the attention of onlookers or the media. The same happens with swinging clubs and other adult entertainment venues. For some unexplained reason, in the general trend of the civilizing process the growing Super-Ego repression of instincts was suddenly overtaken by the so-called sexual revolution only 25 years after Elias proclaimed its unremitting climb. It was difficult to maintain his predictions after the 1969 Summer of Love exploded in San Francisco.

The *pomo* matrix thus travels from a program of unbound relativism to the formulation of fuzzy, but firmly proclaimed, moral and political principles without a roadmap. On one hand, denial of objectivity, grid-reading, the illegitimacy of all power; on the other, liberation of the Other, resistance to every enticement of modernity, nostalgia for the pre-modern past. Elias, as well as Foucault, has contributed heavily to the neo-romantic imagery sponsored by the *pomos*. Ours is a world gone astray in an age of lost innocence, and unbridled abuses of power. There surely was a time when things had not gone so wrong. At least, it can be imagined. From Passolini's dream of a medieval community unfettered by any modern economy of affections (*Decameron*, *The Canterbury Tales*) to *The Da Vinci Code* (Brown 2003) with its evocation of a past paganism, pre-Christian or pre-Judeo-Christian or pre-monotheist or pre-patriarchal or pre-whatever, a significant part of our mass culture reflects the *pomo* nostalgia for a lost time when Arcadia Felix was not just the name of a new theme park. Human history is indeed full of rebels who thought they had a cause; with hindsight, however, one wonders whether they ever had any effect. Effects are what we should to discuss now.

POMOS, POCOS, DECOS

The second half of the 20th century was a portentous time. It witnessed the downfall of the old Western empires, including the Soviet empire, a formidable decolonization process, and the awakening of major social categories that had until then accepted their subordinate status. Women, ethnic minorities, gays and lesbians and transsexuals, people with disabilities—all joined forces in their fight against discrimination, especially in Western societies.

As we have seen, *pomo* offered them all a critical methodology—what it called the new ways of reading or deconstructionism. It also provided a defined object for their criticism—modernity. But the target was too abstract. When Foucault was at his most concrete, he would talk about power, repression, and similar fuzzy categories that, in his view, constrained bodies and made them accept social definitions that unfailingly restricted their best expectations. Who profited from them and to what extent; how could they be best overcome; with what strategies and tactics; all those were open questions. Ideas and theories, however, need the catalyst of concrete experiences and clear goals to gain the hearts and minds of significant numbers of people. Deconstructionism (*deco*) took center stage.

In the past, Marxism had fiercely criticized western political systems, and especially the capitalist economy. For nearly a century, Marxism was the only global intellectual alternative to the dominant ideologies of the West. It had a theory of history, a political economy, and a prime mover for the creation of a fairer order called socialism. It is not a coincidence that some of the first attempts to put together explanations for the subjection of other social categories under capitalism would initially use Marxist concepts and methods. De Beauvoir likened the exploitation of women to that of the proletariat (1949), and some later efforts to build a feminist theory would explore a so-called domestic mode of production (Rowbotham 1973; Rowbotham et al 1981; Hartsock 1983). Even before, some black American writers had gone through a similar evolution. With different degrees of intensity and engagement, W.E.B DuBois, Langston Hughes, and Claude McKay, among others, sought in Marxism and socialism the tools to account for the apartheid people then called Negros suffered in the

United States. Soon, however, it would be felt that race, gender, and class did not make easy partners. More and more it was said that Marxism blunted criticism, and was redolent of ethnocentrism, and patriarchalism. The industrial working class was, after all, an aggregate of Western white male workers not easily found in other parts of the world. Workingmen often had the same behavioral patterns as the rest of the males of the species. Soon, many black Americans would turn towards racial nationalism, and the narratives of feminism would call psychoanalysis onto the stage (Mitchell 1974, 1984).

One can also find a changing attitude to Western models in the theorists of decolonization. Many former colonial Marxists would blindly follow Lenin's definition of imperialism as the senescent stage of capitalism and his ideas about self-determination. The next generation would veer in another direction. Césaire, Memmi, and Fanon were colonials. Soon their radicalism left economics to replace it with cultural analysis. The shift can be clearly seen in Franz Fanon. His best-known theoretical work (1968) brims over with Marxist lingo, but at the same time shows a decided intent to provide a different theoretical basis for decolonization (1988, 1991).

The colonial world, according to Fanon, is a Manichean entity. Colonization usually started with the forceful dispossession of the natives from their land, from their riches and, also, from their cultural heritage, and created two opposed human categories—colonists and colonials. These two worlds would remain separate and mutually exclusive as long as colonialism existed. The asymmetry between the foreign power and the subdued nations, however, is not just a question of naked power. For sure, the colonists have the police and the army in case of a significant threat to their order. But beyond there is a whole world of opposing cultures. The colonists' cultural goal is clear—to deprive the natives of their humanity. In the eyes of the colonists, the colonized societies are a world without values, and therefore a valueless world. They should be destroyed and replaced by the superior civilization the colonists brought with them.

National liberation is the polar opposite of this strategy. The colonial order, brutal and violent at root, should be overturned by a superior might whose task would require a complete overhaul not only on the political level, but also on the cultural front. Liberated ex-colonies have no use for the ideas and cultural institutions of the former power. The uprooting of its alien cultural structures should be as thorough as the colonial onslaught on local life. Even though he pays some occasional attention to the divergent interests of the different fractions of metropolitan capital, the tensions between the colonists and their central governments, and the metropolitan workers' restricted solidarity with the colonies, Fanon often ignores how these realities made the colonial compact less monolithic than he wanted to acknowledge. For him, anticolonial fighters should shun any accommodation with the colonizing powers and their culture, for they are a lethal influence. He warily looks at those sectors of the newly decolonized countries that were more exposed to the influences of the metropolis, as they might be more prone to accept cultural and political compromises with the old order. National bourgeoisies, intellectuals, and even native urban workers should not be trusted by liberation movements, for they were too close to the corrupting influences of the foreign powers. At heart, Fanon—like Mao, like Pol Pot—only trusts the peasants and their urban equivalents, the unemployed city masses, both impervious to the spell of the colonial culture. With Fanon, the decisive danger to postcolonial societies stems less from the economic roots of Western domination than from its cultural ascendancy.

The most influential theories of neocolonialism in the 1970s and 1980s did not follow his footsteps. The dependency school took a more Marxian approach, primarily focusing on the role of the Third World within the international economic order (Baran 1957; Baran and Sweezy 1966), the exchanges between center and peripheries (Amin 1973, 1976; Emmanuel 1972; Frank 1975, 1981; Wallerstein 1974, 1980) or the stability of political domination within the world economy (Bettelheim 1975; Dos Santos 1991). However, Fanon's concept of colonialism as a primarily cultural force that includes but supersedes the economic sphere would soon ride again.

Said imported Fanon's thought structures in the academic environment. For him (1996, 2000), there had been a long debate among Western intellectuals on the economic and political realities of imperialism, but "scarcely any attention has been paid to what I believe is the privileged role of culture in the modern imperial experience" (1994:5). Said unsurprisingly favors the *pomo* technique of filling in the blanks with what he calls *contrapuntal reading*. In this way he thinks he can pierce the silences in the writings of most Western observers of the non-Western world (1994). Their silence reveals an imperialism of the mind that has as its stepping-stone the notion of Western superiority he denounced in *Orientalism* (1979):

> [I]deas, cultures, and histories cannot seriously be understood or studied without their force, or more precisely their configurations of power [...] The relationship between Occident and Orient is a relationship of power, of domination, of varying degrees of a complex hegemony (1979:5).

The Western gazes only at what it wants to see, that is, the signs of its superiority over the rest of cultures. In this way, for Said, imperialism is not only or primarily an interplay of economic forces, but an attribute of the Western mind.

For Said, the superiority of the New over the Old Left lies in the former's skill to detect the iron grasp of culture. The economics-oriented researchers had to go through often painstakingly fact-finding to prove their theses. Were these convincing or not, they had to account for them with hard facts. Said and his numerous followers take a shortcut. Just by probing whether this or that writer or cultural trend is Western or Westernized makes their lives easy. In the end, Said shares with Fanon the dualistic approach that true liberation from the colonial thought structures demands a thorough break with the whole of Western culture and the creation of a new one.

Said has a knack for finding everywhere a contriving West endlessly ready to deprive the rest of the world of its cultural weight. In order to do so, though, he has to have recourse to some very fuzzy notions. Orientalism itself is not a clear historical entity. In different sections of his two main books, Said makes it hark back to 16th century and later travelers (1979:*passim*), the Council of Vienne in 1312 (1979:49–50), Euripides' *The Bacchae* (1979:56–57), even Homer (1979:85). Sometimes it is interpreted as the budding fear from conquering Arabs or Ottomans (1979:58–63; 1994:111–114); sometimes, as the product of Western ignorance or scorn poured on inferior humans or races (1994:132–169). Here it is limited to the West's imaging of Islamic cultures (1979:282–283; 1994:81); there it spills over to the non-Western rest of the world (1979:224–229; 1994:286–291). Orientalism, like in the cream cheese ad, becomes so spreadable that it is incredible. At heart, though, Said has no explanation for the process. Like the Orient of his Orientalists, like Fanon's metropolises, this West has no real inner diversity, no conflicts, no currents, and no divisions.

The later part of *Culture and Imperialism* draws the political conclusions that *Orientalism* had balked at. The new culture must shut down any and all plantations of the mind. Resistance to domination is the new brand's name, and it comes with its own marketing mix. Above all, there is the right to see one's own history as a consistent whole, as an array of rich identities still to be built. "Local slave narratives, spiritual autobiographies, prison memoirs form a counterpoint to the Western powers' monumental histories, official discourses, and panoptic quasi-scientific viewpoint" (1994:215).

Not only does Said reify cultures—he misunderstands the subtleties of their interplay as well. Politics is but a power struggle, and the Gramscian idea of hegemony plays for him the same role that power played for

Foucault. It blurs any differences between *Macht* and *Herrschaft* and with the same consequences. On the one hand, there are many reasons to contrapuntally read him as Huntington in reverse. Identities not only remain equal to themselves over time—they are also ineffable and bound to clash with each other. Whether one accepts the point of view of imperialism (Huntington 1996, 2004) or that of the colonials (Said), the outcome tends to be the same. Both share a common spite for cross-cultural communication and a flippant self-assertiveness. They surely know how to tell the good from the bad without the flicker of a shadow.

Postcolonial studies (*poco*) have taken Said's teachings one step further. As one of his best-known exponents has put it:

> [p]ost/colonialism is now used in wide and diverse ways to include the study and analysis of European territorial conquest, the various institutions of European colonialisms, the discursive operations of the empire, the subtleties of subject construction in colonial discourse and the resistance of those subjects, and most importantly perhaps, the differing responses to such incursions and their contemporary colonial legacies in both pre- and post-independence nations and communities (Ashcroft et al 1998:187).

Hence, unlike dependency theorists, *pocos* believe that conflicts between societies or nations or ethnic groups have for the most part cultural roots. Hence, unlike Marxists, they think that economics counts for very little in provoking conflict, and that it should not constitute the primary object of research and action. Hence, they tend to ignore the real processes happening in the postcolonial world. To them China today or in the 19th century were equally subject to the hegemony of the West. Whether it was imposed by unequal treaties and colonial intervention or by today's increasing consumerism, both situations are the same. Why bother to ask what the Chinese think? Intriguingly, they seem to be as incapable of understanding their consumerist predicament, as their ancestors of governing themselves according to the imperial narrative. Cultural imperialism—so powerful, it lurks even in the *poco* dispensation.

This unchanging structure that underlies all imperialist power games is similar to that described by Lacan in his writings on psychoanalysis (1966). Identity building in Lacan requires from its inception the presence of the other (in lowercase). This other is everything which is not one's self, everything out of the body including the self's own reflections in a mirror. The mirror stage creates a chasm between the self and the rest of the world. The non-ego sphere shatters the initial indifferentiation of the subject, being at the same time an affirmation of the self, and a loss of the comforting whole represented by the union with the mother's body. Loss or lack of this whole plus the desire to go back to the mother's womb will never abandon the individual for the rest of his/her life. There is, however, another type of Other, this time in uppercase—what Lacan calls the Grand Other. Though Lacan gives a rather tortuous description of it, the other Other is a symbolic entity that replaces the mother and her Law of Desire, and chains the self to the requests of the rational order. Although this Other receives the name of Law of the Father, this attribution, exactly like it happened with the Mother, does not reflect an individual or historical predicament. It is an unchanging structural position of the Unconscious understood as Lévi-Strauss' combinatory mind. Individuals may accept it or, otherwise, try to break with it, although in the end, there is no escape from the Name of the Father. Any symbolic order will be replaced by another one as repressive as the previous one.

Although the ontological pessimism that pervades Lacan's idea of identity does not bode well for their emancipatory project, *pocos* gladly bought the notion and imported it to their own research field. Identity structuring of the individual self is not so different from its colonial counterpart (Bhabha 1990, 1994; Burns 2001a; Hall 2007a; Spivak 1988, 1999). Colonials are separated from and marginalized by the imperial language that *Others* or *Worlds* (like in Third World) denies them, thus turning them into subjects. Their options are similar to those of the individuals. They can either remain within the law of desire, and be nurtured by the metropolis, the imperial mother; or they may understand that the colonial order symbolizes the Law of the Father, that is, the rule of an alien power that can be dispensed with. Usually, *pocos* remain at the mirror stage, that is, they prefer to dwell with the strictures of ever-present imperial domination and expose how it works in every corner. A similar framework of reason, desire, and power has been adopted by other postfeminism, queer theory, and other *pomo* critics of modern culture. All of the above study the intricacies of identity building and combine them with the special situation of women and gays and lesbians within both imperial and postcolonial societies. Though they have grown exponentially, they have been unable to avoid an increasing fragmentation of their subject reinforced by dizzying new jargon and endless skills to spot ever-deepening layers of meaning in the commonest of situations. More and more, *pomo* strolls with eyes wide shut through a garden of forking paths and reeks of mannerism. The *pomo* matrix has become banalized into a few slogans.

In the end, the *pomo* matrix wears a formidable armor of self-delusion. It starts with a definition of reality that makes history and human self-interest disappear for the benefit of a grammar of the Mind that cannot explain change. Then, it constructs—or deconstructs—a methodology of self-indulgent selection. Ignoring how easily their starting point may turn into a circular argument, they proceed to state without proof that they can define reality in a better way than scientific methodology. Reality thus becomes a cultural universe populated by good and bad narratives according to their taste. In this way, gains in self-persuasion go in the company of a biased description of reality. In the end, however, the *pomo* matrix pays a high price for its lack of self-control. Facts so easily dispensed with come back as distorted reality.

Chapter 4

The Accidental Tourism Researcher

THE LAST SOCIOLOGIST AND THE GUTS OF THE LAST BUREAUCRAT

MacCannell's approach to tourism is the closest thing to a general theory in a field where one finds few ambitious theories. It is, therefore, no accident that his work is addressed with reverence and profusely quoted. This success does not necessarily mean that it is a definitive benchmark that one should embrace without further ado. In fact, it has been the source of many misguided assumptions that have plagued the field until today. A re-assessment of his work seems long overdue.

MacCannell's work, as noted, is a mandatory stop for general debates on the nature of tourism. However, he makes it clear in many places that *The Tourist* is not a book about tourism. If anything might surprise him, it would be being considered just a tourism expert. By his own autobiographical admission, all his professional life has been like working in other fields (1990b) or, one might dare correct, like working in the various fields of a single master. Although he had a special liking for anthropology, part of his initial career was devoted to rural sociology. However, both anthropology and sociology struck him as too narrow, so he moved into semiotics. According to his website (MacCannell 2008), he is still seeking in other fields, such as landscaping, the unconscious, or the future of the city.

How does tourism fit in this impressive but intricate topography? We only have to follow him to find an answer. He is not interested in what tourism research might add to some general theory of society; on the contrary, what he is looking for (or, after having found structuralist semiotics, willing to tell everybody) is a general understanding of modernity from some specific viewpoints. His best-known work grapples with tourism, but he has covered many other areas of cultural studies—film star cult (1987a), politics (1984; MacCannell and MacCannell 1993b), pornography (1989a), landscaping (1992b), the film noir genre (1993), urbanism (1999b, 2005), semiotics (1989b; MacCannell and MacCannell 1982), marketing

(2002), structuralism and symbolic interactionism (1986, 1990a; MacCannell and MacCannell 1993a) plus *The Tourist* (1976, 1999a), and *Empty Meeting Grounds* (1992a), this last being a kind of synthesis of them all.

But MacCannell aims much higher than expertise in many fields. For all his apparent lack of focus, he, like the hedgehog of Archilochus, only wants to know but one big thing—the texture of modernity with all its entanglements and all its traps. Like medieval troubadours it is Love itself that interests him much more than specific lovers (De Rougemont 1983). The tourist appeals to him inasmuch as it "is one of the best models available for modern-man-in-general" (1999a:1).

Autobiographies do not necessarily bare their subject's psyche, but they obviously indicate how their authors want to be seen by others. Were one so naïve ever to trust the deconstructionist braggadocio that works of art or literary creations disclose by concealing (or the other way around), autobiographies would serve as its epitome. It is always worthwhile listening to what their authors may be ready to show about themselves. MacCannell painted his self-portrait in a collective work under the patronage of the University of California. There he tells a number of interesting stories about some moments of his intellectual career in academia and his approach to life. For our purposes, though, his research strategies come up center stage.

His wager is not for the fainthearted. It will not stop at anything less than a thorough understanding of the fabric of our modern society. He does not provide more new recipes for this or that area of tourism research, which after all is but a section of modern experience. He wants to lock horns with the greatest social theoreticians from Marx to Lévi-Strauss with stops at Durkheim, Weber, Goffman, and Foucault. And still this would limit the breadth of his work in an unwarranted way. Theory is but the waiting room of action.

As he puts it bluntly elsewhere, the foundation of his work lies in tourism (a metaphor for modernity in general as just mentioned), and revolution, those "two poles of modern consciousness—a willingness to accept, even venerate, things as they are on the one hand, a desire to transform things on the other" (1999a:3). Give the tourist, that is, modern-man-in-general, a solid thread and he may be ready to leave behind the labyrinth wherein he is entrapped. For some reason, however, as MacCannell himself has noted, the second item on the slate was adjourned (this will be discussed later). So, let's take MacCannell at his word, let's accompany him in his daring journey and let's make up our own mind whether he proves his mettle. In the end, even if the price of the ride remains immoderate, going along with him is more fun than reading the myriad bland case studies that nowadays parade as tourism research in most scholarly journals.

What does MacCannell mean when he talks modernity? A change of historical period and a new organization of the totality of social life opposed to the previous industrial society where work was life's eminent domain, and centered every other human undertaking. In modernity work has been superseded by leisure. Industrial society that had in Marx its best interpreter was a world of material commodities. On its side, modernity has relinquished this claim. Commodities can still be found in the world of production, but increasingly this sphere has been enrobed by culture. Production nowadays mostly means cultural productions as in "*Lagaan* (a 2001 Bollywood blockbuster) was a great production."

There is a clear chasm between these two eras. MacCannell defines it in different ways, but all boils down to a question of ownership. Classic commodities might be individually owned, but modernity does not allow for so much latitude.

> It is precisely characteristic of tourist destinations, for example, natural famous landscapes, cities, cultures, heritage, tradition, ethnic and racial differences that they are not subject to exchange. Tourists may visit these things, but they cannot buy them and take them home or resell them (2002:147).

In this way, we now have a clear idea of what he will research—leisure and commodities or, better, the social role of modern commodities—in a two-pronged strategy.

MacCannell does not balk at making high-flying pronouncements when it suits him, but these two seem definitely exaggerated. Has work really come to an end with modernity? Did leisure play the leading role in the lives of the 6.7 billion humans that populated the planet in July 2008? Clearly MacCannell cannot not have in mind the millions that enjoy the unwanted leisure of being unemployed; or agricultural workers in less developed countries that till the fields from sunrise to sundown; or factory workers in China and Southeast Asia that put in well over 50 working hours per week; or those who have to waive their right to paid vacations (when they have it) in order to make ends meet.

Even in developed countries, his reports on the demise of work would be greatly exaggerated. Among OECD countries, South Koreans work 2,357 hours per year; Greeks 2,052; Mexicans 1,883; Italians 1,800; and Americans

1,797 (Forbes Magazine 2008). That amounts to 45.3 weekly hours for South Koreans; 39.4 for Greeks; 36.2 for Mexicans; 34.6 for Italians; and 34.5 for Americans for 52 weeks a year. If we leave aside paid vacations, weekends, and national holidays, the intensity of their working periods rises to astounding proportions. Therefore, the assumption that leisure has supplanted work as modern-man-in-general's main occupation seems difficult to sustain. The idea is so outrageous that even calling it ethnocentric would look extravagant. If at all, it would only apply to a minority of rich people the world over—what MacCannell calls the new leisure class— scarcely modern-man-in-general. MacCannell prides himself in his statistical skills (1990b). What prevented him from doing this simple math?

Have commodities changed so much in the age of cultural productions that they cannot be bought and sold? There is no need to dispute that the ambit of cultural productions, including tourism attractions, has expanded precipitously over the last 150 years. Have they, however, lost their relation to their producers and their owners? Are they not exchanged, usually for money?

Today, over the face of the Earth, it is difficult to find what classical Roman jurists used to call *res nullius* (goods with no master). Everything, except the high seas and Antarctica, has been appropriated. Van Gogh's Irises, the Mona Lisa, the Karakorum Range, or New York City belong to definite persons or entities. The Irises are part of the proprietary collection of the NYC Museum of Modern Art, a non-profit institution created in 1929. Adele Levy made a gift of the picture in 1958. She or her ancestors must have bought it somewhere. The Karakorum Range is shared among Pakistan, India, and China. Each one of these countries exerts sovereignty over the areas allocated to them in international treaties. Usually modern constitutions and internal laws will say that they or similar natural areas are the property of the people or the nations that include them in their territory. The latter, on their turn, entrust their management to specific branches of the government. The Mona Lisa (said to have been bought for 400 écus by François I, King of France, in the 16th century) has since belonged to the country, and is nowadays exhibited in the Louvre Museum under care of this governmental organization. New York City was founded in 1613, and was incorporated within the legal framework of New York State and of the United States in 1898. This geographical extension is partly owned by public institutions and partly by private landlords. In this way, every tangible object does nowadays belong to somebody. If this is what defines a commodity, most of the things we see and touch are commodities, including tourism attractions. In this respect, the latter are no different from a car, a piece of silk or a pound of beef, or a brand name.

Why then cannot tourists sell or buy them? The answer is simple: because some, by reason of their legal status, are *extra commercium* (non tradable), as again classical Roman law had it. However, their legal status may change, and often does. They may and do change hands. If they are mobile objects they can be confiscated, or stolen to be sold once they are brought to another jurisdiction. Think of the minor but extremely valuable Cambodian antiques one can find in the backshops of art dealers in Bangkok's Charoen Krung. Take the Nazis. Göring would excel in the top league of great historical spoliators. He looted as many European works of art as he could lay his hands on.

If they are unmovable, some areas and their attractions can be transferred to another sovereign entity. Hitler annexed Austria, the Sudetenland, and Czechoslovakia. He and Stalin, his one-time partner, divided Poland between Germany and Russia in 1939. After the war, Poland and many other countries readjusted their borders, and some attractions found new owners. If they are totally intangible—such as a culture or a religious faith or a given tradition—one may try to do away with them by eliminating their practitioners and by obliterating any remains of their material culture. The Holocaust is the best example of an attempt to destroy Judaism once and for all by exterminating its followers. Indeed, this is an extreme example that furthermore failed. But it shows that cultural productions and tourist attractions, even those that are not amenable to commercial exchange, indeed have owners.

On the other hand, many attractions or works of art are freely bought and sold. Selling artworks and other objects of distinction is how Sotheby's, Christie's, and other lesser dealers eke out a living. When academics complete a book they will—hopefully—sign a copyright agreement with a publisher, and the book will be bought and sold as any other commodity. In 1990, Minuro Isutani, a Japanese investor bought the Pebble Beach Company, owner of a number of golf links in California's Monterey County. The links were, and still are (under new ownership), a famous attraction for well-heeled tourists. One can conceive that even Disneyland might one day change hands.

In fact, however, tourists do not usually attempt to buy or sell attractions. As MacCannell himself notes many times, they content themselves with "experiencing" (whatever this may mean) the attraction. They want to see Angkor Wat, or the New Tate Gallery in London, or listen to Bruce Springsteen, or, if they belong to the "high brow" crowd, they may even buy tickets to enjoy Rigoletto at the Metropolitan. Many people may enjoy a cultural production like "Some like it Hot" by watching it (some do it up to three times over a weekend). It does not mean that the film itself (or, better, the right to show and reproduce it) has no owner. The Mirisch Company that initially produced it and its legal successors have those rights. The person who bought the recorded DVD of the film owns that piece of hardware, and can watch it under some conditions incorporated to the contract she signed when she bought it. Even a live concert that is not recorded has owners—the musicians to their songs and their value, and the producers to their share of the benefits.

Indeed, most people are not in any of those categories. What they expect from attractions and what they usually pay for are just some benefits under the form of services (however, these may be defined), and nothing else, in the same way that they expect that their rooms will be cleaned at their hotel. Likewise for attractions or destinations. MacCannell recalls that millions of people went to Rome in 1975. "Millions of dollars changed hands at hotels, restaurants, souvenir stands, guided tours, etc. Rome was the attraction, but did Rome itself charge admission? No" (1999a:195). Really? It depends. If by Rome we mean the name of a geographical area in which some historical events have happened, it is true because here Rome is nothing. Just a *flatus vocis*, the vibrations of air as it passes through somebody's vocal chords. Rome as the area where some thousands of Romans live is another story. Did not the local government charge hotel occupancy taxes to tourists; did it not levy fees on parking spaces; did not tourists pay dues to many local attractions owned by "Rome"? The same can be said of the goods and services providers that even MacCannell acknowledges made millions of dollars on tourist traffic.

Even when, as it happens in some European countries, one gets free access to beaches or to public buildings or even to museums one has to support some transaction costs in order to "consume" the experience. Tourists have to pay for their transport, their parking, the eventual services of a guide, and so on. There is no free lunch at The Last Supper. Unlike in statistics, MacCannell may not pride himself in his legal skills, but it would have been easy for him to consult with some expert to acquaint himself with the fine print of the law. Why would not he take the pain? This is no trivial pursuit, as in fact the whole issue belongs to the core of MacCannell's research methodology. If we grant that leisure has become the main feature of social life under modernity or that attractions do not have an owner or that no price is paid to enjoy them, the rest of his reasoning can follow more or less seamlessly.

Many details in his analysis surprise the reader as equally unwarranted. He reached his conclusions, we are told, by way of a mixture of ethnographic methods. He carried out distant or participant observation of tourist behavior; he collected and selected notices and commentary about tourist attractions gathered from different print media; he deconstructed a couple of Paris guidebooks dating from the turn of the 20th century (the *Anglo-American Practical Guide to Exhibition Paris: 1900* and the then famous *Paris and Environs with Routes from London to Paris: Handbook for Travelers* of the *Baedeker* guide series). None of these approaches can easily be reproduced independently. His rationale: "[e]ach special informational format presupposes a set of methods and has its own version of reliability, validity and completeness" (MacCannell 1999a:135), which most of the time means that the researcher has a license to say whatever comes to his mind. For instance, that sightseeing "is usually done in a small group of intimates"; that the consensus about the structure of the modern world achieved through tourism and mass leisure is the strongest and broadest consensus known to history (1999a:136, 139); that tourists often placed themselves at scenes of unmarked historic crimes or miracles, though, well, not everyone did—it was just "something of an ideal of a kind of upper middle class touristic travel" (1999a:194); that "[t]he Aztecs were the builders of the mightiest non Indo-Greco-European empire" (1992a:54) Ever heard of the Sublime Porte or of the Middle Kingdom? One can show many other instances of similar hype throughout his work. Few barriers can hold MacCannell when he tries to make an argument that he considers crucial to his specific interest at some point in time. Such small details do not count for much once a subject rises to the next methodological step—an adequate treatment by semiotics that will reverse any previous slips of the word processor.

What does semiotics mean for MacCannell? Above all, it draws a map to escape from the discredited ways of the social sciences—anthropology, sociology, and, above all, economics. This refrain one finds all over his work first hit him when reading Durkheim's *Rules of the Sociological Method.*

> When I read, "Explain a Social Fact with another Social Fact," I could actually feel an old worldview deflate and sense a new direction for thought and beliefs. After such a manifestation, I thought, it was only a matter of time before we would clean up the last vestiges of psychological mystification and associated political beliefs in bourgeois individualism (1990b:173).

It is not that the social sciences necessarily gravitate toward a distorted view of reality. When they do—and they often do—it is because of their methodological limitations and, deep down, of their class ties. They are burdened with a "bourgeois" view that sees societies as made of nothing but individuals, and that speculates that the latter should take precedence in the explanation of social interaction.

He accordingly pounds on the weeds that have colonized all social sciences. He pounds on urban planning.

> In short any causal connection that may hold between x and y is not relevant to statistical significance. Thus, statistically, we have neighbors who are like ourselves in several socio-economic particulars—skin color, income level, life stage, family size, and so on—without ever needing to relate to them beyond the polite exchange of clichéd platitudes. And so long as nothing upsets the balance of life in postmodern neighbor-hoods, the people living in them can pretend that the statistically significant relationships between them are also actually socially significant (1999b:121, 1992b).

He pounds on marketing as it feeds on the narcissistic instincts of our personalities (1987a, 1987b, 2002). He pounds on modern anthropology for having retreated from the study of dependence and disadvantage among Third World peoples. He pounds on mainstream sociology's excessive focus on the Western urban-industrial proletariat even when it was about to lose its key role in the study of poverty, oppression, and false consciousness (1990b). But, above all, he pounds on economics. When the Vietnam war came to an end,

> I also knew that the United States government would take revenge on the universities by initiating an academic repression that would last at least a decade or until the coalition that had formed between intellectuals, Western social scientists, Third World peoples, and marginal domestic groups was broken [...] I was even able to imagine in advance the precise form that the repression would take, namely, the redefinition of development in entirely business, economic, and technical terms, leaving out any serious consideration of culture or social consciousness except as constraints to be overcome (1990b:183–184).

Market economics thus reveals not only its limited cognitive strategy; it becomes an accessory to the program of academic repression planned by the

American government. If this sounds somewhat paranoid, it is because it is. In fact, some, who at the time were academics in societies more authoritarian than the United States, would have felt very happy exchanging their actual repression by a persecution that allowed MacCannell to remain tenured without major problems.

A timely stay in France in the halcyon days of May 1968 set MacCannell on the right track of what he thought to be a new kind of sociology that was truly international in scope, and ready to rescue the excellent tools that academic anthropology and sociology had invented to analyze the shifting base of their own domains, but finally relinquished. The scales in his eyes had already half fallen under Goffman's influence.

> [I]f we follow Goffman into the gap between expression and social forms, between cause and effect, into a space where we have to leave our egos behind and discover otherness without the crutch of determinism, sociology becomes a branch of semiotics (1990a:34, 1992b).

But they would wait to be finally shed until the fascinating discovery of Barthes' work. Semiotics then became the root of his new tree of science.

His was the peculiar kind of semiotics we are already familiar with—the general science of communication sponsored by Lévi-Strauss as the great discovery that would transform all social disciplines. The main twist MacCannell adds comes by way of Barthes. Semiotics must break out of the theoretical box; it will bridge the lasting gap that has pulled its followers away from practice. In this sense, he does and does not belong in the mainstream structuralist mold. He will only accept it if semiotics adds revolution to its research program. Once we possess the key to debrief all types of mythologies, the time has come to hang the last sociologist with the guts of the last bureaucrat or of whoever it is who keeps modern society in its present state of distress. In his words:

> [d]econstruction gives us access to the realm of absolute possibility in theory, in the imagination, and where it exists, in life. But an allied sociology of interaction or dialogue is still necessary to gain access to the realm of contingency and determinism, and especially resistance to, and struggles against, determinism (MacCannell 1992a:3).

Regrettably, it seems unlikely that such a daunting prospect will soon come to fruition, so we will leave it aside until we see how it fits with all the rest of his approach at a later stage of our probe.

What is there in communication that makes MacCannell and many others entertain such high hopes? Communication is indeed a most human phenomenon, although mankind shares it with other species. At any rate, one can say that, until further evidence is proffered, humans enjoy it in its richest possible extent. Merriam-Webster (2002) defines it as "a process by which meanings are exchanged between individuals through a common system of symbols (as language, signs, or gestures)" or, for shorter, information mediated by signs whether written, spoken, or intimated by other means. Spoken and written signs plus the grammar of their use usually conform to what we call a language.

As yet, there is not a single shared theory about languages and their place in human experience. The French structuralist school that stirred MacCannell so much does not delve much into origins. After all, they are historical puzzles that distract our attention from what counts—the randomness of signs, that is, the words and sentences that help us to build our experiences and account for them are decoupled from their objects. The piece of paper that I am now writing on is called a sheet in English, a Blatt in German, and a página in Spanish; the way Chinese speakers organize their sentences differs considerably from that of their French counterparts. Random signs, however, are necessary communication tools thanks to a grammar that holds them together, and makes sense to their users. The grammar of all grammars allows us to account for any possible combination of signs while, at the same time, remains detached from the objects they combine. It is the ideal of a mental structure where history better dare not intrude. Such is also the first part of MacCannell's theorizing, even though his heart is not completely there.

What about prelinguistic communication; is it based on equally arbitrary signs? MacCannell explores the issue in a study of facial expressions in pornographic imagery. Before writing, before even mastering speech, our ancestors obviously engaged in sexual intercourse. Once language was invented, they had to take a momentous decision—to talk or not to talk while making love. The answer, as we know, was an emphatic no. Since then verbal communication between sexual partners is either technically senseless, or fully dependent on some unavailable text (MacCannell 1989b). This seems in keeping with Freud's view that our ancestors were small bands of intimate groups that shared both genetic bonds and sexual love without paying much attention to the incest taboo. Exchanges of individuals among such groups may have started as marauding, child stealing, and rape, or as solitary wanderings of malcontent individuals trying to get accepted by a different group. None of those possible exchanges favored words. They just happened. Speech must have come at a later stage when exogamy became the norm for marital alliances and commerce, activities that request complex negotiations and, therefore, the presence of articulate communication (Lévi-Strauss 1969). The incest taboo now became mandatory to regulate sexual exchanges among groups.

> Sex within the framework of the first marriages was akin to sex with a stranger. Exogamous sex is a sacrifice people make to the language community, and it would seem that humankind has never adjusted itself fully to sexual relations framed by language (1989b:158).

The price for bringing Oedipus onstage was not exactly small change. The pre-Oedipal sex of the primitive hordes is somehow mirrored by the post-Oedipal sex of pornography.

> The obvious difference between the pornographic frame and everyday social life is that pornography depicts behaviors that are specifically suppressed from ordinary public conduct (1989b:158).

Pornography thus provides a clue to understand the explosive freedom of sex in primitive societies and the strictures that have plagued family life since the Neolithic era. It mirrors the sexual trauma that accompanied the invention of language and exiled beyond the pale all sexual activities that did not conform to the new norms of marriage.

The conclusion does not wait: social life as we know it is "fully organized around a required falsification of non-involvement" (MacCannell 1989b:171). Language split the previously authentic and direct forms of sexual expression from our "tolerant" forms of multiple repression—of the intersubjective powers of speech and of sexually based solidarity, now framed as pornography.

> All this is technically a reactionary response to the invention of language, but it is a reaction of massive proportion that has shaped every social institution and the unconscious for more than 30,000 years (1989b:173).

More or less the time since mankind lost its bearings, which incidentally seems to encompass not only modernity but also anything that has happened after the demise of the primeval hunters and gatherers.

MacCannell has thus put together an ambitious research methodology, but at a great cost. As we will see, he cannot extricate himself from, on one hand, the strictures of an antihumanistic structuralist orthodoxy that, in its *a priori* of the randomness of signs, deprives social history of meaning and, on the other, his determination to fight the alleged inhumanity of modernity to the bitter end. This contradiction flows through his views on economic development and consumption, and finally drives him to the outer reaches of dystopia.

A THEORY OF (TOURISM) DEVELOPMENT

As already noted, it is easy to make the mistake that MacCannell just aims at a better understanding of this type of social behavior known as tourism. Indeed he pays a great deal of attention to it, but he never intended to stop there. Tourism is a privileged way to come to terms with modern life in general. In his view, attractions are the driver of tourism development. An attraction, he reckons, is a relation between a sight and a sightseer, usually a tourist. Sights and tourists connect with each other through markers or signs that perform a number of functions. If that was all, MacCannell's position would not be especially noteworthy, and most people would easily agree with him. However, there is much more in his work, and not all of it warrants an equally undemanding digestion. Finding one's own way has been—still is—a complicated task for humans as well as for other members of the animal kingdom. Positioning is often crucial to survival and the complex activities related to it. It was so in olden times when being able to locate hunting grounds, safe shelters, trade routes, or military trails gave to some groups an edge over others.

It is so today as well. From a safe haven when a waterspout lurks on the horizon to smart bombing to hotel sites (*location, location, location*), we need the right directions. Initially, positioning systems were rather crude, but over time different cultures developed numerous better techniques. Polynesians and Vikings knew how to determine latitude, that is, one's location relative to a fixed point, later to be found in the Equator. Captain Cook's observations during his voyages made measurements of longitude (the time difference on an East–West axis point relative to another fixed one) much more accurate (Richardson 2005). In 1884, an International Meridian Conference agreed to make Greenwich in England the universal fixed point and to have the universal day start at the moment after midnight on the Greenwich Meridian. Since that time every location on the planet has had a marker measured by grades, minutes, and seconds of arc in latitude and longitude.

Orientation may thus seem a simple problem, but it is not necessarily so. Markers are not always easy to debrief, especially when visiting a foreign place for the first time. For all their usefulness, if one is a Chinese tourist alone in Rome and not too familiar with the Latin alphabet, there may be markers aplenty for the Pantheon, but still you might not find your way. Not many years ago, only metro stations in Central Tokyo were marked in Western characters, so to those unfamiliar with Japanese script navigating the system was a nightmare. Nowadays, however, global positioning systems (GPS) have made it increasingly easy to precisely find any given place on earth, based on latitude and longitude markers. If one wants to reach Piazza Navona in Rome, one just inputs its coordinates (latitude 41°53′56.66″N; longitude 12°28′22.60″E) into a navigation system and one will be accurately guided to the goal. Nowadays, every point on the planet can be effectively pinned down.

The need for accurate positioning creates a number of relations between tourists and attractions. The obvious one, just described, is recognition—a marker becomes a navigational sign to a site. In recognition mode the marker soon leaves its place to the sight. The newcomer meets objects she had not previously experienced or lived (in the Diltheyan sense of *Erlebniss*), but only knew of through pictures, guidebooks, narratives, and word of mouth, while the old user restores his links with the familiar place. At times, though, a sight may have no marker or the viewer may not have the relevant information about it. MacCannell rather confusingly refers to this as sight involvement, even though it would more properly be described as lack thereof, when recognition becomes benightedness.

Markers, according to MacCannell, have an additional status. They are signs or symbols as well. When one looks for San Francisco in Google Earth, one summons the marker of a locality that occupies the northern tip of the San Francisco Peninsula in California. One could easily find its exact geographic coordinates if so wanted. But this would not be enough to understand the site. San Francisco County covers 46.69 square miles and, according to the 2000 US Census, 776,733 persons had their homes there. It would be plainly impossible for any human being to grasp everything that happens in such a big place at a particular moment.

When tourists say that they spent last summer in Frisco, they are truthful if they mean they stayed for a number of days within those 46.69 square miles; if they imply that this gave them a thorough understanding of San Francisco, they equivocate. Tourists may think they got to know the place, because they visited Fisherman's Wharf, Chinatown, Union Square, Haight-Ashbury, Lombard Street, or the Castro neighborhood, but, in fact, Frisco as any other place (even the much smaller Piazza Navona) is inapprehensible as a totality, and our limited senses and minds cannot boast to have grasped it in full. Even people who spend all their lives there cannot say that they have a complete mastery of the place.

With their stringent time budgets and their limited financial means, tourists only enjoy some places and experiences among the many possible ones. They—as much as locals—have to select what they want to see and do. In this way, the Frisco experience will differ from one tourist to the next, in the same way as it differs from one local inhabitant to another. San Francisco thus becomes shorthand for the relation between my individual experience and the totality that I try to grasp with a necessarily limited glimpse. There are as many Friscos as people that have been or plan to be in the place. Thus, markers not only assist tourists in locating their sights, they also wrap as a whole my share in experiencing the place. In this way San Francisco is a symbol for the knowledge I get when I spend some time within the city limits or for what I anticipate if I ever visit. The marker for the city becomes a synecdoche that allows me to organize and express my actual or anticipated experiences of the place, and compare them with those of other people, transients or residents, dead or alive.

From this point on, MacCannell increasingly loses touch with the marker as a spatial pointer to stress its symbolic iteration with the sight. This relation comes in many shapes, he says. Posters, when they are made part of personal life by someone that uses them as home decorations, are an example of positive symbolic identification with a place, even if the user has not visited it yet. At times, though, markers can be used to discredit their sights (for example, when the Eiffel Tower is said to be just a heap of scrap metal or Venice's Grand Canal a stinking pool of water), and the identification becomes negative. There are also instances of people that participate in an event becoming both a marker and a sight themselves. Carnival revelers at Rio's Sambodromo are as much part of a show as the parade of samba schools. The sight and the marker thus reach their highest level of symbolic identification.

Now he lets his imagination loose. To some extent, we are told, the marker itself not only confirms the attraction; it creates it. A small rock does not usually draw the attention of passers-by; however, if it is exhibited in a museum with a label that marks it as part of the collection that the Apollo 11 crew brought from the moon, its marker makes it different from other common stones. The marker, in this case, becomes more important than the object itself. The tourist sees something as uninteresting as another pebble, but she is warned that this one comes straight from the moon, and that it deserves being appreciated as such. "Even when there is something to see, a tourist may elect to get his thrills from the marker instead of the sight" (1999a:115). MacCannell then quickly jumps to the conclusion that markers make the attraction or that the sign makes the sight. In this way he rids the sign of any concrete reference to geography or history. Markers therefore are more than pointers; they are symbols. A Frisco marker, often expressed in the shorthand of a given object (a miniature model or a poster of the Golden Gate, for instance), stands for a whole that we can only evoke, not seize. For MacCannell, this symbolic facet of markers shapes the very act of tourist sightseeing.

MacCannell's semiotic analysis bears no great originality, though. As signs, we are told, tourism markers have their own grammar or, better, their grammar coincides with the universal grammar of semiotics. He thus treads a path blazed by Saussure, Jakobson, Peirce, Lévi-Strauss, Foucault, and he especially pays heed to Barthes' analysis of myths (1957). For Barthes, a myth is also system of communication, be it a sentence, a writing, an icon, a folk dance, a tale, an advertisement, a picture—in fact, any human action or creation. A myth has the same structure as a language; that is, it is made of signifiers and meaning. In a language, signifiers are material structures (sounds, writing symbols, icons, and so on) through which some sense or meaning, that is, the signified, is conveyed by a communicator to an audience. Signifiers and signified are united in an arbitrary relation that, once created and shared, becomes a stable sign. That a floating vessel is called ship, *bateau, buque,* or *con tàu* has no relation with its function or nature, with the object that the words name, but a listener familiar with the particular structure of meaning of that language will easily debrief the message conveyed.

But with myths there is more than meets the eye. Myths take their signifiers from the world of language and they re-elaborate it into new material for communication to create a symbol. According to Barthes, in so doing, myths interpret facts and events for their audiences with what we might call an ideological technique. Myth deprives narratives of their political edges translating, in the Barthesian formula, history into nature or the present into eternity. In a world defined by capitalism and bourgeois political hegemony myths help to hide the fact that freedom bears chains; that unfairness surrounds equality; and that brotherliness really means self-interest. Myths, such as the invisible hand or the wisdom of the markets, or the consumer's freedom of choice play to perfection their role of explaining the present order of things as the outcome of a human nature that is impervious to change, and close the door to any active agency to replace them with a more trustworthy nexus. Bourgeois society (whatever this may be, for Barthes never makes completely clear his meaning) needs to conceal an essence that otherwise would be easily contested by those it constantly deals an unequal and unfair hand. Symbols and myths dupe us into accepting as invariant all that cannot be justified rationally. Myths are the supplement of false consciousness bourgeois society draws on to sidetrack the majority of its members from their fundamental problems.

Barthes' approach leaves a number of unresolved issues he does not even bother to address. One has to do with human history. The narrow way in which myths are defined—as but ramparts of bourgeois society—does not account for their existence in other past social forms. Which functions did myths perform in what Polanyi (1957, 1968) called archaic or primitive economies and in what way? Will they remain alive if or when capitalism withers away? With a surprising nonchalance to the nature of myth, Barthes uses unwarranted optimism copiously with a vivid prose that has reached premature senescence. He really expected that so-called postcapitalist societies, like the Soviet Union or Maoist China, would become myth-free. Unfortunately, he died too soon to see how his hopes played out.

The other unaddressed issue harks back to methodology. Barthes is supremely confident that there is only one correct way to read and interpret myths. This is rather surprising because his own brand of semiotics can hardly grant this promise. How can he discern which signs are in fact mythopoeic while others can finally be classified in a unique meaning of false consciousness before defining what makes a myth? Such limitations are highlighted because MacCannell accepts them lock, stock, and barrel. His view of the mythical iterative relation between marker, sight, and sight transformation in the tourist experience is but an ersatz of the Barthesian semiotics.

A sight (Eiffel Tower) is a marker or symbol of Paris, whether this sequence is found in the mind of the tourist or is conveyed by a pictorial image. From the interchangeability between the sight and the marker, little by little, MacCannell, after Barthes, builds the same certainty that, in spite of their variability, markers can be interpreted in one, and only one way once we have grasped the basic procedures of myth or marker formation. This is an unwarranted conclusion. Even though it is always hard to reduce the world-out-there to a grammar of signs, linguists have a better case than Barthes or MacCannell. As most aspects of the acquisition and use of language are still unexplained, there is still room for endlessly contradictory hypotheses, and the claim that one's preferred brand holds its mettle.

Forgetting about the difference between the finite means provided by language (in the sense of a universal generative grammar in Chomsky 1975) and the expression of mental states and statements about the world-out-there which are potentially infinite in number (Chomsky 2002), linguists—and deconstructionists in their wake—can pretend to peel infinite levels of meaning in each linguistic sign and, to some extent, in other symbols. In the case of tourism, though, the evidence is more difficult to gather. We more or less know how attractions are generated, and the process does not start with the grammar of markers and symbols—rather the other way around.

Indeed the tourist needs maps, guides, brochures, and other markers of what she is looking for. They may symbolize whatever we want (the Statue of Liberty can bring to mind that the United States is the land of the free or the contrary view; Wimbledon may be seen as the epitome of tennis or not), but above all they are markers for concrete sites and particular ends. Denizens of London's Golders Green may easily navigate their neighborhood, but they are often at a loss when trying to find the All England Lawn Tennis and Croquet Club in Wimbledon. If they have tickets to watch a tennis match, what they badly need is a marker to find it, not whether Wimbledon symbolizes tennis. If they do not find their way to the Club, they will lose their time and their money. What they need is a positional pointer, not a discussion of the layers of symbolism that may be found in Wimbledon as a proxy for tennis.

MacCannell may be eager to lose touch with these material aspects to make his case, but markers' persecute us stubbornly. Their main use is not for symbolizing ("These are the Petronas twin-towers. Welcome to Malaysia"), but to direct the tourist to places he wants to see or enjoy ("This—and not that one over there—is Shanghai's Jin Mao Building. You are right on the money, honey"). Markers, especially canonical monuments or landscapes, can indeed have other functions. They may confirm distinction as the tourist shows her share of financial and cultural capital that made her trip possible ("This is Taipei 101, one of the tallest buildings in the world. Not many US citizens have been here. Well, in this panoramic picture I am the tiny dot at the entrance"). Or they can serve as imagined worlds or objects of desire ("This is a poster of the Great Wall. One day I will be there"). Markers cannot create attractions out of nothing. Behind the colorless moon rock there was the epoch-making space flight of Apollo 11.

This, not the marker, is what made the otherwise nondescript rock different from others. Had it not been because Wyatt Earp, his brothers, and Doc Halliday fought the McLaurys and the Clantons there on October 26, 1881, the marker 326 Allen St. in Tombstone, Arizona (the place where OK Corral stood) would not attract many tourists. It is the most famous shoot-out in the history of the West (punctually re-enacted daily at 2 pm), not the marker, what draws multitudes there. Otherwise Tombstone would be as inconspicuous as any other mining town in the area. Markers, therefore, are but props to the attraction. They will never generate it, always playing an ontological second fiddle.

Their subordinate rank does not mean that markers cannot awaken our symbolic imagination. A poster of OK Corral or an actual visit may unleash an array of different signals. Cowboys come in many shapes. "Over the decades, we Americans have imbued the man on horseback with so many qualities that he has become a whole cast of characters" (Erickson 1999:64). To some the Earps and Halliday represent the dark side of law enforcement, an unwelcome but necessary step in the taming of the Wild West (Anderson and Hill 2004). Or the McLaury and Clanton clans can be presented as practical entrepreneurs with a typically cowboy disregard for the fine print of the law (Wright 2001). Further, one can portray all of them as paragons of the individualistic Wild West (Aquila 1996), or charge their quintessential recklessness as shorthand for the violence white men displayed against native Americans (Limerick 1987). In the congenial plasticity of semiotics, all those symbols and many others have interchangeability that facts lack. But the stream of symbolism would not flow if the sites located by the markers and the actions that took place therein had not happened. They take precedence over meanings that, additionally, can rarely be interpreted in just one way. Many Catholics, Protestants, Jews, Muslims, and other religious and nonreligious persons enjoy a visit to El Escorial Monastery that Philip II erected to commemorate the Spanish triumph at St. Quentin in 1557. Some will see it as a symbol of Spanish intolerance, while to others it just represents a rightful determination to defend the true faith. The markers for the village of El Escorial and the views tourists may have of the sight cannot be subsumed into each other, much less be produced at will.

MacCannell seems to notice the difficulty, so he veers toward a different trail from the rigid predicament that markers generate attractions. Initially, the moon rock mentioned above became meaningful because it was tagged with a marker. Now, the klieg lights will flood another area. Once he has lost this first gambit—that markers can arbitrarily create attractions— MacCannell urges constructivism as the next best choice. In doing so he sings from a song that has become quite popular over time—reality of all kinds (tourist attractions included) is but a social construct. What comes to task now is the shared consensus between the labelers (those who make the markers, not the markers themselves) and their audience. Phenomenology comes to the rescue of semiotics.

At first blush, there is nothing to object to.

> [T]he world of my daily life is by no means my private world but is from the outset an intersubjective one, shared with my fellow-men, experienced and interpreted by Others; in brief, it is a world common to all of us. The unique biographical situation in which I find myself within the world at any moment of my existence is only to a very small extent of my own making (Schutz 1973:312).

This intersubjective world is made possible by different languages such as gestures, expressive movements, and mimetic motions (Snell 1952). Speech and writing, made of linguistic symbols, are the most efficient of all, and this is why usually we call them language in the singular. In fact, most human interaction starts with some kind of language that takes us out of our inner monad. It allows communication, experience sharing, and, indeed, learning. Even when we reflect on our experiences within our own stream of consciousness, we usually talk to ourselves in our mother tongue. Language is the primary social construct. Social constructivism in this sense is a truism. The crux of the matter lays elsewhere, though—in the explanation of how social constructs are built and, in the case of tourism, why attractions tend to have a similar ranking in most human groups.

At the time MacCannell was writing his widely quoted main book, Gouldner had been promoting what he called the sociology of sociology (1973). Behind the outwardly terse and consistent hypotheses of the sociologists (and here Gouldner cast a wide net to refer to all the social sciences), that is, behind their explicitly formulated assumptions, there is

> a second set of assumptions that are unpostulated and unlabeled [...] [and] remain in the background of the theorist's attention [...] From beginning to end, they influence a theory's formulation and the researchers to which it leads (1973:29).

In so doing, Gouldner quarantined the most sacred of all theoretical beliefs—that research findings mirror their objects without unwarranted interference of values or preconceptions on the part of the observer. Gouldner cautiously limited his remarks to individual researchers or to some schools of thought (basically what he called American Functionalism), but MacCannell does not show so much restraint.

> On a more complex level, the field of the sociology of knowledge has begun to discover that scientific theories, in addition to being reflections of empirical reality, themselves reflect the structure of groups and classes in which they originate (1999a:118).

Although the formulation sounds like orthodox Marxism, the generic reference to "groups" opens the door to the inclusion of categories other than class, such as gender, ethnic condition, nationality, sexual orientation, and so on. This is a kind of extreme constructivism that creates serious problems. Initially, it sees the field of theory as a battlefield of contradictions that cannot be rationally solved. We are all eponymous Humpty-Dumpties that can decide what words will mean in each situation. In the next movement, though, it contradicts itself. Yes, it is possible to tell the grain from the chaff. What one hand giveth, the other taketh.

This position has a point. Many have attempted to defeat the human tilt to prejudice, but none of those well-meaning efforts has been particularly successful. The objectivism of most classical and medieval philosophy amounted to little more than a naïve acceptance of our sensorial data or of religious authority. Closer to our times the Hegelian movement contrived to keep an objectivist contraption. On its right, the master himself and many followers would bestow it upon state bureaucracies or, as with Mannheim, to prejudice-free academic communities. On the left, Marxism, with Lukacs as its figurehead, concluded that as the proletariat became the universal class, it would break free from the fetters of bias. Neither side avoided a resounding failure.

Unfortunately it is not possible to escape the trap by purely logical means. If all viewpoints are biased, how could mine not be equally partial? In the end, research, even communication, would be a vain pursuit, and we would face a hard challenge to even decide what "vain" or "pursuit" mean. Trying in vain to sway the skeptic, the best a frustrated Aristotle could offer was a practical answer (1952:Book IV, Section IV). Why do skeptics take the road to Megara (a city close to Athens) instead of remaining in place imagining that they are on their way; why do they avoid falling in wells if they do not know whether it is good or bad? Recently Nozick has argued along similar lines with more modern jargon. Possibly the search for an unchanging objective world is but a chimera. Aspects of the world we know tend to change over time or the way we account for them varies according to new research methods. The best way to cope remains acting on our choices with the belief that, all other things being equal, the structures of the world we know will remain invariant until further notice. This may look flimsy, but is not whimsical. "Evolution provided our ancestors with a fixed (hardwired) capacity to take account of certain kinds of recent varying specifics [...] [C]onsciousness plays some role in the flexible adaptation of behavior to circumstance" (Nozick 2001:179). Consciousness thus makes possible that we learn discriminative behavior to improve individual or collective survival, for instance, by avoiding falling into wells, as Aristotle had it, or by not letting the children play in a river full of alligators.

Social construction of attractions, therefore, appears as the second best choice once the pretension of objectivity is debunked. Attractions indeed reflect a multiplicity of interests, so they resist attempts to be ordered hierarchically. Top ones for this group will be second or third tier for the other. At the same time, they generally follow a hierarchical order in most societies. They do so in our modern societies. They also did in the past or in cultures other than the Western one.

How can we solve this apparent contradiction that plagues not only the ranking of attractions, but more generally all our social activities? In my view, the solution—weak and provisional—requests a generally acceptable definition of the problem and, at least, two subsequent conditions and one basic rule of the game. The basic rule excludes circular arguments and is basic for no rational discussion can exist without it.

The widely acceptable statement is none other than the one we have been talking about up to now. Yes, whatever we hold certain is indeed a social construct. It is possible that a given individual may account better in her mind for a given question or many than the prevailing social constructs or mainstream views; it will not help anybody much if she keeps it to herself and carries the secret to the grave. Without public communication and discussion, social constructs do not exist. As Popper had it, for the hard sciences, objectivity is just intersubjectivity, that is, the beliefs of a given community of scientists at a given point in time. In less truth-oriented social groups this means, more or less, that our everyday world in politics, in matters of taste and, of course, in morals, follows the constructs (in less enlightened times they were just called views) of public opinion. In other words, as it would be extremely inefficient that each of us should reformulate all of life necessities every morning, we trust constructs that have proved useful in the past. In this way, most of our opinions or constructs are based on trust that the world will have today the same general contours it had yesterday, and that we can go about our business taking for granted its basic laws as expressed by successful social constructs.

This initial proviso will not show its mettle without two basic conditions. The first states that we have to accept the existence of diverse, and often contradictory, social constructs, theoretical approaches, or whatever other label we want to use. Even in the best of times, even in the hardest of sciences, not to speak of those with a soft core or of everyday matters, it is very difficult that a group of social constructs, also called theories, may gain general acceptance. Even the highest of theories or hypothetical constructs that, after Kuhn, we call paradigms are provisional—good until contrary evidence debases them, and brings about a paradigm shift. The unfortunate inexistence of social constructs held as uniquely valid by all is hard to accept, as it implies that whatever we hold dearest may be of no consequence to a majority. Unsurprisingly there will lurk in the back of our minds the temptation to circumvent their nagging plurality by sheltering our own sectional constructs under arguments from authority, whether religious or profane, or in self-satisfying solipsism. No matter how heroic we may be on both accounts, we cannot accept that bracketing out of existence whatever we deem inconvenient is an acceptable answer. Some social constructs are more successful than others, regardless of our opinions, possibly because they help a majority to organize their lives in a more satisfactory way.

The second condition is no less stringent. To be successful social constructs have to satisfy the burden of proof. They gain acceptance by showing that they can better explain a number of facts than others. Indeed, some will constitute an exception to this rule by pointing out that facts also need to be construed. However, it is a circular argument forbidden by the basic rule of the game. Both in the hard sciences and in the more anaphoric, soft ones, as well as in everyday wisdom we have learned over time how to adjudge truth value to different kinds of evidence.

With these conditions we can now go back to the more modest issue of attractions. MacCannell errs in his view that anything may become one, "even little flowers or leaves picked up off the ground and shown a child, even a shoeshine or a gravel pit" (MacCannell 1999a:192). All these humble things can indeed be of interest to a child or to a reduced group of people; it is quite doubtful that they would be successful. When Kramer, one of the characters in the Seinfeld series (a successful American TV sitcom from the 90s), tried to turn himself into a marker, and to sell tours to the areas where he had spent his life, he soon found that the attraction did not find many takers. The few tourists whom he succeeded in selling the tour complained of its lack of interest, the bad quality of their lunch boxes, the lousy service, the guide's incompetence, his ignorance of Kramer's history, even though, mark it, the guide was Kramer himself.

This notion that anything can become an attraction has proved deadly for many destinations that have seen their money and their marketing efforts turn to naught. Indeed most of them have attractions. The downside is that many competitors also have them. Because every destination may have attractive tourism products, one cannot naïvely assume that consumers will see them all as equally worth a trip. The glitter of Paris, London, New York, or Tokyo is not easily matched. Even the classical ages were aware of that. In our times there have been quite a few attempts to rank the New Seven Wonders (by New Open World Corporation, USA Today, CNN, even the American Society of Civil Engineers), but the Seven Wonders of the Ancient World were not born yesterday. The existence of rankings is a fact of life, not only under modernity, not only in the West. No single brand, no single marker will create them out of nothing, as implied by MacCannell.

Not only are attractions ranked across many cultures. Their rankings also show a remarkable consistency in what is valued as worth a detour from the asterisk system employed by many guidebooks. Herodotus did not write a Lonely Planet guide, but his *History* (1987) gathers anthropological information about Greece's neighbors (Egypt, Scythia, Arabia, Libya, Persia, and others) that might turn into her eventual adversaries, about their habits, their riches, their form of government, their social customs, that is, he presents a well-organized collection of data that tries to separate the decisive from the banal.

In China, the transition from the 4th to the 5th century CE was a time of political turmoil. Perhaps because of this there was a sizeable number of what today we would call travel writers, as many people would look for safer pastures. The best known among them was Fa Hsien or Faxian (2005). Together with a group of disciples he left Chang'an (today's Xi'an) in 399 CE, and for about 15 years went on a pilgrimage to Buddhist shrines and monasteries that would take him to the Pamirs, Kashmir, Kabul, the Indus valley, Sri Lanka, and Sumatra from where he returned to Guangzhou. In the account of his travels, he dwells on subjects of his private interest: Buddhist monasteries and their activities, but we also find descriptions of cities, monuments, foreign customs, the powers that be, and so on. Fuxian made a considerable contribution to the social construction of the foreign world among many learned Chinese by showing them what they should consider important in dealing with it.

Ibn Battuta would be even closer to the idea of an informed tourist than we have today. In the version of his extensive travels through the Muslim world (1325–54), he does not explain in detail what made him so much on the move. We know that his odysseys started with pilgrimage on the occasion of the *hajj* to Mecca to fulfill one of the duties of pious Muslims. However, he does not offer many reasons for the collection of his destinations or why he elected some places and monuments in his memory, and omitted others. The most we know is what Ibn Juzayy, to whom he dictated his recollections, had to say. To wit, that

> the learned and most veracious traveler [...] known as Ibn Battuta [...] who having journeyed round the world and visited its cities observantly and attentively, having investigated the diversities of nations and experienced the customs of Arabs and non Arabs, laid down the staff of travel in this noble metropolis [Granada JA]. A gracious command prescribed that he should dictate an account of the cities which he had seen on his journeys, of the interesting events that he retained in his memory, and of the rulers of countries, learned men, and pious saints whom he had met (Ibn Battuta 1929:41).

Ibn Battuta faithfully followed the Caliph's will, and he portrayed a great number of cities, monuments, descriptions of customs and traditions, and sketches of notable people; that is, he made a difference between the noteworthy and the insignificant both for him and for his audience.

According to Francis Bacon:

> The things to be seen and observed are, the courts of princes, especially when they give audience to ambassadors; the courts of justice, while they sit and hear causes; and so of consistories ecclesiastic; the churches and monasteries with the monuments that are therein extant; the walls and fortifications of cities and towns; and so the havens and harbors, antiquities and ruins, libraries, colleges, disputations, and lectures, where any are; shipping and navies; houses and gardens of state and pleasure, near great cities; armories, arsenals, magazines, exchanges, burses, warehouses, exercises of horsemanship, fencing, training of soldiers, and the like; comedies, such whereunto

the better sort of persons do resort; treasuries of jewels and robes; cabinets and rarities; and, to conclude, whatsoever is memorable in the places where they go; after all which the tutors or servants ought to make diligent inquiry. As for triumphs, masks, feasts, weddings, funeral, capital executions, and such shows men need not to be put in mind of them; yet they are not to be neglected (1951:21–22).

None of these authors, as well as many others, strayed much from what present-day guides, travel writers, and tourists consider "worth a detour." The issue then is not so much the fact that attractions are socially constructed, but why their constructors seem to have similar interests in constructing them. MacCannell devotes chapter 3 of *The Tourist* to see how "alienated leisure," that is, visits to attractions that highlight workplaces (wherefrom the moniker leisure as the opposite of work) have become popular. Indeed, they are attractions. The fact, however, is that they do not draw so many flows of tourists as Nôtre Dame, the Eiffel Tower, or the Louvre Museum. All of them are socially constructed, but some are more successful than others. I might try to construe as attractions the residence in the Cité Universitaire of Paris where I spent most of summer 1960, or the Parisian street where my then girlfriend used to live but it is doubtful that they would become a magnet for anybody else than my closest friends and relatives, if at all.

A THEORY OF (TOURIST) DEMAND

For better or worse, MacCannell's contribution to tourism research will be attached to the notion of authenticity by an enduring knot. Whatever it may mean, everybody in the field knows that for him authenticity is the prime mover of tourists, and many have adopted it as a satisfactory explanation of their motivations. Not surprisingly, the concept has received so many coats of paint that it has often become unrecognizable or used in contradictory ways. Surprisingly, though, Cohen has a point when he doubts whether diving into authenticity's depths of meaning was ever MacCannell's intention (2007).

A close reading of *The Tourist* makes Cohen's view quite likely. In his Chapter 5, entitled "Staged Authenticity," MacCannell takes the concept for granted, that is, he does not feel the urge to define it. After another quick attempt at separating Industrial Man (whose foremost ties to the world were work and place) from Modern Man (losing his attachment to work while becoming leisured and more interested in the "real life" of others), he proceeds without further ado to show how the latter's interest to enter the deeper recesses of attractions, that is, to encounter authenticity, turns itself into an impossible dream. To state the problem, he turns to Goffman for help.

One of Goffman's tenets in his analysis of the dramaturgy of the self refers to the separation between the front and back regions in everyday life. While individuals and social institutions (including attractions) allow others to peep into some areas of their life, they carefully shutter others from public view. In this way, one can say that all social reality, including the way in which we present ourselves to others requires some degree of mystification. The search for authenticity begets deceit. Is this predicament just a matter of degree so that it might be possible to tell one from the other, and know more or less accurately how they mix in any given situation? Or is it another name for a Jungian wound that will never heal? Is mystification a structural feature of our psyche and the social arrangements that we have to live with, or does it only involve some degree of contrivance that can be researched and exposed?

The existence of front and back regions creates all sorts of trouble in our relations with others. Both for Ego and Thou, it is always difficult to know where their limits lie, how much backstage one is ready to open, what kind of image to project, and how far to push the desire to reach the back. Trespass lurks as a constant threat for Ego at the same time as it spurs Thou's insatiable will to know. Back regions incite curiosity, and the secrets they allegedly conceal entice onlookers. They separate people. On the other hand, when for some reason their walls crumble or, at least, recede somewhat, the new openness creates an exhilarating feeling of fusion that pushes all the parties into unexplored levels of intimacy. Back and front may unite as well. So, might their relentless gap somehow be healed by reconciliation? As we will see, MacCannell stumbles and wavers until finally he decides he can escape this riddle.

At first sight, reconciliation remains a possibility. Even though not all tourists show the same interests, many will endeavor to find what is allegedly occult, trying to engage the back by sharing in local life as it is really lived in their destination. These are the ones that appeal to MacCannell, as they come into contact with "an almost authentic experience" that allows them to recapture primeval sensations of discovery. At close range, though, reconciliation is but a fleeting illusion.

> Touristic consciousness is motivated by its desire for authentic experiences, and the tourist may believe that he is moving in this direction, but often it is very difficult to know for sure if the experience is in fact authentic. It is always possible that what is taken to be entry into a back region is really entry into a front region that has been totally set up in advance for touristic visitation (1999a:101).

There is no sure way to tell one from the other, and MacCannell's tourist finds himself in the same desperate position as the reader of *Beauty and Sadness*, a story by Kawabata, the Japanese author and Nobel Prize winner that may serve to illustrate the point. We will have to summarize it in some detail.

When we first meet him, Oki Toshio, an aging Kamakura gentleman writer, is bound for Kyoto to hear the New Year's Eve bells ring. That is what he said at home, but in fact something different lurks at the back of his mind. Perhaps he may again meet Otoko, his old-time lover. Otoko was 16 when she bore him a child, a girl that died soon after birth. At the time, 24 years ago, Oki was 15 years older than Otoko, already married and the father of a child. Otoko's girl might perhaps have survived had Oki taken her to a better hospital for her labor but he did not, even though he had the money to afford it.

Soon after the incident, Otoko tried to commit suicide, and Oki came to her side, but turned down her mother's suggestion that he marry her and, after Otoko's recovery, they parted. Otoko, nowadays an up-and-coming painter, lives on the grounds of a Kyoto temple sharing her garden apartment with Keiko, a young female artist and, soon we will know, also her lover. Now Oki invites both to enjoy the New Year bells with him. When he starts back home next day, he hopes that Otoko will wish him good-bye at the train station, but it is Keiko who shows up in her stead. She oozes evil fascination, still beautifully enrobed in the same kimono that she had worn the night before, and that Oki had praised. A few days later, she would come to Oki's home bringing a gift of two paintings of her own. She left them there as he was away and went back to the station accompanied by Oki's son, Taichiro. It took Taichiro too long a time to come back home. He had showed her around town, he said.

Back in Kyoto, Keiko confides to Otoko that she wants to take revenge for her. She has a plan—she will seduce the father. Or the son. Or both. She wants to destroy that family. A twisted sort of a plan for, as she explains, it is not so much Oki that she wants to hurt, but Otoko's still smoldering love.

After all her travails, after so many years of suffering, she still cannot tear herself from him.

Some time thereafter, Keiko unexpectedly visits Oki and, according to plan, seduces him. "She acts as somebody experienced in lovemaking", his mind flashes when she forbids him to touch her left breast. Later, in the middle of his embrace, he hears her cry plaintively: "Otoko, Otoko." As his strength ebbs, Keiko pushes him away.

When she tells her the story, Otoko startles with the jolt. May Oki have awakened in her lover the same feelings that she once had for him and are still there? Now it is Otoko's turn to be jealous—a jealousy that is paired at the other end of the story. Recalling his night with Keiko, it suddenly dawns on Oki—he must not ever let Taichiro come near her. Too late. Taichiro has just taken a plane to Kyoto. He has some work to do there, but since they met in Kamakura he has been in touch with Keiko who is waiting for him at the airport. From the very moment, Keiko takes charge of events, making him adapt his plans to hers, and pressing her fancy to go motoring on nearby Lake Biwa the next day. Once they stop at a teahouse by the river, the reader also gets to know that neither has let either his parents or Otoko in on their closeness. Then their talk quickly harks back to their own relation. She tells of her hunger to take revenge on him because of Otoko's abiding love for the old man. As vengeance goes, nothing would beat beguiling Oki's own son, would it? But perhaps she is really falling in love with him, she hints. That night, Otoko hears Keiko arrive home at dawn. When she wakes up early next day, Keiko lets drop that she will meet Taichiro again, even when Otoko entreats her not to go with him. Else she would not need to ever come back, she yells, but Keiko leaves without even stopping for breakfast. The girl said that she hated men, Otoko remembers, but that was nothing to rely on.

Back at the teahouse, Keiko gives away to Taichiro that she feels as though a stage in her life is over. "It hasn't ended, it's begun," he counters. Then, in a taxi, both go visit the old Sanetaka tomb that was his initial excuse to come to Kyoto, for he specializes in medieval Japanese literature. In the secluded woods that surround the temple, her seducing of him ratchets up. While he fondles her right breast, though, something makes him think it is not the first time she has let a man touch her. Later, they move to a restaurant and, from there, at Keiko's prodding, to a hotel on the banks of Lake Biwa. "It is frightening when a woman gives herself completely," she whispers when entering the room that, unbeknownst to him, she had secured. While he is changing to swim in the lake, she calls Taichiro's mother, and makes him come to the phone to confirm that they are together. In their short conversation, the mother shares with Taichiro her suspicion that Keiko has had a tryst with Oki, and pleads with him not to get involved with her. If he does not come back home immediately, his parents will fly to bring him from Kyoto.

But Taichiro stays put. He wants to know. Did Keiko seduce his father, he begs her to explain. She answers with another question ("Did I seduce you? Did I?") at the same time as she starts sobbing. In her shudder, one of the shoulder straps of her white swimsuit slips under his hand. He pulls it down and starts kissing the exposed flesh of her left breast. After a while, they go motoring in the lake.

The last section of the story has Otoko and the Oki couple arriving separately at a nearby hospital. They have been called because of an accident in the lake. Taichiro is missing, but Keiko was rescued and now lies in bed under sedation. While Otoko sits by her, tears sparkle in Keiko's eyes as she awakes.

A clumsy few words will not substitute for Kawabata's bewitching prose, but can help in the discussion of MacCannell's first view of the front/back relationship. One might think that the difficulty in knowing who, if any, among the main characters is letting their back align with their front, stems from Kawabata's subtle nods to the reader; however, they pull deeper roots.

Take Keiko who seems the easiest to read of them all. She pushes her wicked scheme with rightful determination, but her plans could not unfold without a sizeable dose of deception that even seems not to spare her. She deceives Oki by letting him think that he has seduced her when, in fact, it is his gullible male ego that takes the bait plus the line, hook, and sinker. She deceives Taichiro with a no less murky relation. Does she lie when she says she just wanted him to avenge herself on Otoko's enduring love for Oki, or is it when she tells Taichiro of their breakup and her desire to give herself "completely" to him? Why on earth does she let him kiss that left breast that she had held back from his father? Her insistence in motoring on Lake Biwa even when she knows that Taichiro has never skippered a boat—is it craft or just a fateful whim? She deceives Otoko as well. "I never want to hide anything from you again. I have no more secrets from you," Keiko said to her at the beginning of their story, but this is the same Keiko who leaves her in the dark about her ongoing relation with Taichiro. She may be even deceiving herself. As the novel closes, do the tears in her eyes sparkle with the beauty of her accomplished revenge or the sadness for Taichiro's loss? We will never know.

What about Otoko? Hers is the aggrieved role; she is the perennial victim. Is she though really bereft of duplicity? Was sending Keiko to the station to say farewell to Oki on his departure a mere chance or a sleight of hand?

A hint to Oki that her unrelenting love for him would not even stop at letting him have her own beloved; or was she marking for Keiko the kill she should take home? As Kawabata's art translates life so well, quite possibly both Otoko and Keiko would be in a bind to elucidate their real motives. Readers cannot expect better either. All of which seems to strengthen MacCannell's initial position. Authenticity and mystification, with a Chinese twist, need each other as the teeth need the lips. But then the hydra pushes another nagging head. If authenticity, whether staged or genuine, cannot reach the requested structural transparency, then it becomes an oxymoron, or at best a crossword. There is no real truth value to it. Authenticity would amount to just a hunch, a feeling that is not only difficult to interpret—it is also an ontological mirage. Starting his quest for making sense in authenticity, suddenly modern-man-in-general realizes that truth becomes a medley of disparate experiences or, with more technical jargon, that authenticity can only be existential. This first notion of authenticity thus turns truth into a matter of trust. To reach it we can only rely either on our individual experiences or on what we take to be based on other people's word—a seal that comes in too many and all too often contradictory ways to gratify MacCannell's inquisitive mind.

This may be the reason why, after touching Ground Zero, one feels that he downgrades the test so that his notion of authenticity can pass muster. May not authenticity and mystification lie in a different arrangement, one that is not altogether structural; may theirs be but a time-bound relation that pertains to just the modern behavioral arrangements but was different in the past and may be so in the future?

> Primitives who live their lives totally exposed to their "relevant others" do not suffer from anxiety about the authenticity of their lives [...] The opposite problem, a weakened sense of reality, appears with the differentiation of society into front and back. Once this division is established, there can be no return to a state of nature. Authenticity itself moves to inhabit mystification (1999a:93).

At any rate, MacCannell needs this waiver, and for good cause. The existence of authenticity denuded of mystification, even if confined to a nebulous past, carries a double indemnity. One, it provides a badly needed benchmark to discern how contrived or staged each tourist setting is. As if on cue, he feels more comfortable to catalog a limited phenomenology of authenticities based on how far tourists are allowed to enter the local social space, from just front zones to, intriguingly, Stage Six, where he concedes that they may reach Goffman's real back regions. In between lie a number of arrangements that alternate between limited back regions really open to tourists and settings made to look as if they were genuine backs. Showing eventual transitions among those layers has become a trivial pastime for the academic cottage industry grown around the notion of authenticity.

Two, it acts as a gradient that points to the greatest rate of increase of its scalar field or, in plain English, to the point of highest concentration. From humble origins in Neolithic times, staged authenticity has soared to a maximum under modernity. Are those echoes of Norbert Elias's crucible of civilization—that the higher the tide of Western civilization, the more wretched the lives of the people it crushes? To some extent, though unlike in Elias' increasingly repressive world, in MacCannell's there is a place for hope. What man creates, man can change. We'll come to that later.

There are a number of unexplained transitions in this line of reasoning. One wonders how MacCannell concluded that his generic primitives had reached such a happy dispensation. What made their exposure to each other total? The fact that they live in small groups and meet face to face with each other more often than modern people? If so, their alleged authenticity would just amount to increased visibility, but by itself our sense of sight does not penetrate below the surface. We can see others, but their authentic essence, whatever this may mean, may remain opaque to our gaze.

Let us use an example, a bit more concrete than MacCannell's fuzzy primitives. That gossip of the Duc de Saint-Simon acquainted us with the rituals of the court of Louis XIV of France. Here and there he refers to how strict was its etiquettes and gives many details on how the king's activities were rigidly organized (Saint-Simon 2001). One ritual that piques today's readers' fancy is *la toilette du roi*, the fashion in which the king readied himself—was readied, rather—to start his day. According to Saint-Simon, attending this ceremony was a great honor for the people allowed to follow the liturgy.

The first valet would awake the king at eight o'clock in the morning. Once the doors to his bedroom opened, a number of people would be given entry to the quarters by a page standing at the door. They would enter in successive stages (*les entrées*) with only those closest to the king permitted to attend the whole operation. This most coveted circle could enter through a back door at any time, as long as the king was not in council, and they were allowed to remain in the chambers when the king was at mass or even when he was ill (Elias 1998). The whole toilette included witnessing how the king was washed, shaved, and dressed; accompanying him during mass; watching him eating his first daily meal; and even when he would move his royal bowels. It seems difficult to imagine a deeper dive into anybody's back. Everything in the action was visible to the invitees.

Visible yes, but not necessarily transparent. When the king looked at courtiers, many would ignore whether they had sunk or risen in the ladder of royal favor; many were not allowed to partake in the most important royal affairs, like council meetings; and, indeed, most would not stare at the king's antics when visiting some favorite lover. Perhaps they imagined that they were sharing the king's most intimate recesses, but that delusion was all theirs. Actual transparency or authenticity remains beyond the pale of human capacities, and omniscience is the preserve of some superhuman entities, not of simple mortals. Had the courtiers been given total access to each other's front and back regions by one of those benevolent entities, still the condition of total exposure to others would not have been met. The lesser orders of the court and the French populace in general would still be excluded from access. It is difficult to understand how MacCannell's primitives could find themselves in a lesser pickle.

This brings a measure of relief to the reader for MacCannell's dream of transparency/authenticity is disquieting. In fact, it surmises that in their search for understanding, tourists or modern-men-in-general have a right to peep into everybody else's backstage or, what amounts to the same, that absence of privacy should be a necessary condition for authentic social intercourse. His confusion between transparency and visibility creates a logical feeling of anxiety.

First of all, the lust for total exposure of back regions seems suspect. Eroding or imploding privacy characterizes totalitarian societies. The irrepressible panopticon that haunts so many Foucauldian minds, when it is something more than a suitable spook to cheer the boredom of faculty clubs, cannot be easily imposed on democratic societies. Nobody has a right to be shown more back regions than what the counterpart wants. Second but not less, even in totalitarian polities, access to everybody's back regions proves very difficult. Many examples of individuals that did not consent to have their privacy raped even under the most brutal pressure confirm that a degree of uncertainty will always accompany social exchanges.

Accordingly, the gimmick of a waiver bestowed on the primitives does not help MacCannell much to extricate himself from the labyrinth he has created. He wants us to swallow that authenticity always bears a measure of mystification, but, at the same time, that somehow this birthmark can be erased if we avail ourselves of the right historical understanding.

Authenticity and mystification thus become twins joined at the hip in the structural arrangements of all societies and, at the same time, immaterial for some. On the other hand, the only evidence he introduces for his gambit—less ceremoniously, Popper would have called it an adhocism—boils down to the urban legend of the good savage, as popular among the most gullible sections of the anthropological herd as bereft of any substance (Barley 1984, 1986).

So, why am I saying that MacCannell can afford the audacity of hope? Like Siegfried, the Wälsung, all good romantics believe there is always a way to recompose Notung, the broken sword that will slay the dragon and bring the Valkyrie back to life.

A GENERAL THEORY OF (TOURIST) MODERNITY

Let us summarize the argument so far. MacCannell is an accidental tourism researcher. Although his main work deals with this type of social behavior, it only enthuses the author because the tourist stands for modern-man-in-general. Whatever we can say about the tourist applies to him. To understand modern man (which of course serves here as a proxy for both men and women), we need an ambitious research methodology that might free ourselves from the limitations of the self-defeating bourgeois individualist vision that plagues the social sciences, often at the behest of narrow political interests. The social sciences will only fulfill their promise when they place themselves at the service of the subservient majorities the world over.

From there, MacCannell focuses on how tourism develops around an increasing number of attractions. Attractions do not reflect any substantive interest about given objects on the part of people. They become attractions because they are marked as such in a process of social construction. In this way it is their markers that create them. Indeed, there must be something behind those markers; somebody somehow must have named them. Who are they and why do tourists dance to their music? MacCannell has not developed this lead—yet.

Why would tourists want to spend their time and their money pursuing attractions? The new leisure classes have a pressing demand. After having created them, modernity has deprived them of an anchor to their lives. Cohen, after Eliade, prefers to call it a center, that is, the notional space "which for the individual symbolizes ultimate meanings" (2004a:67).

Anchor or center, tourists locate it in something MacCannell calls authenticity. As he does not define it, we are led to think that the moniker refers to the desire of reaching the fullness of the attraction they experience. Following Goffman, MacCannell hints that authenticity means admission to the deepest back regions of attractions, but immediately doubts that it might be possible. Authenticity tends to be interwoven with mystification. If such is its real structure, then modernity's quest shines as a hopeless passion. After reaching this point, he allows himself a glimmer of hope. Under some special circumstances (such as primitive life, whatever this may mean), authenticity was untainted. Could that enchanted space not be revived?

Retracing his meandering train of thought, I have stressed the many empirical hurdles he tried to clear without much success. On some occasions he just pushes his evidence to the outer reaches of credibility; on others, he clearly contrives it. Who are those primitives he knows so well? Where do they live? Are they still alive or extinct? He refers to them as though they were colleagues one meets when walking or in the pub; so familiar with their ways is he, so well does he know that they were totally exposed to each other. But, with a Heideggerian expression, one might argue that these are but ontic trifles that should not make our discussion lose track from the basic or structural issues he raises.

Unfortunately, his tally here fares no better. Its noble structuralist pedigree notwithstanding, the idea that markers create attractions borders on the thaumaturgical. Because of this, he cannot explain why they have been constructed in persistently similar ways through the ages, and across cultures; nor why some are successful while others are not. His notion of authenticity shares a similar predicament. He is not the first, and he will surely not be the last, in cheering the monotony of academic life with the playful ghost of the Rousseaunian Noble Savage that will redeem us from the present degeneration that has taken us away from the Golden Age, a truly Barthesian myth that one can trace back to Tassoni's *La Secchia Rapita* (Bury 1920).

It has also been pointed out that MacCannell would have been better off had he discarded both notions (marker-generated attractions and unmystified authenticity). He was not bound to pay allegiance to them. He could have banked on a different definition of constructivism and of authenticity as outcomes and not conditions, but he did not. So, let us consider what conclusions his twin tracks take him to, and why he had to follow the destiny they chose for him. After all, MacCannell wants to hope against all hope. Here is where the concept of revolution, provisionally left unexamined at the beginning of this assessment, makes an impressive encore. So, let's go back to the beginning.

When someone's goals are as ambitious as MacCannell's, he does not readily compromise with lesser callings; he exposes them. His work on tourism and on other subjects brims over with battles of ideas, all for good reason. His first target in *The Tourist* is Boorstin's notion of pseudo-events. Boorstin's *The Image* (1961) begins with a parable. Looking for improved business, the owners of a hotel hire a PR counsel to help them. In previous times, says Boorstin, a consultant would have come up with ideas such as hiring a new chef, improving the plumbing, painting the rooms, etc. Not in these. What the PR man proposes is a celebration of the hotel's 30th anniversary. A committee of local notables is appointed, the occasion is widely publicized, and the local media broadcast or report the banquet that celebrates it. Such is the fabric of pseudo-events—much ado about nothing. They are not spontaneous; they are produced to be broadcast; they thrive in ambiguity—whether they really happened and their motives always remain obscure; they are self-fulfilling. Pictures substitute for subjects. "Images transfix. Images anaesthetize. An event known through photographs certainly becomes more real than it would have been if one had never seen the photographs" (Sontag 2001b:22). Representation dims their reality. Pseudo-events lack meaning. Boorstin reviews and classifies numerous examples in many avenues of US life, one of which incidentally being tourism. Why have they become part and parcel of modernity?

Between the two great wars of the last century, a clear malaise could be detected among some intellectual circles. Here is how Ortega y Gasset opened his essay on the matter:

> There is a fact that, for better or worse, is nowadays the most important for European public life. It is the arrival of the masses to full social preeminence. As masses, by definition, should not and could not shepherd their own existence, even less lead any society, one can say that Europe today is afflicted by the gravest of crisis that peoples, nations, cultures may face. It is not the first time such a crisis has become apparent in history. Its countenance and its consequences are known. So is its name. It is the revolt of the masses (Ortega y Gasset 1957:49).

All of a sudden, the masses had burst into full daylight and everywhere. Well, not only everywhere. They occupy "the best places, those mostly refined creations of human culture that had hitherto been the preserve of smaller groups; in a nutshell—of minorities" (Ortega y Gasset 1957:52).

It would be a mistake to think of them just as the huddled masses or the working classes; they are more than that—they are the average people or, in today's parlance, the consumers.

The remainder of the argument is well known by now. Societies have always been divided between the leading elites and the rest. In the new period, as in other convulsed past times, this remnant is attempting to undermine such natural order. The masses, however, do not bring anything comforting in their agenda—just rejection of the old, fairer world. Politics, cultural life, and economy will fare better once the masses are prodded to their former and proper status and the aristocrats of the intellect restored to their appropriate station.

Ortega's views, initially expressed as an article in the Spanish daily *El Sol* (1926), would quickly reverberate in the echo chamber of the Weimar Republic. We tend to see this period of German history as a pleasant, energetic lull between the end of a terrible war and the coming of the no less dreadful Nazi state, but there is more to it. Weimar, as Josep Pla (2006) would say of its cousin once removed, the Spanish Republic of 1931–36, was a republic without republicans. In fact, the intellectual elites were quickly disillusioned with it, especially those who had ever harbored any illusions about its future. The *Vernunftrepublikaner* (rational republicans) who had contracted a marriage of convenience, not of love, with it also saw the ground below their feet shake. Both to their right and to their left there appeared many others looking for a divorce (Gay 2001). Whether wearing the SA brown shirt or marching with the socialists or the communists, the masses had come onstage.

The Leftist authors that today gather under the Frankfurt School brand would eagerly search for an explanation of this phenomenon in Marx. Theirs, however, was a peculiar kind of Marxism that would keep the proletariat at arm's length. One never knows whether the stinking heroes, as Flaubert called them in *L'Éducation Sentimentale*, showered and put on deodorant this morning. Deliverance from capitalism's exhausted ways should come from an enlightened anti-Enlightenment or critical outlook that Adorno, Horkheimer, Benjamin, or Marcuse tried but never managed to pin down successfully. Sometimes it veered toward a benign understanding of the Soviet Union; sometimes just to what Adorno celebrated as negative dialectics. Many American liberals signed into their Leftist elitism, and quickly adopted the Frankfurters' views. One only has to think of Lionel Trilling (2000, 2008), and of most of the contributors to *Partisan Review*.

With a wide berth, this is the intellectual tradition that Boorstin contributes to and that MacCannell abhors. Why? The salient reason harks back to elitism or what he calls "the intellectual attitude," which stands for bourgeois individualism squared. In Boorstin's book pseudo-events base their success in giving to the naïve mind the impression that the real or the authentic manifests itself in its immediacy. What you see is what you get. Intellectuals, though, know better, and therefore they have a right to lead. As MacCannell puts it with an unusually clumsy formulation, for them, "[t]he touristic experience that comes out of the tourist setting is based on inauthenticity and as such it is superficial when compared with careful study" (MacCannell 1999a:102). In a nutshell, intellectuals can aspire to a better understanding of social arrangements than any other people, including tourists, that is, modern-men-in-general. They believe in their ability to see directly the interaction of back and front while the vulgar public is unable to pierce its surface. What angers Boorstin and his ilk is the superficiality of the tourist. They are ignorant, they are vulgar, and they are crass. On their side intellectuals, with a Husserlian expression, do tower over appearances grasping the essential by intuition—just by glancing at it.

For MacCannell, the truth lies elsewhere—intellectuals may aspire to the highest insights into reality, but they, as much as tourists, are hoodwinked by the basic mystification of back and front. They think they have a safe conduct to the truth just by being intellectuals, but they cannot avoid the strictures of modern life and its mystified reality.

> Boorstin only expresses a long standing touristic attitude, a pronounced dislike, bordering on hatred, for other tourists, an attitude that "turns man against man as in a 'they are tourists, I am not' equation" (1999a:107).

Cohen downplays the discussion to a generational rift. While an earlier cohort of social critics tended to dismiss tourism as a frivolous activity, "a later generation of social scientists, guided essentially by a structuralist approach, tended in the opposite direction—and identified the tourist as the pilgrim of modernity in a serious quest for authenticity" (Cohen 2004b:88). Cohen chides MacCannell for taking the formula too seriously, but he fails to see how central this is to his research project. For MacCannell, the tourist is not just in a serious quest. She is in a much worse predicament as the quest is always cheated by modernity's structural incapacity to avoid mystification. But MacCannell is not a rebel without a cause who, like James Dean in the eponymous film, thinks that bravery means being the last to surrender. Like Thelma and Louise, MacCannell drives to the brink of the cliff, and then jumps. "Once tourists have encountered touristic space, there is no way out for them as long as they press their search for authenticity. Near each tourist setting there are others like the last" (1999a:106). There is no gain in denying reality.

If Cohen's interpretation were correct, MacCannell's scarcely mannered fallout with Urry would have no sense. Both authors belong to the same generation and share similar views on constructivism as methodology. However, MacCannell sees Urry as an extension of the bourgeois liberal tradition (2001a). Why? Urry is right in his view that research on tourism has weighed too heavily on the production versus the consumption side, he says. The idea of tourist gaze tries to overcome this conflict. Initially the gaze reminds us that different subjects look at their objects in different ways— they construe them in diversity. Once this stated, Urry starts to swerve. He defines tourism as an activity rooted in the separation between ordinary and extraordinary life and explains that the role of attractions precisely lies in their capacity to maintain these two areas independent from each other.

> Urry's tourist gaze, the precise way he has formulated it, is a blueprint for the transformation of the global system of attractions into an enormous set of mirrors to serve the narcissistic needs of dull egos [...] To the extent that this gaze is institutionalized in the arrangements made for tourists, what will be constructed in the name of tourism is a congruence of small selves, and vacuous social representation, an iron circle of narcissistic determinism (2001a:26).

In a nutshell, Urry gains an accolade for his well-meaning constructivist attempt, but he is not radical enough—his is a secondary root. Swimming in Foucault's wake, he unsurprisingly drowns. Like Foucault's, his gaze, socially constructed as it is, remains however on the surface. Surfaces may appear as different to different gazers, but there is no piercing them. Urry's view remains at the same superficial level as the Lonely Planet guides.

It is highly doubtful that this gaze could debunk what MacCannell calls determinism, that is, the alleged impossibility of attaining real authenticity or freedom. Urry's tourists indeed move in a structured space arranged in terms of social hierarchies jealously guarded by their beneficiaries. However, while they are prisoners of such strictures, they, like Foucault's subjects, are supposed to remain free to choose. Their freedom, then, becomes merely subjective. A second gaze is needed.

[This] second gaze knows that seeing is not believing. Some things will remain hidden from it [...] The second gaze turns back onto the gazing subject an ethical responsibility for the construction of its own existence. It refuses to leave this construction to the corporation, the state, and the apparatus of touristic representation [...] It looks for the unexpected, not the extraordinary, objects and events that may open a window in structure, a chance to glimpse the real (2001a:36).

The formulation remains too bland and too fuzzy (how can we open this window in structure when we are told that the structure is always there?), but let's not rush to the conclusion.

It has been said that MacCannell's brand of structuralism owes more to radical Barthes than to tepid Foucault, and he is not shy to confirm this view. To his just mentioned criticism of Foucault he has something even more poisonous to add. In a book chapter written together with Juliet Flower MacCannell (1993a), they express their disappointment with the master. Foucault conceives power as a neutral mechanism, that is, a process that can be unleashd by all and sundry.

Foucault is indifferent to who gets to start power up, to operate it, and for how long: it becomes the great Equaliser. By characterizing all subjects of subjugated knowledge as 'local' he unwittingly undercuts them for being minoritarian not simply in relation to specific oppressors, but in general, in relation to an idealized power (MacCannell and MacCannell 1993a:231).

Nearly the same words he used to chastise liberal social scientists. This hurts.

The MacCannells scold Baudrillard even more relentlessly. In a few words, through despair or whim, Baudrillard comes to the conclusion that the mismatch between authenticity and the human will to know will be never healed. To the postmodern, the modern world shows its emptiness. There is no back, just an endless front that resists all attempts to puncture it. As unmasking the simulacra that jump at us from every corner of reality reveals itself an impossible dream, one should just accept them. Here comes the rub. Baudrillard deserves praise for pointing out the new forms of capitalist exploitation that have introjected class structure into postmodernity, but he does not examine them critically. The uncertainty thus created may make his work an accessory to these new forms of exploitation instead of exposing them to eventual overthrow.

> Ultimately, both Baudrillard and Mickey Mouse insist on a generalized sense of the possible existence not of codes, which would be subversive, but of The Code, a single framework, already in existence for everything (MacCannell and Mac-Cannell 1993b:141).

Being exposed as a twin of Mickey Mouse surely is a worse insult for any self-respecting deconstructionist than being complicit with the repressive government of the United States. This must hurt even more.

Here one sees a relative *volte-face* from earlier times when MacCannell thought that semiotics and symbolic interactionism might have a mutually enriching cross-pollination. At that time (late 1980s), he had a spirited quarrel with Lesley Harman who preferred to have them as separate as possible. The reason for MacCannell's more sanguine view of some deconstructionists (he specifically cited Baudrillard), however, is exactly the same he will use to attack them later.

> There is ample evidence that neocapitalism does reproduce itself symbolically not merely at the level of the determined semiotic sign but in conversations and in consciousness as well. It is precisely the success of capitalism that it can gear intentionality and symbolism to its expansion through the creation of desire; and remake even our conversations in its own image (1986:167).

This quote is not meant to present MacCannell as whimsical; on the other hand, it clearly shows that his intellectual evolution about the value of deconstructionism always circles the same kernel—the intrinsic evil of capitalism, especially in its late stages. But before we can close his argument, we need to follow him in what seems his provisionally last turn of the screw.

The tortured intellectual journey is about to conclude. Once again, MacCannell needs to remind us of the differences between modernity and the rest of social arrangements. And he does so with the usual measure of hype.

> [U]nique to the modern world is its capacity to transform material relations into symbolic expressions and back again, while continuing to differentiate or multiply structures (MacCannell 1999a:145).

One wonders whether *homo sapiens* and perhaps some of his ancestors ever lacked symbolic skills to differentiate the cooked from the raw, and whether our dear friends the primitives did not multiply structures (possibly meaning division of labor, although this is not altogether plain). But let us bracket such excesses of the word processor and not be led astray by their colorful nonchalance; if they are there, it is to render more plausible the argument that follows and it is to it that one should stick.

The preternatural doubt whether the quest for authenticity has a shred of plausibility now braces itself for a happy ending. Undaunted by the Goffmanesque ghost of back and front, and their irrepressible disjuncture, MacCannell swerves to the suspect comforts of economics. "The dividing line between structure genuine and spurious is the realm of the commercial" (MacCannell 1999a:155). The academic cottage industry built around the notions of authenticity and genuineness has interpreted this oracular pronouncement as a rejection of commercialization, commoditization, or consumerism in general. Although such notions are usually left undefined, they usually connote, as in Merriam-Webster's third and fourth senses of the word commercialization, "to engage in, conduct, practice, or make use of for profit-seeking purposes as distinguished from participation, practice, or use for spiritual or recreational purposes or for other nonpecuniary satisfactions" or "to debase in quality, make more conventional and unoriginal, or employ for inferior purposes in the hope of securing a greater or more certain profit" (Merriam-Webster 2002).

However, after what we have seen, this watery notion cannot be MacCannell's. Although sometimes debasing the currency, he is a stickler for radicalism. When he says that "at the heart of the act, the final contact between the tourist and a true attraction, such as the White House or the Grand Canyon, can be pure" (1999a:156–157) he is not betraying himself. This wan Neo-Platonic expression cuts deeper than the usual scorn for kitschy products or bastardized services that one would rather leave to the Boorstins of this world. What MacCannell urges is nothing less than the withering away not just of money, but also of any human relations mediated by interest—a radical approach seldom taken seriously by his self-appointed followers.

MacCannell knows that one cannot wish away transaction costs in sightseeing. Tourists have to pay for travel, food, equipment, accommodations, and all the expenses related to their activities. Often those costs also include fees for access to the attraction. But all of this is irrelevant in relation to the real sight. The fee cannot be misconstrued as the price of enjoyment. "This is a fine distinction to make, and it may not be important from the standpoint of common sense, but like many fine distinctions is a necessary

146 Modern Mass Tourism

one" (1999a:157). Seeing Seattle from the Space Needle, as in the Mastercard advertisement, is priceless.

It does not take the proverbial rocket scientist to insist that this fine distinction does not stand. If there were no fees to pay for at least a fraction of its conservation, the Space Needle would soon fall into disrepair, and it would be difficult to enjoy the view of Seattle it provides. Even when there is no fee, as in a visit to the White House, the site is financially maintained by the public budget underwritten by the American taxpayer. The priceless experience obtained by the sightseer would otherwise be impossible. The argument that experiences have no price or that real attractions may live outside of economic exchanges cannot be easily ascertained.

MacCannell indeed has in mind an alternative to the money link. Just at the end of his Epilogue to the 1999 edition of *The Tourist*, he evokes his maternal uncle, Elwood Meskimen, who had a junkyard that he operated all his life on a strict barter base, or the artist Ann Chamberlain that instead of making her own photo documentary on a New York borough supplemented her work with old photographs provided by the neighbors. It is gestures such as these that he wants to recommend as the expression of a tourism that occurs outside of the commercial nexus. "There are millions of parallel examples accessible for all to see" (1999a:202). One can once again ask for some evidence of those millions of parallel examples; or doubt that the honorable Mr. Meskimen could use his junk as legal tender for provisions at the nearest grocery store; or be unable to find whether Ms. Chamberlain's innovating approach to photo exhibitions was not paid for by some charity.

Let us, though, grant MacCannell leave of such ontic minutiae and follow his logic. Even more, let us take a magic wand and do away with money once and for all. He is versed enough in French sociology to have read Marcel Mauss on gifts. Mauss for one would not be amused with the idea that there was something of a natural economy where exchanges would not be governed by some symmetry between the goods and services swapped, and where the former would be offered free of charge to their members. When they had no markets, our generic primitives apparently organized their exchanges through barter and gifts. Social groups, usually represented by their chieftains, traded goods and other economic values, as well as courtesies, entertainment, women, children, dances, and feasts. For Mauss, this is but the outside of the exchanges. For, he concludes:

> although the prestations and counter-prestations take place
> under a voluntary guise they are in essence strictly obligatory,
> and their sanction is private or open warfare (Mauss 1970:4).

In modern parlance—there is no such thing as a free lunch. Money or no money, the manifold exchanges that make social life possible stand on the trust that people traffic equivalent values. Those Bolsheviks who, in the midst of the Russian Civil War (1917–21), thought the blessed times when money as the measure of value could be dispensed with had finally arrived, soon realized they needed to go back to the old monetary order, now called the New Economic Policy, if they were to avoid a total collapse of the revolution.

The dystopia of a society where not only money but also any symmetrical exchanges would not be needed is not a new idea in social philosophy. Thomas More, for one, describes the possibility in his portrait of the city of Amaurote, the capital of the island of Utopia.

> Every man that will, may go in, for there is nothing within the houses that is private, or any man's own. And every tenth year they change their houses by lot. They set great store by their gardens. In them they have vineyards, all manner of fruit, herbs, and flowers, so pleasant, so well furnished and so finely kept, that I never saw thing more fruitful, nor better trimmed in any place. Their study and diligence herein cometh not only of pleasure, but also of a certain strife and contention that is between street and street, concerning the trimming, husbanding, and furnishing of their gardens: every man for his own part. And verily you shall not lightly find in all the city anything, that is more commodious, either for the profit of the citizens, or for pleasure (More 2001:48).

That this might only happen in a preterhuman world was part of utopian literature until the 19th century, but this would change with the Romantic wave (Berlin 1997). In 1808 Fichte pronounced in French-occupied Berlin his Addresses to the German Nation and things started to move. In his blueprint of the nationalistic fever that would soon inflame most of Central and Eastern Europe (Berlin 1990), Fichte urged the citizens of a future Germany to mistrust any commercial exchange with foreign nations.

> O, that we might at last see that all those swindling theories about world-trade and manufacturing for the world-market, though they suit the foreigner and form part of the weapons with which he has always made war on us, have no application to the Germans; and that next to the unity of the Germans

> among themselves their internal autonomy and commercial
> independence form the second means for their salvation,
> and through them for the salvation of Europe (Fichte
> 1922:231–232).

These ideas were a not too innovative version of the 18th-century
mercantilist creed, but allied to the notion of national identity, they have
haunted many social movements the world over until today. Trade, commercialism, and money thus form an undefined, though threatening web that
may trap the very essence of the people of a nation or, in MacCannell's
version, of modern-man-in-general.

Compared with this ontological threat, MacCannell's subsequent tirades
against corporations as the main conduits of mystification in modern society
sound like a falsetto. In his view, the main change that affected the world of
tourism between 1976, the time of the first publication of *The Tourist*, and
the epilogue he attached in 1999 was the aggressive invasion of the field of
tourism by corporate entertainment interests. In what has later become a
clichéd invective, MacCannell warns us that corporations commodify,
package, and market destinations in such a way that the link between
sightseeing and the specificity of the places gets lost. If this drive becomes
successful, one can wonder whether it "will eventually destroy the reason to
travel" (2001b:380). The question, however, is not so much the economic
misdeeds of corporations, but the fact that no matter how hard they try, they
will never solve the conundrum that the economics of sightseeing is
ultimately dependent on a noneconomic relation.

Why, one feels entitled to ask, have corporations and their definition of
tourism, that is, of modern-man-in-general reached the big success that even
MacCannell does not contest? Little quoted, his response takes us to the
heart of the relation between cultural commodities and the subject that
consumes them. "[C]ommercially successful attractions are those that are
modeled on the structure of the ego, those that stage a narcissistic relation
between ego and attraction" (2002:147). The Disney corporate universe, for
instance, has developed successful theme parks or residential communities
like Celebration, Florida, by mirroring all the qualities of the ego.

> They are well-bounded, organized, entertaining, neat, self-
> made, self-contained, self-sufficient, and fun. They are every-
> thing that a marvelous ego would want to be, and the perfect
> place for an ego to go on vacation. They reflect back onto the
> ego nothing that does not confirm it in its self-satisfaction.

> They constitute an effective field for unrestrained narcissism
> (MacCannell 2002:149).

Egos are the last and best soil for all kinds of corporate misdeeds to flourish. Theirs is a marriage made in heaven.

What is Ego? By now, we should know—it is nothing else than a construct, which at the same time serves as the bedrock of every identity project. Its claim to a firm identity reflects the terrors that haunt us from the day that we are born. Not even the terrors of darkness or of being lost in the thick of the forest compare with the giddy threat of losing our identities. One should look here to understand why people grab them so forcefully. This bedrock, however, is quite shaky. In the past, a firewall surrounded our egos in the shape of the normative injunctions of the superego. In opposing itself to the excesses of the ego, it assured the stability of the sociosymbolic order. However, over the last 150 years this basic arrangement has changed dramatically. The superego has been absorbed by the ego; the moral order now dissolves in the will or the needs of each ego. Consumption has phagocyted morals in a world where brands have drowned all meaningful differences.

Not all faith should be lost, though. We can still dare the audacity of hope. The corporate construction of unrestricted egos faces a number of hurdles. To start with, our selves will still have to deal with strenuous problems such as sustainability, the future, reproduction, etc., not easily amenable to prefabricated scripts. Additionally, the senseless rat race of unbridled consumption often breaks the budgets of its practitioners, creating a desire to escape from corporate environments. Finally, the ego is going out of fashion. The desire for conservation, simple living, and similar movements increasingly curbs the ego and its demands. In conclusion, the ego is but one of the many ways (including the unconscious, neurosis, psychoses, perversion, and the ethics of pleasure) in which individual personalities may be organized. It is not a definitive model.

Once again, MacCannell cannot resist hype as soon as he finds the right window of opportunity.

> The human type that has been put forward as a corporate twenty-first century ideal in the West is "hard-bodied," shallow, acquisitive, uncritical, hedonistic, chauvinistic, selfish and mean. This is very different from the Asian ideal of a chief executive officer who also contributes to classical philosophy, poetry or painting (2002:151).

If the quest for authenticity will frustrate all the efforts of modern humans to solve its riddle, we now know why—it is the new tack started in the West around 150 years ago that deserves the blame. Let it be noted in passing that MacCannell's chronology is comfortably adaptable. As this latter text dates from 2002, we should go back to the middle of the 19th century to follow the trail. Here, malformed Egos start with the Industrial Revolution; there, however, as in the relations between pornography and the origins of language, they hark back to 30,000 years ago or, as in the division of labor, to the Neolithic Revolution; over there, as when relating human thought and symbolism, they may recede to the origins of *homo sapiens*. At any rate, the corporations that have become so central to the development of present-day capitalist economy did not exist 150 years ago. They cannot be directly responsible for the outcome that MacCannell regrets so much. But, in fact, it is not corporations or corporate identities that haunt him. He just detests any Western modernity and finds handy anything that he may try to throw at it, including the portrait of—possibly—Mao Zedong (the Asian CEO above) that even the Great Helmsman's courtiers might find too flattering.

Now the argument comes to a close. Criticism in theory needs revolution, that is, a total change of the ways that priorities are established, and egos constructed. This is the story that the tourist, or modern-man-in-general, tells to anybody who wants to listen attentively and patiently, and MacCannell will not rest until theory and revolution will rest in peace with each other. One can only wish him good luck in this improbable and unworldly mission, only shared by a handful of die-hard *Soixante-Huitards*.

Chapter 5

Liberation Theologies

LIFE'S SURPRISING RECESSES

A powerful current in modern anthropological and sociological research in general and in tourism research in particular nurtures the assumption that their subjects can be studied separately from their economic situations. Indeed, both in the functionalist and in the phenomenological traditions, references to the economy and its importance are typically omitted. In such a manner, modern sociological thought lives the illusion that the ways in which social groups produce their life can be explained satisfactorily by thought processes or the culture people share. As culture is an encompassing word, modern social science does not bother very much about defining its contents. This break with classical economics (Adam Smith, David Hume, David Ricardo, John Stuart Mill) was part of a sequel to the Romantic Movement. Since then, economics has abandoned any aspirations to become a political economy while sociology and anthropology have focused on issues such as power, mentalities, the general grammar of thought, semiotics, and any other subject that supposedly would keep the political economy at bay. This is the kernel of the scissors crisis that plagues modern social science including tourism research (Chapter 1).

However, societies, among them modernity, which is nothing else than the latest successful deployment of human intercourse, do not suffer meekly as they are torn to pieces. In one way or another, they constitute a totality that, even when legitimately analyzed from different viewpoints (the disciplines), in the end imposes their claim to holistic treatment even when researchers imagine that they can dispense with it. We have already seen that underneath MacCannell's predicated quest for authenticity that guides modern people in tourism and elsewhere, there lurks a demand for a radical change in the way modernity produces and reproduces itself. As long as money prevails as the principal social nexus, as long as people relate through the exchange of commodities, authenticity will remain a chimera. Humans will not be able to exert their freedom and give the best of themselves to others unless they replace trade and commercialism with a more complete relational model. This change he calls "revolution" and mightily so it would be if ever attained. To reach its best, humankind needs to steer clear of capitalism. Not only of capitalism. With the whirlwind should also go industry and agriculture, no less. In the end, they are but by-products of the division of labor, which is the root cause of all evil. Given his enthusiasm for the undefined savage mind, one can conclude that MacCannell proposes to replace the Industrial and Neolithic revolutions with Stone Age redux. However, MacCannell's is but one of the two main paradigms to explain modernity in tourism. Sometimes in apparent overlap, sometimes in open conflict with him, there is a second body of theories that we have to turn to now. It has many complex roots that we will follow, but its direct lineage in tourism research begins with the work of Victor Turner.

Turner is not so often quoted as MacCannell. After all, his relation with tourism was at best peripheral. However, sometimes unbeknown to those who adopted his paradigm, he inspired a good deal of what here we will call *liberation theologies*. The critical accent starts in the second part of the expression. This group of theories shares with theological wisdom that their object is ultimately beyond the ken of human minds; they can therefore be interpreted in many, even contradictory, ways; they offer illusory solutions to many of the most intractable problems confronting the human mind; and, because of all of the above, they cannot ever be proved wrong. Nor right. Theology is a matter of belief—not of rational discussion. Lay theologies of liberation are one of the many offshoots of magical thinking still extant.

This strand of thought reaches the opposite boundaries to MacCannell's when trying to elucidate the relation between that odd couple formed by modernity and tourism. For MacCannell, modernity meant the death of the true self, its reduction to an insatiable consumer unable to create dependable links with his fellow humans. Modernity thrives on the death of freedom and creativity. For the motley tribe of Turner-inspired researchers, the outcome is quite the opposite. Modernity and tourism create windows of opportunity for individual freedom and liberation, or at least for social integration. There is no need to cast them into the dustbin of history—only to learn how to use them reasonably. Let us recap Turner's main ideas that for so many provide a better understanding of human life's surprising recesses than MacCannell's devotion to authenticity.

In 1909, Arnold Van Gennep published his well-known work on the rites of passage (1961). With it he aimed at understanding better the structure of some special occasions in the life of the individuals that belong to any given social group. Life is nothing other than a series of transitions like birth, puberty, marriage, fatherhood, diverse occupational activities, and, finally, death. When reaching one of these stages, people go through a number of rites that mark their accession into the new level. In this way, human life resembles nature, as the universe is also governed by cycles and repetitions, stages and transitions, periods of quick activity and of relative calm. Natural cycles often leave their marks on social life as when social groups celebrate moon festivals or the incoming New Year, thus creating some kind of continuity between nature and society.

Such gradation of stages can be found in most societies. However, their importance increases as we go down the scale of what Van Gennep calls the development of civilization. This is probably due to the predominance of the religious aspects of life over secularization. In the simplest communities, every change involves actions and reactions between the sacred and the profane, as no act can break free from the sacred. Each accession to a new stage goes hand in hand with a number of ceremonies that help societies locate individuals in a number of defined positions or roles. These ceremonies have a similar structure, although not all coincide in their goals.

In substance, one can say that there are three main categories of rites of passage—of separation, transition, and incorporation. The former mark the exit of an individual or a group of individuals from their previous subcategories in social life, for example funerals, while marriages typify incorporation into a new category. Transition rites flag the passage from a given status, for instance childhood, to another, for example puberty or old age. In different societies all these rites gain different importance or elaboration. Van Gennep also classifies the different rites along arbitrary lines that look totally obsolete to modern minds (such as dynamic/animist, sympathetic/contagious, or positive/negative). The rest of his work offers numerous examples taken from the anthropological literature of his time for territorial passages, pregnancy and childbirth, initiation, funerals, and so forth. It is not this later refinement, though, that has attracted the attention of other anthropologists to his work.

What attracted people like Victor Turner and his followers was Van Gennep's initial simplification of complex rituals into definite types and stages that unify the diversity of experiences and make them easier to grasp. At the beginning of his classification, Van Gennep states that a complete catalog of rites of passage theoretically includes preliminal rites (rites of separation), liminal rites (rites of transition), and postliminal rites (rites of incorporation). This remark is made in passing and not elaborated throughout the rest of Van Gennep's book. He prefers to stick to his tripartite division of separation, transition, and incorporation rites, and only in the concluding chapter does he mention, equally in passing, "the existence of transitional periods which sometimes acquire a certain autonomy" (1961:191). It is the latter, however, that caused such a stir in the liberationist school.

So let us start where its main representative met it. Turner's initial anthropological fieldwork focused on the Ndembu, an ethnic group living in an area of Africa that straddles modern Zambia and the Katanga region in today's Democratic Republic of Congo.

> [F]rom the very beginning of my stay among the Ndembu I had, on invitation, attended the frequent performances of the girls' puberty rites (*Nkang'a*) and had tried to describe what I had seen as accurately as possible. But it is one thing to observe people performing the stylized gestures and singing the cryptic songs of ritual performances and quite another to reach an adequate understanding of what the movements and words meant to *them* (Turner 1969:7).

If we lay bare the meaning different passage ceremonies have for their practitioners and, additionally, we come to the conclusion that they represent some permanent features that are present in all societies, perhaps we will better understand the way societies coalesce or change. Another way of describing the *emic* position.

In *The Ritual Process* (1969), if not his major work (see 1973, 1974, 1978, 1982) but at least the best structured, Turner, after having narrated some key rituals of the Ndembu turns to Van Gennep and recaps his main findings.

> Van Gennep has shown that all rites of passage or "transition" are marked by three phases: separation, margin (or *limen*, signifying threshold in Latin), and aggregation. [...] During the intervening "liminal" period, the characteristics of the ritual subject (the "passenger") are ambiguous; he passes through a cultural realm that has fewer or none of the attributes of the past or coming state (Turner 1969:94–95).

After the phase of reaggregation or reincorporation, the passage is complete.

However, this is not exactly a true rendition of Van Gennep's thought. What interests him, as we have pointed out, is the description of passages or transitions of different sorts, yes, but above all because they help in leaving behind and reaching to what Turner calls solid states, that is, stages 1 and 3. For Turner, though, rites of passage are defined both from the fixed elements that wait at their beginning and at their end *and,* above all, by the flexible and open-ended stage in between. What in Van Gennep seemed nothing else than the label for a fleeting moment, viz. liminality, becomes for Turner the gist of the whole process. Liminality is *the other* or, as he calls it, the antistructure to the rigidities of everyday life.

> The attributes of liminality or of liminal *personae* ("threshold people") are necessarily ambiguous, since this condition and these persons elude or slip through the network of classifica-tions that normally locate states and positions in cultural space. Liminal entities are neither here nor there; they are betwixt and between the position assigned and arrayed by law, custom, convention and ceremonial (1969:95).

They are a blank slate ready to be inscribed with many variant etchings. Liminality is potential, movement, freedom. And it is this state of dispossession that, in its turn, makes the neophytes develop an intense comradeship among themselves. As Schiller said in his *Ode to Joy,*

> joy [or freedom or liminality] is the magic power that fuses all that custom has divided, the space where all men [*sic*] become brothers [*sic*].

Here shines the special power of liminality. It is at the same time a moment of deprivation and riches, of lowliness and sacredness, whose subjects taste a special bond that ignores the limits of status or roles and makes them one. Fusion of the many into one accompanies it without exception. In this way every group, or community, or society is made of both separation and union, of diverse states, and of the unifying experience that Turner calls *communitas.* Here, in *communitas,* shines the generic link that makes us all human in an indistinct way. It is the moment of liberation from everydayness where freedom begets the deep encounter we call love. It is also the moment of equality. Before being installed as such, the Ndembu supreme ruler has to undergo a number of rites of humiliation. He wears rough clothes; he lives for a while in a modest hut away from the village; he has to accept his future subjects' churlish addresses (talking truth to power); he has to perform a number of menial tasks that he will not perform again once installed as ruler. Indeed, once this rite comes to an end, he assumes his new role with all due pomp and circumstance. In other rites, the neophytes or novices have to adopt the same submissive position until they pass the threshold where they are no longer the image of deprivation but subjects of rights. This moment of submissiveness "implies that the high could not be high unless the low existed, and he who is high must experience what is like to be low" (1969:97).

Communitas shows our shared unity ridding us of alienation, and from the initial and final states that separate humans. It dignifies our true human essence. Morale follows. Social life cannot be seen as an either/or process of separation; on the contrary, it expresses the dialectic of the sacred and the profane, of homogeneity and differentiation, of *communitas* and status, of equality and inequality. Any passage from a rigid state to another needs statuslessness, and reconciles the opposites. "Each individual's life experience contains alternating exposure to structure and *communitas*, to states and transitions" (1969:97). To escape from the Parmenidean trap of perennial stability, one should realize that change constitutes the real stuff of life. This is what Hegelians and, later, Marxists used to call dialectics. Today, a current of thought prefers to talk of *mobilities* (Urry 2000).

Turner waxes long and lyrical on the differences between those phases of social life.

> A mystical character is assigned to the sentiment of human kindness in most types of liminality, and in most cultures this stage of transition is brought closely in touch with beliefs in the protective and punitive powers of divine or preterhuman beings or powers (1969:105).

In this way, liminality reconciles the diversity and oppositions of social life in all its aspects. It is the moment of fusion for beings that are nothing else than human, that is, equals. Why does liminality usually adopt in most groups a sacred aura while it gets perceived as something dangerous or disturbing? The answer does not seem too complicated. *Communitas* reveals the strength of the weak; it is the antistructure that gives away the fragility or the impermanence of seemingly powerful structures. Look at the powers of the court jesters, the holy beggars, the simpletons. They represent the limits of the powers that be and exemplify *communitas*. In Turner's book, these antistructural elements are shown in many examples throughout history. One powerful specimen comprises the millenarian movements that usually deny difference, inequalities, ownership, societal boundaries of sexual love, while requesting the opposite virtues from their followers: no rank, general humility, unselfishness, total obedience to a leader, free love. "*Communita*s, or the 'open society', differs in this from structure, or the 'closed society', in that it is potentially or ideally extensible to the limits of humanity" (1969:112). Going with the powerful flow of the 1970s, the time when he was carrying out his initial research, Turner found a handy example of *communitas* in the hippie movement. "They stress relationships rather than social obligations, and regard sexuality as a polymorphic instrument of immediate *communitas* rather than as the basis for an enduring structured social tie" (1969:112–113).

Turner's basic mechanism does not have many more elements. The rest of his central book simply provides a number of variations on this theme. But there is a twist. Little by little he veers toward a notion of *communitas* that breaks with his initial point of view. From his studies of different African ethnic communities, Turner not only underlines that they all have similar rites of passage; he goes one step further. More than just his objects of study, all people in liminal situations have the same features in common: they either fall in the interstices of social structure or are on its margins, or occupy its lowest rungs. In this way, when we first found *communitas*, it played the role of obliterating the minor features of roles or status to show the common humanity of all members of a society at least at some given times. Even the powerful had to be humiliated to prove their commonality with the rest as happened to the Ndembu rulers.

Now this condition has withered away. Real *communitas* is a call to liberation by the weak, the infirm, and the downtrodden. It may include other members of a society, but they have to have made a definite choice. Here he quotes Martin Buber. Community, more than an instrument of shared humanity that anybody can experience, becomes an unstructured spiritual meeting place for those who decide to leave behind the rigors of structure with its *us* vs. *them* categories to enjoy the encounter of the *I* and the *thou*.

> *Communitas*, with its unstructured character, representing the "quick" of human interrelatedness, what Buber has called *Zwischenmenschliche* [the interpersonal], might well be represented by the "emptiness at the center," which is nevertheless indispensable to the functioning of the structure (Turner 1969:127).

And so that we make no mistakes Turner reminds us that *communitas* is not just a biological drive but the product of human faculties such as rationality, volition, and memory. At the same time as it bets in favor of some human qualities ingrained in all of us, *communitas* is to some extent an option, and therefore it becomes an occasion for liberation.

Turner is no radical, though. After having opened this passage he refrains from treading further. In the end, structure and *communitas* need each other so that societies can grow in a harmonious way. Exaggerated structure may lead to instability, upheavals, and even revolutions from the subdued communities; on the other hand, exaggerated *communitas* may lead to despotism, hyperbureaucracies, or structural rigidification.

> Thus, most millenarian movements try to abolish property or to hold all things in common. Usually this is possible only for a short time—until the date set for the coming of the millennium or the ancestral cargoes. When prophecy fails, property and structure return and the movement becomes institutionalized, or the movement disintegrates and its members merge into the environing social order (1969:129).

From rites of passage as defined moments of social experience, we have reached a theory of social change. Societies and communities move in a binary cycle of structure and antistructure. At any given moment in time, they appear as distinctive entities made of different aggregates of role and status. However, if we follow them over time, we will realize that their stability is only short lived. Suddenly they experiment inner imbalances that push them in a different direction. The antistructure forces start operating. Once a number of changes (that may have a varied range, from small and partial to all-encompassing) occur, or are made to happen by conscious action, a new structure develops. The forces of stability are trumped by those of change; but structure comes back against *communitas* that, after a while, will become once again solidified into a new structure. And so on, in cycles, forever after. *Perpetuum mobile.* A mobility, though, that seems quite capricious. Turner sees that there are deep changes or antistructures at work, but he adopts a passive stance as to the movement. Why do millenarian movements repeatedly show their incapacity to abolish property or to impose free sexual access among their members? Why do they periodically repeat their ritual dance as a moth attracted by a candle? Can people never learn from former mistakes? In fact, Turner has no real explanation for social change.

Although the opposition here is binary (structure/antistructure), the mechanism has a definite whiff of the Weberian continuum tradition/ charisma/bureaucracy or, in more general terms, of status quo/charisma/ routinization. The mediation of what Weber called charisma and Turner calls *communitas* or liminality contrives a mere description of events in the shape of an explanation. Weber never clarified the mysterious charisma. For him, it is but any feature held as extraordinary or a personality considered endowed with supernatural or superhuman or, at least, extra-quotidian forces (Weber 1971). The charismatic says, "You have been told to do X or Y, but I tell you to do Q and R." What really counts is not the essence of the command but the fact that it is considered as extraordinary by his followers or devotees. Why do they oblige? Why do they choose this aspiring charismatic leader and not another? Turnerian *communitas* remains equally undefined. We know that it will flourish wherever (mostly destitute) people meet each other devoid of any other feature than their common humanity as when *I* intersects with *thou*, but do not expect any other refinements. The wind of antistructure blows wherever it wants, whenever it finds convenient. Can we anticipate its movement? Unfortunately, we will know only *ex post facto*.

Initially *communitas* represents a shapeless inspirational moment that allows its participants to look at each other without structural filters and to grasp each other's essential Other, in the same way as Hans Castorp understood in the Berghoff, when his gaze crossed Clavdia Chauchat's for the first time (Mann 1996), that her social *Sie* (marking social distance) had vanished before a closer and more real *Du* (symbolic closeness). Turner calls this experience *existential* or *spontaneous communitas*, and as we have mentioned, this becomes the first stage of social change. However, it is in the nature of this flash that overpowers the performers like a bolt from heaven to be short lived. If it wants to go beyond the interpersonal to become an agent of change, it needs to adopt a less transitive, more stable form. Durable *communitas* needs the encroachment of a timely and normative dimension to grab its participants in an enduring movement and become real antistructure. Therefore, the second aspect of *communitas— normative* structure

> where under the influence of time, the need to mobilize and organize resources and the necessity for social control among the members of the group in the pursuance of these goals, the existential community is organized into an enduring social system (1969:132).

All real antistructure has to somehow imitate the structure it is trying to replace and is tempted by the same forces that keep structures being. As noted previously, this is what Weber used to call routinization. To become a church, the apostolic group around Jesus and the bourgeoning Christian communities (existential *communitas*) had to wait for Paul's organizational and marketing skills that transformed it into a normative *communitas*. Any successful transformational movement reproduces in itself the ways of social structures. Turner also speaks of a third type of *communitas* that he calls "ideological," but this addition only has the ancillary mission of being a label applied to different types of utopian models of society based in existential *communitas*.

The history of the Franciscan order exemplifies the dynamic. Francis of Assisi and the initial circle of his followers represented the fusional or liminal stage. They exalted poverty, that is, the absence of submission to material things in order to concentrate on the real nature of the human soul—the yearning for communion with nature and God. However, as the new order grew in numbers and in influence, it started developing a technical apparatus of vows and superiors and a political structure that attracted money and power. Francis might say that friars should not pay more attention to coins or money than to the dust they trod under their feet, but in fact, monasteries based on hard work and low consumption were bound to accumulate capital, even before counting the donations and bequests of the faithful. So after a while the order would split between the Spirituals, loyal to what they saw as the will to poverty of their founder, and the Conventuals, more open to compromise with their newly acquired riches. Both claimed Francis on their side, as he understood that friars were entitled to the use material goods in order to survive. For the Spirituals, though, use meant consuming a bare minimum; the Conventuals defined it in an easier way. Some Spirituals died because of their strenuous asceticism. Others accused the Conventuals of living in continuous mortal sin. Conflict was bound to appear and it did burst open after a while.

Many other examples of the same dynamic can be produced. Turner refers to the Krishnaic Sahayiha cults that flourished in Bengal in the 16th–17th century. They had as their central act sexual intercourse between male and female followers that simulated the lovemaking of Krishna and Radha. After an initial period where the cult adherents developed their spontaneity and reveled in fusion practices, there again intruded the need for some normative constraints that would avoid social sanctions, and the movement soon split between opposing factions that developed their own structure and imposed different norms on their followers.

Both histories partake of the perennial dilemma between what Weber called the ethics of following one's own convictions or *Gesinninungsethik* and the need to rationally respond to environmental pressures or *Verantwortungsethik* (Weber 1973). For Turner the morale shines glaringly. Franciscans and Sahayihas seemed to be acting on very different levels. "The Franciscans denied themselves property, one pillar of social structure; the Sahayihas marriage and the family, another major pillar" (1969:164). However, both followed a similar path from antistructure and existential *communitas* to a normative stage of acceptance of the world. "Structureless *communitas* can bind and bond people together only momentarily" (1969:153). Enduring social change stands to laws and institutions as the teeth stand to the lips, one dares say in a display of sub-Confucian wisdom. Even more, there appears some cunning of the reason—liminality engenders *communitas* in order to develop a higher level of structuring.

Turner insists. The fusion of *I* and *thou* into an essential *we* has to be liminal, that is, marginal, as permanence over time implies institutionaliza- tion and repetition. In this way, any antistructure is bound to recover some of the traits of the structures it proposes to overthrow. Unlike MacCannell, Turner has no illusions about the possibility of recovering the pristine kind of sociability that allegedly characterized the Golden Age. Any emerging future wants for normative arrangements. "Spontaneous *communitas* is a phase, a moment, not a permanent condition" (1969:140). After that, norms and laws follow and Turner does not see them as noxious apostasy, rather as "the very cultural means that preserve the dignity and liberty, as well as the bodily existence, of every man, woman, and child" (1969:140). Anarchy, in the future or in an idealized past, does not show to true Turnerians the road to human dignity and freedom. Turner believed in the civilizatory powers of the social contract more than in the redeeming virtues of the state of nature.

Turner's maiden trip was long and meandering. His initial demarche followed from a great ambition—revealing the basic rules of social change or history. Social dynamics followed the fault lines present at given times and in most societies between stability and change. Taking his cue from Van Gennep's research on rites of passage, Turner saw the mechanism of social change in a continuum that starts at an initial stage of stability, and is followed by another of uncertainty or freedom that he called liminality, reaching a new balance of forces in the arrival stage. Not all three phases are equally weighty, though. Liminality is the ghost in the machine, being the only instance when change can assert itself. It provides an antistructure to the rigidities of social life and fuels the inner fire that wipes out resistance to change. It creates a deep community among its members—a torrent of spontaneous *communitas* among equals. This *communitas* usually encompasses the powerless, the downtrodden, and those from other social strata that choose to cast their lot with theirs. However, permanent liminality and community cannot endure forever. The existential *communitas* of brothers, sisters, and sundry believers soon morphs into a normative one that in turn begets a new structure, later challenged by a new communal liminality from which stems a new structure, another liminality, and another turn of the structural screw. On, and on, and on.

This theoretical contraption aimed at explaining social change and, beyond, the basic structures of human history. It did so at the great price of homogenizing it into a two-step dance where one could rejoice in perennial rejuvenation through liminality. All this sounds a bit confusing. What is after all this mysterious liminality? As it is not a state but a phase, not rest but movement, as it has begun but knows no end yet, as it is neither here nor there, but betwixt and between, Turner does not bother any more. It thrives wherever a space for change, for freedom appears. As such, it has no history itself; therefore, it can be found at will, in any of life's surprising recesses. At any rate, social processes vacate the scene, while the initially imposing sociology of change becomes a liberation theology that, like all theologies, ranks revealed belief over rationality.

Turner, though, seems aware that his explanation lacks strength, that it looks like a mechanism to acknowledge change without explaining it. Perhaps because of this, at last he introduces a refinement. There is a difference between the liminality we find in rites of status deviation and of status reversal. In the former the novice jumps once and for good from a lower to a higher position in the institutionalized order. They are defining moments with no return. The second type of liminality appears more often in cyclical and calendar patterns, in rituals held at given junctures of the seasonal cycle. Some people or groups of low status are allowed, even encouraged, to exercise ritual authority over the powerful. Such rituals are often accompanied by harsh behavior, verbal and nonverbal, addressed to superiors who leniently accept being reviled. "The stronger are made weaker; the weak act as though they were strong" (1969:168). However, it does not escape Turner's mind that these reversal rituals are but a fantasy of structural superiority.

Turner dispenses a less enthusiastic welcome to rituals of reversal than many of his followers. The rituals and their subsequent license soon go away, while the existent structures remain intact over time.

[T]he masking of the weak in aggressive strength and the concomitant masking of the strong in humility and passivity are devices that cleanse society of its structurally engendered "sins" [...] The stage is then set for an ecstatic experience of *communitas*, followed by a sober return to a now purged and reanimated structure (1969:188).

Rites of reversal just furnish a flickering game and no real change (Caro Baroja 1979a, 1979b).

[T]he liminality of status reversal might provide an opportunity to escape from the *communitas* of necessity (which is therefore inauthentic) into a pseudo-structure where all behavioral extravagances are possible. Yet [...] [w]hat is left is a kind of social average, or something like the neutral position in a gear box, from which it is possible to proceed in different directions and at different speeds in a new bout of movement (1969:202).

But this is not totally satisfactory either. Rites of deviation and of reversal have existed throughout history. Some of them turned into communal movements and engendered new structures. Why were they successful while others were not? Are there not any features that will allow us to understand the process in a more specific way? This is where Turner comes up with a distinction between what he calls the liminal and the liminoid. The liminal characterizes cyclical, repetitive societies that ignore innovative ideas and technological change. These two last features only belong properly into modernity. Modernity has established a clear division between work and play that pervades the most remote areas of social life. The first is the realm of necessity, the second the province of freedom.

The historical watershed between these two ways of experiencing *communitas* or the moment of antistructure appeared with the Industrial Revolution. Turner here gives the impression of correcting or adjusting his previous views.

Failure to distinguish between symbolic systems and genres belonging to cultures that have developed before and after the Industrial Revolution can lead to much confusion both in its theoretical treatment and in operational methodology (1982:30).

Such a stern warning reminds his reader that there is a basic chasm between the inner relations that work, play, and leisure adopt in each one of these two societal forms. Turner has thus quit his initial view of change as an endless retelling of the same story to adopt a more developmental or spiral picture.

For all their differences, preindustrial societies saw work as the work of the gods, that is, the ways in which humans partake of a cosmic order preordained by extra-human instances. No matter the details of each one, what counts is the adjustment between man's and God's work, so that the sacred–profane relation becomes the defining symbolic structure. Rituals braid both regions in harmonious or polemic ways. A badly performed ritual may be the occasion for a show of divine displeasure in the form of a poor harvest, a drought, or any other misfortune, while productive success confirms that humans are doing God's work. There is an additional trait— work includes the whole community. All its members are bound in it; they cannot elect to stay out of the work/ritual.

Industrial societies, on the other hand, act on a different logic; their two main poles are work and play. Turner recalls the many ludic aspects of work in traditional societies, but immediately qualifies them. What we can see as play actually means seriousness. The Ndembu of Turner's initial fieldwork put a lot of apparent licentiousness and aggressive sexuality in their rituals to control twin birth. Giving birth to twins was an oddity that endangered the divine order; therefore, it needed to be exorcized. Too many twins might create economic imbalances in a society with few resources; they also confused the seniority rule—who of the two should have precedence? No matter how much humor and inventiveness went into the ritual, the Ndembu reminded themselves through it of the seriousness of the occasion.

> Joking is fun, but it is also a social sanction. Even joking must observe the "golden mean," which is an ethical feature of "cyclical, repetitive societies," not as yet unbalanced by innovative ideas and technological changes (1982:32).

This is worlds apart from the flow of modern societies where the liminal aspects of rites become liminoid regulatory opposites. In the industrial or capitalist order, the main dividing line does not run between divine and human work; it demarcates work as labor from play as leisure.

So what is play? While work delineates the field of instrumental action that links means to goals with a formally rational bond, play points to an opposite ideal type of action divorced from this kind of rationality. Play is a subjective activity where its components need not follow formal rationality or calculus. If the latter harks back to the economic notion of benefit or the psychological drive to self-interest, play ignores them (Dumazedier 1962; Dumazedier and Rippert 1966). In this way, the distinction between work and play is a thoroughly modern notion. There was nothing like a leisure class (Veblen 2001) in premodern societies.

This seems to run counter to historical evidence (Aranguren 1961, 1976; De Grazia 1964), but on Dumazedier's wake, Turner sticks to the notion, and his is not an idle whim. Leisure means freedom in both the senses highlighted by Isaiah Berlin. It is freedom *from* the rhythms of factory and office, and it is freedom *to* generate new symbolic worlds and to play with all types of entertainment. This dispensation could not exist before capitalism for only here can Durkheim's organic solidarity, that is, a pushed division of labor, flourish.

Modern society offers much more space to discussion, critique, and even radicalism than traditional societies ever might think of.

> The liminal phases of *tribal* societies invert but do not usually subvert the *status quo*, the structural form, of society; reversal underlines to the members of a community that chaos is the alternative to cosmos, so they had better stay with cosmos, i.e., the traditional order of culture, though they can for a brief while have a wonderful time being chaotic (1982:41; emphasis in original).

Modernity not only recognizes diversity or freedom—it bestows on it a permanent and holier aura. While the liminal is but a fleeting illusion, the liminoid is here to stay. Whereas traditional liminality appears like a flicker that quickly runs to its end, freedom is part and parcel of the modern dispensation. Driving another nail in the MacCannellian coffin, Turner concluded that the seeds of cultural transformation, discontent, and social criticism implicit in traditional liminality have turned into permanent and institutionalized features of modernity. These liminoid qualities not only function at the societal level—they give a much wider berth to individual creativity than traditional societies could ever grant. Liminoidness pushed its roots in Western Europe with the Industrial Revolution. It matured later in the contractual environment that gave us the democratic-liberal societies of Europe and America in the 20th century. At any rate, Turner concluded, for most people the liminoid is still felt to be freer than the liminal, a matter of choice not of obligation. The *liminoid* is more like a commodity—indeed often *is* a commodity, which one selects and pays for—than the *liminal*, which elicits loyalty and is bound up with one's membership or desired membership in some highly corporate group (1982:55; Turner's italics).

We have reached a territory that cannot be further away from MacCannell's position.

Turner was well aware when he wrote these reflections that he was treading a new path, but death caught up with him before he could progress much in his scouting. He did not contemplate tourism and travel in detail, but he devised new ways of understanding their relation with the travails of modernity. When it comes to the latter, he seems to have reached the right conclusions. However, one cannot be so sure that he reached them for the right reasons. Even at the end of his work he remained under the spell that work and play obey contradictory logics and that only the second can be seen as properly human. In this way, he opened a door into the same chasm between ordinary and extraordinary life that has plagued Western sociology for a long time and that we can trace to the work of Max Weber.

THE WEBERIAN PREDICAMENT

Even though he is not explicitly quoted, one cannot fail to hear Weberian echos in Turner's division of work and play. Work is but the enactment of formal rationality, the adequacy of means to ends with a view to economic benefit. On the other hand, even though he does not clearly define play, Turner surmises that it breaks free from such constraints. To understand the implications of the argument, one has to go to its source, which is none other than the revered hypothesis of the Protestant roots of capitalism as developed by Max Weber. Not only does it purport to offer the best possible explanation for the advent of capitalism, it is also an epitome for the view that culture is the fundamental engine of history and change.

The thesis has become part of conventional wisdom and has been reverently approached since it reached the canonical stage. In essence, it states that Calvinist theology justified the pursuit of economic success through instrumental or formal logic. Later on, this type of instrumental rationality would shed its theological skin, with bare rational calculus becoming the decisive end of mature capitalism. Weber's insistence on the *ideal* (his word; today we might use *cultural* instead) dimensions of the Big Bang that created the modern world implied a radical bet against what was in his time called the materialist view of history. The Protestant thesis was a combat thesis that, under the antimaterialist label, argued not only against Marxism but also against all explanations that would stress economics as the prime mover of human action.

This was not, though, Weber's initial approach. Earlier on in his career, before his bout of nervous depression in 1898–1904, Weber walked a path closer to the later discarded materialist views. Not that he was a positivist through and through even at that time, but he was looking for a middle ground between the views on Roman history held by the two great German masters of the subject, Karl Bücher and Edouard Meyer, who epitomized economicist and cultural historiography. In an 1896 lecture before the *Akademische Gesellschaft* (Academic Society) in Freiburg, Weber gave his views on the causes of Roman decline. On one side, he maintained Meyer's well-known historicist thesis that historical periods are complex units not easily amenable to comparison. Each has to be understood through its own values or, with more modern jargon, with an *emic* approach. However, on the other side, Weber leaned toward Bücher. Roman decadence had to be understood through the evolution of the empire's key social institutions, especially the exhaustion of slavery as the engine of the economy.

The end of the unique historical cycle that we call Classical Antiquity is marked by the incapacity of slavery to deliver its old economic benefits in a thoroughly changed environment. Throughout the Classic period, slavery had supplied a cheap workforce to the big agrarian estates of the time, thwarting the eventual development of urban trade as an economic alternative. Over time, though, the stabilization of the imperial borders induced a supply bottleneck. Slaves were mostly prisoners of war, so the labor market suffered when wars came to a relative standstill. Slaves were no longer as cheap to come by as in previous centuries, and as a result making agriculture profitable became increasingly difficult. Even when slaves were converted into freeholders, thus passing on to them the costs of their own maintenance and reproduction, the situation did not improve. As soon as many estates were divided into smaller units, it was impossible to produce for urban markets and the faint web of trade possible in olden times was torn and soon disappeared. Previously thriving urban life faded and the army became a mercenary force mostly interested in police work and political intrigue.

Weber recaps:

> the Roman Empire's breakdown was the inevitable outcome
> of a basic economic fact: the withering away of trade and the
> expansion of a barter economy. In essence: this disintegration
> simply caused the collapse of the administrative monetary
> system and of the political superstructure of the Empire as
> they could not adapt to the infrastructure of the natural
> economy (1973:235).

Weber's explanation of this historical process does not carry any Marxist baggage. In fact, Weber's account remains quite close to the classical strand in political economy (Gibbon 1909; Smith 2002, 2007). While Marx insisted on class struggle as the prime mover of social change, classic economics stressed that societies usually change by choosing, even unwittingly, between the economic options that lie ahead of them. That they will make the right choice is a by no means assured.

By 1904, the date when he published his two essays on the Protestant Ethic in the *Archiv für Sozialwissenschaft und Sozialpolitik* (Archive for Social Science and Sociopolitics), whose editorial board he had joined recently, Weber adopted quite a different position. Gone for the rest of his life was his flirtation with economic explanations. For the next 16 years he would try to understand why only Puritanism had succeeded in opening the door to that formal rationality that had resisted attacks by other religions the world over (Hinduism, Buddhism, and Confucianism).

The explanation, as is well known, has to do with some abstruse theological notions about freedom, grace, and predestination. Roman Catholics and Lutherans thought salvation might respectively accrue from good actions and strong faith on their part, but to Calvin's God this was an unacceptable challenge to his omnipotence. Only He, out of unfathomable wisdom, could bestow or withdraw the gift of His grace. He had decided from all eternity who would be saved and who would be damned.

How did Calvinists cope with this harsh fate? One would imagine them mired in despair. Why waste time and effort in living a decent life when this would not in the least improve their chances of salvation? Why respect such a callous lord? No theology can be that coldhearted, and Puritans looked for a crack in the door. Darkness about their role in their God's plan might be the natural environment of the pilgrims, but they should not stop at it. The believer should discount it and behave as though it did not exist. Good deeds may be useless for salvation, but they help to exorcize anguish. Though no creature will know its destiny until meeting its creator, worldly success can provide a glimmer of light. The stricter their lives are, and the closer they are to their faith's ethics, the more the opportunities Calvinists will have to guess God's favor. Success in following one's own calling reconciles predestination with the Puritan's need for intraworldly morals.

This is what gives mettle to the true Puritan—his willingness to collaborate with the economy of salvation in an orderly, systematic way. It is not so much actions that count but how they are accomplished. Order, regularity, system should substitute for goodness. Compliance with the law, respect for contracts, fair trade, and right behavior thus became the supreme norm of an apparently impossible Calvinist morality. Their extended acceptance would seamlessly favor those types of behavior methodically oriented to benefit that are the foundation of capitalism according to Weber. Why did systematic angst turned into morals establish such an important milestone in history? It was but another name for productivity, in the double sense of aversion to excess and devotion for methodic labor. The excesses of the new rich are as much beyond the pale as the knightly fondness for gifts or the precedence of honor. For Weber, Puritan ethics won the day because of its methodic approach to toil and effort, because of its sense of proportion between means and goals, and because of its advocacy of saving.

For the saint, rejection of unproductive behavior should pervade all social relations. There is no objective ranking in labor, as all callings share the same dignity. What counts is pursuing one's own in a cost-effective way, sidetracking both excessive effort and lack of assiduity. In this way, the distinction between pure and impure work that hindered dedication to profitable activities in traditional societies no longer makes sense. Leisure and recreation also deserve a place in the divine economy, but rest or merriment should be proscribed if against orderly behavior. Sexual intercourse, for instance, can be defended only when oriented to reproduction; anything else should beget damnation. Actions do not count; the way they are performed does. In this way, the inner conviction of one's own salvation glides effortlessly into the capitalist mind.

The decisive force in Puritanism flowed from this fixation on order and system. The pilgrims will help destroy the traditional dispensation that did not pay attention to the relations between means and ends. Puritanism believed only in results, so it would pay no respect to the ways of the ancestors when they interfered with rational logic. Take the whole issue of usury. There was an age-old reluctance to accept that money could beget money, and most faiths would consider it a moral transgression.

Not so Puritanism. Lending money at interest lost its sinful lineage and became as respectable a profession as wearing the cassock, running a shop, or tilling the fields. In this way, Puritanism was to bring down all barriers to economic rationality, dooming all previous societal forms that did not accept it. No personal feelings, but if for the sake of productivity old traditions had to die, so be it.

Like most broad-ranging historical explanations, the Protestant thesis has been criticized from many perspectives. Some considered it risky shorthand. It makes all precapitalist societies into a mishmash that lacks clear contours. Indeed, formal rationality did not play the same role in Classical Antiquity or in India or in China than in Victorian England, but its limited presence should not imply that those civilizations were just imperfect forms of the latter. Such a conclusion can be reached only at the price of turning instrumental reason into *the* supreme achievement of mankind, which seems to cozy up suspiciously well with an alleged right to Western supremacy. Well founded as it is (Polanyi 1957, 1968; Tönnies 2001), the objection somehow misses the point. It limits itself to demanding better understanding of historical evolution, while leaving unaddressed why in fact accumulation of capital successfully appeared in Western Europe after the religious wars of the 16th–17th centuries and not at other times or in other regions of the world.

A different critical approach takes for granted that the Protestant Ethic hypothesis is effectively right and has been long in cultural consequences. As seen, Puritanism reduces reason to instrumental reason. If one then identifies instrumental logic with capitalism or modernity itself, one easily concludes that there is no room in their world for whatever cannot be readily submitted to calculus. The Logos of modernity knows no passion, no poetry, no imagination, no Eros—all of them, however, integral to human experience. Modernity thus fights a losing battle for there will always be a Hester Prynne ready to follow her heart over her interests, and even Arthur Dimmesdale, her cowardly lover, may in the end acknowledge that sin was more powerful than the comforts of virtue. But modernity's is a merciless war, and like the Aztec god Huitzilopochtli, instrumental rationality will demand dismembered humans so that the commonweal may thrive.

This line of argument has its radical and moderate versions. Weber himself was quite wary of modernity's charms. Pursuing formal rationality would in the end confine people to an iron cage of bureaucratic uniformity. For Freud, individual goals would always trump the repressive side of civilization but at the high cost of mental pathology. Norbert Elias saw every victory of modern civilization as a loss for the libidinal economy of the self.

Others like Huizinga (1966, 2005) and, as noted above, Victor Turner conceived of a centrifugal force, play, or liminality that might compensate moderns for the hard sacrifices they had to make on the altar of rationality. Whether radical or moderate, however, the dichotomy Logos/Eros seems unable to understand why the process happened at a given historical juncture, and only there.

Weber's insistence on the methodic spirit of modern capitalism does not solve the riddle of accumulation. In fact, modern capitalism broke the Malthusian trap (Clark 2007) that has gripped mankind for centuries. It made possible economic growth that has no paragon in other types of society and, *pace* the theorists of unequal exchange, has extended economic welfare beyond its original cradle. When Weber makes accumulation of capital play second fiddle to the ascetic rationalization of professional life, or when he maintains that the sway of Puritanism derived from the implementation of a rational model of behavior, not from its ability to expand the production of goods and services, he votes for keeping intact the mystery of capitalism; therefore, he falls for the wrong explanation. In the end, economic development is but the upshot of labor and saving, that is, a formal rationalization of the future. Such is the fertilizer that, for Weber, made capitalism blossom.

This is a suspect inference, and it was not necessarily so in the past. Monastic life, in the Christian or Buddhist traditions, stressed asceticism and frugal consumption. However, over time, monasteries started an infernal rotation. Monks produced more than they consumed; abbeys became increasingly rich; the vows of poverty were forsworn; excess became the norm. Convents thrived, but their tide of rising wealth did not lift other boats. Accumulation would not spill over the convent's walls that became oases of opulence in a desert of poverty. Over time, reformers would spring, demanding a return to good old asceticism, new monastic orders would burgeon, and the cycle would begin again. Asceticism did not beget accumulation of capital at the societal level.

Puritanism apparently offered a way out of this seventh circle with its new mode of understanding wealth. Far from being the ultimate evil, to be rich was glorious, as Deng Xiaoping would famously put it a few centuries later. For Puritans, becoming wealthy was a form of accomplishing the divine plan; therefore, they should be proud of their riches. Possibly this conviction brought a measure of psychological serenity to the pilgrims who had for centuries been told that money paved the way to hell. Accumulation, though, has little to do with individual psychology. What really counts is the ghost in the machine that transformed the idle clerical riches into a new type of economy that would offer high rewards for the hoi polloi. Was its mettle just a burst of Puritan asceticism?

Most likely not. At least, so was surmised by others, before and after Weber. There are no serious grounds to defend the view that ascetic savings will provide a shortcut to accumulation. The thesis falls into what Keynes called the paradox of thrift. Saving is beneficial to individuals but detrimental to societies.

> For although the amount of his own saving is unlikely to have any significant influence on his own income, the reactions of the amount of his consumption on the incomes of others makes it impossible for all individuals simultaneously to save any given sums. Every such attempt to save more by reducing consumption will so affect incomes that the attempt necessarily defeats itself (1936:84).

Weber has no real answer to this objection, and his gesture implying that "here it is" cannot be taken as one.

Taken seriously, as Weber undoubtedly did, the Protestant thesis would rather explain stagnation than accumulation of riches. Let us imagine a self-sustaining community that every year produces more than the previous, thus increasing the welfare of its members. Let us imagine that out of a time warp there arrive a number of French Huguenots fleeing from the revocation of the Edict of Nantes and that the dissenters successfully convert the original population to their beliefs. Instrumental rationality and worldly asceticism become the new economic fashion, and the locals increase work, on the one hand, and reduce their consumption on the other. The outcome seems indisputable. The producers will be idle amidst their wares. Consumers will reduce their purchases even more. Order and system will dominate economic life, but at the price of increasing poverty. Asceticism and savings are not good economic bedfellows.

De Mandeville had nearly hit the target in *The Fable of the Bees* (1997). There was a thriving hive well stocked with bees that lived in luxury and ease. It was not perfect, though. All trades and places knew some cheat; no calling was without deceit. Lawyers charged high fees for low effort; physicians preferred fame and money to the patient's health; there were plenty of ignorant men of the cloth; some generals bravely fought the enemy, but others stayed in court or took bribes not to fight; ministers were corrupt; judges let their hands be greased with gold. However, the evil vice of avarice was subject to the nobler one of prodigality, and luxury employed millions of the poor. So vice begat ingenuity, which, together with hard work, made life's pleasures and comforts grow, in such a way that the very poor lived better than the rich had done before.

Unfortunately, the bees ignored that perfection here below is more than the gods can bestow. They ranted about each other's bad habits and denounced their dishonesty and graft in such a pitch that an angered Jove decided to rid the bawling hive of fraud and vice. Then, lawyers and justice became redundant for nobody would cheat; doctors would have no interest in finding new and costlier remedies for their patients, letting them die quickly; repenting officers would now limit themselves to their salaries and they would not increase productivity. The hive thus regained its old moral fiber. Suddenly, disaster ensued. The price of land and property fell; millions were unemployed; those to the new morality gained would not consume; restaurants, bars, fashion shops, and nightspots failed; with no money around, banks would find no customers nor would they lend money to new coming entrepreneurs. An all-too-familiar description of what economic crises bring with them. De Mandeville's morale:

Then leave Complaints: Fools only strive
To make a Great an Honest Hive.
T' enjoy the World's Conveniences,
Be fam'd in War, yet live in Ease,
Without great Vices, is a vain
EUTOPIA seated in the Brain.
Fraud, Luxury and Pride must live
While we the Benefits receive
[...]
Bare Virtue can't make Nations live
In Splendor; they, that would revive
A Golden Age, must be as free,
For Acorns as for Honesty

De Mandeville was still close to the long tradition that viewed luxury as the other face of fraud; therefore, he made no clear distinction between them. However, he was among the first to break with the idea that luxury should be suspect (Berry 1994). Not only did it not support the extension of idleness and effeminacy (a word common in his day to blame weakness of character, which was considered unmanly, therefore noxious)—it was not inimical to employment either.

De Mandeville's views sparked a spirited debate on luxury in the 18th century. Adam Smith and David Hume followed him closely on the economic benefits that follow luxury (the concept of mass consumption, that is, luxury for the masses, had not become widespread in their times), and improved on it. While in De Mandeville it is difficult to discern whether luxury should be confined to the upper classes, Hume adopted a more comprehensive and radical stance. Even the lower orders might benefit from its impulse to economic growth (Shovlin 2008). Smith praised productive investments in education and technology as engines of economic development. Additionally he, together with other authors of the period, also praised consumption that augments the cultural level of society in general, including advances in the arts and refinements in lifestyles. This opens the way to an important formulation—that the difference between necessary consumer goods or wage goods (what we would call necessary or subsistence expenses) and "luxury" goods (in the sense of disposable income) is not cast in stone. Smith and other Enlightenment economists understood that the luxuries of a given era turn into the comforts or necessities of the next (Perrotta 2004).

Along these lines, Werner Sombart raised a double challenge to Weber's argument. He views that instrumental rationality was a Puritan legacy. Systematic savings and asceticism have an old ancestry among other believers. If this is all that capitalism is about, it was born much earlier than the Protestant Reformation. The bourgeois spirit very likely thrived in Judaism (2001), and some scholastic theologians patently advanced it during the Lower Middle Ages (1913). The issue nags Sombart to such an extent that he finds capitalists in the unlikeliest of times and places except where Weber had tracked them. This is the most banal part of his argument. With no other definition of capitalism than the fondness for savings, one can find capitalists even among potlatch addicts.

The second critique stands on firmer ground. Finding more consumers for the goods and services of De Mandeville's bees may dodge market collapse. Consumption, not savings, becomes the engine of capitalist society (1997). To endure, modernity requests increasing consumption, which prompts the next question—what made it possible in Europe at the end of the 18th century? Sombart points first to the sudden changes in the status of Western women (1967). In the Middle Ages and in Classical Antiquity, the natural locus of reproductive sex was to be found in marriage and was subject to its procreative strictures. Beyond this sanctioned boundary, sex had no justification. It amounted to sin, and the righteous must avoid sin. However, since the Renaissance, eroticism and sexual desire found outlets outside of marriage, and often in open contradiction to it. Marriage and love belonged to separate worlds, often rivaling each other. Before, people wed because of reproductive urges reinforced by economic calculus. Good marriage partners should proscribe love and exclusively revel in the joys of friendship. Bringing love as an interloper to marriage somehow desecrated its goals. At the same time, courtesans came to be socially accepted, from the royal courts to the whole of society. Many men lived with their mistresses instead of their wives, and to attract and sustain their fervor, they had to do so at considerable expense. This made the fortunes of an increasing number of providers that, in turn, would create a class of capitalist entrepreneurs.

Why did this increase in expenses beyond the merely necessary not make good the prophecy of the Duke of Saint Simon that the fancy for magnificence in all things could lead only to "general ruin" (1857:143)? Sombart provides an easy answer. Aristocratic displays of luxury provided employment for an increasing number of artisans and ateliers. They created an initial bourgeoisie that would on its turn enjoy the pleasures of consumption. The initial impulse came from people who despised monetary values, and did not understand what savings meant. It is the pursuit of luxury that explains the beginning of capital accumulation.

Quite firm in what his words mean, Sombart defines luxury as "everything that goes beyond the merely necessary" (1987:23), thus placing himself in the camp directly opposite to Weber. Capitalism stems from an ideal-typical behavior that overflows with irrationalism and disorder. In case there was need, Sombart insists on the link between the disorderly drive to luxury and erotic passion—something that Weber, seemingly for private reasons, always refrained from mentioning. Personal luxury springs from the drive to recreation and the enjoyment of the senses that, in its turn, revolves around sexual gratification. Capitalism and modernity, for Sombart, are affiliated with Eros, not with Logos.

Sombart thought to have found the answer to the accumulation riddle, only to lose the right track immediately thereafter. He makes modernity and capitalism repudiate their debts to technology, productivity, competition, comparative advantage, ownership, and wage labor, thus forgiving any reference to their productive efficiency. Sombart sees capitalism as but another turn of the mind—the reptilian brain in his case. However, like savings, luxury thrived in many other cultures than modern Europe. Like savings, though, luxury did not beget capitalism until the long process that Marx called primitive accumulation unwound in a tortuous and painful itinerary that involved millions of people, not just a relatively small number of courtiers and their mistresses.

In 1906 Sombart had asked himself why there was no socialism in the United States. At the time he was a sympathizer of the socialist movement and it was difficult for him to understand why, in opposition to Marx's expectations, socialism was practically nonexistent in the most developed capitalist country.

> If there is anywhere in America where the restless striving after profit, the complete fruition of the commercial drive and the passion for business are indigenous, it is in the worker, who wants to earn as much as his strength will allow, and to be as unrestrained as possible (1976:20).

He said this in a vapid twist that left his question still hanging up in the air.

Why would American workers react in such an unexpected way? In 1908, 2 years after the publication of Sombart's essay, Henry Ford started the production of his Model T. Quite possibly, Ford never read Weber, but Weber might have used him as the poster for his capitalist entrepreneur. Like many of his contemporaries, Ford thought that only work gave purpose to life; he pursued it systematically; he hated tobacco; "the idea of leisure itself or, even worse, a leisure culture was anathema to him" (Halberstam 1986:60); he was frugal and possibly saved a lot; he even once said that alcohol was the real cause of World War One—beer-drinking Germans fighting French wine-drinkers. To the end of his life he had more than a few other loony sallies, though another side of his personality was always quite sober. He will always be remembered for the creation of the assembly line and the conveyor belt. Both innovations, plus Taylor's T&M studies, made it possible for him to lower the price of his cars over time. Fordism is thus usually defined as a highly profitable type of mass production resting on standardization of outputs and minimization of costs, but this is just half the truth of the story. Perhaps because he was not a Calvinist (in fact, he followed the Episcopalian creed), Ford soon understood that the righteous cannot live without sinners or, to use economic lingo, that mass production needs increasing numbers of consumers. Where to find them? In 1914, he doubled the salary of his workers to $5 a day. Soon they became his best customers. Mass consumption thus started the prodigious run that would take it to the furthest regions of the world and would make it reach all economic activities. MMT would be unthinkable without it. Provisionally or for good—the discussion remains open— Sombart's socialism would have to wait for another day.

Now, we can recap. Even though he was probably unaware of its impact, Turner inspired a view of modernity that has influenced tourism research deeply. Ultimately, modern culture allows humans to free themselves from the routine of work-dominated everyday life, and to strengthen the positive drives of leisure and play. Turner thus created an either/or polarization that deprived labor of any meaningful role in the construction of a society worthy of its name. The notion had its roots in the Weberian view of the relation between modernity (Weber usually called it capitalism) and the Protestant Ethic. The former thrived on the intramundane asceticism of the latter. By stressing the need for systematic work and profit-oriented savings (together with some other innovations such as double-entry accounting), the Protestant mentality made capitalism possible. At the same time, it also unleashed a less palatable drive toward routinization and bureaucratic solutions that, in the end, would trap humans into an iron cage.

In tourism research, MacCannell used the latter notion to convey his view that only the abandonment of the profit logic would allow tourists and modern-men-in-general to build a really human environment. Unlike him, Turner and his followers believe, with different degrees of conviction, in the opportunities for liberation provided by all or some aspects of the modern dispensation. But they do so at a price—ignoring the complexity of the markets or, with more solemn lingo, of modernity. Labor is still seen as the biblical damnation that makes of our lives a hard destiny. It is the opposite of leisure or play or extraordinary life. We can enjoy life's hedonistic values only in the absence of work. A fleeting interval or a more stable enjoyment, pleasure must exclude work.

This is not what classical economics had in mind. Productive labor was the initial engine or the necessary way of escape from the Malthusian trap, but it would not have led humans anywhere had it not increased their consumption. Work and consumption can live their separate lives, but they cannot go too far one without the other. That, as we noted, was the basic tenet of Fordism and the key to its success. Without sinners, the righteous would not make any money, their savings only deepening the hole of common poverty; without the righteous and their hard work, sinners would never have the opportunity to consume more. With economic lingo, supply increases demand, which, in its turn, requests more and better supply. To understand accumulation, primitive or mature, one needs to hold both ends of the chain firmly.

It is not easy to follow this capitalist act, for it is counterintuitive. On the one hand, one might think labor and savings should exclude consumption; on the other, consumption might seem to make savings and labor foolish.

However, the history of modernity has shown that, to be successful, the opposites need each other in an ongoing balancing act that can be easily ruined. Too much savings and there may ensue overproduction; too much demand may unleash inflation and financial crisis. Be that as it may, though, modernity, which cannot live without this balancing act, has until now successfully combined these opposite forces and learned how to control them even when faced with serious crises.

Will modernity maintain a successful act forever? This is a thorny issue. It is possible that one day the equilibrium will lose its stability. It is also possible that it will find new ways to rejuvenate itself. For the time being, though, the latter seems more plausible. So let us concentrate on what its endurance may mean for an understanding of MMT.

LIBERATION THEOLOGY. ACT ONE: JAFARI'S LOOP

Turner's is not a paradigm, but a matrix. A paradigm combines a number of hypotheses and theories into a general explanation of an issue or a subject. The given object of analysis is expected to conform to the anticipated patterns of behavior, and only, Kuhn says, when scientists find that some or all of its components do not operate in accordance with it, will they start looking for alternative explanations and better ways to understand it. A matrix is something more flexible. It is a cluster of statements referring to an area of knowledge that do not necessarily fit all the events nor are 100% mutually consistent. A matrix offers a big tent where many different strands of research can find inspiration and shelter.

In a nutshell, Turner tried to provide a (failed) tool to explain social change or history. Its fulcrum was the notion of liminality, the moment in which humans decide to use their freedom in order to make new structural arrangements or change their previous ways. Liminality brings freedom to action. It is an extraordinary and fleeting occasion that allows some groups bound by communal ties to throw off their shackles. In premodern times, it would come in two shapes. In the first, as deviation rituals after which the new order or status would become enduring. The other comprised reversal rituals that would only shake basic structures of power for a short while in the shared understanding that the old order of things would revert to normal once the break was over.

This age-old dispensation changed with the advent of the first Industrial Revolution, capitalism, and modernity. Far from an impermanent flare of freedom, the liminal would become institutionalized in a lasting way, or in Turner's words, it was accepted and arranged in its liminoidness or liminoidity. The opportunity to disagree, to criticize, and to propose different courses of action, that is, to exercise freedom, became a permanent prop of modern societies and found many channels of expression (political parties, independent media, public opinion surveys). This flagged the great divide with the coerciveness of social life in premodern societies. However, it did not cure the wound at the root of social life—the difference between some parts of human life (like work) that can be considered ordinary and less meaningful and others (like leisure and play) seen as extraordinary and liberating remained. How they are conceptualized created great differences among the Turnerian tribes as we will see.

But before continuing, it may be useful to find whether the chasm between work and play, the ordinary and the extraordinary life, subjection and freedom has factual support. We have seen that it is conceptually difficult to maintain their separation. What happens in the real world? Only excessive imagination can lead us to say that work absorbs most of people's everyday lives and that leisure reverses the situation while on vacation. An OECD study (2009) of leisure trends among its members suggests a more complicated story. The study defines maximum leisure time as the amount of time that is not devoted to paid work. Even though there are obvious limitations to this definition (unpaid work and commuting time do not receive special treatment and are included in leisure), data on hours worked are available on a comparable basis for a large number of OECD countries and for long time periods. Taking 2006 as the year for comparison, the mean number of hours per year worked in 25 OECD countries amounted to 1,595, while hours for annual residual leisure were 7,165. Over the year, paid working time then accounts for 18.2% of total time, while residual leisure time makes for 81.8% of it (once again, let us recall that unpaid work and commuting hours are counted as leisure, therefore inflating that category). Additionally, some key OECD countries showed a marked decline in annual worked hours since 1970. Japan cut them by more than 300, Norway by 400, France by over 450. The United States, the country that showed slower reduction over time, shaved 100 hours off the 1970 total in 2006. This should give some pause for thought to those who see work as the predominant occupation of time under modernity, at least in developed OECD countries. This significant decrease in working time, even though some of it may have been forced by rising unemployment in Europe, bucks the trend of alleged dominance of work in the modern societal order. However weakened, one could still make a case for the importance of work in nonvacation periods.

Would it stand? In order to probe the point more concrete, time–budget studies have to be used. In the second part of the study, OECD offers comparable data for 18 of its members.

An average OECD day can be distributed among five main time categories: leisure, personal care, paid work, unpaid work, and unspecified. Of these, "personal care" (including sleep, eating and drinking, medical and personal services) takes the lion's share with 45.3% of the day for OECD denizens. "Leisure" includes hobbies, games, television viewing, computer use, recreational gardening, sports, socializing with friends and family, attending events, and so on. It takes 21.6% of their time. "Paid work" counts full-time and part-time jobs, breaks in the workplace, commuting to and from it, time spent looking for work, time spent in school, commuting to and from school, and time spent in paid work at home. It accounts for 16.5% of the day. "Unpaid work" (household chores, such as cooking, cleaning, caring for children and other family and nonfamily members, volunteering, shopping, etc.) goes up to 15.3%. The remaining 1.4% is spent in "unspecified" tasks.

The average OECD day would thus be distributed between roughly 10 hours and 50 minutes for personal care, 5 hours and 10 minutes for leisure, 4 hours for paid work, and 3 hours and 40 minutes for unpaid work, with the remaining 20 minutes for the unspecified category. Let us remember that this distribution takes into consideration the time use of all the population over 15 years of age, including all those that do not have any paid work time, for instance, many homemakers and retirees. Indeed, real distribution of time among the different social groups varies considerably. Working hours would be higher for the employed population, both male and female. Usually the bulk of unpaid work falls on married females.

The difference between an average working day and one on vacation would not make things dramatically different for the total of the population, although the employed would notice a change in their daily activities. The rest would have more or less the same distribution of time. In this way, in OECD countries the alleged structure of time proposed by the Turnerians does not stand. Work does not dominate the lives of the majority, even in times of high employment, and its duration has dwindled over the last 35 years in many OECD member states. Lacking data for other countries, it is difficult to make a serious argument in one sense or the other, although one would intuitively accept that work represents a bigger burden in less developed countries. But this does not invalidate the argument. The Turnerian hypothesis rests on the separation of work and leisure, and it would be at its strongest precisely in those countries where free time and play take up a great deal of the average day. At any rate, the much-vaunted opposition between work and leisure as a structural component of modernity fades the more actual behavior of people is scrutinized.

The need to maintain the Turnerian division between the ordinary or alienated parts of human life and its extraordinary aspects where liberation can make an appearance dies hard, though. Cohen has often praised the importance of MacCannell's as a key contribution to the study of tourism, but he soon qualifies this view with a Turnerian twist.

> For MacCannell's approach necessarily leaves unexplained an essential aspect of behavior in touristic situations: the suspension of everyday obligations, the freedom enjoyed by tourists, and their license for permissive and playful "non-serious" behavior [...] Such behavior witnesses to the "looseness' of touristic situations, which is well captured in Turner's concepts of liminality and particularly liminoidity (Cohen 2004a:125).

Cohen should not be surprised. As explained in Chapter 4, this is precisely MacCannell's bone of contention with tourism and most of serious tourism research. There cannot be "looseness" or freedom in social arrangements that are structurally constraining or unfree, as social intercourse based on money exchanges and the division of labor need be. And he is not ready to waver on this point under any circumstances. In his vociferous disagreement with Urry, he developed the argument amply (Chapter 4). Turnerians—and on this point Cohen seems to follow the party line—see tourism as a special type of social behavior, loose, unusual, freedom enhancing, something that researchers should be aware of if they want to grasp its substance. The connection between tourism and freedom is the Turnerian perquisite. But it is on the antipodes of MacCannell's.

Turner's followers, however, do not completely agree on its nature. Following the matrix he bequeathed, one can see tourism in, at least, four different ways. We call them liberation theologies not because they have any special link with that theological persuasion that sees a Christian's call as participating in the liberation of people from injustice and taking sides in the class struggle (Boff 1997, 1978; Küng 2008). The reason for the moniker is that both the authentic liberation theologians and the group of authors we will discuss believe that they are entitled to apprehend some essences or concepts, which by their own definition, are beyond the purview of the human mind.

The first persuasion adopts a nearly functionalist attitude. What is extra-ordinary in tourism is its capacity to make people revert to their ordinary work life with renewed energy. This is Liberation, Act One. Liberation, Act Two, adopts the more sanguine view that tourism is one of the great opportunities people can avail themselves of to exert their freedom and "liberate' themselves. There is a third current that sees the separation between work and leisure/play both as a basic feature of an ambivalent reality and as an opportunity to overcome it. Liberation is neither here nor there; it should avoid swimming out of its depth; better a stunted liberation than no liberation at all—Liberation, Act Three. Finally, Liberation, Act Four, maintains a more agnostic view on the thaumaturgical possibilities of tourism, but it cannot cast away the hope that the Turnerian turn allows for a better understanding of the different ways people react to the strictures of modernity. The extraordinary life, though, should remain the preserve of extraordinary people. The different shades of liberation notwithstanding, all of these theories seem unable to offer an adequate comprehension of MMT.

Liberation, Act One, can be best exemplified in an already old but not obsolete paper by Jafari (1987). As a matter of fact, a great deal of literature in the following quarter century has built on this bedrock. Jafari's ambitions in this paper ran high as he proposed not only to understand the basics of individual tourist's behavior but also to offer a general framework for the sociocultural study of the tourist system. There is a lot of drive on Jafari's part that tourism takes people out of their ordinary settings and brings them back to it in a movement that one might describe as a loop.

Enter Jafari's loop; looping the loop is exactly what tourists usually do in their vacation time. They initially take a jump out of ordinary life that is the ground where the need for flight is bred. For some reason, they decide to get out of it. Their upward impulse brings emancipation in the sense of freedom from ordinary-life constraints. Once they have reached their cruising altitude, they incorporate a new role that happens in "a distinctly nonordinary outer time and space." This stage will be followed by the "inevitable" return from their "temporary" position to the "constant" reality of their base. The end comes with the return home and the need to catch up with the novelties that may have happened there since she left base. In this aeronautical metaphor, tourists experience a number of changes that will mark their entry into the nonordinary space and time that belongs into the structure of a vacation. In this way, for Jafari, tourism has a sacred aspect, for sacrality and religion are also defined by their extraordinariness (1987:*passim*).

After takeoff, and now at cruising altitude, the tourist enters an emancipatory state. Not only does she distance herself from her usual residence but, what is much more important, she also gets away from her sociocultural environment. The novice is recognized as such by others as she enters the nonordinary space. And there she floats in a new tourist culture in which she as an actor can define and redefine her rules, her roles, and her expectations. The new tourist space is a space of antistructure. As she progresses into it, she feels entitled to define a new identity and thus partakes of the tourist culture. In this new environment, she can not only break with her at-home culture, but she also feels entitled to forget about the norms in her destination. The new culture becomes a kind of Bizarro World (as Superman comics called an upside-down set of happenings) where the tourist properly is neither here nor there, but betwixt and between, as Turner used to put it. She feels like suspended in the air or at the top of a rolling wave. This space of fantasy that Jafari terms the animation stage of the tourist experience is

> the ink with which tourism's script is written and its magnet sketched. While in this touristic trance, one has entered the "promised" biblical heaven right on this earth—though at times it feels out of this world (1987:153).

Alas, time goes by and reality knocks with its stubborn single-mindedness. Our tourist has to go back home. What goes around comes around. The tourist starts feeling the itch for home. She understands that she has to go back and submit to the old norms. Her older self rises from its temporary grave and home culture beckons the shackles she will don as meekly as she did before. And there she lands right in the middle of her old world. Time to read the stale papers, to open the letters that pile up in the mailbox, to fire up the computer again, to pay the bill that somehow had escaped her careful arrangements before leaving. Because even while she was away, the clock at home continued ticking, and people did not wait for her return to make decisions that may have affected her life. Time to get a grip on everyday life again.

Such is the tourist loop. Why should tourists take it? What makes them go away? What is the relation between their behavior and the system in which it happens? The answer is quite functional. The system's ordinary bounds are unable to accommodate "the unwinding of certain endogenous entanglements"; therefore, its members have to rebalance the wholesomeness of their needs. Even though its expected function was to serve the people who work inside it, the system overpowers them and they end up working for the system. This drains them both physically and mentally. So that they keep on working, they need to lubricate their own individual egos from the dryness of their lives. They need one-eighth of an ounce of extraordinary dope to perform well again.

> The nonordinary treatment for some of its people includes re-creation of the exhausted physique. [...] For others, the treatment may be for anomie—to temporarily become kings or queens [for one day], somebody or nobody, for an elevated sense of fulfillment. [...] When the processing is complete these re-created workers are "readied" to resume their positions in the main system (1987:157).

In this way, tourism appears as a functional condition of the generating system. What happens to the receiving destination? It cannot maintain the totality of its own "local" culture, as it experiences the dynamics of new inputs, the "tourist" culture that vacationers create for themselves and the "residual" culture that they carry from their home base. This is not an easy conglomerate to manage, and the receiving culture may find a lot of difficulties in navigating it.

At any rate, the tourist experience does not leave the generating and the receiving cultures ignorant of each other; it acquaints them willy-nilly in an unequal relationship. In sending its members away, the generating culture expects a re-created workforce to be able to employ new energies in the maintenance of its system, thanks to the ministrations they receive from their hosts. Accordingly, the generating markets are in debt with them and should, within the framework of a fair exchange, pay back their due.

> This calls for a systems-level cooperation and financial involvement beyond the direct expenditure by tourists from the generating and the investment by operators in the receiving systems (1987:158).

Starting from the ordinary/extraordinary, sacred/profane, work/leisure, subjection/freedom diads, we have thus transited from the individual to its system and to their intersystemic fabric. The turn of the tourist's universe is completed with a homecoming for the individual who has to choose between one of the extremes. The final detour through the vagaries of international commerce does not necessarily exceed these boundaries. It is just a practical coda to the basic model.

The need for tourism, therefore, harks back to the need for R&R (the second R meaning re-creation here), and R&R becomes a need for the individual because of the demands that the system puts on him. What "the system" means is not exactly clear, though. On the one hand, it may mean the interaction between the genotype and the phenotype. No animal, including cultured people, can go on indefinitely without rest. Nature or, in other words, our genetic limits impose a break after a period of exhausted energies. But in Jafari's model, the system goes beyond the biological, as it is work, a social activity, what makes some parts of the total "generator" render a subpar performance. One assumes that "the system" is accordingly the basic structure of social relations that we call modernity or capitalism and that this "system" is somehow so demanding that it not only makes breaking out of it mandatory, but also gives its members the means to do so (usually in the form of paid vacations). What is so extraordinary about it? Is it extraordinary at all?

Let us start with the second question—the playful or liberating elements that the tourist combines into the tourist culture in the animation stage.

> The tourist can now play any role of his choice any way he wishes, ranging from the childish games and practical jokes played by the middle-aged conventioneers in hotels, to the loud Hawaiian shirt worn by the conservative bank president, to participating in various kinds of touristic fun (e.g. grandma and grandchild taking rides together in the *Magic Kingdom*), to the "have-nots" pretentiously acting rich or the "haves" acting commoners, to happily married men accepting sex solicitations or female tourists encountering the "black experience." They all know the extent of deviation from their ordinary bounds—"Imagine being this carefree in Peoria." Or "I would be outcast if I did that in Des Moines" (Jafari 1987:153).

Is that "tourist culture," however, a challenge to "the system"; that is, is it what Turner would call a deviation ritual, marking a no-return point in an individual's trajectory or in that of her society?

This would be rather difficult to sustain. A few people may enjoy what has been called extreme or combat-zone tourism where usual norms of security, and practically all the rest, are turned on their head. They will go to areas that are in turmoil to witness or even participate in the events. Many will never reach them because of the threats they pose; others may even get engaged in the turbulences, but their number is surely so small that they hardly can be construed as an example of general tourist behavior. At any rate, in most of those signal cases, such as that of John Reed and the 1917 Bolshevik Revolution, it was not tourism that unleashed their way of getting out of the ordinary life of their societies, rather the other way around. They traveled to the revolutionary acme because they previously felt disenchanted with or ambivalent toward their societies of origin. The functional paradigm would not apply to them.

When unexpectedly they find themselves in the middle of unrest, though, most tourists usually pack for home and leave their destination as soon as possible. Such was the case in Kenya in 2007–2008 and in Thailand in 2009–2010, when political unrest in both countries made many tourists run for the exits. As for the destinations, the tourist culture of safety proved quite damaging. Especially in the case of Thailand (April–June 2009), where they found the international airport closed for days after a sequence of demonstrations, which together with the international economic slowdown, contributed to a serious downturn in the country's tourism industry in 2009. Tourists may like some norms stirred, but they definitely prefer the most basic ones not shaken. Bond, James Bond.

Which are those general norms that they like to stir when on vacation? Do they push for a complete break with the rules prevalent in their societies of origin? There is abundant literature on vacation excess. Some tourists spend beyond their means, follow erratic schedules, overeat and drink more alcohol than they usually do at home, and engage more casually in sex. However, conclusions about the subversive nature of their behavior are difficult to generalize. In many cases, it is just the expression of some youthful subculture that can be found while on vacation or at home. Some soccer fans drink to excess, revel in unruly conduct, clash with the police, attack each other, and exhibit chauvinistic symbols and expressions in international games; they act in the same way at home when the match pitches two local clubs against each other. They do not need to travel to look for trouble. Some youngsters may shock some members of their given destinations (be it in Ibiza, Crete, Goa, Cancún, or Fort Lauderdale) with displays of public nudity or open sexual behavior (Andriotis 2010), excessive drinking (Sönmez et al 2006), use of drugs, or rowdy manners; none of these would be unknown in some areas of their own residential communities at "ordinary" times. And they often have the same protagonists.

Does such behavior break basic societal codes? Turner had a clearer view. Those are rituals of reversal. Like Carnival in Rio, like the Roman Bacchanalia, like the Hindu *Holi* festival, and many others in different cultures, they provide occasions to temporarily change some rules of behavior allowing for hedonic displays of sex, eating and drinking, some disrespect for the authorities, raunchy chanting and posturing, and not much more. Other basic rules such as respect for human life, property, contracts, and orderly traffic remain in place all through. One can discuss their true meaning till kingdom comes, but it is not easy to sustain that such occasions represent a break from, much less a total suspension of, ordinary life.

On the other hand, go to resorts frequented by families and such behavior is virtually nonexistent. There, parents and children follow a very similar routine as when at home on a weekend. Indeed, they all have a more leisurely time than on weekdays, but they all abide as much by the laws and customs of their destinations, domestic or international, as they do at home. It would be difficult to say that eating in excess or having more time for intimacy or sporting a Hawaiian shirt creates anomie, increases ambivalence toward one's own society, or, much less, opens the gates to an outlaw's life. They are just expansions that denizens of many countries often consider as one of the reasons why they are content with their "ordinary" lives. They are part of them. Such excesses are not so different from the ones they allow themselves at certain times of the year when they are at home. Weekends, especially extended ones, or special occasions such as Thanksgiving in the United States, or Christmas or Easter in the Christian world, or the Spring Festival (New Year) in China, or Tet in Vietnam are often accompanied by the same excesses in expenses for extraordinary whims.

It is surprising that so many anthropologists fail to see that in modern societies, work and play are not so far away from each other in everyday life. Indeed this would have to make them reconsider many of their beliefs about the workday being some kind of chain gang. Even in the hardest times of primitive accumulation of capital (Zola's *Germinal* is a good introduction to them), even under the Fordist discipline of the conveyor belt, work and play, asceticism and excesses, subjection and freedom are part of the rhythms of everyday life for most people. They cannot be arbitrarily separated from each other without an explanation of why and how the rigors of the workplace did not cause "the system" to burst, but rather made it prosper and gain acceptance. And its denizens can provide only for a different combination of work and leisure that we call vacations because "the system" offers to many of them increased disposable income, paid vacations, and affordable travel opportunities. In a nutshell—neither can freedom be totally apart from obligations, personal and social, nor could vacations be available for millions of people without the economic success of the markets, capitalism, and modernity.

LIBERATION THEOLOGY. ACT TWO: THE BRIDGE TO NOWHERE

Some starry-eyed seers think that eating, drinking, shopping, and love-making sprees, especially the latter, have the potential of liberating individuals from their chains and/or to blow the social order to smithereens. Which takes us to Liberation, Act Two. Far from the still functionalist or pessimistic undertones that accompanied Jafari's loop, tourism may become an active player for social and, above all, personal liberation. This view has been put forward by Ryan with a particular dose of boldness and, as it seems, considerable success. This is the reason why his views will be given preeminent attention here over some others among the myriad liberation "theologians."

For Ryan, tourism not only opens the door to temporary, marginal reversals; it also contains some life-changing potential. Even more, it may change societies. Using the name of the main character in a 1986 play by Willy Russell, Ryan refers to the Shirley Valentine syndrome. In the play, the protagonist—a lower middle class homemaker obviously tired of her repetitive cooking chores and a boring marriage—accepts the invitation of a female friend to a vacation in Greece, finds her groove back in romance with a local, and decides to stay in the destination—her new home from now on—for good.

This does not only happen in fiction. Ryan constructs his hypothesis on similar but real cases that he eye witnessed. Many a holiday company started like that: people on vacation fell in love with the physical destination, with the locals, with one of them, or with all of the above, and decided to change their lives. The author recalls how, when doing fieldwork in one of his research stints, he even came across an earth-shattering event. A woman he was interviewing said that she was a Shirley Valentine gone through the eponymous syndrome. "She had holidayed in Majorca a decade previously, returned home to the UK, left her husband and returned to the island to take up a new life" (2002:2). The intriguing question comes next. What is it about vacations that can trigger such forceful incidents? Even though the Shirley Valentines of the world cannot be seen as the norm for vacationers,

Ryan warns, leaves of absence from ordinary life have a great potential to sustain or change people's lifestyles. We are gazing upon the liminoid powers that, in a self-reference to the study of sex tourism he and Hall penned (Ryan and Hall 2001), Ryan says pervade all tourist activities.

Why is tourism liminoid? To wit: (1) it is individual and contractual; (2) it happens away from the ordinary flow of natural and social processes; (3) it coexists with and depends on a total social process and represents its subjectivity and negativity; (4) it is profane, consisting of a reversal of roles, an antithesis of the collective, but possessing its own collective representations; (5) it is idiosyncratic, quirky, and ludic; and (6) its symbols cease to be eufunctional (positively functional is what this pleonastic expression seems to mean [JA]) and become instead a social critique, exposing injustices, inefficiencies, and immoralities of mainstream economic and political structures. If in spite of the long series of attributes, the reader still finds it difficult to grasp what liminoid means, she should not blame herself. How the author can fit all these things into one single paragraph without contradiction is incomprehensible. (1) and (3) are mutually exclusive. (4) does not explain why a reversal of roles should be profane and, therefore, an antithesis of the collective. (2) implies that there is something real existing beyond reality (one tends to think that there is nothing tangible beyond the natural and the social worlds). There is no relation between (5) and (6). Why tourism should be (6) and not its opposite, that is, a conformity-enhancing social activity as so many of its critics have claimed, remains a mystery.

Ryan's definition of the liminoid may lack the impressive stateliness of the riddle proposed to Oedipus by the Sphinx, but it beats it for sheer obscurity by far. In the final analysis, however, it only reiterates what we already know. Liminoid are the challenges or "alternative means of ordering structures for individuals, both individually [*sic* JA] and societally" (Ryan and Hall 2001:5). In plain English, the liminoid is something really, really mind-boggling, so much so that Ryan feels free from the need to explain it. The pell-mell ingredients he throws into the mixture are anything but a definition.

One might forgive so many confusing statements, or excuse Ryan's frequent sallies against grammar such as "Mill and Morrison (...) and Leiper (...) have both [*sic*] written books on the Tourist System" (2002:20), or overlook blurbs on tourism's role-switching potential such as

> gymnasia, spas and showers invade the physical space of the office—and in new and imaginative software-based industries young workers create working space within which to skate-board (2002:6).

Perhaps in these new spaces, work and play have finally coalesced under modernity, even though their alleged strict separation was what allowed Ryan to start his drone.

More serious problems unfortunately appear when, leaving aside the caution not to take our by now beloved Valentine as the norm for tourist behavior, Ryan just embraces her syndrome as universal, for "[t]ourism as an educative process, or even as a means of relaxation, implies that it is a process of self-regeneration" (2002:26). Translated into English, tourism and personal liberation go hand in hand.

Some evidence should accompany so much bloviation, but facts remain elusive to Ryan. It would be unfair to forget that, as he underscores, there are people who decide to turn over a new leaf in their lives after going on vacation. Look at Shirley and a few more examples he presents. But Ryan soon falls in a metonymical trap of his own making. A few parts vouch for the whole. A former Marks & Spencer middle manager decides to become a windsurfing teacher in Greece after a vacation? So might, or could, or should do the rest of tourists even if they happen not to be middle managers at Marks & Spencer.

> Here come Proust and his *madeleine*.
>
> Many years had elapsed during which nothing of Combray, save what was comprised in the theatre and the drama of my going to bed there, had any existence for me, when one day in winter, on my return home, my mother, seeing that I was cold, offered me some tea, a thing I did not ordinarily take. I declined at first, and then, for no particular reason, changed my mind. She sent for one of those squat, plump, little cakes called *petites madeleines*, which look as though they had been moulded in the fluted valve of a scallop shell. And soon, mechanically, dispirited after a dreary day with the prospect of a depressing morrow, I raised to my lips a spoonful of the tea in which I had soaked a morsel of the cake. No sooner had the warm liquid mixed with the crumbs touched my palate than a shudder ran through me and I stopped, intent upon the extraordinary thing that was happening to me. An exquisite pleasure had invaded my senses, something isolated, detached, with no suggestion of its origin. And at once the vicissitudes of life had become indifferent to me, its disasters innocuous, its brevity illusory—this new sensation having had on me the effect which love has of filling me with a precious essence; or

rather this essence was not in me it *was* me. I had ceased now to feel mediocre, contingent, mortal. Whence could it have come to me, this all-powerful joy? I sensed that it was connected with the taste of the tea and the cake, but that it infinitely transcended those savours, could, no, indeed, be of the same nature. Whence did it come? What did it mean? How could I seize and apprehend it? (Proust 1982:48).

Eating the pastry was, no doubt for Proust, an event that changed his life, so much so that he gave us his *Recherche* thereafter. Following Ryan's liminoid tourism, one should attribute the same regenerative powers to all specimens of this humble piece of dough—a case of *post hoc, propter hoc*. Some lives change after a vacation; therefore, tourism is a life-changing force. In the past this used to be called sympathetic magic; today we call it postmodernism. But do all *madeleine* eaters feel as shattered as Proust was, and with the same successful results? Only them? What about those who prefer *croissants*? Does Ryan remember that the French writer of the *madeleine*-induced trip spent a good part of his life confined to his bedroom and traveled little? Perhaps tourism is not the only motive why one can Valentinize oneself; perhaps many other forces or occasions will have a similar result. Why lionize travel?

A similar question is raised when considering the numbers of people for whom tourism does not appear as the time to change their lives. Possibly Ryan could not avail himself of consistent statistics. However, had he looked into the passenger numbers offered by different airlines, he would have noticed that more or less the number of departing travelers equals those that come back home. Indeed, some of them may remain behind, or decide to establish themselves in a new abode some time later. But this looks like as small a minority as *madeleine*-eating Prousts. For most, Jafari's loop is just that—a loop. Unlike an arrow, it boomerangs.

However, the issue of size for this minority of future expatriates is not irrelevant. Whether the Shirley Valentines of this world are but a few scores or hundreds of thousands will reflect on the plausibility of tourism's liberating potential. Occasionally, numbers reach critical mass, but below a significant threshold usually they do not register as significant changes. Perhaps some graduate students might devote their dissertations to counting the Valentines and thus help us get a better grip on the accuracy of Ryan's inferred consequences. Until we know more, musing on Shirley and her liberation will remain largely idle talk based on anecdote.

This takes us to another issue. Does a sudden change in one's own life, even if induced by a stay away from home, equal liberation? It should depend on how we define each one of those variables, and Ryan does not show an irresistible inclination to do so. For him, seemingly, liberation comes in two main shapes. Sometimes it looks like change for change's sake. On other occasions, liberation is understood as a definitive break with ordinary life as opposed to leisure.

Let us start with the first. According to Ryan's syllabus, whenever we desire something badly and we get it, we come close to liberation. Shirley Valentine was a creature of fiction, and we can take leave of her in her newly found bliss with the wish that she will live happily ever after. Closer to reality, though, one finds, for instance, Corinne Hofman, the White Maasai (Hofmann 2006, 2009). In a 1986 trip to Kenya with her then boyfriend, Ms. Hofmann met Lketinga, her dream of a Maasai warrior, and she went under the same spell as Ms. Valentine. After settling her affairs in Switzerland, she was back in Kenya, married her warrior, and had a daughter with him. Things, however, did not follow her imagined template, and years later, she broke with her husband and went back to her country of origin bringing her daughter with her. She has written a number of best sellers describing her experience, although they do not seem to have had a bandwagon effect among other white Western women. No rush to Kenya in search of Maasai warriors has been reported, so, perhaps, many saw Hofmann's successful books as a cautionary tale. At any rate, what seems clear is that she understands both of her life changes (marrying Lketinga first and leaving him later) as liberating, that is, leaving behind baggage she was no longer prepared to carry. If that is what liberation is all about, tourism accounted for just 50% of it. For reasons known only to her (no matter how much she records about her life in her books), she was equally unhappy with her life in affluent Switzerland as after deciding to settle with her noble warrior in the Maasai Mara.

Cohen has described something similar in an article on the experiences of former sex tourists who finally married their Thai paramours (2003). Many found their new status as not just liberated, but made in heaven. The male, usually older or much older than his female Oriental counterpart, seems to have found an outlet for his sexuality and/or love needs, not easily satisfied in his environment of origin. For her part, the woman is often able to leave prostitution, improve her financial status, and ascend the social ladder. Perhaps she may in some cases also find an outlet for her sexuality and/or love needs. However, the obstacles to this presumed bliss are many, and not limited to the financial scams some roaming Romeos have experienced.

The extreme heterogamy of these unions is also compounded by the extreme cultural differences between the partners, usually more visible after the wedding. On the one hand, Thai society tends to suspect all Thai wives of *farangs* (foreigners) as being former prostitutes, even when this is not the case, thus creating much embarrassment and misunderstanding for them and their wives. On the other hand, the Western men will not readily appreciate that they are expected to give financial support to their in-laws, that their wives will be so committed to their families, that they may make serious decisions on the basis of divinatory practices shunned in Western societies, or that financial arrangements between spouses can easily be used against husbands because of the strictures of Thai law. Usually,

> the foreign husband met his future wife in a context [...] radically different from that of her rural origins. He thus perceives her as emancipated [...] But his wife, mostly continues to see herself as part of her family group, maintaining [...] not just an emotional tie; her family is also the refuge to which she can withdraw if her marriage fails (2003:73).

Ryan appears so smitten with the view that liberation amounts to definitive life changes that he remains blind to the fact that many are not irreversible and that oftentimes liberation also happens when one becomes once again free from one's previous liberation. At any rate, it is difficult to see the role of tourism in such personal life dramas. Practically, there will be as many kinds of liberations as humans, for only each one of them can tell what makes him or her experience it. And personal liberation may also be redefined many times throughout an individual's life. Can travel or tourism account for all of them? Only if one's imagination matches the dreams that Hofmann or the Western husbands of Thai bar girls entertained when striving for their own liberation.

What about the second sort of liberation? Following what he believes to be the Turnerian Vulgate, Ryan paints personal liberation in a second way—as a breakup with ordinary life as defined by work. However, none of the few nonfictional characters he sees as examples of liberation measures up. Becoming a windsurfing teacher, or starting one's own tourism business in a given destination, or creating a car or a boat rental company does not exonerate from work. The new work can be felt as more pleasant, less constrained, more exciting, more profitable, or all of the above, and a few more things, but most humans cannot do without it. If liberation is defined as absence of toil and labor, it becomes an impossible proposition in social terms.

Ryan travels a third and final way to liberation. According to his definition of the liminoid (above), liberation occurs when tourism and its symbols cease to be eufunctional and become a social critique, exposing injustices, inefficiencies, and immoralities of mainstream economic and political structures. He knows how to please a crowd what with his promises of personal liberation for the price of a package tour, but the eufunctionality of this latter formula goes too far. He is not the first to recommend that tourists cast a critical gaze on their activities and those of the industry that caters to their needs; mainstream literature in this field brims with similar warnings.

Few, however, have dared to recommend to tourists and their symbols to assume the role of prophets. Fortunately. Imagine that some of them were to follow Ryan's advice and seek liberation by publicly exposing the injustices of the Chinese Communist Party on a trip to Tibet, or the immoralities of the mainstream economic structures when on a sex tour of Havana, or decrying the atrocities against political opponents endorsed by the supreme leader of Iran's military theocracy while visiting Qum. Sooner, rather than later, their exercise in liberation would wind up as a not-so-exciting tour of the local prisons. Perhaps Ryan is referring to liberation by social critique just in democratic polities, and this is what he meant by taking tourism to the extreme. If so, he should bear in mind that there is no need to pin the highfalutin "liberation" label on what is just an ordinary, rightful, and legitimate occurrence in such political and social mainstream democratic structures.

Ryan seems to read a lot. His work usually includes an impressive number of references, but one sometimes doubts whether his writings grasp their meaning. To explain the sense of *liminoid*, he quotes from a book on sex tourism that he coauthored with Hall (2001). In the first edition, they claimed Foucault and Marx as their inspirations while they succeeded in not referencing a single work by the first, and in botching the two included mentions of the second (the *Communist Manifesto* got a 4-year face-lift when 1844 was given as its publication date; Engels was made a coauthor of the *1844 Manuscripts*). If he has duly read his classics, Ryan should know that what he means with that awful *liminoid* adjective that Turner put in circulation is exactly the opposite of what Turner was referring to when he floated it. For Turner, liminoid is another form of highlighting the close relation between institutionalized freedom and ordinary life under democracy. Ryans's writings do not convey this meaning.

LIBERATION THEOLOGY. ACT THREE: STUNTED AUTHENTICITY

Wang makes a case for examining the relation between tourism and modernity from a general or sociological vantage point. This seems quite commendable as this book maintains that explanations from this discipline (including anthropology) often were limited and biased. He also starts with the right démarche by sharing his belief that history has to be part of the relation between the two, for tourism, unlike travel, is a type of social occurrence that can be found only in recent times. He does not date its birth, but one would imagine that he accepts it as a post–World War Two phenomenon, as sometimes he vaguely refers to this period (Wang 2000:1). His subsequent treatment of the subject, though, does not fulfill such high expectations.

His initial definition of tourism invokes some sacred names in the discipline (he nods with reverence to MacCannell and Graburn), which should give us some pause for thought. As will be argued later, Wang takes MacCannell's name in vain. Graburn's signal contribution to our understanding of tourism (1977, 2001, 2004)—that it is some kind of religious ritual or pilgrimage—could not be flimsier, so adopting it cannot be of much help. Wang, however, seems to take the phenomenological road; that is, he does not care much about the attributes of the defined objects and takes a shortcut to their essence. Though Wang may not make any special claim to the phenomenological mantle, he avails himself of its latitude.

Born at the turn of the 20th century in Germany, phenomenology concurred in the long-lasting Hegelian impulse to free philosophical enquiries from the strictures of scientific research. Throughout his work, Hegel debased the modern scientific method as rendered by Kant in his *Critique of Pure Reason* for being the product of the lesser powers of our minds—the *intellect* or, with the German word, *der Verstand*—as opposed to *reason* (also known as *die Vernunft*), that is, our highest reasoning power. While the intellect wallows in determination, difference, and detail, reason is but the endless reflection in individuals of the ways whereby some supreme entity that Hegel dubs as the Spirit or *der Geist* takes possession of itself over that process of nature and culture most of us call history and he christened as the phenomenology of the spirit (*Phänomenologie des Geistes*). Reason allows us to grasp the totality of human experience and to overcome the limits of particular sciences that thrive in the narrow world of causality and stunt our most legitimate desires to apprehend and explain the whole of our experience and of the world-out-there (1970a, 1970b). Unfortunately, Hegel never provided a reliable guide to this goal, and soon the universal *Geist* emerged as a pliable tool that allowed the Right and the Left Hegelians to battle heatedly over mutually exclusive interpretations and agendas.

Post-Hegelian phenomenology did not fare any better, though it showed a lot more nerve. Husserl did not hide his will to succeed where the master had let us down, so he resorted to the audacity of hope. While Plato warned humans that they would be blinded if they tried to stare pure essences in the face and thought that their minds limited them to reminiscing about their faint reflections as shadows on the wall of a cavern, Husserl vowed to let humans break out of it and see reality in its naked splendor if they only dared discard their rationalist chains. For Husserl, rationalism, that is, the world of particular sciences, just grasps bits and pieces of the realm of being. At its best, it will reveal only how things come about, not what they are. If one casts off those useful, though ontologically trifling layers of determination, truth will be at hand. All we need is bracketing the world of appearances through the technique of *epoché*, Husserl's gift of a magic wand to his followers. *Epoché* allows us to get rid of determination and particularity and dive into the innermost depths of being. Unfortunately, like Hegel, Husserl was never too specific on how lay folks might avail themselves of this Technicolor Dreamcoat of an epistemology. His long exegesis of concepts such as intentionality, empathy, intuition, *Lebenswelt*, and sundry similar noemata cannot grant that each gazer will independently look at things from the same viewpoint. But if one closes the eyes firmly and chants the appropriate mantras, *epoché* will gratify with a unique delight— one's own definition of the subject becomes the expression of its real essence.

Phenomenology has become somewhat jaded over time. Like Hegel, Husserl did not prepare his followers for the tribulation of seeing the oracles implode in mutually exclusive ways as soon as they were out of the press. The same *epoché* would inspire Heidegger and Sartre to opposite views on the essence of man and its relation to the world-out-there. Phenomenology, though, still retains great power. However, much the phenomenologist tribe may have burst off in pesky fireworks, the chosen disciples can concur on one important dispensation—no matter how much *epoché* can tear them apart from each other, it still remains an impressive gambit to shape the game in one's own terms. Who might dare challenge the runes of those who can look at the essence of things in the face?

All this takes us back to Wang and his view of tourism, modernity, and the complex threads that they weave for each other. He has not much time for statistical distinctions of business, deferential, or leisure travel, or for the details of going to international and domestic destinations. He does not bother much about flows and their changing directions. Those are but mathematical niceties. "In general terms the official, industrial, or economic definition of tourism tends to be a technical and statistical one" (2000:5).

He prefers to grasp its true essence in the act of gazing in *epoché*. Tourism, for him, is

> a religion-like ritual activity and institutions [...], which, through the sacralization of attractions, creates a world of hope, promise and "salvation," or "another world" which is at a certain distance from "This World." Why do people take part in such a distancing action? At least two reasons can be given. First, they have certain problems with 'this world', or with their existential conditions. Second, as a result, people question the taken-for-granted conditions of the existence in which they find themselves, and renegotiate the meaning of their lives through keeping a distance—spiritually, socially and spatially—from everyday life and normality on a regular and annual (or semi-annual) basis (2000:vii).

If the definition sounds like a phenomenological mouthful, it is because it is. It blends religion, anomie, and renewal in a startling mix, but one cannot expect an explanation of how this truth was attained even though common sense would tell that tourists behave in many different ways and that rituals come in many shapes and sizes. Some indeed are ceremonials followed in religious settings, as Wang, on the wake of Graburn, would have tourism be. But when Paul Theroux says that Andy Parent, the main character in his *My Secret Life*, had "made a ritual" of visiting the local brothel at his Peace Corps destination in Africa, possibly he does not refer to the same observances. Usually people are also able to make a difference between visiting a temple and an attraction (which might even be a temple) or a travel agency. What can be garnered by blurring the distinction?

If we leave the religious metonym aside, the rest of the definition becomes even less likely. Do only tourists have problems with their existential conditions in this world? Do people wait to bring them to the front until they take a break once or twice a year? What about those who cannot afford to go away because they are ill, are in prison, just ran out of money, or have no paid vacations at all? Cannot they question their existential conditions and be willing to renegotiate the meaning of their lives? Do they have to wait for changes until they can reward themselves with a vacation? It seems doubtful.

The French Revolution reached a climax in the month of July 1789, but not because the *sans-culottes* had experienced overbooking in the French Riviera. Nobody has—yet—made the case that the storming of the Winter Palace in then Petrograd happened because Lenin and the Bolsheviks decided to renegotiate their lives after a well-deserved vacation over the summer of 1917. Their *datchas* in the Crimea would come much later. Why does Wang need to define tourism in such a bombastic way?

Look at the phenomenological veneer. Tourism is a defining feature of modernity, and modernity demands fulsomeness. After all, it weaves the basic context of present social life. What then is modernity? "In general terms, 'modernity' refers to the period since the Renaissance and is thus associated with the replacement of traditional society (pre-modernity)" (2000:15). It appeared in the West, though later on it spilled over to the rest of the world, bringing about new institutional arrangements such as capitalism, the monopoly of violence by the state (no mention of the rule of law or of legitimacy here), science and technological advances, urbanization, and globalization. Is there an organizing principle to this heap of new changes, some key structure that makes all the rest fall into their proper place? Yes, there is and it is what Max Weber called rationalization, "a process whereby traditional customs give way to contemporary ways of doing things" (2000:15). Not a very encouraging definition. However mangled, tourism deserved one, but modernity does not. Wang's modernity, namely, the waning of the premodern, as rationalization, meaning the waxing of the modern, results only in a circular notion.

This is, however, a minor point. More decisive in the cue from Max Weber is the will to define modernity as a cultural event, a decisive reshaping of the collective mind that has not yet come to an end. Wang does not see any serious reason to maintain that postmodernity (some structural changes that allegedly superseded modernity in the later part of the 20th century) represents a break with its immediate predecessor. Postmodern critics have decried some fundamental flaws in modernity's dispensation that they consider landmarks of a new era in a development marked by ambivalence and, if one believes Baudrillard, the triumph of *simulacra*. Wang, for his part, holds a less unbending view. In spite of their claims to the advent of a new era, postmodern critics should recognize that even in its salad days, modernity adorned itself with the same ambivalence they cautioned against. Postmodernity remains within the same rational order that characterized modernity. Modernity is but an abiding mindscape structure. Both have little to say about how people produce and reproduce their lives. The chasm between the cultural dynamics of modernity and their economic motivation becomes once again as whole as it was in Weber's post-1904 views. This is an albatross placed by Wang on modernity's neck.

Ambivalence sought its academic credentials in psychology, but some sociologists have adopted it warmly. In fact, it is not so distant from the notion of contradiction, or that complex phenomena have different traits and consequences that do not always compose a logically consistent whole. They can be experienced in different ways by different observers, and even by the same observer at different times, like Reims Cathedral as depicted by Monet at different hours of the day. Modernity for Wang is deeply ambivalent and so, for being its offspring, is tourism as well.

Ambivalence and contradiction, though, can be formulated in economic language. Consumer needs are multifaceted, and consumer goods are not only scarce, they also have a limited potential to fulfill those needs. Desire will always exceed supply, and scarcity will always challenge desire for the available resources are finite or limited. Economists have a way to figure out how to strike a balance between desire and reality. They call it cost–benefit analysis. Pareto even designed some so-called indifference maps that allow us to understand the different combinations of goods that a consumer may prefer within the limitation of his means. Wang, though, will have none of this. His notion of ambivalence is quite fuzzy and often misleading.

The most apparent manifestation of ambivalence in tourism, he warns, comes from the interaction between the tourist as consumer and the tourist industry. But Wang casts a wider net. Understanding this obvious display of ambivalence, he says, requests that we go beyond a narrow economic perspective. First and foremost, the conflicting expectations of consumers and the tourist industry hark back to the basic contradiction between people and their desires, between Logos and Eros. Only then can one elucidate the conflict between tourists' search for authenticity and the products offered by the industry.

At first blush, tourism looks like a harmonious totality. A well-performing economy generates higher productivity that enables higher disposable income that in turn yields increases in travel. Tourism thus becomes an indicator of affluence and social well-being—of collective happiness perhaps. However, at a deeper phenomenological level, one can also find in it an expression of the dark sides of modernity. Tourism may lead to disenchantment with the degradation of the environment, with monotony, and with homogenization. Wang segues on a quick crescendo. From his conditional beginning ("Tourism may lead to P or T"), he jumps into factual propositions. Tourism *is* a nonverbal critique of P and T. Even more, by changing their everyday lives during vacations, by escaping, by looking for the extraordinary, by practicing excess, by reveling in anomie, tourism *is* an attempt to change people's existential conditions. Revolution it may not be, but it pushes against the order of things; it tries to quash norms and escape into qualitatively different spaces. It *brings about* change, but regrettably—here Wang offers a less sanguine view than Ryan does—the changes it abets are temporary, rarely permanent.

Maybe, but Wang gets carried away by the plasticity of his words. Tourism indeed may lead to P or T, or G and Q, or to many other sundry features, attributes, or combinations thereof. What counts, though, are not the feelings researchers anticipate people might or should have; rather whether people really do experience them and/or act in a consistent way about them. Do tourists see their travel as a challenge to prevailing social norms? Do they have any idea that what they are doing amounts to a nonverbal critique of their ordinary existence, an equivalent to that kind of deep changes we call revolutions? When discussing Jafari's views, it was suggested that the hypothesis of tourism being a self-sustaining liminal phenomenon does not stand up, and Wang would be more convincing if he could show any evidence for his conjecture. He does not. Intuitively, though, one sees that after their vacation, people in general do not show active resistance to come back to the prevailing social order nor do they usually express any open desire to change it. If at all, collective negotiations about future work conditions have trade unions requesting more paid vacation time—not changes to the system that provides it. To use Ryan's awkward expression, vacations rather tend to be eufunctional.

Wang adds a second phenomenological layer to the macrorelation between modernity and tourism—that it strengthens rationality or Logos at the expense of other sources of behavior that are not directly governed by calculus or the instrumental adequacy of means to ends, which he calls Eros. He warns that the ambivalence between reality and desire (Freud used to call them the reality and the pleasure principles, and he thought, like Wang, that they were a structural component of mankind's inner dispensation) also appears in traditional societies, as much as the separation between work and leisure, but Wang immediately stipulates a difference between both—modernity makes the chasm more evident. It separates both spheres more decisively.

> Whereas industrial, capitalist, commercial and bureaucratic institutions are the sites where Logos-modernity is located, the institutions of leisure and culture are the locations where Eros-modernity resides, though leisure and culture are not exclusively Eros-oriented (2000:39).

Be that as it may, for Wang the Turnerian opposition between ordinary and extraordinary life remains the key feature of modernity, the former controlled by Logos in industrial and bureaucratic institutions, the latter basking in erotic gratification through leisure and tourism. Tourists definitely experience their conflicting drifts.

Can both cohabit under the same roof? The answer should be negative according to what the reader has already been told. Was not tourism a nonverbal critique of society as it is? Miraculously, though, now the extraordinary life of the tourist, his always-malcontented consumerist Id, does not unleash repression by Logos.

> [A] person's Eros impulses and desires can be gratified or released in tourist activity [...] The gratification of Eros in and through tourism, then, releases the tensions caused by the self-constraints imposed by Logos on Eros. In this way tourism helps reinforce the order of the home society that Logos underpins [...] Tourism, so to speak, as a kind of Eros-modernity, coordinates with Logos-modernity organically (2000:41).

And he quotes Urry to the effect that temporary tourist deviance abets normalcy at home. After all, Jafari was not off the mark. Following Wang, one has to accept willy-nilly that tourism has a functional side. But his modernity shines as something really mysterious. It is ambivalence squared. On the one hand, the conflict of Logos and Eros seems insoluble. On the other hand, just by leaving home, tourists can work a way out of such structural ambiguity. Modernity consists of mutually exclusive parts, which at the same time, to the stroke of Wang's magic wand, do not really exclude each other.

Looking at tourism from the microlevel, that is, its institutional or commercial arrangements, Wang makes his views easier to understand while less consistent. The tourism industry is the embodiment of Logos rationality in its rational pursuit of profit while the tourist is Eros bound. Eros pushes tourists toward romantic, authentic, and exotic adventures, but the industry provides standardized, contrived, and commodified experiences.

At the societal level, as we just saw, for Wang there may not be true ambivalence between tourists and their society. In the end, they can satisfy the drives of their Id while bolstering the social order in so doing. But when it comes to consumption, there lurks an industry ready to trump their erotic needs. How this ambivalence or contradiction operates remains an open question. At the lowest level, one might think that it would vanish if the industry lived up to its promises—for instance, when the services advertised in travel catalogs equal those provided at the destination. Being a bit more ambitious, one could propose that the industry stops offering commodities, which would need somewhat more elaborate reasons. Finally, one can suggest that consumers cast away the industry and the social order that supports it. As noted in the previous chapter, MacCannell, always lionhearted, would go for the latter. Much more cautious, Wang just wanders between the two first lines of action.

To understand why this is the case requires a detour along Wang's treatment of authenticity and commoditization. After a ritual acknowledgment of MacCannell, Wang demurs and informs us that the discussion of authenticity needs to be taken beyond its customary limits. Why? Because with so much referencing of it, MacCannell's authenticity has become increasingly polysemous. In a subdued way, Wang prods the reader from the epic of ego-against-the-system to the more limited and mundane goal of truth in advertising.

Some authors, including MacCannell, see authenticity as something that reveals the essence of an attraction or of an experience. Tourists would reach authenticity when they reach its inner truth or, more modestly, consume a genuine product, that is, the real thing or something that reproduces its essential features. The expression "This painting of a smiling androgynous individual I am seeing is Leonardo's work" points toward a real thing. Because of its technique, of some historical evidence and of other anecdotal corroboration, the portrait of Mona Lisa becomes the unique work of a historical individual that collective opinion has constructed as one of the Renaissance masters (Irving 1969).

This is the museum curator's gaze that Wang calls objective authenticity, and, in his view, produces a narrow definition of the issue. His reason is that if this was the authenticity people look for in their travels, they would be looking for an epistemological or bookish experience—how to relate their experiences to some originals or prototypes. For Wang, however, this would make the tourist experience gyrate around the object. To understand authenticity one needs a Copernican revolution. Authenticity does not depend on the objects or places visited, but on what tourists experience. One doubts that MacCannell would accept such cavalier dismissal of the objective impossibility moderns find themselves in to reach the innermost recesses of reality.

Why should objective authenticity not concern tourists? After all, a great part of their experiences harks back to it, and for solid economic reasons.

Attractions have a double objective value. One refers to price. Masterpieces of all kinds that we visit in museums are usually described as priceless or invaluable, but this does not mean that they do not have economic relevance; rather their price tag is usually astronomical. What we mean when using those adjectives is that their market value is difficult to assess not because they are invaluable, but because they are usually kept out of it. When they are on the block, they are extremely expensive but not priceless, though. "Walking Man I," a six-foot high bronze statue of a man cast by Alberto Giacometti in 1960, recently reached an all time record price of $104.3 million at an auction in London's Sotheby's in February 2010. The previous highest bid of $104.2 million bought "Boy with a Pipe," a 1906 painting by Picasso (Crow 2010). Their high prices are a function of their rarity, that is, of their scarcity and, in the case of individual masterpieces, of their uniqueness. There are not so many Leonardos around, therefore, as long as they are considered attributable to him, and as long as Leonardo maintains the esteem of opinion leaders and of informed consumers in the art world, their price will remain sky-high. However, there is a second type of economic relevance for the consumer himself. Masterworks may be copied, even reproduced mechanically, but there is only one Mona Lisa painted by Leonardo and it can be seen only at the Parisian Louvre. This is the authentic object people want to look at. And to experience its authenticity firsthand they are prepared to pay for a visit to the Louvre museum plus a trip to Paris. Consuming or gazing upon authentic objects does not come cheap.

For all the traps that surround the art market, objective authenticity is also possible beyond masterpieces created by individuals, as is the case with antiques that were serially produced and hence cannot be attributed to a known creator. If, while wandering about Hong Kong's Hollywood Road, I want to buy a pair of Lokapalas or a two-humped camel dating from the Tang Dynasty (or just enjoy myself viewing them), I may forever ignore who made them, but I can say that the one I want to buy or see has been certified as made in that period, thanks to some luminosity tests used by a legitimate agency. This makes them different from other similar ones, not easily distinguishable to the naked eye of the uninformed consumer. Therefore, I will buy them from the vendors that can provide such a certificate, and not from the knickknack shops a few yards down the street that stock similar but uncertified statuettes. And I will be right in considering them authentic Tang Dynasty pieces. Mine is an objectively authentic experience.

When it comes to goods produced serially in the present, objective authenticity becomes more complicated, but it is still possible. They can be easily counterfeited; that is, they may quickly lose their uniqueness. Without the intellectual property regulations that protect designer goods or labels such as AOC (*appellation d'origine controlée*) for French wines, or DOC (*denominazione d'origine controllata*) for Italian ones (both usually translated into English as CTO or *controlled term of origin*), it would be nearly impossible to know whether this Chablis or this Sangiovese you are drinking or the Louis Vuitton bag that you just bought is authentic. In this case, authentic means attributable to the grapes grown in Burgundy or in Tuscany or to the unique craftsmanship of the Vuitton factory. Once again the reason for valuing their authenticity has to do with economics. All these goods command high prices because they are relatively rare or scarce. If they are fakes, therefore more abundant, all similar goods, whether authentic or not, will sell for less. Consumers looking to value the money they pay will shun them. This is why it is necessary that they carry the markers of distinction just mentioned.

What to say of the quest, so dear to American lifestyle magazines, for the real *croissant*, the true Hanoian *phở*, or the best Japanese *sushi*? Most of these things can be had in many places and do not have an original with which they can be compared, but they are also scarce. Not so much in relation to their local versions, but to the transaction costs tourists pay to enjoy them in their alleged places of origin. Accordingly, they are relatively more expensive. So-called objective authenticity is thus not an impossible dream or something limited to a few and extremely rare pieces. Through the convoluted bonds between money, travel, and the social standing it provides to different consumers, visiting or consuming objectively authentic goods or services bestows an aura of superiority on some experiences. Nobody will taste again the evolved *kipferl* or *rugelach* that August Zang first cooked in his Parisian *Boulangerie Viennoise* at 92 Rue Richelieu after 1839 and became locally known as *croissants*. Today better *croissants*, that is to say, possibly closer to the original and therefore more authentic, can be found in some *patisseries* in Tokyo's Roppongi Hills than in most French *comptoirs*. However, people remain attached to the French version for it reminds them of their (Austrian) originals in Paris where they first became popular. Their objective experience will tell them that there is no place like France when it comes to *croissants*. *Phở* cannot be tasted any more at the old place in the corner of Nguyen Du and Hue streets in Hanoi; it has become a bank. Many locals, though, swore that it was the real place for real *phở*, and people would pay to go there. *Sushi* comes in many delicious shapes and sizes the world over, but tourists want to try it at *Uogashi Senryo* in the Tsukiji Market. When tourists eat *croissants* in Paris, or *phở* in Hanoi, or *sushi* in

Tokyo, their relative local scarcity confers a higher standing on them than if they can taste only their local Des Moines version. Objective authenticity, therefore, is not just a figment of the tourist's imagination.

Wang identifies a second type of authenticity—constructed authenticity. Here authentic is defined as the projections on toured attractions by tourists or tourism producers of their own expectations, images, preferences, etc. Constructed authenticity does not curry favor with Wang; he blames it for maintaining that there is no independent reality beyond the individual mind or the collective imaginary. Constructivism does not respect the correspondence between the mind and an exterior reality that has to be discovered. Multiple meanings of and about the same things become possible "and humankind may adopt different constructed meanings depending on the particular contextual situation or its inter-subjective setting" (2000:52). Objective authenticity escaped us because it could be applied only in quite limited occasions; constructed authenticity suffers the opposite condition, and worst of all, it can be overly manipulated by marketers. Deep down, Wang accepts constructivism only in a very limited way, which should put him at odds with the *pomo* persuasion.

So Wang introduces a third variant of authenticity. He calls it existential to distinguish it from the other two kinds—objective and construed authenticities. It is

> a potential existential state of Being that is to be activated by tourist activities. Correspondingly authentic experiences in tourism are to achieve this activated existential state of Being within the liminal process of tourism. Existential authenticity has little to do with the authenticity of toured objects (2000:49).

What counts is what the self experiences as authentic when it separates itself from dominant institutions and creates its own space by maintaining a balance between responsibilities and freedom, work and leisure, public roles and authentic self. Always cautious, Wang warns against feeding too much into the notion. It can be achieved only in liminal zones and times; existential authenticity cannot go as far as casting away and for good Logos, social order, routine, and norms. The tourists' existential authenticity is in the end homebound; like McArthur to the Philippines, they will return to the strictures of everyday life. Wang thinks that this notion provides tourists and researchers with a medium term between extremes. Authenticity would go halfway between tourism as liberation, on the one hand, and tourism as functionality on the other. One fears, though, that his tourist, like Buridan's donkey, might see the advantages of both liberation theologies but would perish indecisively unable to move and grab their riches.

More than a halfway house, Wang creates a puzzle. On the one hand, modernity imposes ambivalence on its denizens by the travails of Logos, rationality, production, and work. On the other, they protect themselves with the help of Eros, leisure, play, and tourism. However, the latter does and does not threaten the order of Logos. It is just a liminal space of freedom bound to fade away as soon as Logos runs the clock. Time is over and people go back to their former subjection, only a bit happier than at the beginning. In this way, the erotic pleasures that counter Logos shine as but Logos's own cunning. Liberation in the end begets subjection. Less dramatically and more clearly this is what the functionalist school used to say.

Free time thus becomes a prop for labor. People rest or vacation in order to work harder and better, all of which does not cut much ice as far as liberation goes. MacCannell railed against Urry's notion of liminal freedom for freedom either is an enduring and comforting state or is illusory. Therefore, Urry's and Wang's middle course is just the muddling course. As an aspiration to freedom, authenticity will be complete only when humans liberate themselves from their objective chains—the dominance of corporations; the capitalist economy; trading; in the end, the division of labor itself. Freedom and the humanity it conveys cannot be enjoyed in small doses, 2 weeks at a time per year or semester. One does not have to concur with MacCannell to know that he is right on the conclusion. What kind of liberation is it that can be granted and taken at will? By whose authority? Wang surmises that, ultimately, liberation is but an idle dream. Then why so much rhapsodizing about existential authenticity when Eros cannot finally count as a genuinely liberating force?

In truth, existential authenticity mostly serves as a contrivance to defang MacCannell's radical views on commoditization. Once again, one should remember that he denounced tourism for it has increasingly become a corporate by-product, but that was only for starters. Corporate production of tourism is but the latest innovation on the road to deprive modern-people-in-general of their humanity. The aim predates it, though. Whether knowingly or unwittingly, corporations only prolong the cant of ages. Only when commerce and, in the end, the division of labor wither away will people finally break free. One can agree with MacCannell or not, as is the case here, but no matter how patronizing and dystopian his ideas, they show a consistency and even a grandeur of design patently lacking in

Wang and many others that turn commoditization into a junior-league game. From mankind's Promethean drama, commoditization for them becomes the quest for the medium term. After all the critiques leveled against it, if constrained by a dose of congeniality, or of respect for the Other, or of any other well-meaning combination of words, tourism might still deserve redemption.

This is Wang's next discovery. Modernity, now assuming its proper name of modern capitalism, requests the commoditization of goods and labor. Both become interchangeable. You sell your labor to buy goods and services that you consume to keep on working, that is, to sell your labor force, get paid for it, and buy new goods and services that, as already seen, also include some vacation periods. Such is the predicament of modern-man-in-general. So goods, including one's own labor force, have turned into commodities? To some extent this is nothing modern. Commodities are goods produced with a view not to immediate consumption, but to be bartered or exchanged for money. In this way, commodity production predates modernity by many moons. It was found in Ancient Egypt, in Classical Greece, and under the Roman Empire. For many centuries it contributed a not insignificant amount to the Chinese economy under different dynasties. Limited commodity production added much to the well-being of those societies.

In one respect, Wang is right, though. The main difference between modernity and its premodern social forms hinges on what happened to labor—it has also become a commodity. This is a distinctive feature of modernity that crashes as a horrific hullabaloo in chaste postmodern ears. Let us go for a moment beyond their shock and awe to consider what "commodity" really means, taking a detour through Marx who is the originator of the idea of commodification. Initially, humans tended to their needs, as many other animal species do, by preying on others, eating carrion, or gathering weeds, vegetables, and fruits. Human labor was mostly hunting and gathering, and anthropologists have shown how many different types of society can exist under this label. At any rate, labor was collective, intermittent, and mostly oriented to immediate consumption. Over time, hunters and gatherers would also learn that it might be more profitable to make other humans work for them forcibly. Losers were taken as slaves and their women would bear the children of their new owners. Slavery forced all of the defeated men and women to work for their masters that in turn would provide them with the barest means of subsistence, such as food, clothing, and shelter. Slaves, like chattel, were the property of their overlords and as a rule could not leave them at will, just when sold to another slave owner.

Soon slavery became the most common type of labor, and it has been so for long periods of human history. It has not been completely rooted out yet.

Slavery was closely related to the Neolithic Revolution and the growth of agriculture. It helped to increase its productivity. In some parts of the world, agriculture was better developed later by other means—nominally free farmers. However, farmers needed protection from bandits and from competing landlords. In exchange for it, feudal lords in Europe and other areas charged them with rents and personal services. In China, they paid taxes to more efficient central bureaucracies. Most farmers became serfs, in principle free, but in reality bound to a land that they could not leave, even less sell, without the consent of their masters.

It is only recently that wage labor appeared under modern capitalism as Wang notes, following up on Marx. Modern salaried workers are not bound to the earth, nor forced to sell their labor. When they decide to work (and they would better do so in the majority of cases for only through work can they support themselves and eventually their families), they receive a salary with which to buy the goods, merchandise, or commodities needed for their survival. In this way, under modern capitalism, human labor has become another commodity. It did not happen so by accident or whim. A long process of trial and error (that indeed included much force and violence) showed that it was the technique most conductive to economic growth, so salaried labor has become gradually accepted in most parts of the world. One could think of other ways for societies to produce and reproduce themselves, but the attempts to implement them have been discouraging. Central planning and collectivization, at least in their socialist versions, did not work. They could not cope with a mobile labor force, nor increase significantly workers' standards of living, nor avoid routine and stagnation. All of this may explain the spread of salaried labor, that is, its commoditization.

Marx expected that the wage labor system would keep to a minimum the so-called consumption norm, that is, the batch of goods and services needed to reproduce workers and their families that they can buy with their salaries. However, once again by trial and error (including indeed much force and violence), the Logos in modern capitalism has expanded considerably that consumption norm. It reduced the working week; it increased take-home pay; it augmented disposable income, that is, the part of wages that can be spent in nonessential goods; it created a number of entitlements, from retirement benefits to health insurance to paid vacations. It made possible erotic gratification in the broad sense that Wang gives to the term. This is why so many millions can enjoy travel and tourism today. Modern Eros would be unthinkable without the commoditization of labor and, in general, of most goods and services—something usually left unnoticed by its *pomo* critics, but not by Marx.

MacCannell would have none of it, as we have seen. Better go back to an undefined state of happiness as hunters and gatherers. Wang and many other critics are stunted; they do not dare to go so far. They do not renege on the benefits of modern tourism; they just decry the unfulfilled promises that according to them capitalism has not brought about, its deficits not only in liberty, but especially in equality and fraternal love among humans, its lack of interest in the Other. This is what Wang calls the dark or repressed erotic side of modernity, and the reason why the search for existential authenticity requires a curb on Logos or, with more mundane lingo, commoditization. But how to curb Logos without also curbing the satisfaction of Eros that commoditization has made possible?

If Wang and other critics of mass tourism no longer demand its complete demise, what do they propose instead? Above all, a new and better understanding of the relation between hosts and guests, that is, a renegotiation of exoticism and of the Other. Since its inception, Western capitalist expansion did not only look at distant or exotic places as producers of coveted commodities such as spices or silk. It justified unequal or forced exchanges with the local populations in the name of the universal—and superior—model of civilization that merchants and missionaries brought along with them. The romantic view of exoticism changed that. Now the values and the lifestyles of different cultures were praised as equal or superior to Western ways. This new "orientalist" dispensation (Said 1979), however, did not call for the downfall of colonial goals. Somehow it served them better, for devotion to exoticism precluded any changes in traditional societies. The embrace of distant cultures thus choked them to death. Western capitalism was damned if it did and damned if it didn't.

These two views of exoticism, as per Wang, are not mutually exclusive; they often go hand in hand even today. When tourists react to the disappointing aspects of Western modernity, they often idealize exotic destinations as pristine locales where one can find noble savages, that is, cartoon people that should never disappoint the expectations they project on them. But as often happens, if they do not fulfill those expectations, tourists blame their recently exalted exotics for their barbarism and their backwardness. Once again Wang becomes too greedy. From a molehill in search of some evidence (that some tourists idealize their exotic objects of desire to turn against them when they behave in unanticipated ways), he makes a mountain—no matter how we look at it, modern tourism offers a distorted view of the exotic that, in the end, reflects its incapacity to understand it. The tourist gaze cannot get rid of its scarlet letter. It is always biased, as tourists structure their destinations in terms of binary cultural classifications (advanced vs. developing, civilized vs. primitive, white vs. black, and so on) provided by their own tourist cultures. "A tourist image is therefore a socially and culturally constructed utopian image" (2000:164). In other words, it is a stereotype. Said could not have said it better. Modern tourists being massively Westerners cannot ever get anything right. They always reduce the objects of their interests to banal or contrived remarks.

However, not all stereotypes, not even those of Western tourists, are created equal. *Merriam-Webster* defines stereotypes in two ways. One: "something repeated or reproduced without variation; something conforming to a fixed or general pattern and lacking individual distinguishing marks or qualities." Two: "a standardized mental picture held in common by members of a group and representing an oversimplified opinion, affective attitude, or uncritical judgment (as of a person, a race, an issue, or an event)" (*Merriam-Webster* 2002). In the first sense, all generic concepts, such as male, female, dog, tree, virtue, god, democracy, economy, eroticism, bread, that is, most of the words we use, are generic or stereotypes. Without them communication would be cumbersome and unnecessarily verbose. Picture yourself saying "the 27th day of the fourth month (Gregorian calendar) in the 2008 year of the Common Era the collective and fine threadlike strands that protrude from the skin of humans, and other mammals and mostly grow on the upper part of my body, stood on like the barbs of those nocturnal Old World insectivorous mammals that constitute the genus *Erinaceus* when I heard a quickly approaching, bark-emitting, compact, muscular, short-haired animal genus *canis familiaris* of a breed developed in England and used originally in bull baiting but now usually kept as a domestic pet," when you can simply say "yesterday I was horrified when I saw a barking bulldog running toward me." Stereotypes of this latter kind are good enough to express messages with a great economy of means. Otherwise people might take the speaker for another impossible Harvard don, and the speaker, reasonably, does not want this.

The second meaning conveys the notion of something simplified, contrived, or misleading, and this is what creeps into Wang's definition without further refinement. But it cannot be universally applied to tourist images. Can it really be that a Western tourist uses a utopian image when she says that she likes going to Madagascar because, as Wikipedia puts it, "[its] long isolation from the neighboring continents has resulted in a unique mix of plants and animals, many found nowhere else in the world"

(Wikipedia 2010a). This may be as socially and culturally constructed a notion as they come, but utopian, stereotyped?

Wang, however, does not bother to even think of the difference and how to let the reader know which is which. He needs this appanage so that his conclusions may ring true. For now we are coming close to the home stretch. Once one decrees that all tourist images are both socially constructed and utopian, it can be asserted that all destination images are contrived, commoditized, and can be done even by a toddler, especially when it comes to tourism promotion. An always-cautious Wang immediately distances himself, though, lest promoters or advertisers might feel hurt. What faces us here does not hark back to bad faith on their side or to a compulsion to lie. It is more encompassing. "The production of distorted images requires the complicity of the culture in which tourists find themselves" (2000:166). Once again, here either Wang refers to a platitudinous "my culture made me think like this," or else he has in mind a more specific culture, perhaps the one he calls modernity, which comes closer to his argument.

In premodern societies, travel was an adventurous experience, he says, while modernity has turned it into a form of leisure integrated into its consumer culture. Tourism has thus commodified travel, and made it into an intangible entity consisting of symbolic elements such as images and hedonistic experiences. Commoditization, as Weber reminds us, leads to rationalization that, under capitalism, can only spell maximum profit or, what amounts to the same, minimizing costs. Cost reduction brings about rational design, that is, standardized and routinized products, as epitomized in packaged tours. On the consumer side, standardization evokes value for money, which tracks satisfaction closely. A consumer who receives services according to her expectations becomes a satisfied consumer, possibly a repeat one, and the other way around. Finally, commoditization involves quantification or the skill to manage tourist experiences putting travel in the hands of organizers, that is, corporations such as tour operators or airlines that offer it key-in-hand to the consumer. What a weird argument!

Wang, first, generalizes. Before modernity, travel was not just an adventurous experience. It was a rather hazardous undertaking. Chaucer's pilgrims to Canterbury made their journeys in groups not because they thought that it was amusing and glamorous, but because highways were unsafe and overrun by bandits. However, it does not mean that ancient travel was always adventurous (with the happy excitement and the thrill that the adjective often connotes in today's parlance) while modern travel has become uneventful and colorless just because it is better organized and more predictable. Barring the odd terrorist, planes reach their destinations safely, sometimes even punctually. Apart from overbooking, hotels will keep your reservation. With the exception of accidents, most drivers will arrive safely at their destinations. Is this less adventurous or just more enjoyable? Does it prevent many people from being quite active or even from taking high risks during their vacations?

Travel in ancient times was also quite predictable. Pompey, Baiae and other Roman resorts offered to the elite leisure tantamount to what today's packaged tours offer to the masses—the so-called passive rest. Dwellings similar to our present second residences—not exactly the epitome of adventure—became the playgrounds of, again, some elites in Chang'an under the Tang Dynasty, Kaifeng under the Song Dynasty, or Hangzhou under the Yuan Dynasty. It is difficult to say whether the nature of travel in modern times is more adventurous when compared with former periods. It has definitely made it less problematic and more enjoyable for the consumer.

But, more importantly, Wang's argument attacks the wrong straw man. For Marx, commoditization meant exploitation (1972). By forcing workers to accept a minimal consumption norm, capitalists appropriated without compensation all the remaining value extracted from their work. He called this illegitimately appropriated part of their labor force "surplus value." This surplus value was the essence of capitalist benefits, the root of capitalist injustice, and, in the end, what would make the system itself meet its doom, a final outcome that will not be examined here. Wang does not think along these lines. His view of commoditization fits better with the ideas of some members of the Frankfurt School. A commodity is not a sign of exploitation but of mass production. The problem with commodities is not that they are an exploitative form of human relations, but that they are all equal, serially produced, and trite. Wang describes and critiques modern tourism in exactly the same way. It has become a commodity that people can buy if they have the money; it is designed and packaged efficiently so that services are predictable, reliable, and trivial; its organization is usually left to big corporations that offer similarly meaningless products; it morphs significant human relations into heaps of banal and hedonistic experiences. Ultimately, for Wang, commoditization is to be blamed for being in poor taste and inconsequential rather than for being unfair. It is a matter for the brow, whether high or low, not for rational argument and political advocacy as it was for Marx and, later, for the socialist and communist movements. If consumers had better taste and favored more exclusive products, or these were better designed, or more expensive, commoditization would have less room to hold sway.

This conclusion cannot stand. It is a statistical oxymoron to expect that all consumers will have above-average taste. Moreover, it has unexpected consequences. Marx provided some evidence for his views on how and why commoditization would, in the end, doom capitalism. He was wrong, but one can discuss his arguments knowing their meaning. Conversely, postmodern commoditization is unfathomable. It is a matter of taste, and taste, indeed, always skulks in the eye of the beholder. In a startling exercise of that constructed objectivity he criticized, Wang suggests that when many beholders coincide in their views, one should accept them as the truth. *Eppure si muove* or "show the evidence, not your mainstream consensus" (one's own very free translation) was all Galileo had to say in a similar case.

While tourists demand existential authenticity, commoditizing Logos pounds their hopes unremittingly. Something similar happens to providers of tourist goods. On the one hand, tourist income offers them a way out of the stagnation of traditional societies; on the other, they have to pay the ransom of success. The demands of external agents, who do not even balk at the worst excesses, degrade their cultures and their environment.

> With the globalization of tourism consumer culture, namely the global extension of the reach of tourism, many Third World countries join in with the touristification of their cultures, people, and environments. However, due to a relatively weak position in international competition, a "dehumanizing" form of tourism, i.e., sex tourism, particularly child prostitution, appears in a number of Third World countries such as some in South East Asia (Wang 2000:199).

If the figures quoted in Chapter 2 have any value, these conclusions amount to overblown grandstanding. Modern tourism, even if unduly restricted to international tourism, does not for the greater part involve a relation between developed and traditional societies. It is only marginally a North/South affair. As already noted, most tourism is domestic; it happens in the home country. Most international travel takes place between developed or affluent countries. Additionally, the most recent expansion of capitalism, also known as globalization, has turned traditionally receptive destinations into quickly growing generators of international travel. That "[tourism] is an encounter between the agents of modernized society and the agents of developing society [*sic*]" (2000:221) shines as a figment of Wang's imagination. For its part, sex tourism is indeed a theoretical quicksand

(Chapter 6), but charging venal sex and white slavery exclusively on tourism's account is a fallacy. In Asia and in other continents it predates tourism by far. If at all, sex tourists may have made it more visible, perhaps somewhat more widespread; they did not cut it from new cloth (Chapter 6).

Wang, however, speeds up as the Promised Land beckons. Though not an easy task, he says, commoditization may be duly neutered by reducing the ambivalence of travel and leisure for both consumers and providers, which after all the weight accorded to ambivalence in the noxious development of commoditization comes as an awkward inference. After warning of modernity's ambivalence, of its distortions to the needs of its denizens, of the havoc wreaked over Third World destinations, prophetic determination suddenly abandons Wang. If one thought that he would propose a ban or strong restrictions on tourism to favor the alleged interests of consumers and providers, one would be wrong.

> What is at stake here is not whether tourism should be developed, but rather *how* it should be developed, and how its problematic consequences can be prevented [...] If tourism is the result of people's cultural reaction to the existential conditions of modernity and globalization, then, "alternative tourism" is the result of people's (both tourists' and suppliers') critical response to the negative consequences and impact of mass tourism (2000:222).

Now for the final stage. Being a cultural construct, modernity should be amenable to reformation. Who will enact it? It is a mission shared by all and sundry. Above all, with Weberian overtones, Wang recommends that entrepreneurs and brokers discard the dominance of earnings in order to embrace responsible ethics. They should be allowed to pursue profit, but profit should be subordinated to the interests of tourists, local people, and the environment. This, after all of Wang's tirades against the merchants of commoditization, does not come easy. The reader who has been treated to a short course on the necessary relation between capitalism, modernity, commoditization, and destination mismanagement is now invited to accept that, with the right prodding, entrepreneurs and brokers can be converted to the new vision of responsibility and humanistic concerns. It rather sounds like a case of letting some fake eunuchs loose in the Forbidden City expecting that they will only make the imperial concubines a little pregnant.

The ever-cautious Wang, therefore, keeps a final trump card up his sleeve. Oftentimes markets do not care about humanistic concerns and local providers are sacrificed to the interests of the consumer or they are too weak to advance their own. The state should then step in and fill the gap.

> Tourism development is thus not merely an economic issue; it is often a political issue [...] To ensure that [tourism] becomes a game in which everybody wins, an ethic of responsibility and humanistic concern must be adopted by governments and embodied in public policy [...] The development of humanistic and responsible tourism will help tourists to satisfy their desires in response to the "modernity problematic," and the host community to benefit from tourism under the condition of globalization (2000:224).

It sounds quite beautiful, but a skeptic might think that without appropriate qualifications, Wang's interventionist dream might yield a case of the same dogs *and* the same collars. Can one seriously expect that this role will be fairly played by many a Third World kleptocratic government not responsible to their people because they either do not heed democratic procedures or openly rebut them? Going a rung down the ladder, what makes him think that local communities and their governments will not experience the gale of interests that oppose the powerful and the dispossessed, those who benefit from tourism and those who do not, local entrepreneurs and the local labor force? Reaching win–win results needs more analysis and more thoughtful solutions than highfalutin bromides about responsible tourism and the end of commoditization.

LIBERATION THEOLOGY. ACT FOUR: BELEAGUERED MASSES RATHER STAY AWAY

Cohen has never concealed his esteem for McCannell and his contribution to tourism research. Quite early (1980), he saluted his discussion of tourism as one of the three main currents in the qualitative sociology of tourism, Boorstin's and Turner's being the other two. MacCannell, he noted, had established a crucial link between the study of tourism and that of modernity, thus pushing the former toward the core of the latter's interests, and providing a basic paradigm for tourism research that has occupied the academic scene since the last quarter of the 20th century. The paradigm, known today to even the freshmen cohorts in tourism studies, is synthesized in one word—"authenticity." In Cohen's view, this "stunningly innovative" approach (2004a:120) means that alienated as he is from his shallow world, the tourist looks for authenticity in other times and other places. Cohen has often repeated similar judgments in the 20 years since he first made them (2004a, 2007).

This endorsement comes with a lethal qualification, though. When others tried to make it operative, "[t]he mass of tourists turned out to be neither alienated nor in practice pursuing authenticity" (Cohen 2004a:3). And one cannot but scratch one's head and wonder whether MacCannell's stunningly innovative approach amounts to another case of much ado about nothing, or whether Cohen misinterprets him. When it comes to empirical verification, one can agree that authenticity is burdened with such a Babel of meanings that its users often talk in mutually exclusive tongues (Reisinger and Steiner 2006; Steiner and Reisinger 2006). Cohen rightly notes that tourism is a fuzzy concept usually surrounded by verbal mist. "Different kinds of people may desire different modes of touristic experience; hence 'the tourist' does not exist as a type" (Cohen 2004a:66). One cannot just draw it with a brush that fits all strokes; one should instead classify its epiphanies, and see how many there are and why they appear.

Accordingly and for his part, Cohen has conducted a meticulous analysis. From his earliest writings on the subject, he veered away from stereotypes, looking for a better definition of different types of tourism and showing the variety of tourist roles, why some people prefer to become nomads from affluence, or how recreational tourists behave (2004a:17–36, 37–47, 49–63, 87–99). If he was true to his initial hunch that we have to go beyond single causes in explaining something as complex as tourism behavior, Cohen should have parted ways with MacCannell and his authenticity long ago and for good. However, he comes back to it with the tenacity of a candle-circling moth. Even in what seems a postmortem for authenticity, Cohen cannot remove it from his mind.

> Contemporary tourism may appear to be moving into the "post-authentic" age, but authenticity is lurking beneath the surfaces of post-modern attractions, though in an inverted, and in the eyes of some, perverted guise (2007:81).

Why this lingering obsession? His views on the "Phenomenology of Tourist Experiences" (2004a:65–85) may provide some explanation.

He starts with a nod to phenomenology reminding the reader of the importance of the "center." The notion has entered sociological theory from different sides. Eliade made it the cornerstone of religious experiences and institutions. The center is the eschatological point where heaven, Earth, and hell meet. Shils extended the notion to secular societies—they are all organized around a center where their supreme values and their basic agencies are symbolically structured (the monarch, the flag, the constitution, an icon as Uncle Sam, John Bull or Marianne of the Phrygian Cap). The Durkheim/Parsons tradition in sociology also sees the center as the core values that all members of a group consensually share. In this way, each individual has a socially or communally provided center that he or she accepts, thus solving in one fell swoop the Hobbesian problem of social order.

Cohen accepts the notion with a twist. Far from being central, tourism, as a recreational activity, involves a temporary separation from the center. "This means that tourism is essentially a temporary reversal of everyday activities" (2004a:67). Therefore, it only has peripheral significance on personal biographies, and Cohen does not rhapsodize much about this Turnerian aphorism. However, not all individuals accept their societal core. They are eccentric or alienated from their center, and this is what really needs an explanation in general sociology and in tourism research.

Traditional societies did not feel the urge to travel as much as modern ones do. Following Eliade, Cohen recalls that primitive people had no reason to leave their own life space. Their world was well ordered, a cosmos, while, beyond, chaos skulked. Why venture out? Later on, as pilgrimages developed, the relation changed. A pilgrim leaves the profane periphery to reach the sacred center of a religious cosmos bigger than his own community. Salvation makes his adventure worthy. Modern tourism does not coincide with any one of these two experiences; rather it reverses them, for tourism means traveling from the cultural center toward the periphery. Depending on how this disconnection works, one can think of five types or modes of tourism.

The first is recreational. While the traditional pilgrim is "re-created" in his quest for the center, the recreational tourist just wants recreation, that is, entertainment that will restore his physical and mental energy, and offer a feeling of well-being. Recreational tourists belong to Boorstin's book—they easily content themselves with pseudoevents. For them, travel becomes a safety valve to relieve stress and hardship. They rightly belong to the functionalist cocoon. Next come the diversionary tourists, who receive little sympathy from Cohen. Inasmuch as they do not look for a meaning to their lives, diversionary tourists are centerless persons reveling in meaningless pleasures. In the final analysis, these two types of tourism are barely indistinguishable. Their only difference lies on the vantage point from which we gaze at them. If one supposes that these tourists are not alienated, but firmly adhering to Western values, one can think of them as recreational. If they are seen as alienated, then their travel reflects the anomie prevailing in modern society and they become diversionary. One could say that these two features (alienation and anomie) are different things and that while the former is predicated of societies, the latter mostly affects individuals. However, the distance between the two is not insuperable. In Marx, the unfair distribution of ownership and power creates an alienated social framework that shapes the individual maladjustment of people in both the upper and the lower class. In Durkheim, individuals experience anomie because, for different reasons, they cannot cope with the strictures that their societies impose on them.

There are other, deeper modes of experiencing tourism. Third comes the experiential mode. Alienated individuals become aware of "the meaninglessness and fatuity of their daily life" (Cohen 2004a:73), and they try to put themselves together by either transforming their society through deep changes and/or revolutions, or in a less radical alternative, they look for meaning in the life of others. Experiential tourists move in brackish waters, dithering between going back home as tourists or remaining in their destinations and becoming nomads from affluence. A little further on, one finds the experimental mode. These tourists have already lost all sense of belonging to their societal center and want to get out of it. They may do it through tourism, but also through mysticism or through drugs. Finally existential tourists appear. They are fully committed to a different center; they have cast away their linkages to their previous home society and elected to be part of a different one. They do not come in one single format either. On one side, the exile becomes in fact a member of a different society; he has recentered himself. On the other, there are people who still live in their societies of origin, but their minds and hearts no longer belong there. They conform to the prevailing social norms but are permanently on the lookout for their elected new homeland and travel frequently to it.

This open-ended classification has a clear superiority over the usually binary fixation between tourists who partake of the extraordinary life made possible by the stopgap in work and the rest of people who limit themselves to their ordinary working lives. MacCannell's tourist as modern-man-in-general has too broad a reach, while each one on his stand, Jafari, Ryan, and Wang, cannot break free from a category that embraces too many disparate types of behavior. In doing so, they all adopt a reductionist outlook that has serious difficulty in accommodating the vicissitudes of the world as we know it.

One should not mistake this typology of tourist deportment with another one also proposed by Cohen in an attempt to understand the sociology of international tourism. There he looks at tourism from the continuum novelty/familiarity and its intermediate stages. The first one is organized mass tourism. This is the least adventurous type, usually buyers of packaged tours that keep them inside a bubble when they reach their destination of choice. Familiarity is at a maximum, novelty at a minimum. Next is the individual mass tourist. Here the tourist has some control over the itinerary but still remains inside her tourist bubble. Familiarity dominates, but there is some space to appreciate novelty. The explorer organizes her own trip, opening herself to more novelty; she tries her best to get off the beaten track. However, this tourist still does not completely immerse herself in her destination. The final stage is the drifter. She not only veers off the beaten track, but also tries to live the same way as her hosts. Here novelty permeates everything—travel arrangements, choice of accommodation, the itinerary, modes of transportation, length of stay.

Drifters and explorers, the two noninstitutionalized types of tourism, are the ones who dare tread unknown ground. They often overlap, but one finds some shades and contrasts in their behavior, though mostly in degree. Explorers associate with the people they visit; some even try to speak their language; however, they avoid a complete immersion in the foreign culture. They look for comfortable accommodation and reliable means of transportation. In this way, they remind the observer of the travelers of yore, thus extending their lineage to the Grand Tour.

Drifters have a more modern streak. They are children of affluence fancying a break with it. Usually they take advantage of a gap year between the end of higher education and work. "He prolongs his moratorium by moving around the world in search of new experiences, radically different from these he has been accustomed to in his shared middle-class existence" (Cohen 2004a:44). One might say that they are the spitting image of Ryan's Shirley Valentines, but Cohen does not allow himself so much latitude. Most drifters frown on endless discovery and everlasting liberation. "After he has savored these experiences for a time he usually settles down to an orderly middle-class career" (2004a:44). Many Shirleys often became reincarnated as the ultimate yuppie.

Organized and individual institutionalized tourism lie at the opposite end. They cannot thrive without the mass industry that processes them efficiently.

Efficient here means that the experience they provide will be predictable and regulated, leaving aside risks and uncertainties. The main purpose of mass tourism is to visit attractions whether genuine or contrived. "Contrived" is an adjective one often finds in Cohen. It usually means that attractions must be "suitably" organized for mass consumption, a feature so basic in mass tourism that it even engulfs genuine or authentic attractions. "They are supplied with facilities, reconstructed, landscaped, cleansed of unsuitable elements, staged, managed and otherwise organized" (2004a:41). This need for the least common denominator deprives institutionalized tourism of the taste for the genuine, the spontaneous, the authentic. Its attractions are contrived and tourists are fed the staged authenticity MacCannell decried. As one could expect, Cohen finds its epitome in the different Disney theme parks that have sprouted up all over the world, although he notes that they are not the only places where contrivance thrives. However, staged authenticity predates modernity. "Newfangled devices and fantasy rides have been common offerings at popular fairs for many years" (2004a:138). The difference lies in technology (less primitive in theme parks), in reach (Disney theme parks have become international), in the type of experience (less realistic in old fairs), and indeed, in the providers (theme parks are the brainchild of the tourist industry).

Organization controls novelty and helps attractions to appear familiar to the tourists. The industry looks for attractions and facilities that accommodate the needs of mass tourists and, as they usually originate in Western countries and Japan (a refinement, by the way, Cohen was among the first to introduce), Western-style infrastructures mushroom in even the poorest of host countries.

> However, since the tourist also expects some local flavor or signs of foreignness in his environment, there are local decorations in his hotel rooms, local foods in the restaurants, local products in the tourist shops. Still, even these are often standardized: the decorations are made to resemble the standard image of that culture's art, the local foods are made more palatable to unaccustomed tongues, the selection of native crafts is determined by the demands of the tourist (2004b:41).

All this separates the final product from the local cultures, thus making possible for the tourist to travel in a world of his own, surrounded by but not integrated in the host society. Hence that, promotional literature to the contrary notwithstanding, communication between the cultures of the tourists and those of their destinations does not flow. Instead of destroying myths, institutionalized tourism perpetuates them.

The progression among the four types of international travelers often looks as the vector of tourism development in reverse. Explorers and drifters find places off the beaten track and thus put them in the crosshairs of the industry. Once it finds them and makes them suitable for greater numbers of tourists, the flow of institutionalized tourism, mass and individual, is ready to include more destinations in its reach. In this way the number of contrived or staged attractions will grow considerably. However, one can see an upside in this development, as staged attractions may deflect the interest of tourists toward themselves, thus preventing them from interloping in the life and culture of their communities. At any rate, and for reasons to be developed later, Cohen does not devote much time to the study of institutionalized tourism and one suspects that in fact neither of its varieties (mass or individual) interests him very much.

For Cohen, nomads from affluence are more intriguing. Enter the backpackers. At the time he was writing, their wandering had changed from a minor phenomenon into one of the prevalent trends of contemporary tourism. The trend partially reflected what then used to be called the counterculture, that is, a challenge to the mainstream cultural norms of most Western societies. It came in many shapes, ranging from disregard for what were traditionally known as good manners to confrontations with the more basic rules of family life, private property, or even "the system" in general and its repressive tolerance.

> [O]n the other hand, however, though originally a reaction against routinized forms of travel, it also became institutio-nalized on a level completely segregated from, but parallel to that of ordinary mass tourism (2004b:49).

Institutionalization of drifter travel appeared in different ways. While initially itineraries revolved around free itineraries and no fixed timetables, "routes" that most practitioners closely followed went together with the inception of mass backpacking. While original drifters could not care less for must-see attractions, backpackers soon coalesced around the worth-a-visit places selected in niche guidebooks, "the hallmark of sedate, middle class tourism" (Cohen 2004a:55). *Lonely Planet* would later be recognized as the backpacker's Bible (Chapter 9). The next step would be the creation of specialized infrastructure to cater to these tourists—cheap and specialized transportation systems, hostels and restaurants, special shops and night-spots. A bit yonder some areas in different destinations specialized as drifter communities. Finally, keeping apace with growth, the drifter movement spawned its own inner strands—the "adventurer" or original drifter; the "itinerant hippy," drifting aimlessly from one hippy community to the other; the "mass-drifter," a transient sort mostly interested in cheap lodgings, eateries, and low-cost airfares; the "fellow traveler" or reluctant hippies that occasionally flirt with hard-core countercultures.

Distancing himself from his original environment, like Stevenson coming finally of age in Samoa, or Gauguin among the Tahiti Wahines, or Thoreau in the woods of Walden Pond, or Kerouac's endless sauntering of the Big Sur, was the drifter's prime mover on the road to self-awareness. This inner pilgrimage was often accompanied by travel (*I Wonder as I Wander*, the aptly titled memories of Langston Hughes, encapsulated the usual order of things that Ryan got backward in his Shirley Valentine caption). The drifter would often settle among the people of her elected new abode and live among them, tying a host–guest bond. Happiness is seldom total, though. Often locals would not understand their new guests' fancies—"only weirdos would willingly pass up on affluent life"—and saw them as "cultural pollution" to, later, ostracize them. Tourism in all its forms does not unfailingly translate into seamless cross-communication.

Cohen shows a similar restraint in rushing to judgments on the signal issue of authenticity and commoditization. Authenticity is usually seen as a univocal concept, but this contention lies far off the mark. Although he distances himself from what Wang would later call objective authenticity, he shies away from a purist, museum-inspired definition oriented and from the anthropological tendency to find it in exclusively premodern settings. Both impose more restrictive criteria to demarcate it than those of the ordinary tourist. "Tourists indeed appear to seek authenticity in varying degrees of intensity, depending on the degree of their alienation from modernity" (Cohen 2004a:106). The less aware of their alienation, the more tourists will accept the authenticity of the products offered to them. Therefore, authenticity will summon different degrees of intensity than usually acknowledged.

Something similar happens to commoditization. Sweeping dismissals of it, like Greenwood's (1977) study of Fuenterrabía's (aka Hondarribia in Basque) *Alarde* festival, smack of overgeneralization. Indeed, foreign entrepreneurs frequently market tourist-oriented goods and services, thus opening a flank to the charge of exploitation of their local producers.

But production with a view to monetary exchange does not preclude authenticity necessarily. Local gamelans playing for a tourist audience in Bali or Java may appear to an external observer as changing the cultural meaning of their performance, while the players may perceive it as in continuity with their tradition. In a nutshell, "[c]ommoditization does not necessarily destroy the meaning of cultural products, neither for the locals nor for the tourists, although it may do so under certain conditions" (2004a:113).

Cohen seldom falls for easy solutions. His unbending respect for facts highly contributes to the quality, not to mention the honesty of his work. Occasionally, though, he makes a few exceptions, and a few passing remarks leave a heavy aftertaste. It is difficult to blame the tourist bubble, as he does, for the tourists' isolation from local cultures when they and not the residents are allowed exclusive access to some goods or services, as was the case in the dollar stores of the former Soviet Union or is in present-day Cuba. Here, the bubble should more fairly fall on the rigid governmental control of foreign trade, not on the institutionalization imposed by the mass tourism industry. Even more difficult to swallow appears the contention that cross-cultural miscommunication be pinned down on "[n]ot knowing the [local] language [which] makes forming acquaintances with natives and traveling about on one's own so difficult that few tourists attempt it to any extent" (2004a:43). Mainstream academic literature imposes many surprising demands on the behavior of tourists, but this one exceeds the average. Why should tourists be accomplished linguists? Should they be required to speak Mandarin plus all the languages of the 25 minorities that live there when traveling to Yunnan province in China or high Vietnamese plus the many tongues of the highlanders in their visits to Sa Pa? Should international travel remain the exclusive turf of the few anthropologists-cum-linguists, if any, with a rock-hard grasp of the local folkways as well as profuse verbal skills?

These minor slips of the tongue seem to reflect a perhaps unconscious but clearly conspicuous mistrust of MMT on Cohen's side. In spite of his many fair and qualified pronouncements on most subjects, he looks unable to repress his ultimate scorn for it. One might blame it on the share of Weberian pessimism that pervades his views. An ebullient growth of bureaucracy accompanied modernity's ascent. As much as it imposes increasing doses of formal rationalization, or perhaps just because of it, modernity forges an iron cage for freedom and creativity. The more human activities fall under state or corporate bureaucracies, the more their meaning is lost. Increasingly, modern societies and the lives of their denizens become banal and purposeless. The fate of tourism is no different. Recreational and/

or diversionary tourism, which are but divergent ways of conceptualizing the same phenomenon, cannot divest themselves of their lack of real interest in their destinations and their local inhabitants. Even newly minted drifters, also known as backpackers, share the same liability. They wind up by aping the excesses of mass tourism.

Will there not be 50, 30, 20, not even 10 righteous people in Sodom? Cohen seems as flintily unmoved as the God of Abraham. In the end, tourism speeds the pace of human doom. All his fair distinctions notwithstanding, Cohen's guilty verdict stays by default, and with little margin for escape. He does not share MacCannell's foolhardiness. Modernity and mass tourism are here to stay, and with their expansion, the chances for cross-cultural understanding will dwindle. Little by little, though steadily, freedom and creativity march toward their sunset. Perhaps Cohen is just a well-informed optimist, as the joke goes. Unfortunately the answer to that riddle must be postponed until after the world comes to an end. Let us be patient. Within a few billion years, perhaps even sooner (Chapter 9), we will be able to ponder whether Weber and Cohen were right. In between, there are other sides to his views more amenable to debate. One harks back to facts, the other to interpretation.

Cohen views tourism through a dark looking glass. Countless times he restricts its span to the regrettably incomplete dimension of international flows so dear to most tourism researchers. Not only is tourism international; it travels a one-way road—West to East, or North to South. Old anti-imperialist wisdom dies hard. Or, at least, it clouds the landscape beyond recognition. One can understand that of the few data on tourism in the public-domain UNWTO, figures on international arrivals do have a lot of sex appeal; one can absolve the anthropologist for feeling more at ease when waddling on cross-cultural exchanges, but there is no need to swallow that one and/or the other mark the confines of tourism behavior. Most people move within their own countries and within their own cultures. Increasingly tourists are not Caucasian (if one excuses this misleading adjective) and they do travel in multiple directions. Why is the literature on the Indian traveler or on the Chinese gaze so stunted? For all his impressive contributions to the study of tourism in general and particularly in Thailand, how can one explain that, with some exceptions (1995, 2000, 2008), Thai tourists do not stir Cohen's—or anybody else's—imagination?

Now for the underlying structural argument that mass tourism is banal and meaningless. Here it can be counterargued that many people flock to the contrived attractions they buy and eagerly enjoy their staged authenticity. Why? The explanation might lie in that they do not know what they are doing. Cohen more than once hints so. Most mass tourists (recreational and diversionary ones mostly but also backpackers and other nomads from affluence) know less about their own alienation than the museum curator or the anthropologist, so they content themselves with skin-deep experiences. However, in the absence of an accurate depth-o-meter, comparing the banality endurance of social categories seems either a risky task or a phenomenological outreach. When one remembers that Cohen endorsed Wang's notion of existential authenticity, the argument seems even more tenuous. Although Wang massages it to that normative mishmash he calls responsible tourism, if taken seriously, existential authenticity amounts to but another name for the incommensurability of individual experiences.

Cohen has a less oppressive view of commoditization than most users; for him it comes in many flavors—a wholly commendable nuance. Unfortunately, his notion stops at the outer reaches of the process. What makes a commodity out of a cultural creation is not that it is produced by wage labor, but its seriality. The package tours mass tourists consume exclude novelty or reduce it to a minimum. They imprison their end users in a bubble that frustrates the main reason for travel—getting to know other places, other people, other cultures. Additionally, corporations invest a lot of money in making travel available for all and sundry and foist increasing levels of standardization and contrivance on their products. Cohen, however, does not criticize them for their allegedly exploitative ways. What comes on top for him is the Frankfurtian critique of modern production, later trotted out by Wang, as a loss of the aura that surrounds original creations and genuine experiences.

In this way, one can say that Cohen finally finds his place in the qualitative sociology of tourism that he was among the first to study. Of the three corners of its basic triangle (MacCannell, Turner, and Boorstin), Cohen does not share MacCannell's prophetic zeal nor the audacity of his hopes, and he is wary of Turner's optimism that promises liberationist pie in the sky to all those ready to jump out of ordinary life, in play or in vacations. One dares say that his fatalist phenomenology cannot host any credibility for the eruption of the liminoid as an institutional agency of modernity and that Turner did not exclude anybody from this eventual enjoyment. Cohen suggests that most people, at least when it comes to travel, will never know how to appreciate it. Like Ortega y Gasset, like Adorno (*quello vecchio signore un po' démodé* [that slightly old-fashioned gentleman] in Galvano della Volpe's words), like Boorstin, if there is anything Cohen finds difficult to forgive in modernity, it is its tolerance for the least common denominator so dear to the masses.

Chapter 6

Paleface Does Southeast Asia

EPIPHANIES

The postmodern (*pomo*) methodological matrix probed in Chapters 3, 4, and 5 has undergone countless adaptations in the field of case-oriented tourism research. Not all of them are worthy of their models, which are often distorted in the translation, nor careful enough to follow up on their logical consequences. However, the field keeps on generating new research that relies on *pomo* mainstream wisdom. This chapter and the following ones to the end of the book will track some of its different sequels in a number of research areas: sex tourism, role of identities, languages of tourism, and proposed developmental alternatives to modern mass tourism (MMT).

This chapter starts with a couple of experiences. The first is totally mine. In the summer of 2002, the first night of my stay in Hanoi, I saw in the hall of my hotel an advertisement for a karaoke bar located in the basement. I made a mental note to visit it some time, as I was curious to see how such a quintessential Japanese institution would look like in the heart of Vietnam. A few days later I went to have a look. It was not easy for the lights were dimmed to barely a glimmer. When my eyes got used to it, the picture was totally different from what I imagined. The bar was reached through a long corridor with a bench on each side. Seating close to each other was a sizeable number of young women dressed in night gowns who would respectfully stand up and sit down, with the *Mexican wave* movement of soccer stadiums, every time one or more men walked past them. Except for the smart-clad girls, there were no other women in the place. Once I sat at a table, another woman, neither as young nor as attractive as the rest, appeared from nowhere and accosted me. She said she was one of the in-house *mama-san* and offered me a menu with three basic options: one bottle of whisky (US$80); one bottle of whisky and one escort ($100); one bottle of whisky and two escorts ($120). *Mama-san* also explained in her broken English that prices only included the company of the selected girl(s) in one of the place's secluded singing lounges. Explicit sexual activity was forbidden on the premises, but would it be my pleasure, I could take one or two women with me to one of the hotel rooms or anywhere else for a tag of $60 for two hours or $80 for the night.

Back on campus a few weeks later, I commented on the anecdote with a colleague. He had visited Beijing that summer and had had a similar experience there. Similar hotel, similar karaoke, similar bar, young women similarly dressed, and similar explanations from the local *mama-san*. Prices were the only difference. In China's capital, girls charged $30 per escort hour, $200 for two hours in the room, and $250 for the night.

Neither of these two events might be called an epiphany. If at all, an occasion to ponder that one of the oldest trades in the world was alive in the capital cities of two self-styled socialist countries, or on the vagaries of purchasing power parities for the same type of services in different locations. The epiphany lay elsewhere. My colleague and I had recently discussed a newly published book dealing with sex tourism, where one could read that the institutionalization of sex tourism in Southeast Asia was related to American military interventionism in Vietnam. In this way, prostitution became part of the international tourism industry and an integral component of national and international development (Ryan and Hall 2001:136). This was the real epiphany. To our knowledge neither Hanoi nor Beijing had been locations for American bases. Additionally the majority of tourists to those two cities are not Westerners, but Asians. How could American soldiers or Western tourists be major causes of a sex industry that was so conspicuous in both cities and in many others? On the other hand, for many years there has been a considerable number of American bases in Japan and this country was the cradle of a potent imperialist movement. How is it that those two factors, apparently so powerful in the emergence of sex tourism in other countries of Asia, have failed to turn Tokyo, Osaka, or Kyoto into meccas of international sex tourism? Why should anybody in his sane mind doubt that sex tourism could be a strategic sector for the development of the Japanese economy, as would have been the case had the Ryan-Hall hypothesis had any factual basis?

Before any discussion starts, however, one should warn that sex tourism, at least for the time being, cannot be satisfactorily researched. There is, to begin with, the messy confusion many researchers have turned it into. Some see it as a continuum of sexual activities undertaken at vacation time, from more frequent encounters between stable partners through increased availability of occasional sex to frequenting prostitutes (Bauer and

McKercher 2003). There is limited evidence of some link between vacationing and higher sex activity among reduced samples of people from some given nationalities, age-groups, and cultures (Oppermann 1998; Selänniemi 2003). For others, sex tourism is none of those animals. This shade of tourism is more specific and should relate to trips whose main goal is to engage in sexual relations with prostitutes, whether men or women or transsexual; whether consensual or forced; whether beyond the age of consent or underage. In the real world, there is indeed no Chinese Wall between these latter different types of sexual behavior (Cohen 1993), but one should keep things inside acknowledged boundaries in order to avoid unnecessary mistakes in a field where the lack of reliable data all too often feeds exaggeration, irrelevant notions, and morality tales.

Unfortunately, more than just being unreliable, data are frequently nonexistent; therefore, hard evidence is most of the time elusive. Even where prostitution is legal or finds ample social tolerance, serious research projects are few and far between. Many countries, especially among those used to exemplify the ravages of sex tourism, do not gather statistics on the sex industry; hypotheses tend to be based on limited observations; and conclusions regularly exhibit the moral, religious, or ideological self-righteousness of their authors. Last but not least, sex tourism has become a black hole where sex slavery, child prostitution, and consensual sex are often bound together (Wang 2000).

All of the foregoing remarks advise us to approach the issue with large doses of humility and an acknowledgment of our limits. This chapter cannot be an exception. It does not present a concrete research project—rather some skeptical comments on those who claim to have solved the issue once and for all. It is also a critical reflection on the low quality of mainstream academic research on the topic, and its penchant for neo-romantic visions. Additionally remarks will be restricted to only one dimension of sex tourism, though the most salient—heterosexual and consensual. Finally the quest will also confine itself geographically, as it will only discuss the literature on some countries that have become the target of academic research, such as those of East Asia, even though there are many other venues for this type of tourism—Rio de Janeiro, Havana, Mombasa, among others. However, it is East and Southeast Asia that most academic literature focuses on, with Thailand and Bangkok being the center of attention (Bishop and Robinson 1998; Ghosh 2002; Jeffrey 2002; Leheny 1995; Seabrook 1996; Truong 1990).

Barring some notable exceptions (Askew 1998, 1999a, 1999b, 2002; Boonchalaksi and Guest 1998; Cohen 1980, 1982, 1993, 2000, 2001a), their conventional wisdom has formulated what one might call The Iron Laws of Sex Tourism. To wit:

- Sex tourism in East and Southeast Asia should be explained by nearby causes, not by the traditional family structures widely extended in the region.
- There is a vector leading from the presence of US or colonial troops to present-day demand for sex tourism by Western tourists (Hall 1992; Sitthirak 1995).
- Sex tourism is an integral part of the strategy for economic hegemony imposed on the region by big corporations and global bureaucracies (World Bank, International Monetory Fund [IMF]) in collusion with the interests of the Northern or developed countries.
- Alternately or additionally, sex tourism paves the way for the production and reproduction of Western cultural hegemony and the subordination of regional cultures.
- By implication, those laws equally apply in other areas of the planet that are magnets for sex tourists.
- In a nutshell, through prostitution and sex tourism, Paleface encourages Asia (and other areas) to impose his idea of social order and to subordinate the region and the world to his interests and his cultural hegemony.

Really?

PROSTITUTION, ARMIES, AND LOCAL TRADITIONS

The view that sex tourism in East and Southeast Asia is a contemporary phenomenon seems quite right. It could hardly be otherwise when mass tourism, of which sex tourism is but a part, has been in existence for just about 60 years. To some extent prostitution was present in previous travel forms that included many of the religious pilgrimages of preclassical and classical times in the West and the East or in the patrician Grand Tours of the 18th and 19th centuries. The main difference between those variants and today's sex tourism lies in the sheer dimensions of modern demand and its growing relation with some sectors of the travel industry. In this sense, sex tourism is a modern phenomenon with rather recent roots.

It is not problematic either to accept that many of the three million American soldiers that fought in Vietnam during the years of American intervention in that country (1963–73) created additional demand for prostitution in places like Saigon or Bangkok. Many were indeed sent to Thailand to spend what with a circumlocution was called their R&R (Rest and Recreation). Unfortunately the exact dimensions of this demand remain unknown. One source estimates that in 1957 there were 20,000 prostitutes in Thailand and that their number grew to 400,000 by 1964 as a consequence of American intervention in Vietnam (Hall 1994). In this narrative, the 20-fold increase in the number of prostitutes happened well before the time (1968–69) when the US intervention reached its peak. Only in 1965 did the expeditionary troops in Vietnam reach the 200,000 mark. At this time there was also a much smaller number of US troops stationed in Thailand. Even if all of them had spent all their time there, it is difficult to imagine that they might have created enough demand for the 380,000 prostitutes added to those of 1957. One may wish that it would have been so, for the war in Vietnam could not have happened in the first place— no combat troops available. Commendable as the outcome would have been, the author should have explained where he obtained his figures, but he does not (Gay 1985:34).

Leaving aside moral, politically correct, or gender considerations, it should not come as a surprise to learn that prostitution follows armies. Wherever one finds large concentrations of young and/or lonely men, whether soldiers on leave or on duty, students celebrating spring breaks, or participants in scientific conferences or religious conventions, demand for sex grows. If it cannot be met by regular sex, many of those men will fulfill their needs by buying sexual services. Readers of Thackeray's *Vanity Fair* will remember his description of Waterloo and the number of prostitutes that followed the march of the armies. Any hotelier may tell juicy stories about what in Spain is called "complementary offer" at times of big conventions or congresses. When men alone are stationed in military bases, whether American or of any other nationality, those bases become targets for prostitutes. Even though one should take it with as large a pinch of salt as the growth of prostitutes in Thailand just mentioned, a UNICEF memo on the United Nations intervention in Cambodia at the end of the Pol Pot regime argued that the number of prostitutes in that country had reached 20,000 with a decrease to 10,000 once the troops left (Bobak 1996). Thailand could hardly have been an exception even though the real number of prostitutes between 1963 and 1973 remains unknown.

However, one should not rush to conclusions. As in the case of Cambodia, when the troops retire and demand dwindles, supply—the number of prostitutes—also tends to decline. They have to look for other ways to make a living. One might make a case that in Thailand civilian tourists relayed the leaving troops and allowed prostitution to remain a thriving industry, but the dates do not correspond. The withdrawal of US troops from Vietnam happened in 1973 while the quick growth of international tourism to Thailand had to wait until the end of the 1980s. "In 1980–1987 visitors to Thailand grew at an average rate of 10.53%. In 1980 the number of foreign visitors went up to around 1.85 million, reaching 3.48 million in 1987" (Tourist Authority of Thailand [TAT] 1994). Quick as growth indeed was, the total volume of visitors is hardly impressive. Only in 1987, after launching the *Visit Thailand* campaign did the country start to reach high numbers of arrivals topping 11 million in 2000 and 14-plus million in 2009. The Thai tourism takeoff had to wait for 14 years after the withdrawal of US troops from Vietnam. As sex tourists were—and are— only a fraction of this total, it is difficult to hypothesize about a causal relation between the two events. At any rate, if one wants to maintain a nexus between them, it would be mandatory to provide better evidence. As far as is known, it has not been published yet.

Even if the causal relation between the US military presence, prostitution, and sex tourism to Thailand could be finally proven—a far cry for the time being—one should be able to use the same argument to explain the increase in supply in the rest of Southeast and East Asia, following the Ryan-Hall hypothesis of general application. However, it is a plain fact that there were no significant American forces in China or North Vietnam after the 1950s. Even at the time of the covert intervention in Laos and Cambodia, US troops in those two countries were quite limited. They were not present in Malaysia or Indonesia. South Vietnam and the Philippines might be the only eventual candidates for the role. At any rate, it is not possible to extend the hypothesis to the whole region, making it quite difficult to prove the deep relation between American imperialism and sex tourism.

This may be the reason why Ryan and Hall include Japanese imperialism in the picture. If it is hard to blame only one form of imperialism for its alleged relation to sex tourism, why not charge imperialism in general? Since the Sino-Japanese war of 1895, Japan tried to establish its own empire in East Asia. The 1941 attack on Pearl Harbor showed that it also wanted to control the whole Pacific Ocean. After that, Japan succeeded in taking over most of the colonial British, French, and Dutch dominions in Southeast Asia and included them in its Great Asian Co-Prosperity Sphere (Buruma 2003). Fleeting as its hegemony was, Japan occupied all the Southeast and East Asian lands that are today the focus of sex tourism researchers.

For Ryan and Hall the imperialist Japanese expansion turned prostitution into a formal mechanism of domination and a way to satisfy the sexual needs of the occupying troops (2001:140). The latter part of the statement is a tautology. The former, however, points to some facts as evidence, but at close range they are quite flimsy. Talking about the spas developed by the Japanese in Taiwan after its annexation in 1895 stretches the imagination. More to the point might be reminding of the "comfort women" from Korea and other countries forced to prostitute themselves to Japanese soldiers. However, any similarity between them and the consensual prostitution of modern times vanishes. Even if those events are construed as consequences of imperial expansion, their relation to modern sex tourism in Asia is, to put it mildly, quite fragile. Japan suffered total defeat in 1945, and sex tourism to that part of the world only developed 30 or 40 years later. What kind of present-day causality might link those two phenomena? By the same token one might find harbingers of sex tourism in the Mongol invasions that overran the same geographic areas in the 12th and 13th centuries.

One reckons that it is better to find the roots of sex tourism growth in that part of the world in the economic present, leaving aside such vague and value-laden words as militarism, colonialism, or imperialism, especially when, as in the evidence provided, facts do not match. However, one should not forget how the new demand for sex tourism could be so easily accommodated by the supply. To this end, one has to discuss the role of prostitution in the cultures of the area.

For the accidental tourist, visiting places like Patpong, Nana Plaza, or Soi Cowboy in Bangkok, or their clones in Pattaya or Phuket, easily confirms the stereotype that prostitution in Thailand has followed the path of male Westerners. Those are the areas that attract the great majority of sex tourists. Prostitution in the country, however, also caters to local demand. Usually noted in passing and quickly forgotten to comply with the neo-romantic persuasion, is the fact that a majority of sex customers in Asia originate in the local society. Such seems to be the case of Thailand (Jeffrey 2002:xi–xii, 135). In 1994, the Ministry of Public Health released statistics which showed that 75% of Thai men regularly availed themselves of prostitution services and that 44% of male teenagers paid for their first sexual experience (Wilson and Henley 1999). If these figures are correct, they would buttress the idea that only a small part of Thai prostitutes work for international customers, while the bulk of them caters to the locals. This segment is indeed much more difficult to see for those people that do not have a good command of the local language, are unable to understand the inner workings of Thai society, and do not navigate the country with the ease of a local. Both sides of the sex industry usually ignore one another (Askew 2002).

There is not much better information for other countries of the region, though the little that transpires narrates a similar story. A study of Vietnam concludes that the visible increase of prostitution in the country is mostly related to the expansion of a new class of local entrepreneurs, and to bureaucratic corruption (Nguyen 1997). Something similar apparently happens in China (Goodman et al 2002). In her paper on the place she calls Lakeside, Walsh (2001) noted that the red light district clientele—in this case, red only denotes the usual prostitution areas, not the political ideology of the country—was overwhelmingly composed of Han Chinese, the ethnic group of more than 90% of the population. Another paper (Pan 2002) describes similar patterns in three quickly industrializing Chinese cities. In Beijing, Shanghai, and other big cities, local clients make up the majority of the trade (Hershatter 1999:333–343).

Prostitution is definitely nothing new in the region. Sex traffic before Western colonialism is well documented, especially in the Japanese case. Even though there were prostitutes in the country from time immemorial, the first of the "licensed quarters" was established in Kyoto in 1589. In 1679 there were more than 100 of them in the whole country. In those times, Japan strictly controlled any trade and cultural exchanges with the West. This "world of the flower and the willow" (Saikaku 1969) had as its main clients some groups of local commercial entrepreneurs or *chonin* that were flourishing in the cities as the *daimyo* feudal order started to wither away. *Chonin* spent large sums of money on prostitution. A night with a high-ranking courtesan would cost $429 in 1969 and maintaining one of them might reach $22,400 a year (Morris 1969:7). Below that top group of *toju* or luxury whores, there was a complicated stratification (Ariyoshi 1994) according to the price the women charged (Morris 1969:285–288). This "floating world" persisted until the end of the Second World War, when the American occupation authorities—the Iron Laws of Sex Tourism had not been discovered yet—decided to outlaw the practice.

Japan was, for centuries, the highest and most complete instance of the role played by prostitution in the region, but it was not unique. It was widely practiced in China until the arrival of the communist regime in 1949. A well-documented book on early 20th century Shanghai (Hershatter 1999) shows a panorama quite similar to that of Japan before 1945. The "flower world" there also had a complex stratification that went from highly expensive courtesans that offered company, singing, and acting sessions, educated conversations, and eventually sex to their clients to the lowest rungs that only provided the latter. Shanghai patrons belonged to all social layers, from well-known intellectuals, Chinese opera performers, and sundry artists through rich merchants and high officials to passing sailors and sundry commoners. Relations between the prostitutes and their clients were regulated by a complex ritual; top professionals had wide discretion in selecting their paramours; the most expensive ones were beyond the reach of even rich patrons; and, indeed, the lowest strata suffered the hardest treatment both socially and financially (Hershatter 1999:34–65). Their number at the time is as difficult to calculate as it is today and the data are equally unreliable.

In Japan, China, Vietnam, and other countries of the region (Jamieson 1993:296–297), the well-developed sex trade was a structural complement of the traditional family. One cannot devote much attention to this important point here, but recreational and reproductive sex were clearly separated in most Eastern societies in spite of their cultural differences. Marriages, especially in the most affluent strata, were political alliances. Polygamy was common, perhaps propelled by the desire to ensure family lineages in a world of high infant mortality and overwhelming male supremacy. Contributing male heirs for their survival was the basic role of the female gynoecium composed of the first and subsequent spouses and concubines, while sexual pleasure and overall recreation were to be found beyond the home in brothels and houses of assignation. This dual structure was quite rigid in the geographic arc from Indonesia to Korea (Hyegyonggung 1996).

One might advance the hypothesis that, among other factors, former family structures and the hierarchy of reproductive and recreational sex facilitated a positive response to the increased demand for venal intercourse that accompanied foreign sex tourism. The industry had been in operation for centuries and it only needed some fine-tuning to respond smoothly. Higher numbers of prostitutes (not so high, though, relative to those catering to domestic demand), better vocational training (in Hanoi some karaokes specializing in foreign demand help their workers to gain a basic knowledge of conversational Chinese, Japanese, and English), new travel products (Jago 2003), and new marketing techniques eased the transition from the former licensed quarters to the present-day nightspots. The old sex trade has thus adapted its old pre-industrial activities to the new forms of demand and contact (Internet, cell phones, etc.).

A quick reminder is necessary to conclude this section. It has become quite fashionable among multiculturalist Western researchers of sex tourism (Bishop and Robinson 1998:160; Ryan and Hall 2001:139) to exclude from their interests (Jeffrey 2002:63) any discussion of the role of traditional religious ideologies (Buddhism, Confucianism, Shinto, etc.) in the survival of prostitution in East and Southeast Asia. The issue also lies beyond the scope of these remarks, but for different reasons. For this chapter, subject and space provide the limits; in theirs, it is an ill-conceived idea of what respect for other cultures means. However, one can legitimately ask why those powerful beliefs, so instrumental in shaping behavioral patterns in most areas of social life, should not count when dealing with family structures, sexual identities, and the existence of prostitution. As usual, for all their allegedly best research practices, *pomo* prejudices blur rather than clarify their subjects.

A SWARMING CROWD?

Since 1982 Thailand followed in the steps of the so-called Asian tigers, or the group of Asian countries (South Korea, Hong Kong, Singapore, and Taiwan) that experienced a quick pace of economic development. In spite of the financial crisis in 1997–98, Thai GDP in 2002 was 3.5 times higher than in 1982 (World Bank 2003). In 2008, estimated per capita income (at power purchasing parity or PPP) was $8,400, a fourfold jump over 2002, and higher than that of the countries called "lower middle income" in World Bank jargon. Agriculture's contribution to GDP in 2009 (estimated) was 12%, industry 43%, and services 45%. Thailand has thus gone through to quick economic growth over the last 20 years (CIA 2010), accompanied by rapid middle-class growth.

Changes like these, usually known as modernization, have ample consequences. Some are highly beneficial, others not so. At any rate, modernization usually creates serious social pressures and disrupts traditional social structures (Desai 2002:36–54). Thailand is no exception to this observation. A decline in the rural population has brought about rapid urban growth as millions of peasants tried to find jobs in industrial companies or in the service sector. Many of these internal migrants were young women; many came from the Isan, one of the most deprived areas in the Northeastern region of the country. The majority had few marketable skills. In the alternative between lowly paid and unregulated work in the industry, and a short but eventually high paying career in prostitution, some found more or less voluntary employment in the latter (others were forced into it or sold to brothels by their families).

This growing sex workforce met an increase in demand. The main economic reason for sex tourism in Thailand is arbitrage, that is, the price differential for the same services between Thai prostitutes and those in developed countries. In the United States a patron has to be ready to pay between $300–700 for one hour of GFE ("Girl Friend Experience" as advertised) with an uncredentialed escort (Eros Guide 2010). If the woman is a porn star, prices rise to $1,500–1,800 (Body Miracle 2003). For this last amount, one could find a travel package to spend a week in Bangkok and still have some leftover change to consort with local prostitutes that charge just $30–50 per encounter. No surprise that foreign demand for venal love is higher there than in Chicago, Amsterdam, or Peoria.

How many Thai women took this path is something of a mystery. Once more, researchers are overwhelmed by the dearth of data. Government figures reckoned a number of 77,000 prostitutes in 1992 (Thai Ministry of Public Health quoted in Boonchalaksi and Guest 1998:139). Above this low threshold, numbers escalate according to the imagination or political agenda of the researchers, to 2 million (Hornblower 1993), 1 million (Richter 1989), a 400–700,000 interval (Truong 1990), or another one of 200–250,000 (Boonchalaksi and Guest 1998).

Deprived of reliable data, one can still try educated guesses. According to those estimates the ratio between the number of prostitutes and the general population (an estimated 67 million Thai people in 2010) would be 1:33 (Hornblower), 1:67 (Richter), 1:95 (Truong), 1:268 (Boonchalaksi and Guest), and 1:837 (Thai Ministry of Public Health). The Netherlands, one of the few countries with partial statistics on prostitution, counted 25,000 prostitutes out of a 16 million population in 2000 (data from the Graaf Foundation quoted in Orhant 2002). The ratio there at the time was 1:660, between the estimate of Boonchalaksi and Guest (1998), and that from the Thai Ministry of Public Health.

In 2010 there were 10.4 million Thai women in the 15–34 age group (US Census Bureau 2010), the cohort that provides the largest number of prostitutes. The ratio between prostitutes and the rest of this female group would be 1:5 (Hornblower), 1:10 (Richter), 1:14 (Truong), 1:40 (Boonchalaksi and Guest), and 1:125 (Thai Ministry of Public Health). That same year in the Netherlands there were 2 million women in the same age group (US Census Bureau 2010) with a ratio of 1:40 between prostitutes (supposing their 2000 number had remained stable) and the rest, that is, close to the figure in Boonchalaksi and Guest's estimate. Therefore, the number of prostitutes at a given time should lie somewhere between their estimate and that of the Thai Ministry of Public Health. Indeed, the total number of women that engaged in prostitution some time during their lives has to be higher, but what counts for the economic calculations coming later is the number that actually operate at a particular time. These figures refer to the entire number of prostitutes. For those working in the sex tourism sector, they have to be significantly lower, because sex tourism only represents a fraction of the sex industry. Estimating this part is still more complicated, but again one can use some educated guessing. The number of international arrivals provides the first pointer.

In 2007 the country received 14.5 million foreign tourists, of which 65% were men and 35% women. Altogether, there were 4.5 million more men than women. It seems reasonable to think that most heterosexual tourists in search of sex for sale should be found among this group of men. If all of them were sex tourists (which requires a big stretch of the imagination), and if they were equally distributed over the year, the daily number of men searching for prostitutes would be 12,000. As the average stay in the country is 10 days, maximum daily demand would reach about 120,000. If we estimate that of this entire total, about one fourth might look for sexual activities, they would need some 25,000–30,000 female prostitutes to meet their demand. Sex tourism would therefore occupy between 15 and 20% of the prostitutes estimated in the two counts that seem more reliable.

Many academics, however, are impervious to reality checks. Can there be 300,000 to 500,000 prostitutes in Cambodia? This was the figure proposed by Paul Leung (2003). Anything is possible, but not everything is probable, and this number sounds quite unlikely. In 2000 (taken here as the base year to follow Leung's calculation) the total population of Cambodia was 12.4 million—6.4 million women and 6 million men (US Census Bureau 2003). The number of females between 15 and 29 years, the cohort most likely to engage in prostitution, amounted to some 1.7 million. If Leung's figures are correct, either 1:6 or 1:3 Cambodian women worked as prostitutes. Were it so, the number would be proportionally higher than the most outlandish speculations for Thailand. If there really were 2 million prostitutes in Thailand, only one among four females would do this type of work. Cambodia would have overtaken Thailand in this doubtful ranking.

Let us imagine that this were true. How could all those women eke out a living, even a miserable one? If we detract from the 6 million Cambodian males the group below 15 (2.7 million) and that over 70 (89,000) years of age, not regular users of sexual services, the total of men looking for venal sex would be 3.2 million, including the poor, the chronically and terminally ill, Buddhist monks, gays, inmates, and other improbable clientele. Each prostitute would have a potential daily market of 5.4 clients if their number was 500,000 or 9 if 300,000. So that they might work once a day, each patron would have to visit them 70 days a year (in the higher hypothesis) or 40 days a year (in the lower one). This looks particularly improbable in one of the countries with the lowest income per capita in the world. Most prostitutes would work less than once a week, even though they are in the same uncomfortable need of eating every day as the rest of the population. Anything is possible, let us repeat, but Leung's figures seem highly exaggerated.

If Cambodian demand could hardly sustain such a large sex industry, perhaps sex tourism could come to the rescue. In fact, if one follows Leung, male sex tourists do not only help—they are its mainstay, as local customers are not even mentioned in his paper. Can this be possible? According to the figures of the Cambodia Tourism Ministry (2003) there were 350,000 international arrivals to the country. If the gender percentage distribution were similar to that of Thailand (65% males to 35% females), the total of male tourists would have been 228,000. Let us imagine that all of them, including children under 15 and men over 70, are sex tourists; that they arrive evenly the whole year round; and that each one stays for 10 days in the country. Potential daily demand for venal sex would reach 6,500. So that every prostitute might have one client a day, each sex tourist would have to have intercourse around 80 times a day, roughly one every 20 minutes, without rest and every day of their stay (in the high scenario of 500,000 prostitutes) or 48 times daily, that is, once every half hour (in the low one of 300,000 prostitutes). That would really be a prowess to justify inclusion in *The Guinness Book of Records*, although for all we know about the male sexual response, the mixture of enthusiasm and reliance required for such a feat remains undiscovered. As Rafael *El Gallo*, a famous Spanish bullfighter, used to say "what cannot be, cannot be; besides, it would be impossible".

The magic figure of half a million prostitutes appears to be quite handy. This is the same number of sex workers reckoned to ply their trades in Saigon at the time of the American withdrawal in 1973 (Agrusa 2003). Perhaps they are the same tough crowd swarming through the ages. When the magic wand does not conjure them up, it may be even worse. Nina Rao, a fundamentalist feminist, complained about the 17,000–19,000 *deukis* in Nepal (equivalent to the *jogini* of the *Devadashi* system at work in Maharashtra or Karnataka) that cater to rich men; the 3,138 women (not one more, not one less) from Nepal's Nuwakot district sent to work in the Indian sex industry; the Nepali families that sell their daughters for 10,000–20,000 rupees (US$220–440); or the 20,000 Nepali women that work as prostitutes in New Delhi (Rao 2002). All of that without quoting even one source. Repeating inflated figures when it comes to sex tourism seems to have established a pattern. At the time of the 2010 World Soccer Cup in South Africa, a number of news organizations reported that 40,000 prostitutes had been trafficked to the country to meet increased demand from foreign soccer fans. Unsurprisingly by now, this was the same figure quoted for 2006 when the tournament was played in Germany (Bialik 2010). Are they the same?

Lacking in rigor though they are, such hypotheses play an important semiotic function. They are advanced to make plausible that Western sex tourism generates high incomes for the countries where it has developed, while at the same time creating serious social problems that would not be there but for its mere existence. One can legitimately doubt that any of those two statements can pass muster.

SEX TOURISM AND ECONOMIC DEVELOPMENT

Showing evidence for the allegedly rapid growth of prostitution in East and Southeast Asia as a consequence of Western sex tourism would need better evidence than that examined until now. Let us imagine for a minute that it were accurate. Would that have played a key role in the economic success of Thailand and other countries in the area? The Iron Laws of Sex Tourism answer affirmatively. Sex tourism has been a decisive contributor to the economies of recipient countries, according to Bishop and Robinson (1998:99), two authors whose field of expertise was English literature. Others follow in their wake, adding that sex tourism has been favored as a development strategy for this part of the world by the global agencies that rule international capitalism (Ryan and Hall 2001:141–142). Thailand being the usual showcase, we will deal with it in the expectation that if those two statements are correct there, they will be equally valid for other countries of the region.

Once again we will have to make do with educated guesses for lack of anything better. How big a direct economic impact might prostitution have had on the Thai economy? The different answers for the scenarios can be seen in Table 1. Let us stress that the basic assumptions used to construe it (that all prostitutes work a minimum of 300 days per year and that they make $25 each working day) have been chosen to boost the neo-romantic argument, even though they are counterintuitive.

According to Table 1, prostitution for heterosexual customers, both domestic and international, impacts the Thai economy in widely varying ways according to the number of practitioners forecast by each one of the hypotheses. Their respective economic contribution would go from 5.3% of

Table 1. Contribution of Prostitution to the Thai Economy (2008)

Number of Prostitutes[a] ('000s)	Economic Impact[b] (US$ Bil.)	Thai GDP 2008[c] (US$ Bil.)	Economic Impact[d] (%)
2,000	15.0	285.0	5.3
1,000	7.5	277.5	2.7
700	5.2	275.2	1.9
250	1.8	271.8	0.7
77	0.6	270.6	0.2

[a]Scenarios by Hornblower (1993), Richter (1989), Truong (1990), Boonchalaksi and Guest (1998), Thai Ministry of Public Health (quoted in Boonchalaksi and Guest 1998) ranked by the estimated number of prostitutes.
[b]Assumption: 300 workdays per year at US$25 per day.
[c]Includes 2008 GDP at official exchange rate (CIA 2010), plus estimates for each scenario (Column 2), as prostitution is not included in national accounts.
[d]Column 2 divided by Column 3 (rounded).

the Thai GDP in the highest scenario to 0.2% in the lowest. Even if the obviously inflated numbers provided by Hornblower were correct, prostitution could hardly be counted as a key economic asset. A contribution of 5.3% of GDP is by no means a trifle and if prostitution was to be abolished overnight in Thailand, the national economy would experience a serious contraction. However, if one takes as most probable the numbers in the last two rows, the total contribution of the sex trade to the Thai economy would vary between 0.5% and 0.2% of its GDP—still notable but not substantial enough to be seen as strategic.

Another way of reckoning the sex-trade-related impact can be found following the Tourism Satellite Accounts (TSA) provided by the World Travel & Tourism Council (WTTC), an advocacy group for the travel industry. Its Thai TSA 2010 calculated the added value of travel and tourism in the country (including all direct expenses by domestic and international tourists, plus governmental expenses) at $39.7 billion (WTTC 2010). If the highest scenario in Table 1 were correct, total heterosexual demand for sex services would have reached $15 billion in the same period—a contribution nearly equal to half of all of Thai tourism direct demand, which seems by all means excessive. Even in the more probable scenarios of the last two rows of the table, the impact of prostitution would be quite high—between $1.8 and $0.6 billion, nearly 10–5% of the value added by all the Thai tourism industry (WTTC 2010b), which is the largest in the region.

Table 2. Sex Tourism Impact on Thai Exports (2008)

Number of Prostitutes[a] ('000s)	Economic Impact[b] (US$ Bil.)	Thai Exports 2008[c] (US$ Bil.)	Economic Impact[d] (%)
400	6.0	181.0	3.3
200	3.0	178.0	1.7
140	2.2	177.2	1.2
50	0.8	175.8	0.5
14	0.2	175.2	0.1

[a]Scenarios by Hornblower (1993), Richter (1989), Truong (1990), Boonchalaksi and Guest (1998), Thai Ministry of Public Health (quoted in Boonchalaksi and Guest 1998) ranked by the estimated number of prostitutes. Total number of prostitutes working in the sex tourism trade calculated at 20% of the original scenarios.
[b]Assumption: 300 workdays per year at US$50 per day.
[c]Includes 2008 Exports at official exchange rate (CIA 2010), plus the estimates for each scenario (Column 2), as prostitution is not included in national accounts.
[d]Column 2 divided by Column 3 (rounded).

Similar warnings should accompany any reflection on the impact of sex tourism. As any tourist service consumed by foreigners, sex tourism is considered an export. Foreign tourists have to exchange their national currencies for Thai bahts to hire a prostitute in Patpong in the same way as when they want to buy a fake Louis Vuitton bag in the nearby night market. Table 2 reckons the share of sex tourism on Thai exports.

Table 2 benefits from the same generous assumptions as Table 1. Prostitutes in the sex tourism sector are expected to work 300 days a year at a daily average rate of $50. Additionally, a high 20% of all prostitutes would work for sex tourists. In the different scenarios for the number of prostitutes, their income would reach between 3.3 and 0.1% of all Thai exports, with the most reasonable guess putting it at between 0.5 and 0.3%. At any rate, even if the highest scenario proved true, not even that would demonstrate that sex tourism is a strategic economic sector for the development of Thailand.

Thailand's TSA invites a parallel reflection. According to the WTTC estimate, foreigners will spend $20 billion US dollars in the country in 2010 (2010b). If the maximum hypothesis on the number of prostitutes in the sex tourism sector had a grain of truth, sex tourists would spend around $6 billion in their company, that is, a third of all international visitor exports. It is highly improbable that the inflated number of sex tourists used here for argument's sake might disburse for sex services a third of what a total of

14.5 million international tourists are expected to disburse in transportation, accommodation, restaurants, shopping, and the rest.

Now we can discuss the final part of the argument on sex tourism—that it is a shortcut to development, and precisely favored in the region by the IMF, the World Bank, or the World Trade Organization (WTO). Well, nothing in the copious bureaucratic literature on development generated by those agencies explicitly endorses this goal. Perhaps *pomo* authors have uncommon mind-reading skills that most others lack, which allow them to persist in their argument. If that were the case, however, they would share in the same mistakes that they attribute to others. Do they really believe that sex tourism can make the uppermost contribution to capitalism in Thailand or in any other place? This view, as seen, has no better grounds than the belief in the tooth fairy. If the IMF, the World Bank, the WTO, or any other spectra-sounding global agency ever gave any credence to the sex road to development, this would perhaps be the best reason to campaign for their demise. Sharing such ridiculous notions with its alleged perpetrators does not much help the *pomo* cause.

WESTERN CULTURAL HEGEMONY

Since its inception academic tourism research paid high heed to the *pomo* deconstructionist methodology (Chapters 3 and 4). The field of sex tourism is no exception. However, while modern mass tourism gets decried as its main cause, the economic evidence provided reveals itself as scarcely sound. What about the cultural field? If the economic link between prostitution, capitalist development, and globalization has not proved its mettle, perhaps the cultural or anthropological aspects of sex tourism may make a better contribution. They are more difficult to probe, but as they seem impervious to cost-benefit logic, they are also more difficult to debunk. Therefore, the *poco* school has embraced sex tourism with a vengeance.

A recent version of the argument has been put together by Leslie Ann Jeffrey (2002). In her view, sex tourism in Thailand is at the crossroads of many trends in postmodern societies and cultures—sexuality, the travel industry, political power, and what she calls the "new hegemonic representational order" (2002: *passim*). Within the *poco* template, she sees sex tourism as the main metaphor in the narrative of prostitution in the country, closely linked with the social construction of gender and national identity. To make her point she follows the legal regulation of prostitution in Thailand since the 19th century when the country was finally forced to join the imperialist chain. As her goal is to cover the different forms in which Thai society received and internalized alien cultural norms, any rumination on Thai patriarchy, Theravada Buddhism, or the role of women in traditional society are declared off-limits from the outset.

Prostitution was declared illegal in 1909 with the uppermost goal of limiting the growth of venereal diseases. However, at that time of colonial expansion (1860–1939), it did not bother the imperial powers as much as the local practice of polygamy and concubinage. In their eyes, these two institutions confirmed that Thai men could not dominate their own sexuality, and were therefore unable to govern themselves. Traditional family ways thus became an excuse to interfere with Thai internal affairs. One had to wait until 1960 to see prostitution criminalized in Thailand. Now the rationale was to align the country with the so-called advanced Western nations. The movement is still alive, though it has taken a number of partly contradictory, partly overlapping paths on its way. Some sections of Thai society reacted against the growth of prostitution, blaming it on the presence of American troops on R&R leave. In the narrative of female groups of the elite, prostitution was seen as an assault on Thai women by well-heeled foreigners. This trend could be countered by educating women in a respect for traditional values such as love for the heartland and pride on being a peasant. The practical tool to limit the growth of prostitution was restriction on rural migration to Bangkok. For women who would not heed their advice, vigilance, punishment, and individual reform were the main prescription. The prodemocracy movement of the 1970s shared many of those views, now with a more economic emphasis. Underdevelopment and the strategies of foreign companies now played the role of the usual suspects for the growth, among other calamities, of the sex trade. Under the authoritarian rule of General Prem (1980–1988), undesired exposure abroad of issues such as child prostitution, and women trafficking led to a new turn of the repressive screw. Punishment took front stage.

In the 1990s a new tack followed. Quick economic development unleashed a wave of wellbeing that led to the growth of a new middle class with its own ideas on how to fix the issues of sexuality and prostitution. New narratives weakened the link between poverty and prostitution, and the latter was portrayed as an answer to consumerist pressures encouraged by growing globalization. At the same time, monogamy became a new model for family relations, and masculinity was channeled toward new forms of family leisure (sports, trekking, and domestic and international travel) instead of the old brothels. In the end, however, the new ideologies did not part with the notion that prostitution was a social evil to be repressed.

In 1996 new regulations increased sanctions against parents that sold their children for sexual exploitation, as well as pimps and brothel owners. For the first time, the law punished patrons of underage prostitutes.

According to Jeffrey this is not enough. In fact, the new regulation victimizes poor peasants and women. This repressive model should be replaced by a decriminalization of prostitution, the recognition of sex workers' right to organize against exploitation, and a clear will to stand against abuses. Even though Jeffrey carefully avoids stating so openly, legalization is written all over her argument. One can agree with some of Jeffrey's intended conclusions and still not see their connection with her premises. Paying recurrent heed to *pomo* mantras, she digs herself into a deeper ditch.

Above all, facts do not match well with her explanatory mechanism. For all the Western hegemony, one should not forget that old Siam remained independent until the 1941 Japanese invasion (Baker and Pasuk 2005). Thus, Thai rulers had much more latitude than those in Laos, Vietnam, or India ever had under colonial administration. Among other things, interpower rivalry meant lesser imperial influence in Thai affairs. After the Second World War the country regained its independence and its legal system has been since operated by the national state. Accordingly, Western influence on the regulation of the family, sexual issues, and prostitution can only be second-hand at most. In fact, different governments showed a willingness to legislate in their own way. Indeed, some foreign influence may have trickled down into the debate via global media, but even if it were so, it could not have made itself felt without the consent of important national groups.

The inner logic of Jeffrey's argument is also shaky. Like most *pocos*, Jeffrey wants to make a clear stand on being on the side of the poor and the oppressed Other that often leads her to surprising conclusions. For example, she maintains that the emphasis of the 1996 legislation on the control of brothels and child prostitution favors the rich over the poor, for the latter use child prostitution more often. Other than not showing any evidence for this assertion, it is difficult to accept that in this particular instance "[t]he new law acts as a disciplinary mechanism to force lower-class men into the new man model of the middle class" (Jeffrey 2002:135). If the government leaves child prostitution unregulated, something is wrong; if it legislates, then it is even worse.

The same caring considerations underlie her critique of the 1996 legal text. The law punishes parents that voluntarily sell their children to brothels with steeper sanctions (up to 20 years in jail) than those meted out to clients and pimps. Additionally, it deprives them of the custody of their children when they are recovered from the brothels. To Jeffrey, the regulation should be blamed for it only increases the disciplinary powers of the state over parents and children. Perhaps Thai society, including the many poor who do not engage in child prostitution or sell their children to brothels, would be better served if those who do would remain unpunished or could keep their children's custody until a new business opportunity arises. Indeed, many legal regulations weigh more heavily on some social groups than on others, but this moral issue should not serve as an excuse to request special treatment for them. Most people responsible for fraud during the 2001–2002 financial scandals in Wall Street were very rich. Should they have been excused because rich people are more likely to be prosecuted for financial fraud or insider trading than other social groups?

Jeffrey's argument thus transpires the persuasion that any state intervention will by definition create more oppression. This may be quite gratifying, but she does not give a hint about how modern societies can do without the state. Legalizing prostitution in Thailand, or anywhere else, would possibly be the most sensible course of action, but it is difficult to portray how this might be done without a modicum of that state regulation or normalization that *pomos* abhor. In this case, the state would have the responsibility of defining the age of consent; protecting women (or men or transsexuals) from being forced into prostitution; imposing sanitary controls; persecuting children trafficking; punishing attempts by pimps and brothel owners to control the business; fighting police corruption; and, last but not least, making prostitutes pay taxes on their income. This is what happened in the Netherlands when prostitution was made legal in 1988 and brothels allowed operating in 2000, and the system seems to be working rather well. Indeed, one might say that such normalization is but another way of disciplining the prostitutes' bodies and of imposing a set of alien values on them. Perhaps one should listen to what they have to say.

More complicated still is to understand how all this relates to the alleged Western representational order that, according to Jeffrey and most of the authors already quoted, subordinates the South to the North. If one thinks that prostitution should be legal, one should also follow this position to its logical conclusion. Legalizing prostitution means nothing else than that sex services will be openly marketed or—as per *pomo* lingo—commodified since that point in time. However, how can one draw this conclusion while simultaneously arguing that "politics in countries outside the hegemonic West are fundamentally shaped by the need to contend with—to resist or respond to—Western discursive power" (2002:146)? How to break out of the charade where the West, usually identified with capitalism and globalization and bitterly decried as a consequence, will be resisted by expanding the logic of the market?

This unresolved conflict between ritual disapproval of Western cultural hegemony and the inability to propose solutions other than those already provided by the market rests at the basis of the *pomo* inability to understand the mechanisms of sex tourism. Blaming it all on the hegemony of the Western representational order, whatever that may mean, relieves the authors quoted here, however, from the thorny task of analyzing the role of traditional family systems or of autochthonous religious ideologies in paving its way. Fortunately for them, such generous *poco* generalities compensate for lack of evidence, and simultaneously reward moralistic grandstanding.

Chapter 7

Down the Path of Philosophy

THE PATH OF PHILOSOPHY

The Silver Pavilion or Ginkakuji was built on the slope of the Higashiyama (Eastern Mountains) that surrounds Kyoto, the old capital of Japan, on the east. It was built in 1482 by Ashikaga Yoshimasa, the eighth shogun of the Muromachi period (1333–1573 CE) to serve as his retirement residence. Ginkakuji was built on the pattern of the Golden Pavilion (Kinkakuji) and tried to rival the splendor of its Western counterpart erected by Ashikaga Yoshimitsu some hundred years earlier. Nowadays, both compounds are Zen temples and attract large numbers of worshippers and tourists.

From Ginkakuji, following the Path of Philosophy, one can reach the core of Gion, the populous old quarter on the east bank of the Kamo River. The Path is a pedestrian thoroughfare, less than 1 mile long, that follows one of the brooks coming from the Higashiyama hills on its way toward the river. In contrast with the dramatic appeal of the Ginkakuji, the Path mostly attracts flâneurs. The quaint charm of the tree-lined canal, a famous cherry-blossom view in spring time, invites the tourists to a more leisurely beat than the vibrant shopping area just at the entrance of the Ginkakuji or the throng-friendly Heian Shrine lying at some distance from its southern end. The Path of Philosophy comprises only some minor temples, small shops and cafés, and a number of sheltered residences that become increasingly exclusive as one approaches its last section. It is a place for unhurried walks that invite meditation and intellectual musings. This is what apparently encouraged Nishira Ikutaro, a philosopher in the turn of the 20th century, to bring his students here for some peripatetic sessions that made the fame of the place and contributed to its name.

The Path does not draw a great number of international tourists. In fact, those are always well outnumbered by Kyoto dwellers and Japanese visitors. This is no big surprise. Almost everywhere, domestic tourism contributes more to statistics than its international counterpart. In Japan, the imbalance between internal and inbound tourism ranks even higher than in other developed countries. In 2008, travel expenditures in Japan (rounded) reached ¥23.6 trillion (US$265 billion). The part of international receipts came up to ¥1.3 trillion ($15 billion); the rest were expenditures made by Japanese of ¥22.3 trillion ($250 billion). Japanese expenditures in tourism thus represented more than 17 times what international tourists spent in Japan (JTA 2010a). International tourists to Japan only exceeded the 5 million mark in 2002. In 2008 they reached 8.3 million arrivals, while the number of outbound Japanese nearly topped 16 million (JTA 2010b). In this way, Japan ranks number 15 in the world and number 2 in Asia for outbound tourists; on the other hand, it ranks number 28 in the world and number 6 in Asia for inbound tourists (JTA 2010c). Ukraine, Malaysia, Hong Kong, Canada, and Thailand (among others) beat Japan as inbound destinations by far. The relation between inbound and outbound tourism shows a clear imbalance that has started to close over the last few years. However, it should be noted that the tightening gap owes more to declining numbers of outbound tourists than to a spectacular increase in inbound tourists. Japan reached a peak of nearly 18 million outbound tourists in the year 2000, but after that started a slow descent that was made more visible in 2008 as a consequence of the global economic crisis.

Many factors may account for this imbalance. One was surely the high level of prices in Japan as compared with most countries in the world. Another, the nearly complete absence of promotional activities on the part of Japan's National Tourist Office (JNTO) until 2003. JNTO only assumed an active approach to international promotion of the country after that date, once the Visit Japan campaign was launched on April 1, 2003 (JTA 2010d). Before that, possibly in tune with governmental policy, Japan shunned adopting active promotional policies. For many years, Japan's export-led economy had drawn heavy fire from many quarters, as its balance of payments regularly reflected a sizable surplus, and Japan saved more than it spent on imports. At the zenith of Japan's boom in the 1980s, the national government tried to stem criticism by encouraging Japanese citizens to travel abroad, while limiting inbound travel. At that time, it set a goal of 10 million outbound tourists to curb the surplus accumulated by the country's exports. The 10 million mark was quickly reached and handsomely surpassed during the 1990s. In recent years, it has fluctuated between 15 and 17 million.

Since 2003, as noted, the number of inbound travel has increased, although not at a quick pace. The goal is to reach 30 million international tourists in the future, with a more immediate target of 15 million by 2013 (JTA 2010d). Given the currently uncertain global scene, it seems quite doubtful that this ambitious goal will come on target. Something similar can be said of the objective to attain 20 million of outbound Japanese tourists. At the moment, though, Japan's outlays on international tourism are in the red, or in professional jargon, the country is experiencing a leakage in its tourist balance of payments.

In this way, Japan has become the most extreme case of an imbalance between outbound and inbound tourism among the developed economies of the world. In the recent past, the proportion of Japanese outbound to incoming tourists was nearly 10:4. If one considers only the relation between all Japanese taking international trips and inbound nonbusiness tourists, the relation was 10:2–2.5. This ratio is changing, as the Japanese government has indicated its desire to increase Japan's share of global tourism (Craft 2003), but it still seems that for many years to come, Japan will lag far behind other developed destinations in attracting significant numbers of foreigners. As per Table 1, today there still are half the number of outbound Japanese tourists.

For their part, Japanese tourists have become a notable force that is definitely one of the main engines of growth (Lew 2000) behind the rapid development of the industry in Asia and the Pacific. They are also among the biggest spenders in international tourism (JTA 2007, 2008). Estimates of expenditures per outbound Japanese tourist vary according to the source and how the figures are calculated. Following UNWTO (2004), in 2002, with 16.6 million outbound departures, Japanese tourists spent $26.7 billion for a total of $1,618 per head. The estimated 2008 figure reached $1,743 (UNWTO 2010b) with $27.9 billion in international expenses and 16 million

Table 1. Japan Inbound/Outbound Tourism (2000–2008)

	Outbound (Million)	Inbound (Million)	Inbound/Outbound (%)
2000	17.8	4.8	27
2001	16.2	4.8	30
2002	16.5	5.2	31
2003	13.3	5.2	39
2004	16.8	6.1	36
2005	17.4	6.7	38
2006	17.5	7.3	41
2007	17.3	8.3	48
2008	16.0	8.4	52

Source: Author's elaboration of JTA (2010b).

Japanese outbound tourists. WTTC (2004) estimated expenses of $3,205 per head for 2004 (with a total of $54.5 billion and 17 million tourists).

In general, Japan's competitiveness as a destination for tourism still remains low. It ranks 25 out of 133 countries in the World Economic Forum ranking (WEF 2009), and 23 among the 31 countries of the Organization for Economic Development and Cooperation (OECD) (Table 2). The World Economic Forum classes competitiveness along eight so-called pillars and three main categories. The latter includes regulatory framework, business environment, and cultural and natural resources. Japan rates poorly in areas such as safety and security, prices, and affinity for tourism, while high in cultural resources.

Let us now go back to the Path of Philosophy. With the previous data, it is not surprising that the Westerner strolling along it will have difficulty in finding other Western tourists embedded in the numbers of domestic tourists. This predicament quickly raises the issue of identity. One tenet of the postmodern (*pomo*) paradigm (Chapter 3) in tourism research holds it true that contact between foreigners and locals endangers the identity of host communities. By this token, the low numbers of foreign tourists should pose no threat to Japan and Japanness should have easily resisted the onslaught of foreign influences, or, at least, it should have a high grade of persistence. Does Japan really have a single identity; did Japanese people of the past, and do the majority of those living there today, conform to the same behavioral rules?

MULTIPLE IDENTITIES

Although some contributions take a broad approach to the interactions of identity and nationalism (Anderson 1999; Gellner 1983, 1998; Nairn 1978; Shumway 1991; Spillman 1997), often the discussion of identities becomes entangled with a narrative of deprivation. Quite often, economic dispossession is underlined. Globalization, North–South imbalances, and unequal exchanges cooperate to increase inequality among developed and developing countries, robbing the latter, among other things, of their identities (Britton 1996; Karch and Dann 1981). On other occasions, cultural bonds come under fire for, we are told, they ensure Western hegemony over the rest of the world, thus causing the decay of national or communal identities (MacCannell 1976; McCabe 2002; Munt 1994; Smith 1997). Beyond general assumptions, others have used smaller brushes to paint the different aspects of individual (Dann 1999; Desforges 2000; Selänniemi 2001), communitarian

Table 2. OECD Countries' Competitiveness Ranking

Country	OECD Ranking	World Ranking
Switzerland	1	1
Austria	2	2
Germany	3	3
France	4	4
Canada	5	5
Spain	6	6
Sweden	7	7
United States	8	8
Australia	9	9
United Kingdom	10	11
Netherlands	11	13
Denmark	12	14
Finland	13	15
Iceland	15	16
Portugal	16	17
Ireland	17	18
Norway	18	19
New Zealand	19	20
Belgium	20	22
Luxembourg	21	23
Greece	22	24
Japan	23	25
Czech Republic	24	26
Italy	25	28
South Korea	26	31
Hungary	27	38
Slovakia	27	46
Chile	28	47
Mexico	29	51
Turkey	30	56
Poland	31	58

Source: Author's elaboration of WEF (2009).

(Sofield 2003), gender (Byrne Swain and Mommsen 2001a), ethnic (Fischer 1999), or cultural (Van den Berghe 1994) identity construction (McCabe and Stokoe 2004).

These contributions typically follow two main paths to explain why the search for identity seems so basic to most humans. In the first strand, identity is prior in time to individuals and decisively shapes their behavior. Identities express belonging to a whole (family, nation, culture, race, etc.), which is bigger than its members and provides them with both tangible and nontangible rewards and sanctions, as well as general rules of behavior. Language, religion, traditions, folklore, foodways, sports, and many other dimensions, either separately or together, mold communities and the individuals with a number of specific features that set them apart from the rest. Those features allow them to find a purpose for their collective life and contribute to maintaining and reinforcing their social ties. History or other more or less mysterious agencies such as *Volksgeist* (people's spirit), blood, or people's psychology determine how we should conduct ourselves and keep clear the boundaries between our group and the rest of the world—the "us" versus "them" dynamics. Cross-cultural exchanges tend to endanger this commonality of behavior or to subject it to the culture or the *Volksgeist* or the blood or the psychology or the whatever of some other group(s). This way of gazing at identities started within tourism research with Greenwood (1977). For its followers, the continuum between the community founders and their present members is, in the Burkean convention, a covenant between the dead, the alive, and the future generations around a number of traditions and rituals that represent its history *wie es eigentlich gewesen ist* (as it really happened) in Ranke's formulation.

The other persuasion is constructivist, and it has been writ large among *pomo*s. Identities, in this version, are not inherent to communities and their members—they are the outcome of a process of social construction. "Social construction," indeed, does not mean much. Anything social is socially constructed (Brunner 1991; Brunner and Kirschenblatt-Gimbel 1994; Hollinshead 1992, 1993). Identities, whatever they may be, are social representations; hence they are social constructs by definition. Constructivists usually go one tacit step further in order to assert that identities are ideologies, that is, reified versions of reality that sanction a state of affairs that benefits somebody. That somebody often escapes easy definition, though usually it is code for the powerful (Levinson 1998; Pretes 2003). Other times, as exemplified by postcolonial studies, identity refers to the West and its cultural hegemony. For instance, the identity of the American West serves as a metaphor for the superiority of WASP (White Anglo-Saxon

Protestants) culture over that of women, migrants, Hispanics, Indians, and other people of color (Aquila 1996) and legitimizes their "right" to rule. Similar examples of this fundamentally oppressive brand of identity, one is told, can be found permeating most social institutions (Ferguson 2003). Said (1979, 1994) turned his Orientalist brand into a successful cottage industry quickly and keenly adopted the world over. The exposure of the power-based or political roots of Western hegemony is usually coupled with a call to resistance to it and an appeal to reconstruct the subordinate identities.

Can the case of tourism in Japan substantiate any of the two previous approaches to the issue of identity? Our contention in the following will be that the tradition-as-truth school misses the mark by far and that *pomo* limited constructivism shows the need for a more complex approach to identity in order to discard simplistic notions of unidirectional hegemony. Both versions of the *pomo* paradigm, however, amount to reified constructions that inhibit, rather than throw light on, attempts to understand some of the complicated problems created by cross-cultural exchanges and their latest incarnation as globalization.

WHICH WAY JAPAN?

One leaves the Path of Philosophy, goes west to find Higashioji-Dori, a long North–South thoroughfare on the east bank of the Kamo River, and then turns south on to Maruyama Park. One has reached the heart of Gion and feels close to an important part of Japan's history. Gion was already a site of choice for temple building before Heian Kyo, the capital of peace and tranquility, today's Kyoto, was erected in 794 CE on the template of Chang'an, the Chinese capital under the Sui Dynasty. Still today Gion hosts some of the more important temples of the Kyoto area. Since the foundation of the new capital, the history of Gion has been closely associated with that of the imperial city of Kyoto. It not only contributed to Japan's political and cultural life. Over the centuries, Gion would grow into the largest pleasure quarter in the Kyoto area and the homeland of the geisha, one of the popular symbols of Japan. But well before that, Gion played an important role in the development of Heian culture (794–1185 CE), one of the main sources in the rich history of Japanese traditions. Can one speak of a single Heian identity that would have made a singular contribution to Japanness?

For those who think so, this would have been distilled into the quintessential literary peak of the era, *The Tale of Genji* (Murasaki 1960).

At the time, Japan (at least in the areas controlled by the Kyoto Imperial Court) was a land of gentle people that had developed a special sagacity for beauty and good taste. Highbrow culture, in contemporary lingo, was their stock in trade. They interspersed their active amatory life with many occasions to display their penchant for rich pieces of clothing, the composition of *waka*, striking calligraphy, fancy religious rituals, and the pursuit of splendor and exquisiteness (Varley 2000:58–67). However,

> if we are using Murasaki's novel as a source of history [...] the people in *The Tale of Genji* represent only a minute percentage of the inhabitants of tenth-century Japan. With few exceptions they belong to the aristocracy, who numbered a few thousand out of a population of several million (Morris 2004:178–179).

Other social layers make only a fleeting appearance in the initial story of Tamakazura (Keene 2004:22–23).

Even within the courtier stratum, many had different standards of propriety, and defined their identities in a different way from Genji. Fujiwara Morosuke, Minister of the Right when he died in 960 CE, around the same time of Murasaki's masterpiece, admonished his contemporaries in a different way.

> Reflect three times before you say anything to anyone. Never do anything lightly. [...] From your garments and your caps up to your carriages, use these things only so far as necessity demands, and do not seek for beauty and display (Quoted in Sansom 1999:182).

Morosuke may have been a bore or a bigot, but he nonetheless represented a well-established current of opinion.

We find similar conflicting views some centuries later. At the end of his period of government, Tokugawa Ieyasu proclaimed in 1615 the Rules for the Military Houses (*Buke Sho-Hatto*) that among other things ordained that marriages among their members could not be privately contracted, that costumes and ornaments had to be appropriate to rank, that commoners could not ride in palanquins, and that samurais had to live frugally (Sansom 1987:7–8). Similar laws against the commingling of ranks and the easy life were proclaimed every now and then under the Edo shogunate. However, they were countered in practice and in doctrine during nearly the same time.

The 17th century especially saw the rise of a prosperous class of merchants that patronized kabuki plays and the floating world and accumulated eagerly flaunted riches. Much is nowadays made of the Bushido code and its rituals, but they prescribed only behavioral norms for a section of Japanese society, not precisely the most successful in economic and social terms.

Since the 17th century, Japan tried to live within the feudal identitarian dream, but it was finally put to rest by the arrival of Commodore Perry's black ships in 1853 and 1854 and the restoration of Emperor Meiji in 1867. Under him, the country went through a period of renewal where Western technology, economy, and manners (especially those of Bismarckian Germany) were quickly adopted. However, throughout this period there was an ongoing underlying conflict in the definition of Japanese identity, as noted by Keene (2002). Official ideology sponsored the so-called national essence or *kokutai* that requested the Emperor's faithful subjects "to offer [themselves] courageously to the State" (quoted in McClain 2002:428). On the other hand, sizeable groups of urbanites opted for embracing the bourgeoning mass culture that requested more options in building one's own identity and the extension of individual rights. Thus, national identity could be alternatively defined by Nishida Kitaro's hodgepodge of bureaucratic Prussia, Nietzsche's superman, and Heideggerian authentic life or by the rather weak but nonetheless liberal groups represented by the Movement for Popular Rights and the Kaishinto party (Buruma 2003:50–52).

In this way, and over the years, what we now call Japanness or national identity found at least two concurrent, synchronous and conflicting, expressions, and often many more. Traditions and rituals favored by each one of those alternative ways (and many other minor ones that cannot be retraced here) defined a sharp alternative that did not uphold the fundamentalist strand of identity definition.

A PLURALITY OF ACTORS

Let us go back once more to the Path of Philosophy. Now, after it runs its course, one goes west, passes along the Heian Shrine, and finds the Marutamachi bridge to turn south toward Pontocho-Dori. One looks for the teenager shopping area between Kawaramachi-Dori and the Nishiki Food Market and finds the same fascinating urban youth culture that also blooms in Tokyo's Harajuku, Yoyogi Park, and Takeshita Street or around America-Mura in Osaka. This is "eroganceland," that mixture of elegance and subtle eroticism that characterizes the fashions followed by many Japanese teenagers and twenty-somethings. "Erogance" (Merrick and Parker 2004) includes different styles of clothing and makeup from Elegant Gothic Lolitas or Gothic chic—to be distinguished from Gothic punk—to Gunguro. The first combines tongue-in-cheek Victorian chic (hence the Gothic in the moniker) with a wink and a nod to French maid attire—a look of morbid female innocence that, together with schoolgirls in mini-miniskirts, seems to haunt the erotic fantasies of many Japanese males.

Gunguro is less specific. More than just a clothing fashion, it is a lifestyle; more than a mostly female look, it supplies both males and females with patterns of conduct. Gunguro translates the valley girl cum California surfer lifestyle into the tastes of young Japanese—bleached blond or coppery hair; dark tans; bright makeups in green, yellow, or pink; prominent designer labels; and many hours devoted to personal appearance.

Gunguro has also contributed to changing general attitudes and sexual mores. Gunguro girls go around in groups; Gunguro males are always seen with female companionship, either in pairs or in groups (Park Douglas 2004). Those couples, not necessarily married, can often be seen traveling abroad in Asia with a distinctiveness of behavior that sets them apart from other Japanese tourists. A forceful nonchalance pervades the ways and attitudes of those youngsters that thus want to show their distance with the bureaucratic, corporate Japan mores of the previous two generations. A stronger contrast with traditional fashion for Japanese women and its idea of feminine identity or with the uniforms (gray suit, white shirt, tawdry tie) and ways of the corporate samurai culture would be difficult to pin down. At any rate, they have little to do with the usual stereotypes of Japanese identity, the kimono-clad young beauty.

Yes, one might say, but after all this is fashion—shifting by its own nature. Who knows which lifestyles Japan's youth will favor in a few years' time? Did not the modern boys of the Taisho (1912–1926) and early Showa (1926–1932) periods forget their Harold Lloyd looks and their love of *eru, goru, nansensu* (eroticism, gore, and nonsense) (Buruma 2003:63–84) and the Ginza and Asakusa nightlife (Seidensticker 1990:71–87) to don military uniforms and accept the nationalistic tall tales of the *kokutai*? Did not the modern girls soon change their short bobbed hair and Taisho look (Seidensticker 1983:252–274) to become mothers and ancillary champions of the fatherland in the years of Imperial expansion?

Let us then look at other, more basic features of modern social life. The graying of Japan has attracted conspicuous attention over the last few years. In 2003 Japan had a population of 127.6 million; by 2050 it will come down to 100.6 million. In 2003, 14% of the population was below 15 years of age; by 2050 the percentage will be 10.8. At the other side of the age pyramid, those 65 and older made up 19% in 2003; by 2050, they will be 35.7. The graying runs closely parallel to a reduced fertility rate. In 1950, it was 3.65; in 2002 it had come down to 1.32, and in 2003, with 1.29, it entered the 1.2 range for the first time in the postwar period (Statistics Bureau 2004).

It is difficult to ascertain all the causes of such a sharp decline, but one should pay attention to the attitudes of young women toward marriage and motherhood.

> The general decline in the birth rate is partly attributable to the rise in the average age at which women bear their first child; the average age rose from 25.6 in 1970 to 28.3 years in 2002 and to 28.6 in 2003 (Statistics Bureau 2004).

Not only are women becoming mothers at a later age; many of them are shunning both maternity and marriage. In the year 2000, single women under 29 accounted for 45% of this cohort; 10% of single women aged 35–39 had resolved never to marry; so did a quarter of single women in their 40s—a steep change in a society where in 1950, only 1.4% of women never married (Efron 2001; Orenstein 2001). Divorce, though quite limited (2.25 divorces per 1,000 people in 2003), has been rising steadily since the 1990s. In other societies, for instance in the United States, similar trends have created an upsurge in the numbers of single mothers; not so in Japan, where only 1% of births occur out of wedlock. Here, although the number of unwed women has increased dramatically, they know how to remain childless.

Young unwed women tend to live with their parents (80–90% of them do). Postponing marriage and living in parental homes does not only affect women, though. Many young men share the same arrangements. Hence this group has been called the kangaroo generation or the nestling or parasite singles (Yamada 1999). The latter label, which has proved to be the most successful, is usually used to refer to female singles with an undertone of reproach (Table 3).

Female parasite singles have become the butt of many criticisms, mostly, for their alleged materialistic outlook. They may live on small annual salaries, but they do not have to bother about the paying of rent, food, or even utilities. Their live-in families provide them. Accordingly, nearly all of

Table 3. "Parasite Singles" in Japan[a]

Age	All			Male			Female		
	Total[a]	Parasite Singles[a]	Share[b]	Total[a]	Parasite Singles[a]	Share[b]	Total[a]	Parasite Singles[a]	Share[b]
20–24	9.9	6.1	62.1	5.0	3.0	59.3	4.9	3.2	65.1
25–29	8.8	3.3	37.5	4.5	1.8	39.9	4.3	1.5	35.1
30–34	8.1	1.4	17.4	4.1	0.9	21.7	4.0	0.5	13.1
Total	26.8	10.9	40.5	13.6	5.7	41.6	13.2	5.2	39.4

Source: Masahiro Yamada (Parasaito Shinguru no Jidai or the Age of Parasite Single), and Management and Coordination Agency, quoted in Takahashi and Voss (2000).
[a]Millions.
[b]Percentages.

the money they make is disposable income, and they dispose of it in style. We are told, for instance, of

> Miki Takasu [who] is 26 years old, beautiful, drives a BMW and carries a $2,800 Chanel handbag—when she isn't using her Gucci, Prada or Vuiton purses. She vacations in Switzerland, Thailand, Los Angeles, New York and Hawaii (Tolbert 2000).

All of this on her annual salary of $28,000 as a bank teller.

Most surely Miki was pals with Ronald Reagan's welfare queens from Chicago, who drove Cadillacs on social security checks, but all this media chatter unmistakably shows that the identity of Japanese women is changing rapidly—and that of the traditional family with it. As for the reasons, one should probe beyond the alleged consumerism of young Japanese women. Let us recall that in traditional families, male parasite singles were no exception. Men would live with their parents until marriage and then they would bring their wives home to form two- or three-generation households. At any rate, living with the older cohort would often mean that they and their wives enjoyed the same savings that seem so disparaging in the case of young unwed women, but they were not blamed for their eagerness to consume.

If many young women avoid marriage, there should be additional or alternative reasons. One might be economics. Since 1945, Japanese females have been encouraged to obtain a better education. In the academic year 2000/2001, 40% of women were attending college (Statistics Bureau 2004). Although a better-qualified labor force can achieve higher financial and personal independence, this does not seem to have been the main cause for the decline of the traditional family. Gender participation in the Japanese labor force has not changed much over the last 20 years (60% male and 40% female in 1985; 59% and 41% in 2003), even though since the economic slowdown of the 1990s they have suffered in a lesser way than males from unemployment.

Another explanation mixes economics with cultural reasons. Many young women have not only achieved higher educational and financial indepen-dence; they also consider traditional marriage a bad business proposition. Traditional marriage still preserves many of the obnoxious features it adopted during the Edo period. The neo-Confucian doctrine of the time meted out a hardly attractive treatment to women. They had to accept an arranged marriage and heed the three obediences—to parents when a child, to husbands while married, to (male) children when old (Sansom 1987:89). There was a fourth unrecorded one. Japanese literature brims with examples of the tyrannical figure cut by mothers-in-law to whom the son's wife had to pay allegiance to the point of accepting that mothers-in-law could discipline them even with the use of physical force. For centuries, newly-weds accepted their predicament for lack of any other options, but this has changed. Better educated women will hardly put up with marriages where even today men devote 23 minutes per day to household chores, while women can expect a daily charge of four and a half hours, or 34% of married men declare that they have never changed a diaper. No wonder so many of them vote with their feet—away from traditional marriage and families.

No surprise that Japan, as any other society, modern or old, does not answer to one single identity. In fact, as we have tried to show, the identities that have been assigned to the country, even by its nationals, cannot hide the fact that Japan has offered and hopefully will do so in the future, competitive, even conflicting solutions, for the unknowns of the years ahead. Rea has shown that many other areas of traditional Japanese identity have been quickly changing swayed by unforeseen events (the 1989–1990 burst of the bubble economy, the sarin gas attack on the Tokyo subway organized by the Aum Shinri Kyo cult in 1995, and the disgruntling government's response in the aftermath of the Great Hanshin Earthquake of same year) that gripped Japan at the end of the 20th century (2000:647–649).

CONFLICTING IDENTITIES, MISLEADING PARADIGMS

Constructivists are closer to the truth than fundamentalists. Identities do not lead their existence detached from change, in a kind of extraterrestrial autonomy. In fact, traditions, rituals, and identities can be dated, in some cases with great accuracy. They do not precede the societies that endorse them, while they change to accommodate the new needs of different social groups. They reflect both internal and external influences for change, or to use a *pomo* expression, they are subject to ongoing negotiation.

However, once they reach this bridge, *pomos* show scant resolve to cross it preferring to regress to the conventional wisdom they learned in kindergarten. Lacan, Foucault, and Said, for all their talk about negotiation and diversity, have taught them that identities always reflect a one-dimensional, invariant structure. MacCannell (1992b) translated the notion into tourismese, and for his many followers, identities are always an imposition (when they want to wax Gramscian, they say hegemony) of the powers that be, namely,

> a political process that encodes and reinforces the dominant
> ideology of tourism culture, essentially a global process which
> manifests locally and explicitly involves the construction of
> places (Ateljevic and Doorne 2002).

It seems so evident for them what that dominant or hegemonic ideology is and who imposes it that they deem it superfluous to elaborate further. *Pomo* thrillers, accordingly, tend to be rather boring. From page 1, one knows that the perpetrator is James, the butler—a white, male, Anglo-Saxon, Protestant, loyal servant of the hegemons that through omission or commission flaunts his determination to poison the Other with the biases and prejudices of "Western culture" dating back to the Greek philosophers and the patriarchy they represent, as Garner (1995:x) would put it.

Hegemony's best antidote is said to be the affirmation of identities. Persons or social groups that grasp the meaning of their identities will better understand their present position in any social environment and thus make a better judgment on its legitimacy. In this way, the politics of identity will help women, groups in search of cultural or national self-determination, and other abused or exploited minorities (whether ethnic or cultural), to fight for their rights and curb the exactions meted out by different hegemonic actors. The latter may be men in the case of patriarchal societies, people of so-called straight sexual orientation, dominant ethnic groups, or central or metropolitan powers. At any rate, the *pomo* concept of identities derives from what one could call the Foucauldian worldview of endless power struggles at different societal levels. The final outcome of such a view makes any type of power suspect.

Once again, one should note that this belief cannot stand. If all social relations are based on power, that is, illegitimate domination, it becomes impossible to decide who may be right in any given situation. In the end, any power is as illegitimate (or as legitimate) as the next. To avoid circularity, *pomos* take a shortcut. They think they can decide who has the right to resist and who is the oppressor. This step, however, is more difficult than usually acknowledged, because it requests a reification of categories. Individual identity is relatively easy to ascertain. Fingerprints and DNA tests can contribute to determine that P did not kill S, and there are other trusted tests to determine that this given person P is in fact P and not S. Group identity, unfortunately, does not exist. Skin color did not prevent Haiti's dictator Papa Doc Duvalier to brutally kill many other black Haitians. Not all women accept feminist views of gender, and not all Scots or Catalans support independence for Scotland or Catalonia. One can say that black dictators or nonfeminist women or integrationist Scots or Catalans do not in reality belong to any of those social categories (blacks, women, Scots, or Catalans), but this legerdemain does not resist much testing.

Life is both more complex and entertaining. In fact, for ages, white, male, Anglo-Saxon, Protestant dominant ideology has been at odds with itself. This was also the case, as we have seen, of non-Western, male, Japanese, Buddhist-Shinto ideology, and possibly of every other society. Most human cultures are made up of conflicting interests, contrasting currents of thought, and opposite subcultures retrospectively streamlined by researchers into a single paradigm. No matter how necessary this stereotyping may be (Pinker 1997:308–313), one risks losing sight of specific histories when one adopts the *pomo* limited constructionist view. Social constructs are not good or bad in isolation from historical situations, and even more decisively, those that become more successful tend to be the result—the constructs—of majority views that represent compromises between individuals and groups. These become more and more complicated as modern societies include in the workforce and in the political franchise groups that in the past were easily cast aside, such as women or minorities that, in their turn, are also characterized by increasing inner diversity and diverging agendas.

Quite frequently—ritual invocations of endless negotiations that make identities notwithstanding—this complex panorama gets lost in the *pomo* translation that boils the complexity of economic and cross-cultural exchanges—today's globalization—down to a misleading paradigm of identity. They cast identities in bronze or rushmorize them with the help of dualistic deconstructionist techniques (powerful/oppressed, Western/non-Western, Ego/Other, and so on) that subdue or omit unruly or inconvenient facts. For instance, that those family structures so unappealing to young Japanese as well as to other young Asian women (Ganalh 2004) do not hark back to Western hegemony. For instance, that tourism is not the sole globalizing pressure felt by less developed communities in the days of satellite dishes, instant messaging, and the Internet.

Our constructs usually reflect oppositions and negotiations, but also, and above all, points of view that cannot solely be seen as domination narratives. Many individuals, irrespective of the social groups they may belong to, may and do accept a number of key constructs that they do not see as impositions, but as rational and/or acceptable definitions of a given situation. The paragons for this category are scientific concepts that any independent observer can ascertain following some established procedures. Indeed there will always be some people that reject, for instance, evolution in favor of creationism, but their number has been dwindling significantly since the 19th century, and the same can be said of other scientific notions. Additionally, sometimes individuals that think "out of the box" may be right, and their views, initially rejected and even persecuted, become the mold of future constructs. This is the perennial tension that affects human societies, and that *pomos* hide behind their endless war between domination and resistance.

Below scientific constructs, one finds a number of beliefs and institutions that a majority of people find acceptable to organize common living. At the top of the pyramid appear constructs dealing with the basic norms of what is usually called the social compact. The United States Declaration of Independence summarizes them as the right to life, liberty, and the pursuit of happiness. Most constitutions go into details in the so-called Bills of Rights usually enforced by democratic polities. Then come the laws that shape different areas of social intercourse. Many societies also recognize customs and traditions as part of the social contract and expect that citizens also abide by other accepted moral rules and social conventions. The further away one goes from key rules, the wider the latitude societies have in organizing themselves; therefore, their diversity. Diversity, however, does not only operate in the international arena; it is also crucial within nations. Democratic polities allow for a wide variety of choices in religion, in political orientation, in tastes, in consumer choices, and in many other arenas.

The wider the choices, the more legitimate they usually appear to a larger number of citizens. Indeed, in all societies some individuals and groups of people do not feel bound by majority rules and, accordingly, their societies threaten those who break the rules with a wide panoply of sanctions that may go from the death penalty or life imprisonment to light social sanctions such as estrangement or stigmatization. All this is Political Sociology 101.

Why does a majority of citizens abide by the rules? The sanctions just mentioned count, but they are not the sole reason. Most people also believe that compliance with the rules is another way to obey themselves. In democratic polities the legal network reflects the popular will expressed in free elections of its representatives. Indeed not everybody will be happy with every regulation, but still most people will find majority rule the least bad method to organize social life in a peaceful way. Pace *pomo* views, such respect for the rule of law and the ways it will adopt at given conjunctures does not reflect naked power or a false conscience, nor is it but the product of manipulation. If it were, it would mean that the oppressed they purport to defend are unable to use the power of their own reason.

This brings us back to hegemony. Social constructs are not just superstructural endorsements of crass economic interests that a good sleuth will always track to their class origins. Only Bourdieu (1984) and some of his more naïve followers will think, as they do, that any cultural manifestation, for instance the meat stew that French cookbooks know as *blanquette de veau* (a kind of veal stew), stems from and reflects the tastes not just of a social class, but specifically of one of its inner sections—the industrial proletariat. On the contrary, *blanquette*, as well as many other and more fundamental social constructs, appeal to broad swaths of people irrespective of their social origins. The talent of some people or ideas or institutions in successfully answering collective issues is exactly what hegemony means.

Even though many of the gentlemen that approved the American Declaration of Independence in 1776 practiced slavery and did not consider necessary to include women in the compact, the ideas it contained opened the way to successive, though often painstaking and painful, extensions of the franchise. It was not by attacking or by heaping scorn on them that blacks or women would finally reach legal parity with whites or men. Many of the social constructs originated in the European Enlightenment (freedom, democracy, the rule of law, markets based on private property, and the nation-state among others) had this capacity of garnering approval of people from different classes, genders, ethnic origin, and religious persuasions. When the suffragettes started campaigning for female voting rights, when African Americans fought against the local version of apartheid, when the Thai Red-Shirts movement demanded democracy in 2010, when many other social movements expressed similar requests the world over, they were not discarding those universalistic ideas; they just wanted them implemented in a true way. When Chinese consumers want to have a better home, or a car, or just a rice cooker; when Indians and Arabs buy tickets to watch Hollywood movies; when Southeast Asian youngsters wear Western fashions, they do not bow to imposition; they just want to follow their choice.

Hegemony creates imagined communities (Anderson 1999) of many shapes. People from diverse backgrounds join to accept, manage, or defend common projects, and their leaders exercise a hegemony that most of the time is the outcome of free decisions. Hegemony, therefore, can translate as leadership and be found in many areas of social life including pop music or sports. However, the name usually applies, in a more restricted way, to political hegemony. This is how Gramsci (1970) would use a concept that nowadays touches nearly every single power relation. Let us follow his thoughts.

Marx was certain that he had discovered the laws that govern the evolution of human societies in the same way as Newton had unearthed the basic principles of physics, or his admired Charles Darwin ascertained the mechanisms of biological evolution. So, in spite of his conviction that the transition from one mode of production to the next would come about through revolutionary conflicts and that the same would happen in the foreseeable advent of a higher stage of human development—what he labeled socialism—his theory of history was evolutionary in the sense that it did not make room for unexpected leaps and bounds for individual societies. Even though he never formulated a definite prognosis, he intimated that socialism would be viable only in those societies where capitalism was at its most advanced and mature, and where salaried workers made up the overwhelming majority of society. Sometimes, Marx hinted that the first historical shift to socialism might happen in the United States, but his sustained bet was that it would first bloom in the most developed society of his time, in the United Kingdom.

This is the predicament that the first generation of his followers inherited. For, no matter the expansion of capitalist markets and the growth of industrial workers in the United States or the United Kingdom, socialist transition or revolution was never a serious possibility in either one of them. The march to socialism might be slow, but if one had to take his cue from the momentum it had in the United States or the United Kingdom, the highest stage of social development would have to wait many decades, centuries, or eons. That's why Lenin (1965) and other equally impatient revolutionaries jumped onto Hobson's theories (1967). They would not find in them a ready-made revolutionary handbook, but they could see in his work a silver lining for their expectations of a quick end to capitalism.

Not only were Marx's transitional blueprints scarcely developed, they were also piecemeal. Socialism would start at the top of the developed countries, but how would it spread to the rest? Should all societies go through the same long historical process of shedding feudalism through bourgeois revolutions first, and growing to maturity later on their own different paths? What did this mean, for instance, for Czarist Russia that had just seen the emancipation of serfs, and could by no means be considered a full-fledged capitalist system (Trotsky 1996)? What about those countries where the proletariat consisted, if at all, of a few urban islands in a sea of backward and illiterate peasants? Should revolutionaries wait or strive for the advent of bourgeois society, even though in such a stage they would definitely be out of cue? The notion of imperialism seemed to offer an eventual answer to many of these complicated riddles.

Above all, imperialism offered an architectural alternative to Marx's somewhat abstract depictions of the future. World capitalism was not a disjoint ensemble of individual narratives, but a structured system of parts. In the oft-quoted Leninist metaphor, it was a chain made of different links, that is, a unique entity. Capitalist societies formed but a single world system. But, second, if world capitalism was a system, it was an internally contradictory one that was far from developing harmoniously. Some of its parts lorded over the rest, and at the same time they often had contradictory or mutually exclusive interests. The reason of this dialectic formation, for Lenin, lay in that nonsocialist societies are based on the premise of unequal access to the means of production, which pits class against class, nation against nation, and even sections of the same class against each other. Finally, these conflicts are exacerbated, as the system grows more and more mature. In order to counter unbridled competition, ensure privileged access to basic commodities and increase their markets, capitalist trusts and cartels go through a process of increased concentration, create big monopolistic groups that combine industrial and financial capital, and carve the world according to their own interests. Latecomers find themselves increasingly excluded from this arrangement and often resort to threats, even to open violence, to secure part of the spoils for their national capitalist classes. Thus imperialism, the last stage of capitalism, would grow increasingly bellicose.

An important consequence followed. If imperialism is the capitalist system at its most rapacious and aggressive, it also follows that its end is at hand, that backward or less developed societies do not have to wait long to be ready for a socialist transition. If capitalism is a unifying chain, it may be broken wherever its weakest link lies. That's how Lenin conceived the theory and encouraged the practical possibility of starting revolutions against *Das Kapital* (1965). Gramsci did not see events in a similar way (1949, 1970). For him, the Italian *Risorgimento*, the protracted historical process (1815–1861) that produced the unified Italian nation-state, was somehow a failed revolution. It could not have been a proper socialist upheaval as the industrial proletariat was practically nonexistent in the country, but even the most radical elements within the *Partito d'Azione* (Action Party), the followers of Mazzini and Garibaldi, did not find the key to solve the historical puzzle of disparate forces (small states, cities, local bourgeoisies, and peasants) of prenational Italy. It was left to Cavour's cautious diplomacy to coalesce all those forces around the interests of the capitalist classes of Northern Italy. They were able to create a framework where, for some decades, most other social forces would find an acceptable place. In this way, it was not impossible for similar unexpected actors to lead different historical processes that go beyond their social class. One can thus infer that for Gramsci, Lenin's theory of imperialism was a simplistic analysis of the evolution of capitalism and that the latter might have a new lease on life, as it really happened. After World War Two it would be up to the United States to grab the banner of political and cultural hegemony. As beleaguered as it looks nowadays, the historical period still has to reach an end.

Benedict Anderson (1999) produced an interesting memoir of the birth of contemporary nations and nationalisms. For him, they initially are the precipitate in the British and Spanish colonies of today's Americas, of a number of changes in mentality and technologies. The modern nation epitomized by the Thirteen Colonies in their rebellion against the British crown was possible only after a new conception of duration set in, where homogeneity and horizontality, toward both the past and the future, replaced previous notions of cyclical and repetitive time. This new vision abetted and, at the same time, was encouraged by the extension of printing that helped to extend normalized languages in areas where previously only local speechways dominated. The normalization of printed language, in turn, made possible new bureaucratically efficient administrations and the creation of those imagined communities (how else define ample groups of people that would never have a chance to personally know the overwhelming majority of their fellow citizens?) that we call nations.

This poses a riddle.

> [W]hy was it precisely *creole* communities that developed so early conceptions of nation-ness—*well before most of Europe?*

[Anderson's italics] Why did such colonial provinces, usually containing large, oppressed, non-Spanish-speaking populations produce creoles who consciously redefined these populations as fellow-nationals? And Spain, to whom they were, in so many ways, attached, as an enemy alien? (Anderson 1999:50).

In a more general formulation, what made people from all classes and even different ethnic origins, then and later, be ready to make sacrifices and even die if required for an entelechy called "the nation"?

Anderson takes an interesting trip into a subject that still remains poorly mapped, but he does not answer his own riddle. He starts with the alienation of the creoles in both North and South America. Creoles were people of metropolitan origins (in Britain or in Spain), but born in the colonies. Although they shared a similar identity, their aspirations to equality with the metropolitans were curbed in many ways. In essence, while the top echelons of the administrative and economic system were reserved to the British or the Spanish *peninsulares* (born in the Spanish peninsula), creoles could only become lesser players in their own lands and were not allowed the same rights as the locals when they moved to metropolitan areas. Additionally, creoles did not enjoy horizontal mobility. Someone born in Chile could not be employed in what then was known as New Spain (later Mexico).

Creoles, especially in South America, faced a further problem. They might be increasingly alienated from the mainland, but they were a minority within the local population. There was no census in Spanish America at the time of the Napoleonic Wars in Europe, but it was reckoned that out of an estimated population of 15–16 million, 6 million were Indians, another 6 million were *castas* (people of mixed ancestry), and the remainder creoles or Spanish residents (Elliott 2006:loc.6744–6765). If they wanted to be successful in their aspiration to independence, creoles had to enroll many other people on their side. It was not an easy task. As Nairn (1982) put it, the creoles could not break from their predicament without the concourse of the masses in their surroundings. As we know, they ensured it with varying doses of forcible imposition, but this does not tell the whole story.

Waving the national flag, they made their domination acceptable or, at least, tolerated by a majority. Many saw the nation, in opposition to the old colonial regime, as a better arena to reach equality before the law and, therefore, as the legitimate turf to vent their aspirations and find fair solutions to the conflicts created by social intercourse. This was also the same process that swept France after 1789 where the revolutionaries also offered a design for justice and democracy superior to the particularities and status differences of the *Ancien Régime* (The Old Order). The nation beckoned a new stage where the old unbridgeable differences between actors and spectators, between nobles and commoners, disappeared into a collection of *citoyens* (citizens). This is the basic pull factor of the national dispensation. Nations, those imagined communities, derive their appeal of this simple notion—that all their members can expect to be equally treated by the law, their objective differences in many other areas notwithstanding (Malia and Emmons 2006).

Anderson equivocates in describing the process as a mostly bureaucratic revolution driven by the printing press and the normalization of language. Indeed both contributed to the popularity of the new political framework, but they were not enough. Not many people would offer their lives for administrative machines. In fact, after the 1941 German onslaught into the Soviet Union, Stalin did not call the Russians to defend the Communist Party, but the motherland—the nation by another name (Judt 2006). At times, Anderson, like Bauman (2001), points to the family-like qualities of nations to explain the attachment, otherwise difficult to understand, of people to them, but this is also misleading. Families are not imagined communities; their members do know each other and have firsthand experience of their mutual bonds, even when they diverge. The imagined national communities do not solely hark back to emotional or blood ties. Their collective appeal is based on the new way of preserving and conciliating the different interests of a diverse populace through the rule of law—a system characteristic of what we call modernity, which is deemed to be superior to any other known until now.

Hegemony, that is, the capacity to create stable interest coalitions around political and national goals shared by ample sections of a society, is not a quality based exclusively on emotions nor is it just an exercise of naked power. It is a hybrid of the qualities that Pareto attributed to his lions (strength) and foxes (cunning) (1935) that gets sorely lost in the *pomo* translation and its Marxian subtext. Hegemony serves well most human ventures as it creates unity, also known as sinergy, in pursuing collective ends. It is the cooperative face of evolution.

Acknowledging the key role that it has played and still plays in most societies does not entail a denial of diversity, of contradictions, or of eventual bouts of violence along history or in the foreseeable future. No social groups, institutions, and agencies can accurately read the future or totally conciliate differing interests; therefore, they face continuous tactical and strategic unknowns. Even agencies that put a premium on uniformity, such as religious institutes or communist parties, usually have at least two factions *vis-à-vis* any course of action—in favor or in rejection of whatever may be the bone of contention at any given time. Often subcurrents that stray from their center surround each one of them. In this way, they socially construct their respective arguments and decide about actions by opposition, and by trial and error. And we know that at some juncture the conflicts between them may become so intractable that splits, quarrels, and eventually violence inevitably flare up, although it is usually quite hard to forecast the exact moment when this will happen. Such are the feared divisive drives that compose the contradictory path of societal evolution.

Unfortunately the limited notion of constructivism accepted by *pomos* falls short on both aspects. Their politically correct bedtime stories are misleading in a fundamental sense. Their social constructivism entraps itself in a logical dilemma that is finally inextricable. If the role of all identities is merely to reflect illegitimate power struggles, as *pomo* theory demands, it is difficult to understand, barring a leap of faith, that some of them might avoid such fate. With the logical tools it has created, constructivism cannot make, for instance, a compelling case against Huntington's argument (1996, 2004; Fleishman 2002) that the real American identity is precisely the one that Aquila tried to expose for the American West (1996).

The other side of the equation is equally complicated. If one accepts *pomo*'s limited constructivism, once one of the candidates is crowned as the real representative of a given identity, it will become difficult to avoid that it curtails, persecutes, or even proscribes the rest of untrue displays. Limited constructivism opens the way to cleansing, whether ethnic, religious, or ideological. One only has to recall that the principle *cujus regio, ejus religio* (people should follow the religion of the area where they live), enshrined in the 1555 Peace of Augsburg between Catholics and Protestants—and quite similar to *pomo* constructivism—far from ensuring religious peace directly led to the bloody and terribly destructive Thirty Years' War in the following century (Parker 1997; Wedgwood 2005). Should one provide examples of equally devastating events in recent history, there would be not enough space to narrate them in this book.

However, once the usual suspects have been rounded up, most *pomo* narratives maintain that some alternative ideologies (Foucault's creative follies) or identities (some prevaricating Japanness, or Germanness, or Kenyanness, or whateverness), through the touch of a magic wand (they serve, we are told, the resistances of the oppressed), would be immune to hypostatization. One has to be careful, though, with what one desires. Sometimes those alternative identities come true and all of a sudden the conductor with the magic wand is none other than Mao Zedong, or Pol Pot, or Khomeini, and the rest have to countenance their notion of identity whether they share it or not. If they are still alive in the latter case, that is.

Chapter 8

The Languages of Tourism

FROM BABEL ...

L'enfer c'est les autres [hell is the others] opined Jean-Paul Sartre in *Huis-Clos* (a play literally translated as "Closed Door" that he wrote in 1943–44) and the infernal apothegm soon became quite trendy. Some years later, Sartre would explain that he meant it in a different way than that usually held. It is not that our social relations will always reveal a blasted streak, or that we will always have to suffer others as an anticipation of hell. Rather:

> [w]hen we think about ourselves, when we seek to grasp who we are, we ultimately wield other people's views; we judge ourselves with materials that others have already used—and have so proffered to us—to appraise us. Anything I may say about myself calls for other people's wisdom. In other words, if our rapports sour, I will appear totally dependent on them, thus effectively landing in hell. Many people are in a similar situation because they rely too much on the judgment of others. This by no means implies that we cannot weave different ties to them; only that all the others have capital significance for each one of us (1964).

In a nutshell, though not too clearly formulated, Ego and the rest are bound to live together. We cannot escape society, and societies bind humans in many ways, most of them communicated through language.

A language is above all a means of communicating information understood in a broad sense. Usually, language refers to verbal utterances and written statements. However, it may come in many other shapes, such as body language, audiovisual media, and, with the advent of structuralist linguistics, any sign, including natural objects when taken as signs, may become part of a language. Even though languages convey information, this is not limited to factual statements. It also covers states of mind, nonverbal communication, commands, feelings, etc. Furthermore, languages encode their components under constraining rules in order to impose under-standable meaning. Linguistic codes receive the name of grammar, that is, a system of inflections and syntax that allows the use of words to make sense of our lives. Grammar not only comprises verbal and written language; movies, performing arts, comics, love—all have a grammar of their own.

Today, we know that many animal species use language to communicate (biocommunication), but we think that human languages come topmost in complexity and wealth of resources. Societal bonds adopt many forms and most of them are expressed by language. If Sartre is right, this means that not only is language a social construct, as the ritual postmodern adage has it, but—much more importantly—that language always travels a two-way road. No individual, no social group, not even the most totalitarian of governments, can shape language and meaning at will. In authoritarian polities there will be a relentless pressure for people to abide by what the powers that be, Humpty-Dumpty style, want words to signify—a pressure often countered *sub rosa* and/or through humor. Democratic societies understand that language, and the objects it refers to, are a shared field, though often *shared* only means an agreement to disagree on meaning.

Nowadays all social subsystems are expected to display an ensemble of words and signs that, correctly interpreted, provides a better understanding of their relation to a wider social totality, be it the bounded geographical area of a country, the world, a particular culture, a number of cultures, or universal culture as such. The tourist social subsystem is no exception. It is widely accepted that if one grasps its basic elements of meaning and the way they are combined, that is, their grammar, both modern mass tourism and the social system that makes it possible will surrender their true structure and that, accordingly, we will be able to grasp and eventually shape it in an efficient or sustainable way. Under the present scissor crisis (Chapter 1) in tourism research, this goal tends to be interpreted in two mutually exclusive ways. It either becomes relevant for the purposes of marketing or of semiotics. While the former concentrates on how to use tourist language in order to increase productivity, maximize benefits, improve destination management, or adopt efficient branding techniques, the latter usually attempts to reveal the mystifying ties that bind it to modernity under capitalism and/or Western hegemony.

Communication theory has evolved to great complexity in the second half of the 20th century, after Shannon and Weaver proposed the simplest model of the process (1949). In their version communication was a unidirectional flow of messages from a sender through a medium to a receiver. The medium, which they portrayed as a phone, no doubt because of their experience at Bell Laboratories, was the central element of their theory. At more or less the same time, Lasswell proposed a similar model, though somewhat more elaborate. Communication theory should study the five Ws: who said what, to whom, by what media, and to what effect (Lasswell 1950). He would also apply it to the study of politics (Lasswell 1952; Lasswell et al 1968). Following this template, communication was later coded as the relation between an ego/author/emitter that transmits information/content/ messages to a receiver/audience/decoder through some medium.

Being forms of communication, messages from and about destinations, tourist, "vacation factories," local communities, and the rest of tourism subjects, though open to many other types of analysis, can be studied following this simple generalization. It is only a start, though, for the process just mentioned remains formal and atomistic. It is formal because, to make it operational, we have to flesh it out with different instances and practical evidence. It is also atomistic because it takes into consideration only the smallest bits and pieces of communication. If we want to get a better understanding, we should add that, in reality, the tiny elements that constitute the basic pieces of every process of communication are usually involved in feedback, that they piggyback on each other, and that in this way they unleash macroprocesses that resemble a shambles made up of countless skeins whose threads intertwine pell-mell with each other.

This chapter will look at some elements of the language of tourism, or, more accurately, adopting a caveat, perhaps we should speak in the plural— the languages of tourism. The contention means that thinking of tourists and the tourism world as using a limited number of resources grouped in a closed collection of encoders, messages, and audiences often betrays in its simplicity. Above all, it does not consider the everlasting contradiction between Mespeak and Thouspeak (more later); additionally one should never forget that message encoders usually relate to types of rhetoric or narratives that have different goals, use varying types of syntax, look to induce different effects, and address audiences accordingly.

"Enough talking about myself; now let us talk of what you think of me" may seem a joke but, flattering or intriguing as the statement may be for its author, both sides of the proposition will not necessarily coincide. De Unamuno, the Spanish philosopher, took a cue from Oliver Wendell Holmes to suggest that there is a trinity in each one of us—the Three Johns and the Three Thomases (De Unamuno 1998). One is the real John or Thomas that remains unknown even to himself; another—John's ideal of John or

Thomas' ideal Thomas, that is, the person each one of us presumes oneself to be and tries to project to the rest of the world-out-there; we have John's ideal Thomas and Thomas' ideal John or the self of the other that they have constructed, and that do not necessarily coincide or overlap. One could embellish the conundrum by distinguishing another pair in the third state— John's ideal Thomas and the Thomas John lets himself talk about in public or the other way around. At any rate, to keep it simple, leaving aside the first John or Thomas that by definition should remain opaque, the other two elements usually display a lingering state of dissonance. When John speaks from his ideal self, we say that he uses Mespeak; when Thomas refers to John, then we understand this as Thouspeak. Most often they do not coincide. A tourism application of the framework can be found in a paper by Karch and Dann dealing with the problematic process of role negotiation between female tourists and beachboys in Barbados (Karch and Dann 1981).

This is a nagging state for, ideally, we would all prefer that the person we want to project should be accepted without further ado by all and sundry. But, to concentrate on tourism, destinations and attractions, as defined by their promoters, seldom coincide with the perception of the rest of the gazers. Images are definitely constructed in alternative and variant ways by authors and audiences. Neither side holds complete control over them. Images move restlessly. They are in a state of flux or, alternatively stated, they are cockpits where opposing forces clash—a point often overlooked (Chapter 7).

Finally, most perceived information, some under the guise of gossip, relates to facts (including feelings and held opinions) that allow navigating the rapids of the natural and social environment. In this way, communication and language have a clear evolutionary edge and are intimately linked to survival. However, as already observed, not all communication refers to facts. Parts of the messages we receive on a daily basis include a persuasive element. They inform us of the alleged advantages of consuming such and such goods and services, or present them in such a way that we feel attracted to future consumption. This is the language of advertising, which even conspicuously present in other historical periods, has reached a special peak in market-oriented societies based on mass consumption, that is, in modern mass societies. Maybe because of its ubiquity, maybe because of its intensity, it is easy to mistake it for language as such, especially in areas like tourism where establishing the image of a product or a destination often becomes a make-or-break issue. This would be a huge error. In the motley collection of statements referring to tourist behavior and activities, one should keep fact-based communication separate from suasion. It is not an easy task, but there is much to be gained in understanding their inner difference.

Dissonance traps more easily narrators that have to construct and maintain positive images and brands. In the tourist system they are mainly vacation factories (tour operators, travel agencies, airlines, hotel chains) and destination management organizations (DMO). Their job revolves around spinning yarns about the quality of their products, the unique attractions of their places, and so on. That must be a story of unmitigated success, even clairvoyance, on the part of the firm or destination they are promoting. When the message comes across successfully, it generates a relation of trust that will make the consumer buy the offered product or service time and again.

Image building and branding have been mostly used to sell products and services. In the world of tourism, airlines, hotel chains, tour operators, even travel agents have successfully used branding techniques (Morgan and Pritchard 2000). With an eye on their positive outcomes, other actors started using them in order to increase business. Over the last few years a growing number of destinations have thus tried to establish their own brands. Does destination Mespeak fulfill the expectations? It seems doubtful. To start with, destinations cannot easily extricate themselves from being identified with nation states (Ansholt 2002, 2005, 2006; Lee et al 2005). When asked about where they vacationed last time, many will say China, France, Thailand, or the United States, if they do not wax even more general: "I went to Europe"; "We toured Southeast Asia"; "Island-hopping in the Caribbean". It is obvious that they did not. They went to some resort, or covered some places in a region, or visited a few towns in a number of countries, but in everyday language they take a shortcut through nations, geographical areas, and even continents.

This connection is as vexing as difficult to avoid (Papadopoulos and Heslop 2002). On the one hand, most destinations carry baggage that is not directly related to tourism. Most nations have an image imposed by historical events and their popular interpretation. Resorts in Turkey can be similar to those in many other countries, but still many feel wary of going to them because one of the features they identify the country with is its religion (Baloglu 2001). Seldom political turmoil wreaks havoc in proper tourist areas; however, as in the recent cases of Kenya and Thailand, it can harm incoming flows of international tourists for a long time. Most destinations might gain from breaking the association with their national history, but in fact this is an unrealistic expectation. Some destinations are islands, but none is totally severed from the historical baggage they carry.

Some geographic areas in the world, like the *Côte d'Azur* in Southern France, have achieved general repute, but they are an exception. For most, name recognition is limited to just a few markets. Majorca may accommodate 10 million international tourists in one year, but not many people beyond Western Europe would know it. Additionally, destinations do not cater to the same customers. The Northern part of Majorca around Deià may be an elite destination for writers, artists, celebrities, and other jet-setters, so it does not easily mix with the masses that pack to El Arenal or Magaluf during the summer. There are many difficult issues trying to create a single brand for those two markets (Castro et al 2007; Morgan and Pritchard 2000, 2002). Destinations come as a medley of different locations and different products, and their different stakeholders have interests and expectations that are difficult to reconcile.

Most importantly, destinations do not have direct control over products, pricing policies, or distribution systems (Prideaux and Cooper 2002). One should acknowledge that, no matter how customer loyalty can reward brands that provide pleasing experiences, still most tourists' budgets are limited, and they have to reckon with the value their money is buying. There is a difference between acknowledging the emotional tie between customers and brands, and concluding that disposable income has disappeared from most people's radars. Inasmuch as DMOs cannot control most of market-ing's 4 Ps (product, price, place, and promotion) as by definition happens in market-based systems, it seems wise to tone down the talk about the paramount role of emotions in consumer decision-making. Marketers should acknowledge that, because of it, destinations are less amenable to branding than business. This makes the danger of dissonance rise exponentially (Pike 2004a, 2005).

The initial boom of mass tourism in Spain (1959–79) offers a good example on the limits of destination imaging and branding. One can discuss endlessly whether the activities of the specialized Spanish agencies of the time were really branding (concept which had not yet gained the traction it would later) or just image building (Gartner 1993). Given the fuzziness of both concepts, one should rather take a flexible position. However, if we attend to the gist of the matter, whatever the label, Spanish National Tourist Agency ([SNTA], a name used to cover the many denominations and acronyms that have accompanied it throughout its history) covered the same bases one expects from branding. It followed a consistent market action, using the best promotional tools of the time, mostly based on distribution of posters and brochures. Posters and brochures provided a more efficient way to communicate with the target public than expensive advertising campaigns spread thin over many markets by budget strictures. SNTA also tried to create an emotional bond between (mostly European) consumers and the destination. It finally tried developing their loyalty so that customers would make repeat visits to the country. At face value, whether branding or image building, given its economic accomplishments, SNTA's strategy of the time looks extremely successful. However, there are good reasons to doubt the correlation between the plan and its outcome.

SNTA has recently published a number of volumes containing most of the posters printed since this medium was first used in 1929 (SNTO 2000a, 2000b, 2005) up until 2000. Later on, another volume (SNTO 2007) appeared that contains a larger number of posters of the same period, including some missing in the previous editions, and extending to 2005. In addition to their documentary interest and artistic value, the now available collection of posters provides a clear view of the communicational strategy developed by SNTA at the time when Spanish mass tourism started its takeoff (1959–79). An analysis of those materials offers a number of significant pointers.

Above all, it is clear that SNTA made a big effort to publicize Spain. From 1959 to 1979 it published a total of 550 posters with an annual average of 21, nearly one poster printed every other week, although production did not maintain a regular schedule and went in cycles. Spain thus tried to create its own branded products. However, what was that brand SNTA was so eager to create? A couple of basic statistics will make it clear. Making the distinction between nature- and culture-based posters, one can see a clear bias towards the latter. Of the 550 posters published during the two take-off decades, nearly 80% had culture (monuments, museums, paintings, traditions, cultural activities, etc.) as their main subject. The trend was obvious—nature was below SNTA's radar. When it appeared, however, Spanish communications did not have a clear sense of direction either. Out of 137 nature-based posters, only 89 represented beaches and sea resorts, with only 74 of them devoted to the Mediterranean, the Balearic Islands, or the Canaries. The rest depicted imposing mountains, snowy landscapes, flowers, forests, dramatic sunsets, roaming animals, and the like. Overall, the sea, the coastline, and the beaches definitely took a back seat in Spain's image. Of the total 550 posters of the period, less than 15% associated Spain with sand, sun, and sea.

SNTA had fallen into the DMO trap. In a nutshell, it allowed the brand it wanted to project to overwhelm the image perceived by the target. If the message and the image are not well calibrated, they will create a degree of dissonance. This danger, as has been pointed out, plagues DMOs more easily than other branding agencies. In the Spanish case, especially until 1975, SNTA tried to define the country in a totally unilateral way with scant regard for consumer expectations. From 1959 to 1975, SNTA was in denial that its best selling product was the sun and the sea, and that its consumers were the European middle and lower middle classes. The strategy that underpinned Spanish promotion turned its back on the majority of its customers. Neither posters nor brochures had them at the top of their list. A contemporary analysis of Spanish brochures (Febas 1978) had already pointed out such shortcomings. Only 11% of texts and 20% of the iconic material paid any direct attention to the audience.

Additionally, Spanish posters and brochures prioritized the arts over any other features. The country was "museumized" and packaged as a place where art, above all religious art, reigned supreme. It was supposed to epitomize the unchanging features of a perennial Spanish identity. Imposing churches and abbeys, ascetic saints, heroic warriors—such was the essence of an Eternal Spain that required men (not much was said about the role of women) to be half-monks, half-soldiers. In the self-made SNTA symbolic universe, chauvinism and disdain for modernity went hand in hand. Were incoming tourists really motivated by all that old-age paraphernalia?

When SNTA started work on its first marketing plan (1985–86), data showed that international tourists to Spain were not exactly looking for the culture and the history of the country. Over 85% of them spent their vacations on the Mediterranean littoral and the islands enjoying sun and sea vacations (unpublished data from the first Spanish Marketing Plan 1985 known to the author). The projected brand had definitely not seeped deeply into the consumer consciousness. However, tourists would come and come back to Spain in droves. What happened was obvious. DMOs can project as many images as they want. However, they are neither the sole nor the most important source of information for the consumer. In fact, the public is always surrounded by a steady flow of advertising stimuli, educational sources, and interpersonal communication. Therefore, DMOs are but one of the sources of information and not particularly reliable for different reasons (from limited budgets to bureaucratic guidance and inadequate market knowledge). SNTA's goal of turning tourism into one of the main sources of foreign exchange was completely successful. In this way, the outcome validated the political strategy. However, as a matter of fact, European tourists, the bulk of foreign inbound, clearly voted with their feet away from Eternal Spain. Most were looking for sun and sea family vacations at affordable prices, just what foreign tour operators were offering them. Their catalogs displayed a number of products, and projected a definite image of beach products that fitted the expectations of many Northern European consumers. Whether they accurately represented the country in their brochures (Dann 1996c; Gaviria 1975, 1996) was of little or no consequence to them.

   The complete success of the overall political strategy has precluded a foregone conclusion—SNTA branding strategy during the take-off period of mass tourism to Spain (1959–79) was an unmitigated failure. Indeed, after 1979, under democratic governments of different shades, SNTA improved its communication policies to the tastes of increasingly educated consumers (Gnoth 2002; Haug et al 2007). These policies have been quite successful until the present, as the country consistently ranks among the top destinations in the world. Still, a doubt lingers at the back of the mind. Was the Spanish success in the new phase of maturity a product of the brand-new new-brand (Joan Miró's inspired logo; the initial slogan "Everything under the Sun"; attention to the beach and family vacation customer) or just the fact that Spain offered the right experiences at the right price to the right customers? Possibly there cannot be a clear-cut answer to the riddle that is independent of the circumstances of the context. Taken in isolation, any of the two sides would be misleading. As noted previously, if there is a lesson to be drawn from the Spanish case, it is that branding always travels a two-way road. Neither can one single agent control its own image, nor will the latter remain unchallenged by many other market pressures. Seen from this point of view, the discussion whether DMOs, tour operators, airlines, hotel chains, and, in general, any tourism-related agency can control the image of their product or destination seems to have an easy answer—no, they cannot.

... TO THE LANGUAGE OF TOURISM

Graham Dann has devoted much attention to studying the language of tourism, and his work has inspired a great deal of the later discussion. Other authors (Blichfeldt 2005, 2007; Pike 2004b, 2007, 2008; Tasci and Gartner 2005) have treated the subject as well, but in general, none has shown the depth and breadth mastered by Dann. His main work (1996a) uses an impressive collection of materials and, what is more decisive, advances a few hypotheses to summarize the inner system one can find in the language of tourism. His was an innovative approach to tourism analysis that has not been equaled yet.

   In a number of other papers (1996a, 1996b, 1996c, 1999, 2002, 2005a, 2005b; Dann and Parrinello 2007), Dann applied his sociolinguistic approach to items as varied as brochures, posters, tourist ads, guidebooks, travelogues, and even notices in tourism zones. He later extended his views to the Internet's ways and protocols used to convey information on diverse aspects of tourism. His work deserves to be probed in detail even if the reader may think that, for different reasons, it does not pass muster. In a nutshell, the capstone of his theoretical work is that tourism communication, otherwise known as, the language of tourism, treats tourists as children in need of social control. This central thesis is amply developed in an elaborate way using scores of materials and an impressive amount of examples. For all its wealth of evidence, though, the final result falls prey to the reductionism of the basic pattern.

At the beginning of Chapter 4 of *The Language of Tourism*, Dann announces to the reader that the notion "the language of tourism is one of social control" is so important that "it may be considered as the central thesis of this presentation" (1996a:68). However, he keeps close to his chest what he means by it. Control, social control, and power are words that deserve a clear treatment as they suffer so much from polysemy. Power, as defined by Merriam-Webster (2002), means the ability to produce a given physical effect, as "in the earthquake had such a power that it destroyed all the houses within a radius of ten miles from its epicenter," as well as the ability to direct or to influence other people's behavior or a course of events, as in "the leader imposed his will on the assembly," or "the democratic party has won a number of elections over the last few years." When we say that something reflects social control, we usually use it in the second sense. But not all types of social control are created equal. When we say "the Führer decided to send all the Jews to extermination camps," we usually understand that this type of power is not the same as in "parents decided to send their children to a summer (boot) camp." Both are instances of social control, but most people realize that while parents can legitimately decide what their underage offspring must do over the summer vacation, disposing of other people's lives without their consent brings illegitimacy to the decision even though, in the first sense of "power," the Führer definitely had the power to do so.

The notion of legitimacy and the fine print of how to define it, as we saw in Chapter 3, get no real space within the *pomo* matrix. By definition, it sees all social relations reflecting a power structure that cuts both ways. The notion has been around in philosophy for many centuries, but its latest and more cogent version harks back to Foucault. Either you are dominant or dominated, but you always participate in a power struggle; what counts is the position where you find yourself, either as the powerful party or the other side, that is, the Other. This initial situation, however, may be affected by the negotiations that take place between the two of you, so much that it may even be completely reversed. Both Ego and Alter vie for recognition and for power over each other; both use all the weapons at their disposal, in a new edition of the Hegelian master and slave dialectic. There is no other way—both will acknowledge each other, which to some extent makes their power struggle redundant. But, if one forgets about this striking conclusion, ultimately neither Foucault nor Hegel have any feeling for the eventual asymmetry of power. The notion of legitimacy has no room of its own in their theoretical constructions. All that counts is power; whether the master dominates the slave or, as in Joseph Losey's *The Servant*, the slave finally overcomes his former master, both are equally availing themselves of power.

This approach irked some commentators. Dean and Juliet Flower MacCannell countered that this was not the way it goes between rapists and their victims. Their remonstration showed some mind-reading skills not usually available to common mortals, as when they said that

> [w]e are concerned [...] that Foucault's vision [of rape] may have been prematurely Utopian: that redefinition of sexual and other identities remains subject to ancient power relations and violence even, or especially, in our postmodern epoch; that if some appear to escape tyranny based on their categorization it is because they have been allowed to escape only to serve power by masking its effectiveness (1993a:205).

Like many other of their usual suspects, the MacCannells portray Foucault as providing excuses for power. However, they effectively score a point in saying that "power is not neutral, diffuse and freely available but fiercely protected by those who hold it and their agents; and finally that threats and the actual use of force and violence remain essential to the exercise of power" (1993a:205). They may have not anticipated the consequences of their views (the need to elucidate what legitimacy means), but the conclusion seems flawless. There is a difference—one to be understood and retained— between the legitimate and the illegitimate uses of power. Power and legitimacy cannot survive one without the other.

Dann does not show any special disposition to Foucauldian orthodoxy; he is not particularly fussy when it comes to social control either. He does not define it and stays comfortably away from the discussion. Why? One suspects that Dann belongs to what might be called the Durkheimian Left. After Parsons and other American sociologists successfully hijacked the French master's "solidarity" brand, Durkheim has usually been interpreted as an advocate of social conformity. Parsons read him as meaning that core societal values will always trump individual will (1937, 1991). Irrespective of their individual inclinations, most people in most circumstances, if not always, will gladly, or at least passively, accept the different roles they are expected to play in the organic division of labor proper to modernity. This disposition, together with other main "social facts," creates a successful coercion that binds together any given social order. Societies cannot live without such constraint and control; however, abiding by their core values appears to most people as the most expeditious way to solve the Hobbesian problem of order. Most accept all power as legitimate and thus find a reason to obey it. To leave behind the nightmarish state of nature, they are ready to pay any compliance tolls to the powers that be without much ado. Control in this Durkheimian interpretation comes naturally to societies as it does to people. After all, the latter just obey themselves when they follow societal rules (Lanfant 1981, 2007; Lanfant et al 1995).

Does anybody remember Durkheim's study of suicide (1997)? Those in the Durkheimian Left do. For them, the more social control pervades collective life, the more people will resent it, consciously or unconsciously. Conformity is not a given; one has to pay a high price for it. Durkheim may not have put great faith in heroic resistance against social control (after all he had seen the 1870 Paris Commune and its sequels), but he knew that in every modern society some or many individuals are to be found in a state of *anomia*, of normlessness, meaninglessness, and lack of belonging. Individual disillusion with the anomic social system reveals itself in many varieties, ranging from the nomadic escape from affluence to suicide. Even though seemingly confined to individual decisions, widespread social anomie represents a challenge to the prevailing order. Durkheimians of the Left equate social control with anomie and, even though they do not entertain great expectations about radical change, they analyze social life through this dark looking glass—the ubiquitous and noxious consequences of social control. Depending on their point of view, Durkheimians of the Left will paint their canvas with either the cubist shades of gray of the eponymous Juan Gris or the desperation of Edvard Munch's many versions of *The Scream*. Social life is in no way a bed of roses. If this interpretation is correct, it would provide the key to why Dann does not feel pressured to define social control. Just open your eyes and you will feel it. This is exactly what he does with an impressive plethora of information.

Social control is essential to all language, and the language of tourism is no exception. Dann feels it has been so since ancient times. According to him, Greece and Rome regarded early forms of travel as escape from what today we would call urban blight. For many Greek authors, going places would counter the overcrowding and the violence of established *poleis* in Hellas and in Asia Minor. Not everybody saw travel in a positive way. Plato recommended that overseas visitors be quarantined so that they would not corrupt the minds of Athenian youths—an ancient case of divergence among stakeholders, as the local innkeepers did not appreciate his views much. In Rome, places like Baiae or Pompei, which were in essence akin to present day resorts, awakened the same confrontational views as today about the economic and social dynamics of travel. Similar developments followed during the Middle Ages, through the centuries of the Grand Tour, and, later, at the birth of mass tourism that Thomas Cook introduced to Britain and the railways in the United States. In all those instances one can see how different authors not only discussed tourism's pros and cons, but also established a cannon of objectives and required behavior for tourists. No strangers to this story were the agencies that provided the wherewithal to vacationing, especially in modern times. Cook's organized travel started with trips to temperance meetings. But even more than his moral undertow, Dann highlights the organizational skills that allowed Cook and his successors to flourish. Organization mirrors social control even more than the ethical underpinnings of the harbingers of modern mass tourism. This is where danger mostly lurks.

The relation between tourism and social control deepened quickly with the advent of mass tourism. It is often said that travel gives ample opportunity to exert individual freedom, but one should take it with the proverbial pinch of salt. Some authors point out that tourists feel trapped in their decisions; that they have to abide by the stringent rules imposed by tour operators about timing, places to be visited, the services provided during the trip, etc. Turner and Ash (1975), for example, saw control as a consequence of the social corrosiveness of tourism or, otherwise, because tourists requested order to ensure their own safety while on a trip. They even went a step further, arguing that this drive to order may have been the reason for the success of tourism in places such as Spain under Franco, Portugal under Oliveira Salazar, and the Philippines under Marcos.

But, Dann notes, it is not so much political power that counts for social control in the tourist system as the sheer economic power of the industry that organizes tourist consumption (2003). Hotels and restaurant chains, tourist-oriented shopping malls and entertainment venues, theme parks, and, above all, the tour operating companies that design vacation packages look for maximizing their benefits and impose a framework for tourist behavior that will always beat the expectations of either hosts or guests.

> It is from such an asymmetrical relationship of power that they mould the wills of receiving societies and tourists [...] Not only do they popularize models which facilitate such control, but they manipulate attitudes to conform to these models [through] advertising [...], [thus] redefining situations, setting parameters and altering consumer behavior in the desired direction. Since clients are disorganized and lacking any coherent agenda, they come under the control of a discourse which asks questions, provides answers and speaks to them in a series of commands (Dann 1996a:76).

The rhetoric of advertising hides the subtle domination of those big corporations that grow and grow as their help is presented as necessary for the successful organization of tourist trips. The corporations are the real owners of the tourist gaze. The language of freedom they so conspicuously use in their ad copy hides the reality of control.

Social control is not only evident in advertising. Dann highlights its footprint in many other recesses of tourist communication. One of them is the guidebook. In his probe of Baedeker's guides, Boorstin pressed home how, below the descriptions of places and attractions, one can find his admonishments on how tourists were expected to behave, to dress, to avoid talking loud, "in short, to be decent, respectable, model representatives of their own country" (Dann 1996a:84). Baedeker was also the creator of the star system to rate attractions, thus telling tourists exactly what they should see and what was not worth a detour. Even residents in the visited places (including Old Faithful in Yellowstone National Park) would follow the routines assigned by Baedeker. Dann, together with Boorstin, gets a bit carried away. *Feldmarschall* Göring is said to have been so enthralled with the guide that in 1942 he ordered the *Luftwaffe* to raze every place in Britain distinguished with an asterisk in it. "In the days before the Second World War no less a person than Kaiser Wilhelm felt obliged to perform for tourists" (Dann 1996a:84), by showing up for the concert that the imperial band held daily at noon in front of the imperial palace, "because it says in Baedeker that at this hour I always do" (Boorstin 1961:104). Indeed, the guide must have been quite powerful. If the story is true, it even forced the Kaiser to go through his antics when he was no longer Kaiser. He abdicated his crown in November 1918, many moons before the Second World War started.

Not only guidebooks qualify for the imposition of social control. Travelogues are full of advice, and what can be more oriented to control than advice? So do pictures and videos that accompany advertising and pictorials in travel magazines. The way in which they present tourists corroborates the previous depictions one can find in the travel catalogs produced by vacation factories or the images displayed by destination management agencies. Dann takes an example (provided by O'Barr 1994) from an Indian tourist authority ad that shows a white couple sitting on top of an elephant led by a mahout in his best regalia as the best way to visit Jaipur—another instance of the ideology of photographic colonialism "where the sahibs and memsahibs are treated as maharajahs and the locals are portrayed as their servants" (1996a: 87).

Social control extends to many other components of tourism (Dann 2003). Take the aforementioned star-rating system for hotels and attractions. It not only informs about their most important features, but also categorizes them in such a way that closes them to the less affluent classes. The top rungs are symbolically beyond the reach of all those lacking the cultural capital to follow the appropriate codes of behavior. By offering better rooms than the ones many people have at home, good hotels confine guests to their bedrooms. Or, in another twist, they enclose their properties in such a way that the outside is presented as dangerous or boring for the customers. They thus become a captive clientele that will not leave the resort's bars or swimming pools during their stay, thus running an ever-higher drinks' bill. This strategy, successfully adopted by Club Med since it started business, not only improves the company's bottom line, but also makes the clients submissive, and therefore, more amenable to accept the rules of the resort. Some may be quite obnoxious. One travelogue quoted by Dann tells of a Dominican Republic resort where guests were made to wear ID bracelets fastened to their wrists; otherwise, no services were provided, not even could they open their rooms without them. Even a former Miss Bristol had to wear the bracelet over her otherwise much desired and admired suntan! Another writer compared his stay at a Caribbean resort with being under SS control.

Social control encapsulates tourists while they are supposedly free during their vacation. Must-see attractions, guides' views, imposed routes, visiting schedules, hotel and resort regulations, all these and many other allegedly benign rules of social intercourse end up by leading the tourist herd toward the only pastures on which they are allowed to graze. Packaged tours epitomize this predicament. However, as soon as travel organizers take the place of the individual will, even the allegedly freest and most open-ended of tours become tools of control. Adventure tours, safaris, hikes, white water rafting, and other extreme sports—all go down the same broad path.

What could be less constraining than a walking tour? But, if you take one, outfitters' brochures will tell you that good boots are needed in certain areas and that some trails demand more strenuous effort than others. Some former pilgrim routes, for instance, have become increasingly popular. In 1987, the Spanish Camino de Santiago (St. James' Way) became the first European Cultural Route designated by the Council of Europe. In the past, *peregrinos* (pilgrims) could wander as their fantasy took them; nowadays, proper routes are marked by its own Camino brand-signs (a pilgrim's scallop shell). If participants want to spend the night at one of the hostels reserved for pilgrims, they need a pilgrim passport. Where formerly one could walk it at leisure, nowadays many travel companies offer Camino products that are thoroughly regulated. A similar story can be told of many other attractions.

> Thus, whether one is talking about social control in hotels or in the various forms of touring, whether one is dealing with the relatively unexplored control imposed during the travel experience or commands issued by notices at the resort or destination, whether one is referring to historical or contemporary tourism, an overriding message of order and control is both omnipresent and perennial (Dann 1996a:100).

Dann rightly pursues the problem raised by his conclusion. How is it possible that the reality of social control can coexist with the perception of freedom held by many tourists and so often noted—even celebrated—by many researchers? Answer—because the language of tourism succeeds in treating them as "children." To prove the point, Dann gathers a sizeable number of examples and avails himself of as many explanatory theories as he can lay his hands on.

Exhibit A—the alliterative triangle formed by the Three Rs of romanticism, regression, and rebirth. Romanticism provides the themes tourists should covet: freedom as the enjoyment of the pristine (MacCannellians, proper or phony, would say the authentic) whether in social intercourse or nature. The oppositions of civilized/savage, town/countryside, hectic/bucolic, and bureaucracy/quaintness so eagerly used to sell the travel products convey the message that travel can reconcile modern city dwellers with a deeper reality either in the simplicity and exoticism of the savage mind or in a bountiful and benevolent nature. Possibly in both, for exotic people are often imagined as living in nonpolluted spaces.

This romantic vision thus urges us back to the comforts of the maternal womb (regression), unfortunately sealed by a Lacanian Law-of-the-Father that denies our innermost drives. Dann approvingly quotes from Dufour that tourists protest against this dreadful ukase by sheltering in myth.

> Thus tourists seek to discover the good old days and a return to nature via the myth of the Golden Age, a rich, abundant, and luxurious nature (the myth of the Horn of Plenty). They long for childhood (the Myth of the Fountain of Youth). They seek their mother in the inner recesses of cities (the myth of Heliopolis), in the mountains (the myth of Olympus) and the Ocean (the myth of Poseidon). Holidays, he says, can never be devoid of myth, just as myths themselves represent a regression of humanity, a form of infantilism, a return to Mother's breast (Dann 1996a:105).

So, Mommy Dearest has as many incarnations as the Hindu Vishnu—here as sea/womb, there as mountain/breast, and beyond as a male Poseidon. In a nutshell, the language of tourism succeeds because it promises rebirth, often wrapped in sexual fantasies. The white bikini worn by a young woman in an ad evokes virginity; travel literature is full of mammary representations such as mountains, domes of mosques and churches; mammary glands do not stop at those convex representations—they can also be seen in Baudrillard's (1995) world supermarket of consumption (Dann 1996a:60, 108, 127).

All this seems a bit overdone, both as imagery and as explanation. Indeed overt or implicit promises of open, duty-free sex rewards are used by promotional literature, but pop Freudianism à la Barthes soon leads to excess. One can recall here an old joke. Father takes his young son to a psychoanalyst. "I am worried, doctor. My son is obsessed with sex. We have some masterpieces at home. He looks at one of the Mirós and says it is of a couple making love; he looks at a Mondrian and there is a naked woman, he...." "What can you expect," cuts in the psychoanalyst, "if you expose him to such filthy pictures?"

This new scientific explanation to end all myths, the longing for vacations included, is nothing else than a remake of another, not so motherly myth: that of Otys and Ephialtes told by Aristophanes in Plato's *Symposium*. Those two miscreants wanted to scale the heavens and lay hands on the gods. So Zeus hatched a plan to enfeeble their strength and extinguish their turbulence. Always the economist, he ran a cost-benefit analysis. He would not annihilate mankind for, he pondered, who would offer sacrifices to the gods if humans vanished from the face of the earth? Better cut them in half, which would make them more numerous and also weaker. They would no longer entertain any more crazy ideas about carving a new subdivision to build a few MacMansions on Mount Olympus. Also more humans meant more sacrifices. A win-win situation for the gods, isn't it? The plot thickens, though. Always the dismal scientist, Zeus forgot about externalities. Instead of offering more sacrifices, humans started searching for their lost halves and, when they found them, they embraced them and longed to grow into one with them. Unfortunately this was impossible for, cut in half, their organs of generation could not find each other, and humans started dying of hunger and self-neglect.

Being masters of mass entertainment, Zeus and pop Freudianism tweaked the initial plan to a happy ending. They re-engineered the previously mentioned unmentionable organs of generation and put them in front. In this way, each human only has one side. It is the half in endless search for the other half, becoming in fact one in a lover's embrace. Men and women sectioned from an androgynous being are heterosexual, while men grown from other men and women cut out from other women will count as homosexual. We endlessly feel the missing Other (whether man or woman) in ourselves because they are there, like the missing leg that aches to the sailor who lost it in a storm. Anything concave represents a vagina/womb; anything convex, a penis. Yes, but everything is not just convex only on one side, for it recesses on the other, just like everything that is concave. The concave is also convex and the other way round. These inversions have been endlessly exploited by psychoanalysis and marketing. They can be put to nearly any use. Whatever works, like in Woody Allen's eponymous movie.

From the three Rs, Dann introduces the reader to other complementary and pedagogically alliterated threesomes—the three Hs (happiness, hedonism, heliocentrism), the three Fs (fun, fantasy, fairy tales) and the three Ss (sea, sex, socialization). In the end, they all hark back to the first theme. The tourist is a child in search of gratification and afraid of deprivation. There are many ways to phrase it. One can wax Freudian (pleasure vs. reality principle) or Jungian (intro- vs. extraversion) or Lacanian (mother vs. father laws) or Left-Durkheimian (freedom vs. organization). Economists and down-to-earth sociologists prefer to talk about the conflict between expectations of plenty and scarcity. While Freud's, Jung's, and Lacan's problems can always find a literary solution for they deal in intangibles, scarcity is regrettably concrete, palpable, and impervious to the magic of words.

Is the language of tourism the only one that offers imaginary solutions in exchange for social control? This would unfairly lionize the industry. In fact, the illusions created by advertising in general and for tourism in particular are quite minor when compared with the illusions peddled to humans by many other institutions of their making. Regression and rebirth/resurrection are the stock-in-trade of religions. They play with the most serious and the most inescapable ailment of the human condition—death—and, though they cannot promise that our life in this sublunary world will be limitless, most pledge eternal life and/or peaceful annihilation in a future one. Dangling this reward in front of our desperation, they have built a number of extremely successful brands over the centuries. Their market share of aggregate social control totally dwarfs that of tourism promotion, and the best ad agencies only ape them clumsily.

Should the blame for winking at increases in power, in wealth, in status, and in sexual access be exclusively limited to advertising? Are they not the stuff politics, cultural life, academic progress, and even family-life thrive on? One does not need the proverbial rocket scientist to know that; just a modicum of evolutionary psychology will do. Offering rewards to survival (i.e., better opportunities to fit and reproduce) or threatening to withdraw them (via starvation, discredit, poverty, castration, or denial of tenure) are very effective ways to control and shape human behavior. Promotion and advertising employ them to sell. Wherever there has been human life, power and control have not been very distant. This is a given.

There is something highly commendable in Dann—his adamant suspicion of power. He looks with a wary eye on all institutions and agencies that claim superiority over the individual. Behind every prohibition, behind every command, behind every ad, and even behind seemingly friendly advice (2003), an attack on individual freedom may lurk. However, possibility does not necessarily entail likelihood, even less necessity. Accepting that "may" and "be likely" are interchangeable, Dann easily falls prey to the liar paradox ("Believe me, all language is social control"). If the assertion is untrue, it defeats itself; if true, why should we believe that Dann would not try to have his share? Readers thus reach an impasse. However, like Achilles' hapless pursuit of the turtle, the conundrum cannot be solved by formal logic alone; otherwise, language itself would be unnecessary or redundant. Language, indeed, can be put to many purposes, but there is one that trumps them all—stating facts. Without this informational component, language would have no evolutionary or adaptive value. If I think that social control is embedded in every message and that it curtails my individual freedom, quite possibly I will disregard the person who tells me "Beware, this part of the beach is full of big lizards". But if we both happen to be in Komodo Island, I may quite well end up as fodder for one of the namesake dragons. Every year the media report a few attacks on tourists and locals there. So, under normal circumstances I would be better off if I heeded the advice.

More in general, complete mistrust of social control would make any social contract moot. Social compacts rest on both trust and suspicion, not just on one of them. This does not make social relations easy. Indeed in this sublunary world of ours, social control pervades all human relations, but not all social controls are created equal. The problem, once again, lies with legitimacy. We usually give the benefit of doubt to most messages until further notice. We also trust some sources more than others. We feel that we are exercising freedom when we go to the voting booth after a free electoral campaign. We know that we are free to spend our hard earned money and on what. We have choices, and when we have them, we think that the type of social control that allows us to go for one or the other is more legitimate than others based on slavery, feudal exactions, or one-party rule. Legitimacy based on people's consent is one of the things that make modernity so resilient.

Are any choices always possible for all? Not necessarily. Sometimes, nature partners with social control to limit options. People less than six feet tall cannot usually play in the National Basketball League. People over five make poor jockeys. Social control is also present in many other societal regulations. Citizen rights and freedoms, plus the state structure derive from a constitution freely adopted by the people of a country or their ancestors. The Bill of Rights, as interpreted by the courts, decides the limits that can be imposed on the exercise of freedom. In this way, most modern constitutions enshrine economic freedom regulated by the market. This means that human beings are free to work and to sell their labor, even though at times they may find no takers. Slavery and undue exactions are thereby forbidden. Without these and other manifestations of control, social life would be more hazardous and unpredictable. No need to quote Hobbes about the hardship in the state of nature. These and other regulations that make the exercise of individual rights possible in a democratic society usually find ample popular support. Some people, or many, can feel displeased with this or that aspect of life in democratic polities, but they can associate to defend their points of view and eventually change them. In the end, the legitimacy of democratic governments remains high because they allow people to do much of what they want. Markets may not be so widely accepted as representative democracy; however, many people understand that the freer they are, in the end the more efficient they become. For all its failures and foibles, for the entire hubbub about the need to regulate them, most people would also accept that they perform better than controlled or planned economies.

This covers a large area of legitimized social control. The rule of law and the markets, however, can only do so much. Within their framework social intercourse finds many ways to express itself in customs, in trade, in creativity, and in new ways of work and leisure. However, not every individual has the skills, the capital, the perseverance, or the stamina to be a landmark in any one of those social venues. Individual opinion tends to be expressed in collective ways via the media. Not only do we voice our points of view, we want to feel our opinions shaped into currents of public opinion and we identify with gatekeepers. We trust the media, or the bloggers, that express our thoughts and feelings in a more coherent way than we are willing or able to do. Tastes and consumption decisions are shaped by fashions, fads channeled by the media through information, and opinion and advertising. Moreover, humans often need guidance about which products and services are reliable and which are not. They can find it among friends and relatives, by word of mouth, in consumer magazines, or in the literature of different providers. All of them exercise some form of social control.

Many times, the big players that have the money to push their products efficiently, that is, corporations and conglomerates, overwhelm the public with advertising. However, people do not seem to resent the control they exert as long as they offer them the products they want at the right price. Consumers often feel something akin to religious devotion for the brands they trust. Does it mean that they have no choice? The evolution of many products (from cars to hotels to airlines) shows that the big corporations never control the market and the consumer so much as to make crises impossible, postpone renovation endlessly, offer poor customer service, or avoid going bankrupt. As long as there are a sufficient number of providers, no matter how big some of them may be, and as long there are good rules to regulate competition, consumers will definitely exert their choices. Indeed, some people, even many, especially in times of economic crises, will feel splenetic or alienated and will show their disgust with the system in telling ways. A majority, though, accept the mainstream way of life without too much questioning. Stasiology, the science of revolutions, explains why most people accept social control from the powers that be either meekly or enthusiastically.

This is a point Dann tends to overlook. Tourists may be cajoled into buying their packages by corporate advertising, but they choose them freely. They have options. They can organize their trips individually, either with a travel agent or more directly using the Internet. This last modality is becoming more and more popular. However, individual travel cannot take advantage of the economies of scale enjoyed by big vacation factories. Even on the Web, hotel rates for individuals are in the end higher than those tour operators offer when one includes transaction costs in the total, negotiating airline schedules and rates is not easy, making arrangements for side trips or excursions in a faraway venue with a local provider may create much frustration because of cultural differences, and finding a price adjusted to the consumer's needs may involve complicated operations in foreign currencies; in a nutshell, organizing a vacation may be far from simple. Possibly this is the reason why many would-be individual tourists finally use Internet facilities to research the websites of big tour operators. Indeed, the latter will exercise a degree of control over the package; the cheaper the price, the more rigid the schedules, products, advance payments, cancellations, and so on. Tourists can avoid all this aggravation by just taking it on themselves. They usually end up paying a higher price. In this way, many prefer to relinquish control to the providers as part of a game that most tourists gladly accept. Ultimately, the logic of Dann's argument about social control pays little attention to the capacity of tourists to decide what is best for them under the circumstances. They are turned into defenseless pawns in the hands of authoritarian corporations that decide on their behalf. The history of travel organizations tells another story. In spite of their power, many of them either disappeared or were bought by other, more efficient ones. No matter how much money they might spend on advertising, they did not curry favor with potential clients.

Often it looks that academics that criticize mass tourism may have attended too many scientific conferences—probably the most obnoxious form of packaged tourism. They are well known for rigid schedules, poor accommodation, substandard food, final gala banquets of nondescript soups or salads followed by rubbery chicken, authentic local shows performed by third-rate troupes, plus the cultural-capital-enhancing field trip to an allegedly high brow local venue usually included in all the cheapest of itineraries. Not all mass tourism products are that controlled, nor are all mass tourists that gullible and conformity prone as academics in conferences. One can empathize with the feeling of anomia that they create among perceptive observers. Perhaps a good trip to an attractive destination bought on Internet from an inventive tour operator at prices that even academics can afford would help lessen it.

So as to express their disillusion with the lack of more opposition or collective rebellion to social control in any shape, Durkheimians of the Left finally opt for an old position. People accept being manipulated and controlled because they ignore their real interests, or their genuine desires, or their authentic drives. Tourists let the industry run them the way it does because they accept that they are acting like children. However, if, for one second, one grants the conclusion, the options ahead do not look too appetizing. On the one hand, tourists might look for new guidance, though more objective and less manipulative this time. But, after the predicated ubiquity of social control, chances are that they will exchange one type of control for another. On the other hand, there is St. Anselm's ontological argument for the existence of God. We can think of a perfect and benevolent authority (an academic, perhaps?) that is unwilling to manipulate unsophisticated people in their travels. Therefore, it exists. As is well known, Kant would not be amused.

So, in the end one is back to the inexorable conclusion of Square One—promotion and advertising, like religion, are but the opium of the masses. However, why should not the masses enjoy smoking opium? In fact, going by the results, most people are religious and are proud of it. When it comes to that, promotion and advertising are usually less noxious and toxic than opium and much less so than religion. Considering the conceptual and methodological theme advanced so far, it is important to ask whether the entire tourism industry speaks with one single voice and if its audience accepts it.

THE PROOF OF THE CAKE

Much of published tourism research consists of case studies. There is a serious problem with them—they are not easy to replicate. They usually require stays in faraway destinations, quite often also they necessitate command of a foreign language whose mastery is not always easy, and they may need a number of techniques of participant observation that vary considerably from researcher to researcher. Sometimes, when attempted, replication leads to conclusions that openly contradict the previously accepted ones, even though the object of study is the same. Take the polemic on Margaret Mead's work in Samoa (1928) started by Derek Freeman (Côté 1994; Freeman 1983, 1999). While Franz Boas claimed that her book was a painstaking investigation, Freeman maintains that

> [i]t is now known from detailed historical research that the extreme environmentalist conclusion to which the young Margaret Mead came in *Coming of Age in Samoa* is based

on evidence that is quite unacceptable scientifically. [It] is in
certain vital respects [...] a work of anthropological fiction
(2001:111).

Finding contributions to tourism research that can be replicated, if not in
their entirety at least in their methodology, is not easy and models to this
effect are welcome. Dann's study of the people of tourist brochures (1996b,
1996c) is one of them. As the author says in a different context, the content/
semiotic analysis technique that he uses in that study has relatively few
drawbacks. Being scarcely demanding in terms of time and money and easy
tore-start if design flaws appear clearly, content/semiotic analysis combines
both quantitative and qualitative approaches and is not obtrusive when
applied. Content/semiotic analysis is a combined methodology in which the
former establishes quantitative patterns and the latter focuses on qualitative
meaning (2005a).

One of the areas where the technique can be used, as Dann did, is to
research destination images. His pioneering research was based on "11
representative summer-holiday brochures targeted at a cross-section of the
British public, comprising some 5,172 pictures featured on 1,470 pages of
visual and written material" (1996c:63). The study progresses in two stages.
It starts with a quantitative analysis of the pictures in the brochures
examined and their classification in categories according to whether images
include people or not. Where people are represented, pictures are
subsequently categorized into tourists only, locals only, and locals and
tourists together. His data show that the main category of icons in the
brochures analyzed belonged to tourists only (60.1%) followed by no-people
(24.3%), locals and tourists (8.9%), and locals only (6.7%). The pictures
mostly represented hotels and beaches, which together accounted for some
70% of them. Local scenes were the third main category (11.5%). Tourists
appeared mostly in beach and sports activities and in hotels while the other
categories overlapped in local scenes, sights, and other.

Aramberri and Dao (2005) followed Dann's model to study a different
type of tourist communication. The archive consisted of all the icons
contained in the promotional guide to Vietnam found on the Internet site of
Vietnam's National Administration of Tourism or VNAT (2004). Unlike
British tourist brochures, this website was addressed to foreign and resident
audiences. It had versions in English, French, and Vietnamese. Indeed,
the Vietnamese pages may also have had in mind the considerable number
of Vietnamese speakers who either no longer maintain this nationality or, if
they do, live permanently out of the country (*viet kieu*). Additionally VNAT

did not make a distinction between foreign and domestic tourists. The 2003–04 iconic files were the same in all three languages with the exception of a few additional ones in the English and French files (less than 10 in each case). They projected the same tourism image of the country to all audiences. Here lies a disparity with the brochures in the British market that primarily targeted British tourists and not the locals in different destinations. Therefore, the expectation that image-building strategy in the Vietnamese tourist site would be different from the British one.

There was an additional element. Dann's work revolved around the tourists/locals divide. Whereas he studied a number of tour operator catalogs, the narrator for Vietnam was a public sector company not directly involved in sales. Even though they had an undeniably promotional aspect, the icons did not include addressees of travel companies or invited to buy anything. They relied more on pull than on push. The second expectation then was that they would not only reflect a different order of priorities, but also project it with images at variance with those of commercial companies. The basic hypothesis was that local people would be paramount in display, and hence represented more profusely than in the British brochures. The archive analyzed contained a total of 1,008 pictures and icons. Results confirmed the first hypothesis. VNAT's image-building strategy was different from the British brochures. On the Vietnamese site, the "no-people" category eclipsed the rest by far. It made up for 72% of the pictures in the files. "Locals" followed with just 19%; "locals and tourists" (5%) came a distant third with the ranking closed by a paltry 4% of "tourists". The comparison with Dann's results seemed telling. However, within the category "people," the results were exactly the opposite of the British brochures. On the VNAT's site, "locals" came first in number of pictures, "locals and tourists" in the middle, and "tourists" occupy the lowest rung. Additionally, in contrast to Dann's study, no servants were found in the "locals" category.

This may be due to the fact that the same happens to hotels, where people portrayed in that role would most likely appear. There was only one hotel picture on VNAT site and it showed only the facade, belonging, therefore, to the "no-people" section as an urban sight. It is difficult to conclude that the absence of locals as servants reflects a clear change in iconic strategy without knowing what would have happened if the Vietnamese site had depicted hotels in detail. Indeed, while a tour operator brochure would make no sense without hotels, image-building kits can dispense with them. However, any customer of Vietnamese hotels and resorts can attest that almost all servants are locals. Concluding that, had hotels been depicted, a sizable number of locals on the site would have appeared as servants does not seem an uncontrolled flight of the imagination.

For the rest, "locals" on the VNAT site closely reflect the rest of Dann's categorizing. One finds a high percentage of performers and vendors as such (together they account for 27% of all pictures), but their number would increase significantly if we merged with them crafts people and festival paraders. A clear case can be made for this approach. Though they may not be professional performers, festival revelers actively participate in a performance that keeps some distance between actors and spectators. The case of crafts people is not dissimilar. Artisans, though still constituting an important part of the Vietnamese economy, increasingly feel a shrinking pressure elicited by the growing number of industrial workers and the flight to cities that Vietnam has undergone since the *doi moi* (New Deal) policies were introduced in 1986 (Hiebert 1995; McLeod and Nguyen 2001). Vietnam's population is still overwhelmingly rural. In 2001, of its 78.7 million inhabitants, 75.2% lived in the countryside. However, the latter had decreased by 7.4% since 1990, and the trend seems poised to deepen as annual urban growth rate accelerated from 2.4% in 1990 to 3.6% in 2001, while rural growth rate decreased from 1.8 to 0.6% (GSO 2002:27; Khanh et al 2001). Census data may even ignore the strength of the flight to cities. Other sources reckon that Ho Chi Minh City alone received 700,000 migrants between 1996 and 1999 (Le n.d.).

Though still numerous, rural crafts people are on a gradual wane. They, together with their technologies, belong to a pre-industrial age increasingly foreign to many city dwellers. To this extent, they come quite close to entertainers. In the Vietnamese files, their pictures regularly ally a staged setting with old-fashioned clothes and obsolete tools. They embody a reality that is more and more exotic for urbanites, precisely the population group most likely to engage in domestic tourism.

Many of the "locals" in the Vietnamese site are ethnic minorities. The *List of Ethnic Groups in Vietnam* published in 1979 officially recognized 54 ethnic groups. Dominant are the *Kinh* or *Viets* that account for 87% of the population. The diversity of ethnic groups—many of them inhabitants of the poorer mountain regions of Vietnam, some still eking out a living from hunting and gathering—creates many problems for the integration policies pursued by the national government. Minorities are usually portrayed in individual pictures wearing their best attire against an undefined background or in "spontaneous" scenes of everyday work life where they invariably use pre-industrial tools. It is not the implement in itself that creates the atmosphere, but the eye of the beholder. As a matter of fact, many minorities people do use obsolete technologies, but the pictures are hinting at the cleavage between, on one side, the Vietnamese who work in an urban environment, don Western clothes in everyday life, speak the national language, and therefore quite likely are the domestic tourists served by VNAT, and, on the other, minorities impervious to change. They are exotic and, in this way, their icons are exciting and entertaining even though they are not professional entertainers. Exoticism not only beckons in far-off destinations most Vietnamese cannot yet afford—it is just a stone's throw away. Occasional talks with Hanoians on weekend trips to Sa Pa, a mountain resort in the nearby mountains where members of a few ethnic communities live, reinforced this conclusion.

In a nutshell, the findings came close to expectations on the order of priorities of commercial tour operators and a DMO like VNAT when constructing the attractions and activities they want to promote. The former emphasize tourists in facilities and settings they are enticed to consume. The latter suggest a general product through depictions of nature, beaches and seascapes, urban and rural sights, and history. However, when it comes to the key issue of the role of locals in the imaginary universe of tourists, both commercial companies and VNAT coincide in presenting them in similar roles and use them as exotic markers that introduce a definite cleavage between tourists and tourees (this neologism used to refer to the local populations visited by outside tourists was first used by Van den Berghe 1994).

What about image construction by agencies that are not directly involved in promotional activities? Aramberri and Liang (2009) have researched the way some Chinese travel magazines presented the province of Yunnan to Chinese audiences. Modern mass tourism is a recent occurrence in Chinese social life. It was only after the "open door" policies initiated in 1979 that tourism grew exponentially (Sofield and Li 1998). Inbound tourism, both by Chinese living outside the People's Republic of China (PRC) borders and by foreigners, replaced the formerly tiny groups of politically motivated tourists (Zhang 1997) and the urban populations forced to go into rural exile by the Cultural Revolution (1966–76). Domestic and outbound tourism grew by leaps and bounds in step with an economic growth that has induced deep and rapid social changes. Above all, a tidal wave of migration from the countryside flooded the cities. Together with urbanization, consumption standards have risen. Urbanization and new consumption patterns usually go hand in hand with an expansion of the middle classes. A local study (CASS 2003; Hodgson 2007) estimated them at 19% of the population—around 250 million people. The study also forecast that in 2020 the middle classes would comprise 40% of Chinese population, that is, somewhere between 500 and 600 million people. Increasing numbers of Chinese have the disposable income to engage in tourist activities, either as direct consumers or as beneficiaries of incentive travel provided by their companies or the public sector. Household tourism expenditures have risen to 14% of disposable income in urban areas (Gu and Dake 2004).

It would, therefore, come as no surprise that many Chinese consumers want independent information and advice on where and how to spend this part of their income and that is where travel magazines come into the picture. They offer both on a wide range of destinations, domestic and international, and in so doing they contribute to tourism education. Aramberri and Liang (2009) selected for their study icons and articles referring to Yunnan province that appeared in the issues of three travel magazines between 2003 and 2005. The three publications used to create this universe (*National Geographic Traveler*—hereinafter NGT—*Traveler*, and *National Parks* or NP) were selected because of their perceived leading position in upscale markets, which are the most likely to engage in travel behavior. The time boundaries considered for research (2003–05) responded to the need of having an ample, though manageable, iconic archive including the latest issues available at the time of starting the project.

What are the main features of their audiences? There is no information on NGT's circulation in China. Its website only refers to the 5.3 million readership that *National Geographic* enjoys all over the world. NP publishes 80,000 copies every month. *Traveler* boasts of a monthly circulation of 338,000 copies and an audience of over three million—nine readers per copy. It is also *Traveler* that offers the most complete picture of its followers. Its median reader is both male and female in nearly identical proportions; lives in Beijing, Shanghai, or Guangzhou; is between 25 and 44 years old; is well educated (98% have a college degree or higher); is a high-level manager and official; and makes between CNY40,000 and 120,000 (US$6,000–23,000) per year.

Yunnan came uppermost in the exposure ranking of all destinations offered by the selected media. There are good reasons for this. This province, with an area of 394,000 square kilometers and 43.3 million inhabitants, matches on both dimensions some of the biggest countries of Europe. It has a number of well-known attractions such as the Stone Forest near Kunming, Lijiang, Dali, Jiuxiang, Guangdu, Zhongdian/Shangrila, and many others. The province is home to 25 ethnic minority groups out of the 56 officially recognized by the Chinese government. Over 13 million of Yunnan's people (roughly 30% of the population) belong to ethnic minorities.

The total number of icons devoted to Yunnan in the analyzed series was 547, and the number of articles about the province reached 49. The magazine that devoted more pictorial attention to Yunnan was NGT with a total of 284 icons, followed by NP with 172, and *Traveler* with 91. In the three of them, the main category was "no-people," followed by "locals." Depictions of tourists and of tourists mixed with locals were quite limited relative to the two previous categories. Putting together the three magazines, the total distribution of icons in percentage was "no-people" (48%), "locals" (39%), "tourists" (10%), and "locals and tourists" (3%).

Let us now look at the inner structure of the two categories that attract a higher percentage of icons—"no-people" and "locals." The first category was further broken down into three additional groups: "nature" (including animal icons), "heritage," and "modern cityscapes." The last two refer to built structures diverging by being either historic or contemporary. Differences of approach among the three magazines become relevant here. NP and *Traveler* have no interest in depicting contemporary city life, while NGT devotes much more attention to it (albeit many of the 26 icons in this category appear in one single article devoted to Kunming City). On the other hand, NP is more interested in nature than heritage, while the opposite is true of *Traveler*.

The "locals" category in turn was classified according to the activities locals were performing: "vendors/servers," "entertainers," "premodern tasks," and "other." *Traveler* is the medium that depicts fewer locals in any category, while they have more presence in both NGT and NP. NGT comprises 51% of the total, NP 38%, and *Traveler* only 11%. Differences become more significant when looked at by subcategories. NP and *Traveler* mainly depict "locals" as "entertainers" (56 and 34%, respectively), while NGT allocates very little space to them. For NGT, it is the "other" subcategory that draws most attention. In this subcategory, people are usually portrayed as modern urbanites. The Premodern category, usually encompassing ethnic minorities (many times overlapping with vendors, servants, and entertainers) is more or less evenly distributed among the three media.

In general, the overall distribution of icons in the Chinese magazines was quite different from the icons in British tour operator brochures analyzed by Dann. It also differed from the priorities of a DMO like VNAT. The proffered visions of Yunnan present an inner structure that is quite the opposite of British travel brochures. The Chinese magazines devote very little attention to the "tourists" themselves (only 10% of their space) and to the interaction tourists/locals (3%), focusing mostly on no-people (48%) and locals (39%), thus reverting the proportions allocated to those categories in British brochures and coming close to that of the Vietnamese

DMO. To explain the relative weight of these categories in the British tour operator brochures, Dann argued that it reflected the contrived view of reality conveyed by promotional tourism literature (1996c). In other contributions published at the same time, he identified promotional media as the only language of tourism (1996a). Additionally, when it came to the "locals" category, he emphasized that British brochures mostly portrayed them as vendors, entertainers, or servants, and explained such bias by an alleged postcolonial mindset among British tour operators.

On their side, Chinese magazines take a clear distance in the way they apportion their icons. They devote more space to no-people and to locals, which pace Dann makes it difficult to maintain that the language of tourism speaks with one single tongue. On the other hand, when it comes to locals most icons in the Chinese travel magazines portray premodern ethnic people, entertainers, vendors, and servers, as much as British brochures. This also coincides with VNAT's strategy. How can one explain such differences?

SPEAKING IN TONGUES

It would be easy to dismiss the problem with the apples versus oranges argument. That tour operator brochures and travel magazines belong to different promotional media seems a trifle simplistic. However, this is not so with Dann's hypothesis that, as noted, has become widely accepted as paradigmatic. After deconstruction of its iconic or literary categories, for him the language of tourism reveals itself as another tool for audience control. The conclusion does not specify why this should be so; it just sticks to the counterintuitive notion of a single language of tourism. Additionally, it surmises that messages and promotion go hand in hand, thus concluding that the language of tourism always ends up as duplicitous, or misleading.

From the diverse viewpoints that communication can be looked at (as in Laswell's five Ws), this view just focuses on the "what," that is, on the message itself. However, if one goes beyond it to other aspects of the communication process, the language of tourism reflects more shades, that is, it no longer operates under a single logic. One travels from the "language" to the "languages" of tourism. In fact, the statement that all tourism-speak is promotional does not conform to experience. Travel guides, travel magazines, newspapers travel sections, TV programs, Internet travel blogs, Web 2.0, word of mouth, and other tourist information sources are not directly promotional. The way in which iconic categories are used by British tour operator brochures, the Vietnamese DMO, and Chinese travel magazines highlights this commonsensical difference.

Even what is strictly considered as promotional literature does not adopt the same communication strategies. Package-tour catalogs and DMO materials are the two most common sources of promotional communication. Let us call them Promotion 1 and Promotion 2. Tour operator materials, printed or online, aim at closing sales using unique selling proposition (USP) advertising techniques. "That's what you will be getting for your money" sums up the message they address to potential consumers. Accordingly their materials will mostly show, as Dann rightly stresses, pictures of tourists in hotel settings. They also include an even more ubiquitous piece of information that Dann omits—the price list. Different vacations have different prices, but under market conditions no travel will take place if there is no exchange of money between the provider and the consumer.

On their side, DMO have a different approach that also drives their iconic and textual mix. As nonprofit organizations, they do not engage in hard selling. They promote their destination in general, not particular resorts, hotels, or any other hospitality businesses. The study of the VNAT website found an imaging mix clearly different from that of British tourism brochures. Pictures with no-people (nature, heritage, urban views, etc.) were widely used, followed by pictures of locals, while depictions of tourists were negligible (Aramberri and Dao 2005). The disparity can be explained by their diverging promotional strategies. While profit through sales drives vacation factories, DMO are content to just register in the evoked set of potential consumers.

Effects of different languages are quite variable. No matter how hard they try, tour operator and DMO promotional communications tend to have low credibility (Gartner 1993). Consumers usually reach travel decisions after a meandering process in which many other sources get involved. The languages of tourism thus follow a pyramidal structure where each level releases different messages and has a varying degree of reliability. Intuitively, one can say that word of mouth, nowadays exponentially amplified by Web 2.0, lies at the base, in terms of number of messages and reliability. Over this basis stem other levels with narrower reach and credibility as they get close to the top. Travel guides, travel magazines, and newspapers' travel sections, as well as educational audiovisual productions are the next step up, followed by Promotion 2 or DMO communications and Promotion 1 or vacation factories' promotional materials. A similar structure is usually accepted in the general literature (Chías 2005; Gartner 1993, 1996; Gartner et al 2007; Hsu and Powers 2001) and supported by local surveys.

In Germany's case, for instance, word of mouth comes first, followed by educational media (guides and TV/Newspapers reports), while DMO and tour operator catalogs and websites come a distant last (FUR 2008).

Each one of those stages has its own logic, grammar, and rhetoric. While in the two basic ones tourists find mostly accurate and general information used to map their mental worlds, the two at the top, especially Promotion 1, are more present at the time of actually buying a vacation. Promotion 1 makes known the conditions offered by providers. That commercial brochures mostly depict actual venues and activities that tourists will enjoy (like hotels and beaches) only shows that their authors know what they are doing. Though also part of marketing, travel kits provided by DMO follow different rules. In marketing lingo their main object is to successfully place the destination in the tourist's evoked set without mention of specific products. Above all, they stress the generic and multifarious possibilities that their destinations provide.

Educational sources occupy a different narrative level. They aim at making their readers conversant with the natural and social environment they will find in different destinations of their choice, Vietnam or Yunnan in the Chinese case. This explains the differences in the iconic structures of Chinese travel magazines as compared with tour operators' catalogs or DMO materials. Potential Chinese tourists need accurate information in their burgeoning "tourist careers" (Pearce and Lee 2004), and travel magazines like those analyzed help them in constructing their attitudes and expectations. In this way, it should be stressed again that there is no such a thing as a unique language of tourism, but a plurality of them. If one wants to put it so, one might even say that there is one language of tourism tiered in different ways. Both formulas would not be that far apart from each other, and Dann could likely live with the second. The problem, though, does not go away so easily. After recognizing the inner differences of the way in which one talks about tourism, there still remains the issue whether the shades of tourism language(s) can be trusted and, if so, by how much. Information and promotion blend in different ways according to the type of messages conveyed and the audiences targeted.

How do the Chinese travel magazines construct Yunnan? In the qualitative analysis of 49 articles that the travel magazines devoted to the destination, it is portrayed as timeless, ethnically diverse, and tradition-oriented. However, NGT's feature on Kunming City adds a different perspective. Yunnan can also be a place where the global influences on its capital and biggest town are a complement to the region's age-old quaintness. The feeling of timelessness springs from the weight of the "no-people" category and is reinforced in the copy of most articles. Yunnan is seen as a place where time is of no consequence. Mountains, valleys, rivers, and other natural attractions do not change, at least do not change quickly, and their towering presence among the icons contrasts with the daily experience of an urban audience inured to the sudden modifications their cities have gone through. Beijing, Shanghai, Guangzhou, and many other Chinese cities have seen whole old neighborhoods pulled down in order to make room for new high rises and apartment buildings. Something similar can be said of heritage. In contrast, the slow pace of cyclical time and the resilience of country life offer a stark contrast to the strictures of modern urban life. Yunnan thus becomes the antithesis of urban China.

Ethnic diversity also differs from the alleged standardization of urban life. As previously mentioned, Yunnan is a region where one can find a great number of non-Han groups. The "locals" category, with a total of 219 icons, allocates about three quarters of them to show people in ethnic attire and/or executing premodern forms of labor. Once again it should be noted that NGT takes a different stance from the other two magazines. While the latter have practically no space for nonminority people, NGT reserves nearly half of its depictions of locals to people who do not belong to minorities.

It has already been mentioned that Chinese travel magazines, as well as British brochures and Vietnamese DMO literature, mostly portray locals as servants, performers, and vendors, many of them members of minority ethnic groups. In our view, this similarity in treatment illustrates the fact that in their short stays at the destination tourists that have no other links to it and no further interests than having a good time will mostly meet locals that perform those roles. Encounters with locals, when they happen, are fleeting and epidermal, though exceptions may and do take place; therefore, most locals, whether in the First World or in the Third, are portrayed as servants, entertainers, and vendors. But there is more to it.

In community-based tourism, such as it usually happens in Yunnan, local populations and ethnic minorities are the main attractions. However, vendors, entertainers, servants, and premodern artisans are not just a fact of life for the city dweller. They represent traditional society, and attractive as it may be, their exoticism also shows a lifestyle impervious to modernity— either as an unrealized potential or a threat to its expansion. In this way, the insistence on people discharging menial, though hard tasks somehow protects urban audiences of eventual shocks when actually meeting them. Doubts about the superiority of modern life are in this way exorcized even before they arise. This may be the reason why NGT, the most global-oriented of all three magazines insists in showing chunks of Yunnan's urban life. The cityscapes and the modern locals that appear in the articles devoted to Kunming are a reminder that even in that timeless and remote corner of the global world grows along its own negative image, both alluring and disquieting.

At any rate, in the case of the three Chinese travel magazines, their educational goal is difficult to miss. They offer information about destinations (in this case Yunnan) as well as a reference framework their audiences can use to build their own mental maps of different destinations. Their audiences belong to the upper social layers of present day Chinese society. They tend to be affluent, well educated, and urban. These features are usually accompanied by exposure to economic and cultural globalization, plus access to independent sources of information. Such social groups also are at the beginning of their careers as tourists. The education provided by the selected magazines helps them to define their expectations, gather practical pointers to the attractions, and prepare them for the environmental and social differences they will find when traveling.

In the case of Yunnan, timelessness/modernity is the pivotal relation. It plays a double role. On one hand, it exposes the affluent urbanite to a world whose values fully differ from those at home. People wear different clothes, mostly work in agriculture, their tools are not machine-made, they have different and colorful rituals and festivals, they may not be as money oriented as town dwellers, and their ways differ from urban mores. It may not be completely so in reality. Below the traditional clothes so many people working at local attractions wear, one often sees the hem of blue jeans that will appear in full as soon as working time is up and the locals can stop performing and become their own selves again. This usually causes several ethical problems for researchers (Brunner and Kirschenblatt-Gimbel 1994), but does not seem to pose so many for the guide/performers. Most enjoy the higher pay and the easier work they have as compared with that of the real peasants. Do they impersonate, and to some extent, contrive their real selves and their community life? Well, is that not how many artistic performances and their performers started?

Therefore, education, as understood by travel magazines, is a way of softening the culture shocks that may arise on both sides of an interaction. The tourists thus will know—to some extent—what to do, what to refrain from, and how to behave when they find themselves in an unknown place. On the other hand, future tourists will also understand themselves—how they differ from the visited—and, eventually, they will find reassurance in the values of their own culture supplies. In this way, providing independent information for affluent tourists and helping them navigate the eventual pitfalls of social intercourse comes topmost in the value ranking of the travel magazines. Unlike promotional literature, whether directly commercial or brand-building, educational sources thrive in making accessible to their readers as many destinations as possible in as independent a way as possible; unlike word of mouth, whether from friends or relatives or from the social Web, they offer standardized and stable inputs useful to ample numbers of consumers. In this way, neither their goals nor their practices can be easily reduced to peddling tourism products or to abstract notions of social control. The notion that there is one vertical language of tourism should be revised. No language can successfully impose total top-down social control on the audiences. Seldom has promotion been so powerful or consumers so gullible. In this regard, let it be noted that Dann has shifted his position of late to acknowledge that the language of tourism has become more dialogical, and that the Web has made it possible for it to even be trilogical (Dann 2005b).

Dann has an additional and more encompassing explanation for the idea of a single language of tourism co-equal with promotion. As he recapped in a later text, his main aim in 1996 was to elucidate the relation between tourists and locals in order to highlight the promotional structures of "Othering" and the controlling discourse through which it operated. [T]he imposition of imagery by the superordinate First World on the subordinate Third World constitutes the asymmetric and selective manipulation of the latter by the former (Dann 2005a:32). His semiotic analysis ignores that promotional materials such as travel brochures or image-building kits are only one form of presenting reality or "Othering" that reacts to some specific needs of their audience and employs well-known suasory techniques. On the other hand, his idea that brochures and kits impose the asymmetric and selective manipulation of the Third by the First World needs more precision.

Let us start with the first issue. Commercial brochures are advertisements. As their main goal, they aim at making known the conditions (types of accommodation, means of transportation, conditions of stay, and prices) under which the advertiser will sell some goods or services (in our case, packaged vacations) to a consumer or group of consumers. They are a form of communication, indeed, but with a view to persuading the potential customer to buy their specific product and not a different one. They do not speak to reason only; they compel or push to buy a product. The only differences between old rhetoric and modern advertising lie in that the latter has learned to muster a great number of sophisticated persuasion techniques and in that advertising must drive to closing a sale. If tour operators forget this, they would soon go bankrupt.

If they want to be effective, advertisers must know their target audiences, and tailor their messages to them. A vacation brochure, therefore, has to tend to the tourists' needs, whether real or contrived. That commercial brochures mostly depict venues and activities that tourists might enjoy (like hotels and beaches) only shows that their authors know what they are doing. That locals mostly appear as servants, performers, or vendors only illustrates the fact that in their short stays at the destination, tourists that have no other links to it and no further interests than having a good time will mostly see them in this condition.

The diary quoted by Selänniemi (2001), which seems quite consistent with a great number of surveys on tourist behavior, allows a glimpse on why many tourists have very little interest in the place they vacation in or in the locals who reside there. One might desire otherwise or disapprove of their lack of curiosity when "Othering," but we should bear in mind that the same happens in everyday life at home. We usually do not engage in social intercourse with many people we meet (bank tellers, sales attendants, vendors, policemen, entertainers, passers-by, etc.). One could maintain that vacations and the opportunity for cross-cultural exchanges they provide should be used in a different way; that tourists should interest themselves in other relations with locals than mere utilitarian exchanges with servants, vendors, and performers; that vacations should be more meaningful and so on. Soon, however, one finds oneself going down the slippery slope of prescriptive reasoning. Why ask tourists, especially those in cultural areas remote from their own, to behave as one deems academics would do?

Though also part of advertising, travel kits provided by public bodies such as VNAT follow different rules. Now the main object is not to close a deal, but to successfully place their country or region in the tourist's evoked set, as marketers say. Any NTA representatives that join forces in promotional campaigns with airlines or travel companies will immediately notice the disparity of goals. They want to position their destination no matter who sells it; their partners want to advertise and sell only their own tickets and packages. They address two diverse, though not disparate audiences, and this demands different types of rhetoric. NTAs will stress the generic and multifarious possibilities that their destinations provide. So, while vacation factories push, DMO try to pull. The former use Thouspeak, the latter love Mespeak. In marketing lingo one can say they brand themselves.

Dann follows up with another critique of the language of tourism. Commercial brochures, he says—and generic promotional kits, we might add—create an ideal world. They sanitize nature forgetting to tell that it not only includes beaches and romantic sights, but also mosquitoes, scorpions, and skin cancer. They, we are told, brim with stereotypes. For instance, Rio is conjured up by reveling Cariocas while pollution, violence, and favelas are glossed over. However, the rhetoric of advertising does not coincide with that of the social sciences or professional journalism. Social sciences aim at firm conclusions that can be accepted by any dispassionate observer; journalists report events. Reputable media try to keep a clear demarcation line between news and opinion. Through different languages, then, social scientists and journalists have created grammars to define reality, which are accepted as objective by most users of their services.

This does not apply to advertising, whose success is measured in units sold. Even general image building such as carried out by NTAs provides a very selective image of reality. So do infomercials and infotainment used by other advertisers in travel and many other fields. Most people targeted by advertising are perfectly capable of understanding that advertisements try to persuade them by hook or by crook, and react accordingly disconnecting in a nearly automatic way when they are assaulted by advertisements instead of information. When they want hard facts about a destination, most people will look for them in a reputable travel guide, not in promotional literature. In spite of NTAs efforts, their materials rank quite low in credibility (Gunn 1972).

Something similar can be said about the expectation that stereotypes might be radically excised from advertising and even sociological pursuits. In fact, many of our unquestioned concepts are nothing else than stereotypes. There are good reasons for that. Referring to oaks, willows, spruces, and pines as "trees" reduces their specificity for the sake of expressive economy. One may answer that stereotypes are something else—concepts that lack precision, mirror reality in a crooked way, or diminish their tagged objects. But then stereotypes come in many shapes. At any rate, one can understand that academics in the social sciences would have more employment opportunities if brochures and promotional kits were made to read as economic, sociological, or anthropological treatises, but it is difficult to see why tour operators and NTAs should accept such broadening of their call.

The second general issue raised by Dann is also highly debatable. That the imagery of people in tourist brochures constitutes an asymmetric and selective manipulation of the Third World by the First does not fit well with the other findings referred to here. If treatment of people, especially local people, in VNAT's Internet kit and in Chinese travel magazines shows some striking similarities with that of British brochures, there are only two alternative explanations. One might argue that Vietnam or China have become part of the First World and contribute their share to the manipulation of the Third. Both countries, however, are still far from being developed societies. If words have any meaning, this explanation is out of kilter.

VNAT and Chinese travel magazines use their own rhetoric to position the country or other destinations. This rhetoric in part coincides with the one used by tour operators in commercial advertising; in part it does not. This explains the imbalance of focus. Tour operators will stress hotels and beaches occupied by tourists; NTAs will play them down. On the other hand, NTAs and educational media coincide in their interest to devote a great part of their icons to the generic attractions of the selected destinations and in showing their exoticism (whatever that means) for both foreign and domestic tourists.

It is to rhetoric, therefore, and not to narratives of international relations that we have to turn in order to understand the functions, similarities, and differences of approach between these two breeds of marketing agents. Modesty about the capacity of tourism marketing to shape the international scene is also highly recommended, especially when dealing with those techniques that Gartner calls "Overt Induced I" (1996). They are the least effective tools in image building.

Chapter 9

Alternatives to Modern Mass Tourism

ANYTHING BUT ...

As soon as modern mass tourism (MMT) started to show considerable economic strength, an adverse reaction set in. Although not limited to the academic world, it was there where it gained considerable momentum. Initially it came from the area of cultural studies (MacCannell 1976; Smith 1977), but it also spilt over to other disciplines, including economics (Brown 2000; de Kadt 1979; Young 1973) and sociology (Krippendorf 1987). As already argued (Chapter 1), the real scissors crisis in tourism research only has a slight relation with the disciplines. Rather, it harks back to a chasm in paradigms. Whatever the discipline cultivated in each particular case, the basic difference lies in the final acceptance or rejection of modernity and the market economy (lately baptized as neoliberalism) as the framework to explain our recent history, and to plan the near future. Accordingly, it comes as no surprise that many tourism economists are as opposed to it (Sharpley 2010) as its cultural critics or even more so. This geological fault runs throughout the academic disciplines that focus on tourism, and for the time being, though often concealed behind a MAD policy (Chapter 1), the naysayers run the general discussion with nary a murmur or complaint (Butcher 2002, 2007) and quickly muffle the slightest show of disagreement (Butcher 2006; Wearing et al 2005; Wearing and Ponting 2006).

Many tourism researchers have become enthralled with the rejection of MMT, but not everyone in the outside world has followed suit. The industry, the public, and even the media usually show a milder and more balanced disposition toward it. Some academics beyond the tourism preserve, even when they are not particularly enthusiastic with the development of capitalism (Löfgren 1999), express more sanguine views.

> Mass tourism [...] may be environmentally insensitive but it has distinctively re-distributive benefits. As prosperous north-erners flocked to hitherto impoverished Mediterranean lands,

jobs opened up for building workers, cooks, waiters, chamber-maids, taxi-drivers, prostitutes, porters, airport maintenance crews and others. For the first time, unskilled young men and women in Greece, Yugoslavia, Italy and Spain could find low-paying seasonal work at home instead of seeking it abroad. Rather than migrating to the expanding economies of the north, they now serviced those same economies in their own lands [...] Foreign travel may not have broadened the mind [...] Indeed the success of large-scale tourism in the 60s and after depended upon making Brits, Germans, Dutch, French and other neophyte tourists feel as comfortable as possible, surrounded by fellow-countrymen and insulated from the exotic, the unfamiliar and the unexpected. But the mere fact of going somewhere distant on a regular (annual) basis, and the novel means of transport used to get there—private car, charter flight—offered millions of hitherto insular men and women (and especially their children) a window into a far bigger world (Judt 2006:loc.7641–7697).

One does not usually encounter such arguments among tourism researchers, but apparently the general public understands them quite well. A sociology of the tourism academia might explain the reason for this dissonance, deepening an attractive topic for discussion that has not been especially enlightened by the limited contributions made up to now (Ateljevic 2009; Tribe 2009, 2010). However, such an analysis would overreach the scope of these pages. Let us just remember one fact. Not only was the expansion of MMT quickly followed by an adverse academic reaction (what Jafari called the Cautionary Platform); the 1980s witnessed a blooming of endless new forms of tourism (Eadington and Smith 1992) that shaped Jafari's Adaptancy Platform, and were seen as so many alternatives to MMT by academic audiences celebrating the long-awaited demise of their nemesis. Since that time, academic praise for all types of tourism that proposed to veer away from MMT increased considerably (see, for instance, the collection of the *Journal of Sustainable Tourism*, widely considered the best academic publication in this subfield). Deep down, one feels among most of its contributors a not-too-muffled wish to finish off, once and for all, any MMT display or, short of such a praiseworthy goal, to impose drastic reductions to tourism as we know it.

Initially, conventional wisdom adopted the notion of carrying capacity, that is, the maximum number of tourists per day that could be admitted to destinations without causing excessive stress, together with the view that slow or uncommodified development (Wearing et al 2005 Wearing, McDonald and Ponting 2005) should be favored. Thus, demands for eco-tourism, special interest tourism, alternative tourism, low-intensity tourism, responsible tourism, or green tourism became increasingly heard among researchers, and became popular among some media. More recently, the trend has found allegedly better grounds in a notion of sustainability that, by definition, sees the most popular types of tourism as unsustainable. The tourism academia and some of the highbrow travel and general media thus oscillate between general reproof and/or the imposition of so many strictures to any tourism development that would render MMT mission impossible.

The trend has only grown over the years as better-designed, multi-dimensional products found their way to the traveling public—minitrips, city tours, an increasing number of MICE (meetings, incentives, conferences, and exhibitions) activities, farm- and agrotourism, wine tours, gastronomic tours, cooking courses, festival and concert trips, hiking, high-risk sports tours, equestrian gymkhanas, deep-sea fishing tournaments, photographic safaris, diving excursions, speleological trips, visits to theme parks and to cultural capitals of this or that, and scores of other tourism products have replaced the rather limited choices available at the inception of MMT. Critics of the packaged tours of yore thought that finally they had reached the public's ear.

Often as well, disabuse followed elation once the new products set in. Ecotourism, for instance, promised to make both MMT consumers and providers more attentive to the natural and cultural environments of their destinations, but would soon be exposed as another marketing trick (Honey 2008). Other new products and shapes would travel the same path from praise to disparagement as, unbeknown or unrecognized by their initial supporters, they did not involve a rejection of the MMT business model. They were just the expression of increased volume and deeper segmentation of solvent existent demand both in the domestic and international arenas (Plog 2003). The initial academic beguilement could not displace the realities of the marketplace and the wishes of the consumers. A few years later, one can contemplate somewhat ironically the geological strata of so many fossils as quickly adopted by academics as suddenly discarded thereafter.

Some basic economic and demographic factors would help them to understand this unrelenting discomfiture if they wanted to take them seriously. Far from stagnating within a limited redoubt of well-off areas, the middle classes—the foundation of mass tourism—have expanded. Their growth in China and in India, though not only there, has been amazing.

In China, they went up from 65.5 million in 2005 to 80 million in 2007. They are expected to reach 700 million in 2020. In 2007 it was estimated that Indian middle class had climbed to 50 million or 5% of the population. For 2025 the forecast goes to 583 million or 41% (Beinhocker et al 2007).

Paid vacation days have increased considerably in many European countries (Schmitt and Ray 2008), lately even as a way to mitigate unemployment. In Italy they reach as many as 42 workdays, that is, about 8 weeks per year; in France, 7 weeks and a half; in Germany and Brazil, 7 weeks; in the United Kingdom, 6 weeks; in Korea, Japan, and Canada, 5 weeks. The only developed country that keeps paid vacations low is the United States, at just 2 weeks (although this minimum ratchets up with seniority and individual contract clauses). Developing countries are not there yet, but many hope that increasing vacations will shorten their long working days and years.

Finally, disposable income has been on the rise in many developing countries, thus making it possible for middle class tourists to be on the move. Even the economic crisis of 2008–2009 may not have deflected this upward trend significantly. Tourism contracted 4.8% in 2009, but it is expected to recover along with global economic activity. The contribution of travel and tourism to the world's GDP is forecast to be 9.2% in 2010 (US$5.7 trillion) and rise to 9.6% in 2020 ($11.5 trillion) including both direct and indirect contributions of the industry (WTTC 2010).

These numbers, however, do not quench the Canute-like determination of many researchers to flog the waves. Without further ado than a horror of middle class life and the compassion inspired by small communities allegedly at risk of seeing their environment ravaged and their culture ruined by uncontrolled flows of tourists, academics keep on looking for the real alternative to mass tourism—from backpacking to CBT to different forms of local empowerment to sustainable development. One day, perhaps, they will find it.

THE BACKPACKING ROAD TO TOURISM DEVELOPMENT

Backpackers have come to be seen as one of the alternatives to MMT from the demand side. The underlying hypothesis goes something like this. Many small and still pristine communities see tourism as a way to increase their collective welfare. If they open themselves to mass tourism and the travel companies that control it, the barbarians at the gates will invade them at an extremely high social cost. However, if they position themselves on a market segment that favors slow but steady development, they may reach their desired goal without being defiled in the process. Which should their target market be? The large numbers of young people who travel the world before entering the labor market in their countries of origin are also known as backpackers.

To add some history, at the beginning of 1991, under the auspices of the Government of India, UNWTO organized in Delhi a conference on youth tourism. As the norm usually goes with bureaucratic venues, the hidden agenda of the conference went a bit further than addressing the many faces of an important sector of tourism customers. The Indian Government, as well as many other governments of less developed countries with a long history and old traditions, found themselves in a bind then, and still do today. On the one hand, they are eager to develop tourism, especially international tourism, as a source of economic benefits, employment, and foreign exchange. On the other, they want to lessen as much as possible its impact on the traditional ways of life of local host communities and, quite often, are also eager to protect the burgeoning national tourism industry, as well as their own roles in economic planning, including tourism.

Unfortunately, there is no easy fix to the quandary. International tourism, above all to destinations that require long-haul travel from the main generating markets (that is, from developed countries), is an industry where the rules of the game are well delineated. International tourism demands comfortable accommodation, new resorts, enhanced sanitation and safety, infrastructural investment, etc. that are often beyond the pale of the local industry. Furthermore, the expectations and behavior of affluent and mainstream tourists often conflict with the expectations and behavior of the locals. Coveted as it is for its economic benefits, international tourism has definite costs in terms of power for the national government and allegedly generates decay in local lifestyles and traditions.

Can a third way be found? That was the real goal of the Delhi conference—international youth tourism in the shape of budget or back-packing travel might offer a shortcut to the best of both possible worlds. On the one hand, youngsters from affluent countries, even though traveling on a shoestring, have massive purchasing power when contrasted with the local communities that they favor. Their local expenses are a shot in the arm for these indigenous economies. On the other, with their low budget, they do not require the usual Western frills, patronizing local hotels and guesthouses, and paying heed to local lifestyles. In a nutshell, less developed countries and their fragile communities might safely become pregnant with international tourism, though just a bit. In spite of some cautionary notes (Aramberri 1991, 2000), the backpacking strategy loomed large, India included. Did it fulfill its promise?

There is a sizable literature on backpackers and their traveling styles (Elsrud 2001; Hampton 1998; Loker-Murphy and Pearce 1995; Murphy 2001; Richards and Wilson 2008; Scheyvens 2002; Sørensen 2003). Usually authors specify a number of features that characterize this type of tourism, among them, shoestring budgets; long duration of trips; use of local transport and low-end accommodation (Hannam and Atejevic 2008); and a desire to engage in educational, cultural, and adventurous travel experiences (Loker-Murphy and Pearce 1995; Maoz and Bekerman 2010; Pearce and Foster 2007). They do not shun unknown geographic areas and often enjoy engaging in social exchanges that are liminal, out of the ordinary, or uncertain, if not utterly risky (Elsrud 2001; Adams 2001). Other features include the existence of specific communication networks, own "watering holes," or backpacker ghettoes, plus the developments of intense inter-personal relations among backpackers who only a few days before were total strangers (Uriely et al 2002).

At a level that reflects their subjective experiences and attitudes, backpackers, as opposed to other types of tourists, are said to be ready to adapt to local culture and mores and to have a role distinct in relation to mainstream vacationers (Murphy 2001:61–64 offers a detailed discussion of backpackers' perceived goals and means). Loker-Murphy and Pearce see the image of this type as "a return to the earlier values associated with the Grand Tours and the educational value of travel" (1995:827). Many youngsters either postpone for 1 year their entrance to college or delay for a long period their entry in the labor force after completing their degrees, to engage in this rite of passage (Caprioglio O'Reilly 2006; Brown 2009). In this sense, the most recent image of this long-term low-budget segment is a favorable one (Ooi and Laing 2010) that contrasts with the more severe tones used by Cohen (1982, 2001b) or Riley (1988) to refer to them.

The discussion has focused much less on other dimensions of back-packing, or its economic role in the chosen destination and its contribution to development strategies. Hampton (1998), in his study of Lombok, Indonesia, underlined that for the locals backpackers, demand is an opportunity to embark on a number of business ventures, as its minimalist infrastructure is less capital intensive than other tourist developments. He concluded that, even though it needs more detailed study,

> [b]ackpacker tourism could increase local participation in real development, part of a more sustainable long-term strategy

which attempts to balance local economic development needs against powerful interests wishing to build large international tourism resorts (1998:655).

Wilson (1997), in his otherwise remarkable paper on tourism in Goa, also sounded an equally favorable note.

Scheyven's contribution was even more upbeat—for her backpacking was demonstrably beneficial to local communities. Given their long stays in place, backpackers finally spend more and in better ways than other tourists, as they travel to remote areas; they bring economic benefits to communities that otherwise would be outsiders to development; they consume locally produced goods and services; investments to cater to their wants need not be capital intensive (therefore, entry costs are affordable to many local small entrepreneurs); imports are minimized. Other intangible benefits usually accompany those economic ones. Scheyvens points to the increase in small ownership that contributes toward involving locals more deeply in their communities, the revitalization of local culture and traditions, and more respect for the environment. She concludes that

> [t]here are positive signs, however, which indicate that by catering to backpackers, Third World peoples are able to gain real benefits from tourism and control their own enterprises. [...] National and local governments as well as non-governmental organizations can play important roles in facilitating a process to enable local communities to maximize opportunities that international backpacking presents to them (2002:160).

These conclusions seem a bit too bullish. Not only because, as Scheyvens notes, citing Hutnyk (1996) and Noronha (1999), there are many differences in backpackers' onsite behavior. Although it is a fact that many respect local cultures and their environment, others conduct themselves with the same aloofness to both as they do when in Cancún or Fort Lauderdale for the spring break. But furthermore—and this should be forcefully underlined— Scheyvens does not seem to have thoroughly understood the political economy of the proposed backpacking road to sustainable tourism. What is the position of the backpackers in the economy of the locality where they are staying? Their standing comes close to that of rentiers-cum-arbitrageurs. In fact, they derive their incomes from external sources and most do not engage in any other productive activities locally, while taking advantage of the difference between their home-earned proceeds and the price level at the local markets. In this way, their income goes much further while away from home—sheer purchasing power parity magic.

These remarks should not be construed as derogatory. In their own way, backpackers are very savvy consumers, haggling their way through the host community, at least while their income source lingers on, in the same way as informed agents pursuing a rational strategy would do. That might offend only those who bear moral grudges against self-interest and consumerism. The economic issue, however, lies elsewhere. If arbitraging is the main rationale for backpacking, this group of tourists will be better off the longer the host community remains in a state of underdevelopment when compared to their own. Whether they like it or not, and many would be sincerely appalled if they knew, they have an objective stake in the economic backwardness of their hosts. When the price differential between the affluent countries where they come from and their destination of choice softens, they respond by either shortening their stays or by booking alternate destinations where arbitrage may still work to their advantage.

There is also some evidence to support this argument on the cultural level by looking at one of the basic tourist tools—travel guidebooks—and the way some destinations are presented to backpackers (Enoch and Grossman 2010). What is a guidebook? Usually, a printed database about one country or a region that provides information and advice on a range of subjects of interest to potential tourists. The bulk of most guidebooks discusses attractions, transportation, lodging and food, usually flanked by an introduction with practical advice on how to get to the destination, do's and don'ts, plus sections with summary information on the country or region (history, religion, society, etc.). By no means can this last part substitute for thorough or accurate information on the destination, but quite likely this is what most potential tourists will ever learn about it, and is thus a key component of the destination image and of mass culture (Reichel et al 2009).

Guidebooks are important travel tools. Usually, they do not come first in the ranking of information sources, as most tourists say that their decisions are mainly influenced by word of mouth from friends and relatives or from the Internet, but they are used in conjunction with other sources and may carry a lot of weight. Some researchers have recalled that many off-the-beaten-trackers refer to their *Lonely Planet* guidebooks as "the bible" (Spreitzhofer 1998:980), both a treasure trove of factual information and a code of manners including even morals. Quite often the travel guide is crucial in closing a sale and, even when it is not, it helps in positioning a given destination in the evoked set. In the case of India, for instance, 19.1% of the audience sampled by Chaudhary (2000) reported that guidebooks were part of their basic information package.

Aramberri (2004a) studied the different images of India projected by two guidebooks that addressed different segments of the market. They were *National Geographic Traveler* (Nicholson 2001) and *Lonely Planet* (Singh 2001), both from the same year (2001). By far the most popular one in 2004 was *Lonely Planet* that ranked among the best-sold 10,000 books in the inventory of Amazon.com at the time. Both guidebooks addressed different publics. *National Geographic Traveler* aimed at upmarket or affluent tourists, while *Lonely Planet* mainly addressed budget tourists and backpackers.

Other than written information, the *National Geographic Traveler* guidebook relied mostly on visual iconography to accompany its text. It included 286 photographs (plus four on the cover) in 400 pages of the text. *Lonely Planet* included 163 photos (plus the cover) in 1,080 pages of the text. The more upmarket guidebook thus showed the greater number of photographs per text page. But there is a still more important issue, that is, the way in which pictorials were used to convey the message. The total number of photos used by each publication was divided into four main categories bound in two continua. The first continuum related nature and culture to pictorials of natural attractions, such as mountains, parks, and agricultural activities, on the one hand, and built monuments on the other (temples, palaces, and forts). The second continuum moved between, on the one hand, modern India and traditional lifestyles on the other. In modern India were included pictures that showed the impact of modern cultural icons (high-rise office buildings, designer shows, and information and communication technologies) of everyday life or, to put it in a widely used phrase, of the markers of globalization.

Lonely Planet focused overwhelmingly on images of traditional India (114 images out of 163 in total), followed by cultural attractions. For its part, *National Geographic Traveler* put cultural attractions first and then traditional India. It also paid much more attention to modern India with a total of 36 photographs (13% of the total), while in *Lonely Planet* it only scored a total of 7 (less than 5% of the iconic archive). If one looked at the inner balance in the continuum tradition/modernity in each of them, the outcome was even more significant. While *Lonely Planet* pictured modern India at a 6% rate in comparison with traditional India, the proportion for *National Geographic Traveler* was close to 40%. In the *National Geographic Traveler*, one also found the image of a country with a long history (both in monuments and in traditions) but increasingly impacted by global forces that were quickly leaving their footprint on the frame of traditional routines and attitudes.

This impression was reinforced by the written text that looked at India's present-day reality with a dynamic opposed to *Lonely Planet's* propast gaze. *Lonely Planet* reveled in a visual image of India that rated stolid nature, static monuments, and age-old traditions over new lifestyles—the old over the new, the past over the future. Though it is a sensible rule of common sense never to take polysemic symbols as having one single meaning, in this very context, the backpacker bible seemed to project a nostalgic (imperial?) preference for a timeless India, a country that remained unchanged, among other things, regarding the poverty that usually is the companion of the low prices so important to backpackers.

The copy in both guidebooks deepened a similar division. How to define India today? "[A] place to expect the unexpected," as per *Lonely Planet* (Singh 2001:17). *National Geographic Traveler* shared a similar view, defining the country as "a land of contrasts" (Nicholson 2001:14). Where both guides parted ways, though, was in locating the unexpected and the contrasts. For *Lonely Planet*, one could find the latter in sacred sites, in historic places, and in scenic nature. *National Geographic Traveler*, for its part, also noted the dissonance between old and new, but it made of it the crucial element to understanding present India. A long introductory section insisted on how the forces of globalization were affecting Indian life, with silk weavers in remote areas selling their wares via cell phone, or young university graduates forbidding their families to arrange their marriages. *National Geographic Traveler* also devoted a long section to the biggest democracy on Earth that departed from the short remarks devoted to the issue in *Lonely Planet*.

Bangalore has become the poster child for modern India. *Lonely Planet* acknowledged the fact and provided information on how the IT industry developed. *National Geographic Traveler* was both more precise and enthusiastic, pointing out that in the past, Indian brains went to the United States to work and learn, but today the tables have been turned with the homecoming of many of them and their setting up new companies busy "buying out weaker US firms" (Nicholson 2001:227). It is difficult to dispute that India is an ancient society with many cultures and traditions widely different from Western ones. What happens, then, when both clash in the everyday traffic of tourists and locals? *Lonely Planet* operated from a conceptual framework adopted from cultural criticism and postmodern cultural anthropology. The key tenet of its approach was the *emic* persuasion that cultures can be understood only from the inside, that they are the best judges of their own values, and that outsiders will never be able to capture all their dimensions thoroughly. Tourists should not be judgmental and should try to adapt to local mores.

When one reads the small print, this initial stand appears somewhat shaky. Take women's issues—it is not easy to reconcile local behavior with the Western tenets of women's liberation. One either opts out of the discussion or has to defend rules that will make one of the parties unhappy. *Lonely Planet* adopted a "just-the-facts-ma'am" methodology and lets it be known that, even though urban and middle class Indian women had made inroads in the professions, in the armed forces, and in politics, the rest of the female population had not improved its position; that traditional families still preferred to have male children; that female infanticide and abortion of healthy female fetuses, though banned, were common practice; that arranged marriages were the norm rather than the exception; that married women faced a lot of pressure if they wanted to divorce; and that, according to recent surveys, two-thirds of urban men thought that female willingness to adjust to male desires was very important. A box informed on sati and how this tradition died hard. *National Geographic Traveler* was more outspoken. Though some privileged Indian women have occupied important places as company directors, surgeons, filmmakers, and politicians, "life for the vast majority of Indian women is different, full of inequality and deprivation. Even in India's more emancipated urban areas, tradition remains strong" (Nicholson 2001:68), and tradition did not show a pleasant face to women.

The conflict grew deeper when both guidebooks offered advice on how to avoid eventual collisions between different cultural norms and practices. In fact, then and now, a sizable number of backpackers and low-budget tourists were Western or Westernized women who did not share local mores or values. The advice given by *Lonely Planet*, however, was not encouraging. Again, facts were let to speak for themselves. Indian streets, it was said, are male dominated—therefore, expect some measure of being stared at, suggestive comments, or even sexual harassment. It is better to dress modestly and refrain from smoking and drinking in public, counseled *Lonely Planet* (Singh 2001:113–115). One can understand that common sense may persuade in offering directions to avert unwanted or unpleasant consequences to female readers; however, not offering any mental reservation on the discomfiture of being bound to forget about their hard-won rights at home when they cross a foreign border seems a bit more difficult to excuse.

Can backpacking be construed as a blanket way to less painful tourism development in poor countries or destinations (Teo and Leong 2006)?

It looks as though it would rather lead them astray into a blind alley partially successful in the short run, though eventually followed by quick decay. Arbitrageurs are not investors ready to stay put with their resorts, casinos, theme parks, or hotels, but highly volatile consumers sensitive to the least changes in prices. They do not directly create employment in their destinations; they just help to develop it on a small scale. With an expression typically used to refer to highly volatile capital flows in financial markets, they are "swallow" consumers—here today, gone tomorrow. As soon as the local community starts to thrive in its budding prosperity, and as soon as this trend brings about increased prices, off they go to less pricey places. The low capital-intensive investments made by the locals would soon get low rates of return and become stagnant, while there would be hardly anybody to substitute for the backpackers gone to greener pastures. One might call this drift, *pace* Urry, *The Tourist Graze.*

Should backpackers be accordingly cast off from their Garden of Eden? Only the operation of the market will tell. A business as complex as tourism can always accommodate many demands and many income groups. The previous argument only means that the backpacker sector cannot be expected to play a key role in the development of tourism in India or anywhere else. Backpackers' economic contribution to local communities is usually low, does not call for strong work opportunities, and does not create heavy investment opportunities. Something similar can be said on the cultural side. Important as it may be under certain circumstances and occasions, it is far from being the economic alternative to MMT touted by its practitioners and their academic admirers.

Unfortunately, the same may be said of other alternatives to standard mass tourism, such as volunteer tourism, also known as voluntourism and pro-poor tourism (Ashley et al 2001; Deloitte and Touche 1999; Wearing 2008). Both have more or less the same goals—contribute through tourism to poverty alleviation in depressed areas of the world. There are a number of small differences between both practices, with voluntary tourism (Sin 2009) favoring that practitioners participate in the implementation of projects that help the local community while pro-poor tourism would take a less engaged participation in the life of the communities. Advocates for both types of tourism celebrate, though, their economic value for the local community, their low footprint, and their opposition to allegedly neo-imperialist practices (Gard McGehee and Almeida Santos 2005). In this way, it is surprising how once highly celebrated ecotourism has been downgraded at lightning speed to eco-colonialism or eco-imperialism (Butcher 2007; Cater and Lowmann 1994). Many now see it as a scam or a marketing ploy, even though not everybody completely agrees (Fennell and Dowling 2003). Could this be a morality tale for future voluntary tourism and pro-poor tourism?

At any rate, their advocates see them as definitive alternatives to MMT (Clarke 2009; Gard McGehee 2002). Really? One empathizes with their good will. Take, for instance, the definition by pro-poor tourism partnership.

> Pro-Poor Tourism (PPT) is tourism that results in increased net benefits for poor people. PPT is not a specific product or niche sector but an approach to tourism development and management. It enhances the linkages between tourism businesses and poor people, so that tourism's contribution to poverty reduction is increased and poor people are able to participate more effectively in product development. Links with many different types of "the poor" need to be considered: staff, neighboring communities, land-holders, producers of food, fuel and other suppliers, operators of micro tourism businesses, craft-makers, other users of tourism infrastructure (roads) and resources (water) etc. (2010).

Only Dr. Evil could be against that.

Unfortunately, there is little contributed by way of hard evidence (Blake et al 2008; Hawkins and Mann 2007) to the economic success of such types of tourism. After the usual tirades against mass tourism, capitalism, commoditization, banality, and the like, numbers are not easy to come by, though the devil, as usual, lies in the details. Can these types of tourism find much demand? Can they elicit the necessary investments to make such commendable intentions come true? Almost everything is possible, but the likelihood of turning pro-poor tourism into an alternative to mass tourism seems quite limited. Should therefore people be discouraged from engaging in pro-poor tourism? Of course not. It definitely may help to increase the number of jobs in some locations and develop community income, but in order to be successful PPT, as well as voluntary tourism, have to attract investment and also be able to motivate the number of tourists necessary to sustain it. Will it become, as some dreamers expect (Wearing 1999 Wearing 2001), an alternative to mass tourism? One can doubt it. Small-scale development may be beautiful. It is much more difficult to make it profitable.

Some final words have to be devoted to other alternatives that propose the acceptance of dubious products in the marketing mix of destinations that desperately need tourists to alleviate the extreme poverty of many of their denizens. Faced with such a problem, Kibicho (2009) proposed the legalization of prostitution in Kenya, and to promote some areas of the country as sex tourism destinations, expecting that such steps would increase the number and the expenses of tourists, diminish risks for its practitioners, increase their earnings, and let the state tax their activities. Once again, even if one understands the logic of the argument and is not opposed to a measure that would make the life of prostitutes easier, it is quite doubtful that it might become the silver bullet to alleviate poverty in Kenya. According to the latest data available in the UNWTO database (2010), in 2004 the country received 1.2 million tourists who spent $486 million. Even if the number of sex tourists had increased to the same numbers in 2008 and even if they had spent a similar amount of dollars in the country as all tourists did in 2004 (so that we can use World Bank 2010 data for 2008), they would have added but 1.7% to the gross national income (Atlas method). Not a pittance, but definitely not a lot. Far from Ryan and Hall's (2001) epic ruminations (sex tourism is the way to development chosen by the World Bank for the economic development of a number of countries), sex tourism would not be a magic shortcut to development for Kenya or any other destination (Chapter 6).

COMMUNITY-BASED TOURISM AND EMPOWERMENT

If the demand side does not offer much hope in finding alternatives to MMT development, perhaps one could find a solution on the supply side. That is what different solutions such as bottom–up development, CBT, and local empowerment propose. With different names, what advocates of the idea have in mind is to give decision-making power in product development to the local communities. The program harks back to a popular idea initially circulated by Murphy (1985) that the latter know best what to offer to tourists, and will do it more efficiently than outside actors.

Once again, the idea looks quite appealing. It would be difficult to deny that local people know their communities and their products well. However, as soon as one tries to go a bit deeper, things become fuzzier. The basic postulate from which all the rest derives is that communities do speak with one single voice. As noted in Chapter 7, this is not the case. Additionally, Bauman (2001) has rightly noted that the concept of community itself talks more to our heart than to our reason. It evokes affective fusion, cozy feelings, and a yearning for the security of the maternal womb. However, passion and feelings do not provide the best financial advice. Quite often they encourage an irresistible drive to romance local communities, and when one tries to implement courses of action in the real world, the outcome may be unrecognizable or discouraging, as measured by the initial expectations.

Locals, almost invariably, have divergent and often conflicting interests. Stonich (2000) documented the contradictory goals pursued by different social sectors in the villages of the Bay Islands, Honduras. Whether it is Central Florida (Milman and Pizam 1987) or Samos, Greece (Haralambopoulos and Pizam 1996), there is a marked difference of attitude toward tourism and tourism development between the two sectors (nontourism- and tourism-dependent subgroups) characterized by Canestrelli and Costa in the case of Venice, Italy (1991). Similar conflicts are also found in developing countries, such as China (Byrne Swain and Mommsen 2001b; Cohen 2001b; McKhann 2001), and in areas of developed societies where tourism is not the major industry. In the wine-growing Napa Valley, California, wineries, environmentalists, and the tourism industry are in a tug of war around the issue of who should determine the use of the land. Their divergent interests have even made their way to the courts (Kahn 2002).

Sofield is one of the first and firmest advocates of CBT, and his study of tourism in the Kathmandu Valley, Nepal (2001) is a case in point. He starts by stressing the need for local empowerment especially in those communities that are traditionally oriented, though living in the social and political space of a modern state. Following from a muddled characterization of Weber's forms of domination (compare Sofield 2001:258 with Weber 1971:122–148), his article suggests that empowerment is a multidimensional process that, in the end, should leave decisions in the hands of the local communities. No reference to the role of the state or the local government of the area where they are located is made, perhaps because his unqualified idea that "empowerment must be able to counter dependency" (2001:258) would make the centralized power irrelevant. In fact, however, the latter usually shows an understandable resistance to accept similar limits to its sovereignty, and so we face the first theoretical quagmire for CBT and the empowerment theory. Can local empowerment, whether in theory or in practice, make hay of other power centers (the central government, provinces, states in federal regimes, local administrations)? One should prove it.

Though important, however, this is not the main problem. Sofield describes the different ways of travel to the most sacred sites in Kathmandu Valley (Svayambhunath and Changu Naryan) and how the UNDP (United Nation Development Program) sponsored a plan to make those forms of tourism a sustainable undertaking. He stresses that the plan was "more of a bottom–up rather than a top–down planning process, with the community empowered from the beginning to participate in decision-making" (2001:268). One should reasonably expect that, under these premises and after the adoption of the plan, all the parties would live happily ever after. By early 1998, most project objectives had been achieved. The contests over space still continued but had diminished. The UNDP-sponsored Partnership for Quality Tourism Project (PQTP) intervention had significantly improved the physical site, and its hillsides, and the village site management. Residents, pilgrims, and tourists all expressed satisfaction with the results (2001:269).

In fact, the bliss was short lived. In the last section of his analysis, Sofield cursorily informs his readers that only a few months later the plan was petering out. Apparently, the PQTP had relied too heavily on a local cluster of interests organized around the Community Development Committee at the expense of a Village Development Committee. According to Nepalese law, the latter had a right, among other things, to oversee the channeling of funds that the PQTP had transferred to the Community Development Committee without its approval, whereupon the Village Development Committee closed the Community Development Committee's Tourist Information Office, one of the PQTP's key props, and approved other measures oriented to curtail its powers even more. Some local powers apparently resisted the empowerment process devised in the bottom–up project.

It is difficult to ascertain who was right in this dispute without a background on Nepalese jurisprudence, which is not easily obtainable. The clash, however, states openly that there were, at least, two conflicting interest groups in the local community and that one of them felt unfairly excluded from the solution promoted by the PTQP. Empowerment of the locals was clearly trickier than initially expected. Consequently, the conclusion—the interests of the local stakeholders constitute a harmonious whole—is either a figment of the imagination or, worse, a way of rewarding the stakeholders favored in stealth by the researcher and/or the plan consultants. In both cases, it should not come as a surprise that conflicts would ensue.

The issue, however, is not just that there will always be conflicts among the different groups of a community—they will. Conflicts of interests are not fleeting misunderstandings that will go away once good communication is restored, as international bureaucracies often surmise. Conflicts are, rather, as we have been stressing, the stuff of everyday life, given the fact that the interests of participants in both local and broader communities do not usually coincide. When romancing the locals is not the main inspiration for researchers, this fact comes quickly to the surface.

A more developed attempt by Sofield to apply his empowerment theory does not reap a better harvest (2003). The author employed three case studies centered on the South Pacific, to illustrate what he thinks to be a good theory applicable to all tourism development. "[It] constitutes a synthesis of the concepts of empowerment, tourism development (especially involving indigenous communities), and sustainable development to take account of the political and socio-economic environments" (2003:8–9). In spite of the clumsiness of the last clause, let it be said in Sofield's defense that he does not fear to go down the road less traveled by so many academics that have turned *pointillisme* (pointillism) into their technique of choice. Their devotion for minute case studies resembles the neo-impressionist technique that uses tiny brush strokes to be constructed as a whole by the viewer's eye. Take our academic publications and you will find a near endless stream of minute case studies unable to sustain even a mid-ranged hypothesis. Thus, Sofield's stab at dusting the barely existing theoretical credentials of tourism research has to be praised and commended. The best homage to be paid to his effort is to discuss it in detail, even if one finds it falling well short of the mark.

In his effort to construct the aforementioned synthesis, Sofield starts with two basic policy propositions that can be summed as sustainable tourism development cannot be reached without empowering local communities, and it cannot be solely achieved by letting them follow their traditional ways, but also needs state sanction. Apparently, the Kathmandu lesson was not to be forgotten so that the new dispensation could navigate a less choppy sea. Such postulates do not bear being examined in their inner logic, though; instead, we are prompted to accept them because they have been endorsed by some authoritative sources. Short of revelation or dogmatic infallibility, Sofield finds solace in bureaucratic consensus. Oftentimes, when asserting the legitimacy of a given concept or theory, the author defers to different international documents. For instance, the notion of sustainability or sustainable development should be adopted because it was enshrined in the 1987 Brundtland Report; the need to link economic development and equity sprang from the International Labor Organization when it adopted it in 1976, or the definition of indigenous peoples and their common features should follow what the UN General Assembly or the UNDP had approved. However, one does not have to be an Aristotle to realize that the argument from authority is the weakest argument of all.

Sofield, who served as an Australian diplomat for part of his career, is well aware that those documents are more of an exercise in horse trading than in scholarly debate—nevertheless he invites us to accept them without the shred of a doubt. He knows that the notion of sustainability or sustainable development adopted by the Brundtland Report (sustainable development should meet "the needs of the present generation without compromising the ability of future generations to meet their own needs") is so unspecific that it cannot answer most of the questions that follow attempts to implement it. It rises at least as many questions as its proponents think it answers. However, Sofield embraces it lock, stock, and barrel, adding a few holes of his own. What does it mean that policies aimed at sustainability should err on the side of caution or that social equity should be a key principle of sustainability, as he advocates, when those notions are admittedly open to multiple interpretation, and he makes no real effort to adjudge the merits of the different contenders.

Indeed, there is a rather long chapter apparently devoted to this task, but one would look in vain for any substance beyond some stereotypes summarily dispatched. To wit, that while economic growth, a notion well defined in economics, is quantitative, that of development is qualitative, as though those adjectives were not so loaded that they do not mean much without further clarification that the reader will await in vain. Or that in discussing less developed countries one can skip Keynes or Marx, the former more interested in mature, industrialized capitalist societies, the latter in "the ideology of centrally controlled economies" (2003:32). One would think that, in fact, Keynes tried to identify general laws for any society that would have to deal with employment, interest, and money, while a sizable part of Marx's work is devoted to the problems of the transition from precapitalist modes of production to capitalism itself, exactly the juncture at which so many less developed countries find themselves today. If one skips such basic discussions, what is there left by way of theoretical discussion?

Not much. Above all, the ritual exorcism of modernization theories; then, a qualified critique and validation of the tenets of the postcolonial school of thought.

> Dependency theory, had it persisted, may [*sic*] have eventually got around to consider empowerment of the nation state as a way to break the chain of dependency; but it would not have incorporated community empowerment in its thesis (2003:56).

In plain English, with some refocusing, albeit not a complete overhaul of its hypotheses, dependency theory might still flex its muscle in a new lease of life.

Sofield's cosmetic surgery, though, looks surprisingly problematic. Did not dependency theorists do a bit more than eventually consider the empowerment of the nation-state? If one accurately remembers them, the writings of Bettelheim (1975), Frank (1975, 1981), Amin (1973, 1976), and Dos Santos (1991) precisely made national liberation into a precondition of any type of independence, including community empowerment. Sofield grants that dependency theoreticians did in fact overlook the actual diversity of roads taken by the search for development and made some too broad statements, but one should not forget that they carved for environmental and cultural factors a role that one would seek in vain among the modernizers, whose evolutionary schemes equated development with the expansion of Western capitalism.

This last is a stereotype that, as former President George W. Bush might put it, misunderestimates modernization theory. After the demise of the Soviet Union and its planned economy, after the opening of party membership to capitalist entrepreneurs in China, after the failure of the experiments to dispense with capitalism in Africa and in the Islamic world, after the incomplete but nevertheless unmistakable Indian resistance to abandon its inefficient command economy, the notion that a modern economy has to be capitalist may not be so misguided after all. Why does Sofield discard it in such a cursory manner? He favors what one might call a compassionate progressivism, that is, the idea that environmental and cultural dynamics, not necessarily economic imperatives, should lead sustainable tourism development. This is in the end what he means with his notion of empowerment.

Empowerment, however, assumes different shapes in his work. Here, taking a cue from its use in rural development, Sofield believes that empowerment means that

> the desires and objectives of the rural poor must be put first
> and the capacities, views, and values of the professionals held
> in abeyance and only harnessed to assist in bringing to fruition
> those desires and objectives of the poor (2003:91–92).

There, he likens it to total quality management and *kaizen*—which by the way does not mean empowerment as he translates, but "continuous improvement" (iSixSigma 2004)—two techniques increasingly used by big business. Over there, he celebrates the bottom–up approach he used in Kathmandu as the allegedly best tool for empowerment as proven by repeated nongovernmenal organization practice.

One cannot be sure, though, that all of the above have the same meaning. While the second incarnation is but a way of improving the performance of companies without ever giving to the rank and file a say on key issues such as investment, product development, marketing strategies, and so on, the great-leap-forward undertones of the first would require that exclusive protagonism on all those issues be given to the poor. Compassionate as this may be, it does not enlighten us much as to how the category should be constructed. Take Australia, for instance. Who are the poor to be put first—the 13% of people who lived in poverty there in 2000 (The Smith Family/NATSEM 2001), or also the working poor just over the official line of poverty; the rural poor and/or the urban poor; the white poor and/or the aboriginal or indigenous poor; if the latter, all in the community or just the poorest within it, as usually not all of its members have the same access to resources? As for NGOs they are a motley array where antiglobalizers brush up against market enthusiasts and a myriad of shades in between. The tool of empowerment thus looks more and more like a sorcerer's apprentice's broom.

Eppur' si muove (However, it moves), Sofield insists. The theoretical parts may not fit seamlessly with each other, but he offers the evidence in his tale of three tourism experiences. Exhibit #1, the *Ghol* performance in Vanuatu, proved sustainable as well as Exhibit #2, the Mana Island Resort in Fiji. Exhibit #3 is, or better was, Anuha Island Resort in the Solomon Islands. After a few years, it went bankrupt. What did the first two ones have in common that was missing in #3? You guessed it—local empowerment. To understand their diverging courses, let us start with the winners.

Sa people in some villages of Pentecost, one of the islands in the archipelago that forms the territorial base of Vanuatu, celebrate the annual ritual of the *Ghol*, a ceremony in which "specially selected initiates leap headfirst to the ground from a platform about 25 meters high, with vines lashed to their ankles so that their foreheads just brush the earth" (Sofield 2003:261). Beyond its significance for the natives, the *ghol* is one of those *morceaux de bravoure* (stunts) that like the running of the bulls in Pamplona (Spain) or the Palio race in Sienna (Italy) excite the interest of a wide public or, in marketing jargon, have a strong pull factor.

For a time, tourists willing to attend the event were channeled through a foreign travel agency, but a few years later the locals started having qualms about whether to allow foreigners to watch their prowess; finally they agreed to sell their culture by the ounce—by the pound, as Greenwood (1977) would put it, seems too grandiose a word here, as the event can accommodate only a few dozen spectators at a time. They would let the foreign travel agency sell tickets to the event, but they also decided to take control of all the other aspects of the ritual themselves. The main reason provided for commercializing the event was that it could make them more money than sticking to cash cropping or accepting wage labor. "Since the Sa themselves took control of the touristic exploitation of the *ghol*, direct annual income for the villagers has exceeded US$20,000" (Sofield 2003:267). At the same time, we are told, Sa control of the *ghol* vouched for the authenticity the tourists are said to look for. In this way, the *ghol* successfully marries local customs with tourism money, ensuring its sustainability. This first tale, in true Aesop tradition, carries a moral. "Indigenous ownership and control is absolutely fundamental to empowerment in terms of cultural or ethnic origin" (Sofield 2003:276). However, a question lingers—is this empowerment or just the fact that Sa people have become entrepreneurs of their performance while outsourcing ticket sales to a third party? After all, they do not need to be empowered by anybody— they are the *owners* of the attraction.

The second success story was that of Mana Island Resort, in the Fiji archipelago. The resort was built on a plot of land (around half of the surface of the island) leased in 1971–1972 to an Australian company. In 1988 this company sold its interests to a Japanese enterprise that proposed to develop up to 600 tourist units with a total capacity of 2,600 beds. Its 30 years of life attest to the sustainability of the resort. What accounts for this longevity? Above all, "[n]ot one single household in Yaro lives in poverty" (2003:302). Besides the rent, the lease provided that the local community, the owners of the land, would be hired in preference to any other workers. Additionally, it confirmed public access to the beach and other marine resources. As a consequence, either by direct employment or by exploiting resort-related business (deep-sea fishing, a backpacker resort, craft shops, and a mini-mart), the locals experienced tangible benefits accruing from tourism. All is well that ends well.

However, one might ask, what, if anything, did empowerment contribute to this happy outcome? That the locals would become satisfied wageworkers or small entrepreneurs, as any economist might have forecast, is the consequence of good market economics. Indeed the good will of the strong men in the community smoothed the process, but it is difficult to picture it as anything else than a welcome fifth wheel or, in economic jargon, reduced transaction costs (Williamson 1975) for the managing company. The locals' control of the resort operation, however, cannot bear a comparison with that of the Pentecost islanders and for good reason. They are not owners, but employees. While no *ghol* would be possible without the Pentecostians' involvement, the continuance of the Fijian resort might be ensured even in the case of a refusal to cooperate on the part of the people of Mana. If no conflicts have appeared for years, one would think that this was due above all to what we can call a business-friendly environment where the lease and other obligations would eventually, in the case of conflict, be enforced by Fijian legal institutions (Soto 2000).

This was lacking in Exhibit #3, Anuha Island, in the Solomons. In 1981 an Australian company decided to lease it and build a small resort there. The lessors were the local community, the Nggela people of Rera village. Since the beginning of the new business venture, under the leadership of one of their strong men (Father Pule), the community, invoking traditional rule or *kastom*, imposed on the resort developers a consultative management committee to supervise operations and control job allocation. Father Pule had definitely decided to empower himself and his family for "[s]everal of Father Pule's nine sons and daughters and their wives and husbands were employed by the resort, Pule's eldest son being the most highly paid local" (2003:231). In time, new lessees succeeded the original managers, disbanded the joint committee, and fired some of the local workers. The result in following years and through new changes in management was an increased level of conflict that in December 1987 led to an invasion of the resort by Father Pule's warriors (Sofield's expression), who therewith proceeded to expel the managers from the island and to hold 40 guests and a construction crew hostage for several days. In shorthand, following Sofield's own narrative, the local community tried by all means, including low-intensity terrorist techniques, to impose its will in a way that any reasonable investor would have resisted. During this long process, successive Solomon Islands governments failed to impose the rule of law, and in July 1992, Anuha Resort ceased to exist as no new investors were found to resume operations.

At this juncture, Sofield's analysis of the conflict takes a surprising turn. After a long excursus on social exchange theory and plenty of graphics to describe expectation levels, power differentials, conflicts between actors, transaction evaluation, and other theoretical frills, he concludes that

> [t]he now defunct Anuha Island Resort provides a graphic example of the drastic consequences which may occur when the host community is disempowered, alienated and margin-alized from the development process (2003:345).

It is difficult to read this sentence without assuming that the collapse of the operation might have been avoided had Father Pule and his "warriors" been given total satisfaction.

Let us, for argument's sake, skip the fact that a similar solution would have had to quash a court ruling that rejected Father Pule's claims and acknowledged the lessees' rights and let us concentrate once more on the consequences of this theory of empowerment. Sofield is free to think that his conclusion is consistent with his postulates of giving priority to ecological and cultural factors over the economy. He is also free to portend that the Anuha Island case is a good example of the need to err on the cautionary side in order to preserve the rights of dispossessed indigenous communities. He is even free to believe that the latter can do no wrong. Unfortunately, stubborn economic factors, once shown the door, creep through the window, and threaten to turn Sofield's compassionate embrace of the underdogs into choking them to death.

As he acknowledges, after the conflict, it was not easy for the Solomon Islands to regain the trust of tourism investors, thus depriving the locals of badly needed investment—a premium one has to be ready to pay when one allows compassion-*cum*-cultural-factors-*cum*-political-correctness take the driver's seat in theoretical issues. One wonders if Sofield's conclusion would have been the same had Father Pule and his "warriors" been a bunch of Aussie rednecks (to avoid hurting sensitivities, the term is used after Cowlishaw 1998) like the tormentors of Priscilla, Queen of the Desert. In the end, however, we come to understand Sofield's insistence on postulating a causal relation between empowerment and sustainability—there is no way to prove it with compelling logic.

Sofield is not the sole example of how passionate love for the idea of community can lead to ostracizing their denizens, and scorning their attempts to take their lives in their own hands. Some anthropologists become so enthralled in their tough love for a given community that they will even deny them the right to choose. Empowerment is fine as long as the locals do not insist on making their own decisions, and follow academic advice. This is at least what one deduces from reading Pi-Sunyer, Brooke Adams, and Daltabuit's essay on the Mayas of Cancún (2001). Their subject is the growth of tourism in Mexico's Yucatan Peninsula and its costs to the local populations, although quite quickly only the indigenous Maya are considered under this rubric.

Tourism growth has had dire consequences for them, we are told, even though most holidaymakers in the area enjoy the old sun-and-sea formula, or the new ecological offers without the slightest idea of what is happening around them. More and more, the new economic and cultural forces marginalize the remnants of the old Maya community to a point where the indigenous population becomes a minority in its own country. The new enclaves of marginality that they occupy have little in common with the traditional Maya peasant life in isolated and homogeneous communities that had a strong sense of solidarity. Is this due to the rapid tourism development that started in the 1970s around the then quaint fishing village of Cancún, in the Mexican state of Quintana Roo, and has attracted over 2 million visitors a year in the late 1990s? Yes and no, say the authors. Let us begin with the no. The marginalization of the Yucatan Maya originated well before the first tourist set foot in one of the area's beautiful beaches, though they will not tell how this happened. In a few perfunctory remarks about the Caste War (1847–1855) and its aftermath until 1901, they just state that the Mayas were confronting the Mexican Army, as though the latter was just a ghost, was operating in a vacuum, and was not supported by the then popular ideology of nation building, or by the Creole and *mestizo* non-Maya people that occupied the coastal areas, and were introducing new modes of production. Below the political conflict, there was a social and economic one that pitted those two groups against the Maya. The Maya lost the war, among other things, because their slash-and-burn crop system demanded an extended agriculture, and also because it was inefficient and unsuited to the more complex economy espoused by the non-Maya (Dumond 1997; Reed 2001). The beginning of the Maya marginalization, therefore, predates by many years the tourist development of the region.

Undoubtedly the latter has left its mark. The demand for new resorts and services attracted many job seekers from other parts of Mexico and abroad that quite often displaced the old labor force, in part because of employment policies that discriminated against the Indians, in part also because they were better trained, or had skills attuned to the new service economy that the Maya lacked. The Maya, then, suffered the tough lot that awaits those who, for whatever reason, lag behind in times of rapid change or, in evolutionary lingo, are reluctant to adapt to a new environment. To their moral credit, the authors lament this outcome, but moral self-righteousness hardly changes the issues. They, therefore, seem to be in denial of the fact that the service economy will not go away, and prefer to wrap themselves in a cloak of nostalgia, even though their narrative is overly at variance with the reactions to modernity of the Maya. The latter or, more properly, many of them have a different way of figuring out costs and benefits. It may not be easy for them to go from collective owners of the *ejido* (communal land) to wage laborers, and they may resent it. But, on the other hand, there is no longing on their part for the old subsistence agriculture of the *milpa* (Mayan traditional crop system). Of those who participated in the authors' survey, 78% said that things would not be better without tourism.

The authors, however, go on to deplore that the old structures of the Maya communities are crumbling and that consumerism has permeated social life. They do not consider even for a second why so many Maya have no qualms about it. Pi-Sunyer, Brooke Adams, and Daltabuit just complain. Western casual attire has replaced traditional dress codes; modern medicine and commercial drugs have debased the authority of the h-men or Maya curer priests; the print media and, above all, television are the new sources of entertainment and news; people consume Coke, Nestlé, and other big commercial brands instead of following the old diet, which according to the authors was healthier. Not a single comment on the fact that jeans and t-shirts may be cheaper and more functional than the old *huipiles* (tunics and blouses), that modern medicine has a better record in fighting diseases than traditional practices (by the bye, where do the authors go when they have a medical emergency, to the neighborhood healer or to the nearest University Hospital?), that ready-made tortillas and tacos save many hours of hard labor for women, that branded foods usually have a better quality control than unbranded ones, or that Mexican *culebrones* (TV soap operas) may be more entertaining for many Maya than the oral folkways of yore. In this heartfelt epitaph for Maya culture, though, there is room for everything but present-day Yucatan Maya. Maya culture may speak with one single nostalgic voice if we belong to the same anthropological tradition as Pi-Sunyer, Brooke Adams, and Daltabuit, but the real Maya seem to understand that their lot would be much worse were they to take the wager of old times the authors propose.

Yucatan Maya seem to be adapting to modernity in the same way and with troubles similar to those experienced by millions of other people the world over. One may not like it, but it is difficult to see why this would contribute to their marginalization. As a matter of fact, the Maya seem to have a pretty good sense of reality. They know that the old times are not coming back, that they should adapt to the new circumstances, and that they have to maximize their meager social capital. This looks like a better way to surmount marginalization than denying the changes—and the opportunities—that come with the new times. The authors may state with a straight face that "[in Mexico] the post-World War Two development model has minimally improved the living standards for the majority of the population" (2001:128), even though World Bank statistics or United Nations' human development indicators claim the opposite, but there is no need for the marginalized Maya to believe them. The Maya may not read arcane data and reports, they may get angry at the mostly small opportunities that the new service economy gives them, but they know that they are better off than they were yesterday. One cannot blame them for not sharing the implicit theoretical assumption that modernization and the service economy are but a fable invented by some arcane institutions just to dupe and exploit them even more.

Something similar can be said of Jurdao's work (1979, 1990) on the Spanish village of Mijas, a book that has experienced a degree of popularity in the Anglo-Saxon academic media, thanks to its enthusiastic endorsement by Nash (1996). According to Jurdao, Spanish tourism development brought a number of social consequences especially hard for the people, mainly peasants who had traditionally inhabited coastal areas. Their rural culture made them defenseless before the foreign developers that many times acted in cahoots with the local power brokers. Fraud and graft unleashed tourism developments that would decimate agriculture and turn the peasants into construction workers.

Jurdao followed the process and its alleged dynamics at the microlevel of the Andalusian town of Mijas, a small inland city in the area known as Costa del Sol in southeastern Spain. Together with Majorca, Costa del Sol was the cradle of foreign mass tourism in the 1960s. Before that, Mijas was a sleepy backwater in a mostly agricultural area. Like most of Andalusia, since the mid-19th century, it was torn by landlord–peasant conflicts similar to those described by Brenan (1990). After the Spanish Civil War (1936–1939) and under General Franco's dictatorship, the town seemed poised to reproduce inequality and poverty as it had done for generations. Then the masses of tourists arrived and, with them, Jurdao's research on the impacts of tourism (see Aramberri 2009 for a full account).

In the years before the advent of mass tourism, sharecroppers and day laborers represented a social majority that could not make enough to feed their families with their work. However, at the end of the 1950s, the construction of new hotels and condominium blocks on the Costa del Sol required a growing workforce, thus offering new jobs to peasants in nearby areas such as Mijas. The old traditional order started to crumble. According to Jurdao, villages that had developed more or less harmoniously over the centuries, each proud of its culture and its identity, were replaced by suburbs alien to their old world. In many cases, the peasants sold their holdings for a pittance thinking that they were doing an excellent business. Damages to traditional society did not stop at the economic sphere. "Because of the division of labor introduced in a few years by tourism development, the peasant family was broken" (1990:199). Mijas was now a dual society. On the one hand was the autochthonous Spanish population of laborers and peasants; on the other, were the planned communities with their villas and bungalows inhabited by foreigners who usually enjoyed a higher standard of living than the locals. The process, says Jurdao, developed with the complicity of the Spanish Government during Franco's dictatorship and under the democratic governments that followed. From Madrid, the Spanish administration looked at the tourist towns of the Mediterranean seaboard as at so many other colonies. It allowed foreign colonization to deepen without caring to protect the native communities, to prevent the disappearance of Spanish villages, or to hold back the sale of land to foreigners at bargain basement prices.

Among Anglo-Saxon academics, Nash has insisted that Jurdao's is a genuine denunciation of tourism and its imperialist dynamics (1996). In the final analysis, however, the prime mover in Jurdao's argument is not an evaluation of national interests at a time of growing international integration—rather nostalgia for the passing of rural society and the old communitarian order. Jurdao, however, refrains from providing an understanding or explaining the process. According to him, the Spanish actors, especially day laborers and poor peasants, made the wrong choice. They exchanged the ways of their traditional communities for the deceptive comforts of the new towns.

Asking "why?" does not interest him, though he might have found the reason just by reading what he wrote himself. Many workers in old Mijas were unable to cater for most of their families' needs. Hunger, early death, and squalor were their everyday lot. Leaving their land in droves, they acted out of the conviction that the old order definitely was the worst possible of two evils. Even at their low-level skills, construction and the tourism industry offered better living opportunities than tilling the fields in endless days of misery. It was a voluntary choice. Nobody forced the *Mijeños* to sell their land or, in the case of the landless majority, to abandon it, except the desire to have a better life in places where good schools and adequate health care would be provided. The vaunted old communitarian order seemed to them less fair than the new one; accordingly they voted with their feet. This is something Jurdao, or Sofield, or Pi-Sunyer, or many other collectors of case studies prefer to forget. Deep down under the communitarian vocabulary, their classical populism dies hard. They share the illusion of rural society's moral superiority over modernity and do not want to understand the economic reasons that led many poor peasants the world over to choose wage labor and urban life over the peasant commune. For them, the latter are but fare for accountants, not real arguments. If the peasant commune suffers because of the unreachable goals they propose, let them eat cake.

WHICH SUSTAINABILITY?

An interest in sustainability started long time ago, indeed as far back as one of its first modern promoters, Thomas Malthus. Malthus forewarned his contemporaries of the oncoming clash between population growth and the increasing inability of agriculture to feed the newcomers. The forecast was sustainably wrong for a couple of centuries and turned him into an intellectual liability. Few wanted to be associated with his inheritance during this period. However, Malthus touched on one of the most ancestral fears of individuals and social groups—that whatever we may have achieved in terms of well-being or success today might be suddenly swept away tomorrow by unforeseen events or by our ignoring of recognizable threats such as population growth. No matter how disputed the causes, the Roman Empire collapsed, and so did the Tang and Song dynasties of China, the Mayan polities of Central America, the Polynesian culture in Rapa Nui (Easter Island), and many others (Diamond 2005). Ancient Greeks and Romans warned of the power of change, or of luck (Tyché or Fortuna); in Heian Japan they parsed the impermanence of human lives; today, closer to our subject, Urry (2000) and his followers speak of ceaselessly wavering mobilities. They all remind us of something similar to Malthus's jitters when they try to preempt with sustainability the optimist's reaction when his pessimist colleague confided that his problems could not get any worse—"of course they can!"

The latest interest in sustainability can be traced to the publication of *The Limits to Growth*, a book commissioned by the Club of Rome (Meadows et al 1972). The study stressed the threats to natural resources available to sustain the growth of world population after World War Two and the need to control unbridled economic development. Similar concerns were popularized in a number of contemporary books (Carson 1962; Nordhaus and Tobin 1972; Schumacher 1973; Singer 1979) that elicited an intense debate that is still alive. In a nutshell, and as noted earlier, sustainability as defined by the Brundtland Report is "development that meets the needs of the present without compromising the ability of future generations to meet their own needs" (WCED 1987:6). Born as many a cautionary notion with the goal of preventing unchecked economic growth, along the years sustainability would fuse with another major issue—global warming or, as in today's favorite expression, climate change. Economic development not only consumes too many limited resources, it is said; it has also unleashed a number of trends that threaten our natural environment and, eventually, life on the planet itself. This is the specter that has replaced among contemporary humans that of the long-ago dead communist movement conjured up by Marx and Engels. As any specter worth its salt, it frightens otherwise shrewd observers, for nobody knows with any certainty what it hides under the shroud. Might it not even be the imminent extinction of human life?

There has always been some bad news in this department. Human life is not sustainable. One day the sun will die. In between, as it becomes a white dwarf star, it will possibly absorb the Earth. One day, whatever remains, if anything, of Nineveh, Jerusalem, Alexandria, Rome, Chang'an, Kyoto, Istanbul, New York City, and San Francisco, even of Peoria and Pontoise, will disappear with nobody left to keep alive the memory of things past. Some optimists expect that an in-between Armageddon will take all of us humans, past, present, and future, to a world yonder, wherever it may be. Some eschatologists tried to be more precise—they predicted the Rapture that will separate good from evil for different dates, some of them unfortunately past without consequences. Unaware of later postcolonial strictures, some Buddhist traditions had the Buddha speaking of a paradise somewhere in the West (Manhattan's Upper West Side? California? A Caribbean island? There is no agreement among scholars). At any rate, the bad news is here to stay—the planet is as sure as doomed and humans will have to live happily forever after in a different abode if they can find it. Every cloud has a silver lining, people used to think. The sun that makes life possible has been around for 4.57 billion years, and it is expected to be still there for another 10 billion, give or take. There remains plenty of time until the final stage and, additionally, none of us or of our nearest descendants will see it. Or will they? The persuasion that the end of the world might be nigh has found increasing followers of late. If no solution to the anthropogenic increase in greenhouse gases (GHG) emissions comes on time, we are told, human life may vanish within the course of a few generations or, at least, it will become even more painful and conflict prone than it has been recently. Estimates of how bad and/or how sudden the outcome may be, as well as of the measures to duck or mitigate the danger, vary, but the threat hangs over all human activities, tourism and leisure included.

All this has added urgency to the discussion of how tourism might affect sustainability and climate change and has broadened the horizon of the academic tribe. What in the past was but an in-guild discussion of the alternatives to MMT has today grown in scale and solemnity. This time we are not just talking about consumer banality or corporate benefits; now it is all about saving mankind or, for those who think that it should pay for the doom it has brought upon itself for trying to yoke Gaia to its base needs, about making the planet still inhabitable for other, more considerate species that will succeed the human one. At any rate, the calling of tourism researchers has become higher and now we are discussing issues beyond the hitherto limited field. To some extent, this should bring comfort to the author of this book, as he has been claiming for increased exposure to political economy and social history. Unfortunately, it does not make the task any easier, for now we have to confront matters many of us only have a limited knowledge of. The dissonance between authorities that profess to know exactly what will happen with climate change and which are the true parameters of sustainability, on one side, and the opinion of academics and the general public, on the other, has only grown wider.

Initially, it is the jargon. Permaculture, green technologies, the three pillars (not one more, not one less, like in the Christian Trinity or in the Hindu Trimurti) of sustainability, the I-PAT formula (if you do not know what it is, you will not find an explanation here—nor there), lifecycle analysis, Triple Bottom Line accounting, Happy Planet Index, comparative ecological footprint, photochemical smog, albedo, evapotranspiration, sodification, waterlogging—this is a short list of the ample vocabulary on sustainability one finds in such websites as Wikipedia (2010b) that has been chosen because of its well-known use as reference of first resort by wide audiences. Such definitely uncommon parlance among the general public worsens when filtered by the media and the bloggers. Both usually interpret those arcana and the feeling of undefined doom they convey with relish. You do not need to be an expert on American TV to understand why anchors look much happier when they can start their newscast with a calamity, usually overblown—ratings go up.

Serious scientists often cannot resist contributing their own modicum of gloom. Possibly persuaded by the advice that one should be ready to err on the side of caution when discussing "serious" matters, they do. The stance taken by WHO (World Health Organization) at the first outbreaks of the so-called swine flu (influenza strain A/H1N1) definitely did. Since it declared it a pandemic in 2009 (the first in 41 years), people feared that it might become a catastrophe on a par with the Spanish flu of 1918–1920 that infected one-third of the world population and reportedly killed between 50 and 100 million (Barry 2004). WHO's decision was later blamed for alleged lack of transparency, for wasting large sums of public money, and for provoking unjustified alarm (AFP 2010). No matter how valid such claims may be, WHO's verdict was definitely blown out of proportion by many media (Stephens 2009). A similar dissonance often appears with reports on climate change and its foreseeable consequences. While they may be more temperate (many times they are not) in their scientific journal form, many media only highlight their most frightful features. Once again, terrified audiences listen more attentively.

The discussion of climate change has been led by the Intergovernmental Panel on Climate Change (IPCC), an agency established by the UN Environmental Program (UNEP) and the World Meteorological Organization (WMO) "to provide the world with a clear scientific view on the current state of climate change and its potential environmental and socioeconomic consequences" (IPCC 2010). IPCC received an accolade from the Nobel Foundation when it awarded its 2007 Nobel Prize to the agency jointly with former US Vice President Al Gore. IPCC's contribution to the discussion of climate change appears in its Assessment Reports (AR). Up to 2010, IPCC had published four AR, numbered from AR1 (1990) to AR4 (2007). As of this writing AR5 is getting under way. AR gather what is considered to be the scientific consensus on diverse aspects of climate change, defining its trends and making prognoses about its evolution. The degree of confidence in the evidence contained in AR varies for each one of the areas examined, and the agency states its position on how shared that confidence is.

The IPCC "standard" scenario reckons that median temperatures have been on the rise since the mid-19th century. This development followed from an increasing concentration of GHG in the atmosphere. CO_2 levels have gone from 280 ppm (parts per million) at the starting date to 380 ppm today. Current GHG levels are higher than they have ever been in the past 650,000 years, and most models show that a doubling of preindustrial GHG levels will induce a rise of 4–7°F in global mean temperatures, with some predicting that it might be bigger than that. A wide consensus maintains that this change is anthropogenic (built). From this notion IPCC details its effects, usually disastrous, on numerous areas of human life between now and the end of the century. It is beyond the scope of this book to analyze or summarize them.

At the end of 2009, a file with emails and documents from the Climate Research Unit of the University of East Anglia (UK) made the rounds of the Internet. This research agency had contributed significantly to IPCC's AR, and some of the messages exchanged by its members might be interpreted as though they had tried to silence or muffle the opinions of other colleagues who were more skeptical about climate change. The Select Committee for Science and Technology of the British House of Commons (Lower House of Parliament) and a Science Assessment Panel set up by the University of East Anglia investigated the matter and found no malpractice on the part of the

Climate Research Unit, although they criticized some of its working practices (Wikipedia 2010c). The incident, baptized as "climategate" by some media, is brought about not to cast unwarranted doubts on the existence of global warming, but to show that sometimes the discussion of conflictive subjects suffers from the passions awakened by self-righteousness and, not least, by the huge amounts of money and prestige that surround them. None of the ingredients is missing in this instance (Lindzen 2010).

What is really worrisome about this episode and much of the research on climate change (including its tourism counterparts) is the religious fervor professed, above all, by the defenders of the mainstream position. Environmentalism plays for them a role similar to that of a tribal identity that will not stand challenges to its beliefs, even the smallest of them. As Paul Rubin of Emory University, Georgia, put it in a discussion of the Climate Research Unit incident, for climate change defenders "[s]keptics are not merely people unconvinced by the evidence: They are treated as evil sinners. I probably would not write this article if I did not have tenure" (2010).

People tend to believe that ideas live in a special region beyond our sublunary world, but ideas do have real consequences (Weaver 1984), and here one can find some. The postmodern (*pomo*) matrix (Chapters 1 and 3) has tried to debase in many ways the notion that science and politics should be kept as far apart from each other as possible. Among present-day academia it has become a fundamental belief that science (especially social science) has to not only discuss solutions to problems, but also to do so in a way that favors the chances of the poor, the oppressed, the Other (whoever they might be as required by the definition). As previously noted, the *pomo* critique of value judgments finally boils down to the view that only those favored by the members of the guild have a right to stand. Even initially, "objective" quality-control procedures like double-blind peer reviews help to do the job smoothly. As the majority of reviewers share the same deeply felt certitudes, the chances that divergent opinions can be published tend to diminish. They do not understand that majority views do not necessarily enjoy wisdom, especially when it comes to very complex matters. In 2007, the International Monetary Fund majority consensus had it that the financial turbulences experienced by the global economy would pass without serious consequences. We know what happened one year later. Let us mention in passing the more mundane but no less angst-causing global collapse of computers announced for the year 2000. Surely the consensus about its likelihood was quite high.

IPCC data and consensus do not escape this trap. It is not only that they may contain some errors (such as the prediction that Himalayan glaciers would melt by 2035); it is that its whole institutional framework does not pass muster. Why not? IPCC basks in UN legitimacy, as it was jointly created by UNEP and WMO, two of its daughter agencies. Who could ask for anything more? If one thinks that bureaucratic committees are not the best judges of truth value, one could. The best of the UN is its record, checkered though it is, in dealing with peaceful solutions to international conflict, which was and still is the main reason of its existence. One should not extrapolate from there. The UN is not, as claimed by Paul Kennedy (2007), the parliament of man (*sic*). Parliaments are elected democratically; the UN General Assembly just includes legal representatives of all the countries that belong to it, whether they are democratic or not. The majority is not. According to Freedom House, a nongovernmental organization that tracks the evolution of political freedom in the world, only 89 countries can be considered free (2010). The rest are either partly free (62) or not free (42)—however, most of them are UN members.

Over the years, the UN has created a large number of specialized agencies in many different fields and, in their turn, these have spawned a dense network of subagencies, programs, internal *apparatchiki*, and external consultants who design and develop studies, projects, and consensus. IPCC is one of them. One may understand, though not condone, that expecting from governments to get rid of such costly paraphernalia would be naïve. However, one should also understand the forces that drive bureaucratic institutions and their underlings—they tend to operate in agreement with the anticipated goals of their paymasters. In this case, the governments, democratic or not, that contribute to the maintenance of the network with the taxes they make their citizens pay.

One of those governmental goals is to make the agencies work as clearinghouses for transferring funds from the UN treasury, or from donors, to projects in less developed countries (Easterly 2007). Therefore, the more serious the problems, the more money will payers be ready to contribute and transfer. There is a vested interest, though not explicitly formulated, for bureaucracies to find and deal with really, really big problems—the eventual extinction of humanity definitely looks like one suitable candidate. Sheer magnitude also helps bureaucrats to fulfill another of their major dreams—no external control. Who would dare discuss the amounts of money they spend and on which ways when the potential risks exceed the imagination? One, though, would feel a higher degree of readiness to believe their scientific consensus if institutions like the IPCC operated outside this bureaucratic loop. It would make its conclusions less vulnerable to disbelief.

These are some of the reasons why one should discount from the scientific consensus the part, not easily quantifiable, of the interests that surround it. This is what Lomborg has proposed in a number of instances (2001, 2007, 2009a, 2009b) with his suggestion to cool the heated claims in the climate change narrative. Cooling everything off should be the first commandment of scientific reasoning. Even if the ghost of the warmologists keeps on wondering whether or not to spook us, instead of panicking, one should first look into all of its dimensions, both ecological and economic. As this book does not claim any particular authority on the former, it will not be amiss to refresh some of the views held by Lomborg and the Copenhagen Consensus Center, as well as by a minority of scientists ready to look under the ghost's shroud. When it comes to the key issue of global warming, they are not deniers; they just cast doubts, as it is their wont and their right, on the doomsters and their apocalyptic predictions.

> T[heir] kind of language makes any sensible policy dialogue about global choices impossible [...] Of course, if the deadly description of global warming were correct, the inference of its primacy would also be correct, but [...] global warming is nothing of the sort. It is one—but only one—problem of many we will have to tackle through the twenty-first century (Lomborg 2007:loc.1581–1608).

Doomsters usually include too vast an array of problems with different causes and effects in the same narrative. Many of the problems mankind will face over the century do not ensue from global warming. Less developed countries, for instance, will become more dependent on food imports from the developed world, but this will be due to increased births and to relatively less availability of arable land in these parts of the world. The basic warmist argument also forgets that many processes are Janus faced. For instance, global warming will cause a higher number of deaths due to heat waves, but it will decrease the number of those due to extreme cold, which causes many more. Finally, gloom and doom language does not make room for the relatively inexpensive measures that can be taken against some of the calamities forecast. Sea levels will rise, as they have from the 1850s, but also since that date the land surface lost has been minimal.

> With global warming, rising sea levels will mean many more people will get flooded—if we don't change. More than a foot of sea-level rise will cause about one hundred million people to

get flooded every year. These are the numbers you will often hear bandied about, but of course they entirely disregard the fact that societies will deal with the issue. If they survived over the past 150 years in relative poverty, it is likely that they will do so much more effectively when they are more affluent (2007:loc.888–919).

For better or worse, the human factor does not count for much in warmist literature.

The issue does not seem to be whether we can expect an increase in global temperatures throughout the coming century—most likely they will rise. What counts, however, is forecasting their foreseeable effects and how to combine limiting them together with the many other problems humans will have to face in the same time span.

What we have to come to terms with is that even though CO_2 causes global warming, cutting CO_2 simply doesn't matter much for most of the world's important issues. From polar bears to poverty we can do immensely better with other policies. This does not mean doing nothing about global warming. It simply means realizing that early and massive carbon reductions will prove costly, hard, and politically divisive and likely will end up making fairly little difference for the climate and very little difference for society. Moreover, it will likely take our attention away from many other issues where we can do much more good for the world and its environment (2007:loc.1487–1517).

The fight against global warming will not be costless, and the final check should be taken into consideration. The initial Kyoto Protocol would only have reduced the impact of global warming by 0.3°F at a cost of 34 cents for each dollar spent (Lomborg 2007). By all means, it was poor business.

There are more recent cost estimates. The Stern Review on the Economics of Climate Change (SR) was produced in 2006 for the UK government by Nicholas Stern (later Lord Stern of Brentford), Head of the Government Economic Service and former World Bank Chief Economist (OCC 2010). The printed SR edition comprises as many as 692 pages (Stern 2007) with a thorough review of the subject. (Quotes in this text will follow the digital edition of 2006). Both IPCC's AR and SR cover similar ground, with IPCC providing the basic science for the latter. However, they differ in their goals. While IPCC aims at providing a consensus digest of the mainstream scientific literature on the areas it was mandated to cover, SR is above all a policy position paper to estimate the costs of mitigating the effects of climate change.

What would be the immediate consequences of business as usual, that is, of maintaining the prevailing level of GHG emissions?

> We estimate the total cost over the next two centuries of climate change associated under Business As Usual emissions involves impacts and risks that are equivalent to an average reduction in global per-capita consumption of at least 5%, now and forever (Stern 2006:x).

Even so, it is said in the same stretch, the estimate is low because the "nonmarket" impacts of climate change (on the environment and on human health) could raise the total to 11%. It might even go to 14% once one adds "positive" feedbacks due to higher-than-expected release of GHG other than carbon dioxide. The loss would not be equitably distributed, with the heaviest burden falling on the poor regions of the world. With the latter in mind, the loss in global per capita consumption might reach 25%. If annual emissions are maintained at today's levels, a 4–7°F increase might occur by mid-century.

Climate is a public good, meaning that it benefits those who pay for it and those who do not. Climate change is an externality, that is, a cost imposed on the world and on future generations but not faced directly by those who create it. "All in all, it must be regarded as a market failure on the greatest scale the world has seen" (Stern 2006:25). Additionally, it does not only have local effects. An extra unit of marginal damage affects everyone no matter where it comes from. In this way, climate change poses a global problem and solutions should consider what might be called global ethical imperatives. "[A]nalysis of policy cannot avoid grappling directly with the difficult issues that arise" (2006:28).

Stern's approach differs from the "consequentialism" often used in conventional economics.

> [A] standard welfare-economic approach has no room, for example, for ethical dimensions concerning the processes by which outcomes are reached [...] Deciding what values should be applied is difficult in democratic societies. It is not always

consistent with ethical perspectives based on rights and freedoms. But the approach has the virtue of clarity and simplicity [...] Simple thought experiments can calibrate the social welfare function's treatment of income differences. For example, suppose the decision-maker is considering two possible policy outcomes. In the second outcome, a poor person receives an income $X more than in the first, but a rich person receives $Y less; how much bigger than X would Y have to be for the decision-maker to decide that the second outcome is worse than the first? (2006:30).

If this sounds like a Paretian indifference map, this is because it is. Unfortunately, neither Pareto nor James Buchanan thought that the maps would solve in one single stroke such basic ethical and political dilemmas, for the social utility function may be measurable, but nobody has yet come with an effective contraption to measure it. Stern should produce his, but he does not.

When he tries to delve deeper, the reader is not much better off. After having contrived the solution to the social utility function, Stern introduces the notion of discounting. This last word means for him something already found in the Brundtland Report definition of sustainability: that our understanding of it should include the views and decisions of future generations. If we did not value the long run, "then climate change would be seen as much less of a problem" (2006:33). Erring on this outsized issue would cause much havoc; societies should conceive of it as an insurance premium paid on behalf of future generations. Once again unfortunately, neither Brundtland nor Stern tells us how many generations should be included in the picture or how we can figure out what their needs, even less their decisions, will be. Both Brundtland Report and SR flaunt a gift for extrasensorial perception usually beyond the human purview. A counter-factual would not be amiss here. Would the Industrial Revolution have ever happened had people in mid-18th century known and accepted their dispensation? As for the insurance premium, one doubts whether our descendants would not consider that paying an outsized premium on their behalf—such as one that would ruin some or much of their future well-being—might be seen as anything short of profligate and/or reckless.

Ethics settled, here comes the check.

Overall, the model simulations demonstrate that costs depend on the design and application of policy, the degree of global policy flexibility, and, whether or not governments send the right signals to markets and get the most efficient mix of investment [...] To put these costs into perspective, the estimated effects of even ambitious climate change policies on economic output are estimated to be small—around 1% or less of national and world product, averaged across the next 50 to 100 years—provided policy instruments are applied efficiently and flexibly across a range of options around the globe [...] The numbers involved in stabilizing emissions are potentially large in absolute terms—maybe hundreds of billions of dollars annually (1% of current world GDP equates to approximately $350–400 billion) – but are small in relation to the level and growth of output (2006:248–249).

It is not surprising to find a former World Bank chief economist who believes that costs basically vary in relation to policy—the *pomo* matrix looms large and, as noted, respects no disciplinary boundaries. The problem, though, lies with what auto dealers call "sticker shock," so much that Stern does not dare quantifying it. One can easily do the missing math for him. At official exchange rates (lower than PPP) the gross world product for 2009 was estimated at $58 trillion (CIA 2010). A median 3% rate of growth over the next 50 years would make it $254 trillion, or around five times bigger; over the next century it would reach $1,115 trillion, that is, 20 times more. Stern's proposed 1% levy to mitigate climate change would respectively go up to $2.5 trillion a year by 2059 and $11 trillion a year in 2109.

Can one find alternatives to such fearsome amounts? According to Stern, no. The BAU mentality will definitely make the rise of future threats more likely. Could not adaptation reach the same goals as mitigation? Adaptation here means financing only those measures needed to resist increases in global warming, not to decrease them.

Adaptation reduces the damage costs of climate change that does occur (and allows beneficial opportunities to be taken), but does nothing direct to prevent climate change and is in itself part of the cost of climate change. Mitigation prevents climate change and the damage costs that follow (2006:305).

Adaptation is necessary, admits Stern, for even if all emissions stopped tomorrow, their cumulative momentum would make global temperatures keep on rising over the next 30–50 years. But it does not come free; it also generates costs, and it cannot cancel out all the effects of climate change. Stern has no doubts—climate change policies should be more ambitious. "Uncertainty is an argument for a more, not less, demanding goal, because of the size of the adverse climate-change impacts in the worse-case scenarios' (2006:284). Mitigation is need. More or less what Sofield had to say about erring on the side of caution. To this end, beyond ambitious GHG reduction targets, climate change mitigation requests a three-pronged approach: new pricing systems for carbon (either new taxes or cap and trade plans), supporting technological innovation, and subsidizing commercialization of new techniques.

From the time of its publication, SR has been criticized (Mendelsohn 2006; Nordhaus 2005)—and vindicated (Ackerman 2007)—from many angles. In general, critics coincide with what has already been noted. SR usually presents the most alarming scenarios to be found in the climate change literature; accordingly, it gives an exaggerated idea of the future costs of global warming (including the discount for future generations); at the same time, high as his anticipated mitigation expenses would be, they could not cover those costs. Should humans make the sacrifices he hypothesizes and how?

The latter part of the question preempts the first. Stern's answer is well known—mankind faces either higher taxes or higher costs in the form of a cap and trade system. Taxes would directly increase final prices; they are quite visible to the consumer and risk a potential backlash few politicians are ready to withstand. Cap and trade (tradable permits to generate given amounts of GHG) would have the same effect—consumers would pay more for the final product—but the relation between both ends would be less obvious. In both cases, though, consumers would have to face increased prices.

Saying that the allegedly necessary sacrifices will be borne by humans sweetens a hard choice these same humans will have to make. Polluters should pay for the externality they create and enjoy. The more the pollution generated by a country, the higher the check its taxpayers should underwrite. Developed countries generate most GHG; the conclusion flows smoothly from the premises. Things, however, are not so easy. In 2007, China, not the most developed country in the world, became the biggest global polluter in absolute terms. As Chinese society tries to catch up with other, more affluent ones, her CO_2 generation will increase even more, though people in China will reasonably think that they have a right to improve their lot. India, Brazil, Southeast Asia, and Russia lurk behind. Therefore, as seen in the Copenhagen Climate Change Summit at the end of 2009, agreeing on how much each party should contribute to global GHG mitigation is not about to happen. Additionally, if most of the levies finally go to the people of the poorest regions of the world, who will ensure that this goal comes to fruition? Many poor countries are undemocratic polities where governmental corruption is rampant. Would anybody say after the fiasco of the UN Oil for Food program implemented in Iraq after the first Gulf War (1991) that international bureaucracies are immune to corruption and that mitigation money should flow through them? No surprise that so many taxpayers in the developed world are against such arrangements.

Lomborg and associates are not so far of the mark when they go off the beaten track. Climate change should not be mankind's main preoccupation. It is indeed a problem, but there are many others and transfers of money would be better spent in addressing malaria, malnutrition, illiteracy, and equality for women on a global basis.

> Specifically, we should radically increase spending on R&D for green energy—to 0.2% of global GDP, or $100 billion. That's 50 times more than the world spends now—but still twice as cheap as Kyoto. Not only would this be both affordable and politically achievable, but it would also have a real chance of working (2009).

Breaking the dependence on fossil fuels will not be easy or immediate, but many taxpayers would be ready to fund research projects to this goal, provided that they are cost effective (Calzada et al 2009).

These are remarks on the broader discussion of climate change. What about sustainability in tourism research? One of the sectors SR analyzes—transportation—is basic to tourism. Transportation CO_2 emissions (including rail, road, maritime, and air transport) accounted for 1.6% of total GHG generation; under business as usual the figure will raise to 2.5% in 2050, but aviation not only emits carbon dioxide—it is also responsible for other GHG that would raise its total to 5% in 2050. There are additional singularities to aviation. International flights emissions double those of domestic ones. And, at the same time, the former grow faster than the latter due to new low-cost airlines. ICAO (International Civil Aviation Organization) has received a petition from UN to take action on emissions considering the need for a global approach.

> The EU (European Union) Environment Council has suggested some preliminary guiding principles to be taken into account for its inclusion, so that it is a workable model that

can be replicated worldwide. For example, coverage must be clear (options include domestic, intra-EU, or all flights leaving or landing in the EU), trading entities should be air carriers and aircraft operators, and the allocation methodology should be harmonized at EU level (Stern 2006:485).

The future carbon price for aviation should reflect its full contribution to climate change. In plain English, here, as in other economic sectors, this means increased costs and/or taxes, and possibly a decrease in the growth of air transport. Long-haul destinations will probably be the hardest-hit while some low-cost airlines will have to consider changing their names. Even though excerpts from a general research, such considerations are more accurate than what one can usually find on the sustainability issue among tourism researchers. Once again here one is overwhelmed by its popularity and, at the same time, by the lack—or the richness, according to the definition—of specifics. One small exhibit: if one classifies the main articles (excluding editorials, book reviews, and conference summaries) published in *The Journal of Sustainable Tourism* from 2006 to 2010, the total dealing with either case studies or conceptual models reaches 70%. One cannot find much by way of general conclusions.

It looks as though sustainability has become so popular in tourism research for it is the definitive wild card to exorcize MMT whenever it is deemed necessary or convenient. Unlike other forms of tourism examined in the previous paragraphs, it does not have to prove being an alternative. As noted, it was not easy to find one. But being a concept without content (as in Brundtland or in Stern), sustainability does not need to pass such muster. Its mark of distinction can be attached to, or withdrawn from, whatever the academic mainstream likes or dislikes.

Additionally, there is a basic inconsistency in the concept. Sustainability cannot be predicated without implying a time dimension. Sustainable, as per *Merriam-Webster*'s definition, is whatever endures (2002). One can discuss how long the duration should be, but one cannot do without it. In this way, it is difficult to understand why we should consider that destinations MMT has favored since its inception, such as Las Vegas, Venice, Majorca, Orlando, Cancún, and a few others are supposed to be unsustainable while a small place far away from main generating markets and with flows of, at most, a few thousand tourists a year will have a longer life. Their future performance will not be for academics to decide. Like it or not, it will depend on whether and where modern mass tourists decide to spend their hard-gained money.

Finally, there is something important. One could imagine that MMT structure might change if, in the not-so-distant future, drastic taxes are levied on air transportation, as anticipated by SR and later by the "Helsingborg Statement on Sustainable Tourism" (Gössling et al 2008 Gössling 2008), or if the economic crisis that started in 2008 becomes sustainable, that is, endures. Perhaps. However, if the MMT trends described in Chapter 2 also endure, it is difficult to see how they would make the small developments favored by academics more sustainable. If long-haul transportation is heavily taxed and if low-cost airlines have to increase their fares, no prophet is needed to forecast that the allegedly sustainable destinations will suffer long before the allegedly unsustainable ones.

Afterword

MODERN MASS TOURISM AND THE FUTURE

In 2001, MacCannell (2001b) took a turn of host–guest land in a book edited by Valene Smith and Maryann Brent (2001). His subject was the future of tourism and his thesis, to use Wang's expression (Chapter 5), objectively authentic. Not just because his name appeared in the Table of Contents. Even if it had not, one could easily have traced the piece to his authorship. It talked like MacCannell; it read like him (since he customarily writes well); it was ambitious as his work has always been; it contained arguments made in the past by him. The article also had the same flaws one can usually find in MacCannell's work: facts only made cameo appearances and conclusions amply obliged with the right doses of hyperbole.

In a nutshell, MacCannell maintained that MMT was bound to disappear shortly. Cultures, he warned the reader, have become standardized. Because of the global reach of modern corporations, cultures and destinations look more and more like each other: one finds the same brands, the same malls, and the same theme parks all over the world. Not only are attractions cloned, they have also become accessible to everyone equipped with a computer from any point in the planet, courtesy of Internet. With the universe within easy reach, there is no reason to move around and spend one's money in tourism. A few clicks and the Taj Mahal, the Iguazú falls, Kathakali dancers, Bruce Springsteen, the Bayreuth production of Wagner's *Ring*, etc. will come to your screen like the mountain to Mohammed, not only in beautiful but static pictures. Now they move. They are as good as real. Additionally, most of those productions come free of charge. They will not force you to leave your desk or your couch. So tourism will soon be dead and one can easily name the offender—an unbridled capitalist expansion that is quickly killing diversity and authenticity. The usual suspect has now a technological accomplice—Internet. The easy access it provides to all kinds of documents, written or audiovisual, will wreck any curiosity and any further intellectual challenge. No more surprises worthy of their name, so why go to look for them? Whatever remains comes alive at the touch of your fingertips.

It is not the first time that new technologies have been chastised for their sins or that their creators and users have received a deserved punishment.

One still remembers how the gods treated Prometheus after he stole their fire—Pandora being not the least of his troubles. Younger generations will be more familiar with the reactions to radio and television. The radio, according to Riesman et al (1950), bore a huge portion of the blame for the increasing turn of the American psyche to other-directedness. As for television (Postman 1985), this is still a matter of heated discussion even though TV, as we used to know it, is on its last legs. The Internet now shares with both a similar scarlet letter (Carr 2010; McKenna and Barg 2000), and MacCannell could not resist probing the cultural effects of the new technology. To a sigh of relief from the audience, his prognosis was negative as predicted. The Internet will replace the need for tourism in a world of abolished cultural differences.

Is the Internet really the definitive nemesis of all human skills, except the one to put our intellectual capacities in the idle position? MacCannell's conclusion, however expected, seems wildly exaggerated. The Internet has received many critiques—among the chief of which is the widespread consumption of pornography. However, so much erotic interest does not necessarily foretell the end of the sex drive—more likely an eventual increase, or at least an enhanced awareness of its appeal (Aramberri 2004b). If one image is worth a thousand words, an experience, in sex or in tourism, must have a similar multiplier over simple visual exposure.

One might add that the Internet will not extinguish a deeply felt human need for distinction, whether in its high-brow form of cultural capital (Bourdieu 1979) or in the more modest form of not letting the Joneses keep up with us. Traveling widely stamps a mark of good taste and social superiority on people who can afford it—another important reason why people go away. But one should not delve too long on distinction, for MacCannell had settled accounts with it many moons ago (Chapter 4). It is but another ego malformation typical of modern-man-in-general. It would be cured if we were ready to go ahead with the only tourism worth its name—a trip to the remote past or, even better, to a Golden Age of dedifferentiation where everybody would be exactly like the rest and, therefore, equally impervious to temptations of obtaining comparative advantages. However, such dispensation, which looks excellent to MacCannell, can only be attained in contradiction. He forgets the small print on the wall—that, would it ever come to fruition, dedifferentiation would even improve on the loss of cultural variance allegedly caused by globalization and the Internet. Tourism would be as pointless in that happy past as it is supposed to be in the not too distant future.

Pace MacCannell, MMT should have a longer lease of life. Cultures may become better known to increasing numbers of people as they are watched in action on the Internet. As long as disposable income and paid vacations are there, few people will resist the temptation to ascertain by themselves whether they are as attractive as they look, and, given the noxious dispositions of modern egos, we will still want to show our distance with the Joneses. No cultural malaise will make tourism wither away. Not even among its critics. They will always find in lambasting it a reason to attend conferences and to undertake faraway fieldtrips. Like Mark Twain's demise, the death of MMT has been prematurely reported.

Sometimes friends or relatives ask me for advice on whether they should invest their money in tourism companies, naively thinking that a professional interest in tourism should give me the allure of a financial guru. To their disappointment, I have no insider information to offer, and I have to limit myself to generalities as the one just proffered about the health of MMT. Will it be a reasonable investment to buy shares in Starwood Hotels or in American Express? Perhaps. In legacy airlines? Definitely not. You should have been attentive when Tony Ryan and his colleagues founded Ryanair or when Tony Fernandes started Air Asia. Today it might be too late to invest in these two companies, but not for the cultural reasons flaunted by the anthropological crowd. Heavens, no. Had the financial climate remained as it was in 2007, just before the economic crisis broke out, investing in companies that work for mass tourism might have been wise, but today many clouds darken the horizon. "It is the economy, stupid," as Bill Clinton's slogan said in 1992.

Let us for a moment turn back to precrisis times. MMT, both international and domestic, thrived (UNWTO 2010a). There were many reasons to explain such excitement. Developed economies had an increasing number of paid vacation days; a huge middle class; graying, but healthy, age cohorts with sound retirement benefits, mounting disposable income, relatively low air- and rail-travel fares, and many cars running on affordable fuel. All of them were factors that favored tourism expansion. Far from limited to affluent societies, similar trends appeared within less developed countries, especially in East Asia. Urbanization, a quickly expanding middle class, rising living standards, paid vacations, more disposable income, a pent-up desire to get acquainted with the neighborhood, and even with destinations further away—all were felt in the triangle that had its apex in South Korea and two sides respectively reaching south to India and to Australia. Today half of mankind lives in this area. Expectations of endlessly growing MMT for the foreseeable future reflected this sunny disposition.

All this was thrown into disarray in a very short period of time. Between the summer 2008 and the spring 2010, first the United States and, then,

Europe pushed the global economy into deep turmoil. The history of this crisis cannot be written yet, as by mid-2010 it has not unfolded completely. One has to read the tealeaves to debrief its future, and this is a most futile sport. All one can say is "expect that the crisis will put considerable stress on tourism" and follow with a few easy remarks.

Within 10 years, MMT may not be too different from precrisis times as far as main trends are considered. This is the forecast from World Travel and Tourism Council. After a poor 2009 where it underwent a 4.8% decrease, world tourism should recover with somewhat slower growth in 2010–11 and renovated vigor as the developed countries leave the crisis behind. "Overall, the T&T economy is forecast to grow by 4.25% per annum in real terms between 2010 and 2020, supporting over 300 million jobs by 2020—i.e., 9.2% of all jobs and 9.6% of global GDP"(WTTC 2010:7). This industry will thus continue to be one of the main economic activities of the future. The forecast, however, was not particularly convincing, as it took for granted that the expected return to growth had already taken place in 2010 and that it would not falter in the near future, which was a tall order.

Let us assume the prediction turns out to be correct. Will this growth take place in the same geographic clusters as in precrisis years? As noted in Chapter 2, this is how it should be, but quite possibly the balance among the three main ones (North America and the Caribbean, Europe and the Mediterranean basin, and East and Southeast Asia) will change at a quicker rate than anticipated. Prospects for the Euro-Mediterranean generating cluster are not rosy. It is not because elderly people will increase their share in the demographic pyramid, as has been stressed often. After all, this worrying trend should not be necessarily dire for tourism. The older segment of the population enjoys a longer life expectancy in good health, so its members have become avid tourists. The problem, though, lies with the drastic decline of the welfare state that has just started. If something seems really unsustainable today, it is the European lifestyle—its financial weakness there for all to see. Huge public and private debt, gigantic budget deficits, higher taxes, growing limits to the social benefits Europeans presently enjoy, high and sustained unemployment levels, sluggish economic growth, possibly longer working hours, and shorter paid vacations, all of these will loom large and will visibly reduce the disposable income that financed, among other things, the impressive expansion of European MMT. Vacations will still survive, but they will not be as prone to easy-going expenditure as in the recent past. They will be taken closer to home and in cheaper places. Faraway destinations will not be visited as frequently.

Similar trends have materialized in the United States and they also create concern, though on a lesser scale. The American safety net, not to speak of the rest of social benefits, does not compare with the European one. The American economy has also been proven more dynamic and productive over the last years. Though considerable, the unavoidable pain caused by the fiscal deficit already existent before the crisis of 2008 and highly increased by the Keynesian response to it, may not cut so deep as in Europe. But Americans will still be more likely to enjoy their leisure time at home than abroad.

The horizon clears somewhat when one looks at East and Southeast Asia. China and India will be among the 10 quickest growing tourism economies within the next 10 years. China's forecast expansion will reach 9% in cumulative annual growth until 2020, while that of India will be 8.5%. These relative terms tell much less of the story than some absolute figures. By 2020, the top 10 earners in tourism exports (international tourism receipts) will include three Asian countries (China will come second in the world with US$177 billion; Hong Kong number 8 with $51 billion, and Thailand number 9 with a slightly lower figure). Between 2010 and 2020, tourism capital investment in China will grow 3.5 times, the volume of direct tourism GDP 4 times, and tourism exports 3.5 times. Capital investment in India will be $110 billion, the same as the volume of its total direct tourism GDP, while its tourism exports will rise to $1.9 billion. The whole region will feel the impact of these two colossi (WTTC 2010).

At any rate, if the immediate future of MMT looks less optimistic than it did only a few years ago, this in no way makes good the prognoses of so many postmodern (*pomo*) academics. MMT-diminished expectations cannot be traced to blase feelings after discovering that one can eat a similar Big Mac in Austria or Australia, as MacCannell surmised. The foreseeable millions of future Chinese tourists will not complain because it tastes the same as in Shanghai. Schönbrunn Castle and the Belvedere Palace, or the Outback and the Sidney Opera House, however, cannot be so easily cloned in Pudong. Diminished expectations cannot be traced to commodification either. If its proponents would ever agree to define it in less simplistic terms than they do (travel should not be bought and sold like apples or oranges), economic crises would push people to complain that MMT is not commodified enough, as they cannot find offers within their purchasing power, and they will ask for more, not less commodification.

Diminished expectations also bear little relation to feeling aghast with Western cultural hegemony. I am writing this afterword at a resort in Nha Trang, Vietnam. It is an urban resort, for Nha Trang Beach has not been manufactured as so many other enclaves. Hotels and resorts have grown in a ribbon pattern along the axis of an existing maritime promenade called Tran Phu Avenue. They take advantage of the urban infrastructure and services of a town founded long before tourism arrived. Nha Trang has indeed changed since 2003 when I visited it for the first time, and its popularity as a tourist attraction was not yet established. The town has expanded considerably along its South end, where one can meet many people recently migrated from the countryside to work for the tourism industry. By the way, the latter caters to a domestic clientele. In 2003 the overwhelming majority of the public who frequented Nha Trang Beach was Vietnamese. This remains unchanged today.

Nha Trang Beach is not a totally sun and sea destination. In a surprise to the participant observer, the beach empties itself as soon as the sun becomes strong in the very early morning (around 7 am) and stays like this until late afternoon when the sun weakens. The few scattered beachcombers that remain in between are foreigners, mostly Westerners in the "mad dogs and Englishmen" mode. One reason for the sudden and concerted flight from the sun is work related, as local people have to go back to their chores. However, this condition does not apply to the Vietnamese tourists who, even so, also flee the sunrays. Let us give the culturalist her pound of flesh. Many Vietnamese women do not want to be tanned. Dark skin is still seen in the country as a mark for poor peasants, thus hardly attractive to most men. This, and not only modesty, explains the surprisingly retro (*circa* 1900) outfits Vietnamese women wear at the beach to cover their bodies almost completely. It also makes understandable why, in Nha Trang and in all the country, they ride their motorbikes wrapped in hats (nowadays helmets are mandatory for both genders), mufflers (also used as a protection against polluted air), and arm-length gloves that elsewhere have not made the rounds since Rita Hayworth starred in *Gilda* (1946).

The complement to the limited attraction of sun and sea in Nha Trang is family life. Like many Spanish beaches *circa* 1970–80, this is a family beach—a space where children can play at ease and safely under the gaze of their mothers and relatives, where one meets other people with the same interests, and where one can gossip with the neighbors or make new friends. The beach accommodates many extended families made up of two or three generations, and the social scene reflects their interaction. A few meters across Tran Phu Avenue, back from the beach to my resort, one enters an intriguingly different world. Not so much in social composition. Vietnamese clients comprise the bulk of the transient population but, even though the hotel belongs to an American chain, this seems in keeping with the dominance of internal tourists in the destination. The hotel enjoys a high occupancy rate in spite of its steep prices, even steeper when power purchasing parity enters the picture. However, it is nearly full. Who are these people? The obvious answer—they are the members of the country's quickly growing upper-middle classes. They are a few economic rungs over the commoners on the beach.

There are also some changes in behavior among guests at the hotel and beach users. Most of the former come as family groups as much as it happens at the beach, but in the hotel these are nuclear families. Young mothers, mostly without help from other siblings, take care of their noisy offspring who run without a break all over the dining room, and cause all the mischief that goes with their age. After the breakfast buffet where a majority chooses *phở* and other Vietnamese fare over Western staples such as bacon and eggs or continental breakfast, the swimming pool beckons. The big infinity pool offers an even more secure space for kids than the beach and they revel there for hours. On her side, mom (as well as other single women) now dons a two-piece swimsuit similar in shape and size to the ones the few Western female guests also use. The modesty defense of the old-fashioned gear Vietnamese women don at the beach seems no longer well placed here.

This glimpse—short and limited as it is—on some food- and beachways of a small and well-to-do stratum of Vietnamese vacationers remains but an anecdote. However, if their behavior were seen as a trend, it would shed light on a couple of intriguing things. Increased body exposure to casual third-party viewers in the restricted pool area seems easier to accept than more ingrained and genderless habits in food. While the latter can be easily negotiated into the ever malleable limits of an imagined Vietnamese identity (our food is better, healthier, more delicious, or more whatever than the Western one), the former involves a display of intergroup distinction (we, guests of this hotel, both Vietnamese and Western, are different, possibly better, than the beach crowd; by the way, the shaded areas and wide parasols around the pool also allow us to avoid tanning). If this interpretation carries any weight, this acceptance of a modicum of Western cultural hegemony would be volitional, not subservient. Additionally, the cultural in-group difference flaunted would mainly relate to an alleged superiority grounded in financial, not cultural capital (we can wear Western-style bikinis because we pay here in one day as much as Westerners do; it would take the beach crowd one month to top it).

Back to June 2006 and to a short course I was teaching in Sa Pa at the time. This is a small town nestled in the Hoang Lien Son mountain range in Lao Cai Province around 350 kilometers northwest of Hanoi. A number of minority ethnic groups live in the area, and have become one of the main draws for the number of tourists, mostly Vietnamese, who roam the place in summertime. As per the course program, audience and teacher all went together on one fieldtrip to visit some small communities, and a couple of newly built eco-resorts.

Our guide was a young Hmong woman who spoke very good English. I asked her where she had learned it. A nongovernmental, she said. She was sitting by my side in the bus during a long stretch of the excursion and we carried on with the usual small talk—living conditions in the place, the lure of migration to Hanoi or Saigon, the barriers ethnic minorities found there, and cost of living comparisons. Throughout our chat, the NGO footprint displayed itself not only in her language, but also in her train of thought. No, she would not leave her village. She and her peers had a lot to do to preserve their own identity and traditions. They were endangered by the strength of Kinh culture (the ethnic majority in Vietnam) and of Western-style globalization.

I had recently read Cohen's excellent essays (2000) on Hmong arts and crafts, and I asked her about the complicated patterns of Hmong embroideries. Our conversation went like this:

> It must be quite difficult and time-consuming to stitch your clothes. Do you do it yourself?

> No, in my village only a few old women know how to darn.

> So you buy your clothes from them?

> No. If you look closely at mine, you will see that they are not embroidered; the pattern is traditional, but it is a transfer. They make the fabric somewhere near Guangzhou and the garment also comes from a Chinese factory. We buy them in Hekou, the Chinese town on the border at Lao Cai City. There is more choice and they are much cheaper.

A few days later, when the course ended and we were on our way back from Sa Pa to Hanoi, it would be no mystery for me why most of the students would take one day off at Lao Cai Town before homecoming. They wanted to buy souvenirs in Chinese Hekou. "Do not forget some authentic Hmong stuff, please," I said as a guise of farewell.

From this "fieldwork" example, we can widen the scope of our view to capture all that has been argued in this book, a volume which has striven to take a look at MMT that strays from the academic mainstream. For the author, MMT is just one of the many benefits that accompany the development of modern market-based societies.

A market society does not just mean capitalism. Not all versions of capitalism have the same profile. The one favored here corresponds with that of classical political economy, which for the author is also the best sociology. Individuals follow their interests and, in so doing, most of the time, contribute, willingly or not, to general well being. De Mandeville's formula is not obsolete yet: private vices, public virtues. This is liberal capitalism (in the European meaning of the word). Although it understands the need for public intervention, it maintains that government should be as limited as possible (a clause also open to different interpretations). American liberalism and European social democracy have a much more expansive view than this. At times, as in the present discussion on sustainability and climate change (Chapter 9) or the one on the ongoing economic crisis, they look ready to stifle most private action and replace it with governmental fiat. Most of the time, such a view will restrict individual initiative to a bare minimum—to the disadvantage of the common good. If the opposite view expressed here runs counter to this general—and academic—mainstream, including that of tourism research, and is subsequently labeled as neo-liberal, so be it.

Disagreement with the conventional academic mainstream does not stop at labels. In fact, the *pomo* matrix favored by most colleagues, beyond its disciplinary purview, does not care much about differences in economic paradigms. As discussed in earlier chapters, most academics limit their account of behavioral variations to cultural factors, whether a general grammar of signs; or, closer to the earth, the excluded Other in its manifold avatars; or identitarian politics; or metaphors; or empowerment; or wholesale notions of hegemony. Against the grain, this book advocates that classical political economy and social history, that is, general sociology and, beyond it, evolutionary psychology (less frequently invoked because of the author's limited skills in the discipline) should be preferred as paradigmatic, since they place individual interests and the innovations they induce at the center of social action. In this vein, it is also suggested that liberal capitalism procures the maximization of social benefits better than other alternative blueprints.

Capitalism has an obvious, though complex relation with modernity. Modernity is made up of many other layers of action that need to be distinguished for analytical purposes, for instance, the political and the cultural spheres. Indeed, capitalism cannot be explained without them. Innovation and the dissemination of knowledge will only thrive in societies where people can freely research whatever they want and communicate their discoveries publicly. Otherwise capitalism will stagnate. For all her decisive bet in favor of it, China will find it very difficult to create the harmonious society her present leaders want if she has to keep the authoritarian straightjacket they impose on innovation and communication. Decision making may be quicker and more unyielding there than in other, more open and more cantankerous polities (trains in Italy, so the story goes, started running on time under Mussolini), but in China and elsewhere only democracy can ensure that capitalism will deliver its best promises. When one talks about democracy, experience tells us that there is only one version of it—government of the people, by the people, and for the people (popular sovereignty, free elections, political parties, a bill of rights, the rule of law).

Some *pomos* do adopt a more relativist view.

> If we take the original meaning of "democratic" to mean "rule by the people," it might be argued that planning under Vietnam's communist system is no less democratic than planning in some other, more substantial concerns, for example, making us aware that community participation in planning does not need to follow the Western multi-party democratic processes. In India, for example, the most senior tourism technocrats in some states are members of the elite Indian Civil Service (ICS) and appointed by the government of India (GOI) (Burns 2001b:294).

Indeed relativism cannot see reasons to care about small details, such as the differences in legitimacy, though they make the stuff of Political Science 101. Perhaps Burns was too busy to address them, urged as he was to share his next big discovery—that "democracy remains a social construct with more than one interpretation" (2001b:296). No doubt Hitler, Stalin, Ngo Dinh Diem, the Castro brothers, Franco, Khamenei, the endless parade of tyrants and autocrats of modern history, and, more fearsome, their would-be future inheritors will bless his soul. Those of us who have lived under one of these regimes can easily point some decisive differences between them and democratic rule. The real problem with this widespread and so-cheap *pomo* constructivism cuts deeper than *ad hoc* examples, though. When words are defined Humpty-Dumpty style, the quest to make sense of reality loses all urgency. One way or the other, we will allow the powers that be to construct reality—and our lives—the way they want.

This is not just a mind game for idle academics. Efficient economies—and decent living standards—require free and democratic polities. As we have tried to show in this book the fair play of individual interests, especially when not totally eclipsed by the so-called cultural values of postmodernism, will provide higher yields on all accounts—in theories, in real life, and, indeed, in explaining why people like MMT and will not heed academic advice to change their ways. MMT is not the most decisive social activity, not even the biggest industry in the world, much less a key component of globalization, but like all of the above, it will be better understood from the paradigm of modernity and with the help of classical economics and social history—not with narratives of the Unconscious and sundry archeological contraptions that make no room for human subjects of any gender.

Let us, for once, be radical—let us work and research at the genuine roots of social action. If we want to understand the riddles of modernity, MMT included, looking at its sociological genesis will warrant our best hopes.

References

Ackerman, F.
  2007 Debating Climate Economics: The Stern Review vs. Its Critics <http://www.foe.co.uk/resource/reports/debate_climate_econs.pdf> (28 May 2009).
Adams, K.
  2001 Danger-Zone Tourism: Prospects and Problems for Tourism in Tumultuous Times. *In* Interconnected Worlds: Tourism in Southeast Asia, P. Teo, T.C. Chang, and K.C. Ho, eds., pp. 265–281. Kidlington: Elsevier.
Adorno, Th., W. Frenkel-Brunswik, and D. Levinson
  1964 The Authoritarian Personality. New York: Wiley.
Afary, J., and K. Anderson
  2005 Foucault and the Iranian Revolution: Gender and the Seductions of Islamism. Chicago: The University of Chicago Press.
AFP (Agence France Press)
  2010 WHO slammed for handling of flu pandemic. June 4 <http://www.google.com/hostednews/afp/article/ALeqM5htt1btsuNKD-O2MlbiblXHv6AH_g> (9 June 2010).
Aghion, P., and P. Howitt
  1998 Market Structure and the Growth Process. Review of Economic Dynamics 1:276–305.
Agrusa, J.
  2003 AIDS and Tourism: A Deadly Combination. *In* Sex and Tourism: Journeys of Romance, Love and Lust, T. Bauer, and B. McKercher, eds., pp. 167–180. Oxford: The Haworth Hospitality Press.
Allcock, J. and K. Przecławski, eds.
  1990 Editorial. Annals of Tourism Research. 17:1–6.
Allen, D.
  2004 More FAQ. *In* Foucault Resources <http://www.qut.edu.au/edu/cpol/foucault/faq.html> (23 November 2004).
Althusser, L., and E. Balibar
  1970 Reading Capital. English Translation by B. Brewster. London: New Left Books.
Amin, S.
  1973 Unequal Development: An Essay on the Social Formations of Peripheral Capitalism. New York: Monthly Review Press.
  1976 Imperialism and Unequal development. New York: Harvester Press.
Anderson, B.
  1999 Imagined Communities: Reflections on the Origin and Spread of Nationalism. London: Verso.

Anderson, T., and P. Hill
2004 The Not So Wild, Wild West. Property Rights on the Frontier. Stanford: Stanford Finance & Economics.
Andriotis, K.
2010 Heterotopic Erotic Oases: The Public Nude Beach Experience. Annals of Tourism Research 37:1079–1098.
Ansholt, S.
2002 Nation Branding: A Continuing Theme. Journal of Brand Management 10:59–60.
Ansholt, S. ed.
2005 Editorial: National Brand as Context and Reputation. Place Branding. 1:224–228.
Ansholt, S.
2006 Why Brand: Some Practical Considerations for Nation Building. Place Branding 2:97–107.
Aquila, R.
1996 Introduction: The Popular Culture West. *In* Wanted Dead or Alive: The American West in Popular Culture, R. Aquila, ed., pp. 1–20. Champaign: The University of Illinois Press.
Aramberri, J.
1991 The Nature of Youth Tourism: Motivations, Characteristics and Requirements. Paper presented at the 1991 International Conference on Youth Tourism, New Delhi. Madrid: World Tourism Organization.
1999 El Gran Puzzle Americano [The Great American Puzzle]. Madrid: El Pais-Aguilar.
2000 Youth Tourism. *In* Encyclopedia of Tourism, J. Jafari, ed., pp. 633–634. London: Routledge.
2004a Reading the Tourist Mind. Indian Tourism: The Next Decade. Tourism Recreation Research 24(1):1–13.
2004b Will Travel Vanish? Looking beyond the Horizon. *In* New Horizons in Tourism: Strange Experiences and Stranger Practices, T.V. Singh, ed., pp. 195–227. Wallingford: CABI.
2005 How Global is Tourism? *In* Tourism Development: Issues for a Vulnerable Industry, J. Aramberri, and R. Butler, eds., pp. 127–152. Clevedon: Channel View.
2009 The Sociology of Tourism in Spain: A Tale of Three Wise Men. *In* The Sociology of Tourism. European Origins and Developments, G. Dann, and G. Parrinello, eds., pp. 243–274. Bingley: Emerald Group.
Aramberri, J., and R. Butler
2005 Tourism Development: Vulnerability and Resilience. *In* Tourism Development: Issues for a Vulnerable Industry, J. Aramberri, and R. Butler, eds., pp. 293–308. Clevedon: Channel View.
Aramberri, J., and T.T.M. Dao
2005 Vietnam for the Vietnamese. Tourism Recreation Research 30(2):69–75.

Aramberri, J., and C. Liang
    2009 Educating the Chinese Consumer. Visions of Yunnan. Journal of Tourism
       Travel Research 4:282–296.
Aranguren, J.
    1961 La juventud europea y otros ensayos [European Youth and Other Essays].
       Barcelona: Seix Barral.
    1976 Etica [Ethics]. Madrid: Revista de Occidente.
Aristotle,
    1952 Metaphysics. New York: Columbia University Press.
Ariyoshi, S.
    1994 Kabuki Dancer: A Novel of the Woman Who Founded Kabuki. London:
       Kodansha International.
Ashcroft, B., G. Griffiths, and H. Tiffin
    1998 Key Concepts in Post-Colonial Studies. London: Routledge.
Ashley, C., D. Roe, and H. Goodwin.
    2001 Pro-Poor Tourism Strategies: Making Tourism Work for the Poor.
       A Review of Experience. Pro-poor Report No. 1, 23 April.
Ashworth, G.
    2007 The North: Playground for the Netherlands? In A Compact Geography of
       the Northern Netherlands, G. Ashworth, P. Grootte, and P. Pellenberg, eds.,
       pp. 77–80. Assen: Boekvorm Uitgevers BV.
Askew, M.
    1998 City of Women, City of Foreign Men: Working Spaces and Re-working
       Identities among Female Sex Workers in Bangkok's Tourist Zone. Singapore
       Journal of Tropical Geography 19:130–150.
    1999a Strangers and Lovers: Thai Women Sex Workers and Western Men in the
       "Pleasure Space" of Bangkok. In Converging Interests: Traders, Travelers and
       Tourists in Southeast Asia, J. Forshee, Ch. Fink, and S. Cate, eds., pp. 37–70.
       Berkeley: University of California.
    1999b Labor, Love and Entanglement: Bangkok Bar Workers and the
       Negotiation of Selfhood. Crossroads 13.
    2002 Bangkok: Place, Practice and Representation. London: Routledge.
Ateljevic, I.
    2009 Transmodernity: Remaking Our (Tourism) World? In Philosophical Issues
       in Tourism, J. Tribe, ed., pp. 278–292. Bristol: Channel View.
Ateljevic, I., and S. Doorne
    2002 Representing New Zealand. Tourism Imagery and Ideology. Annals of
       Tourism Research 29:648–667.
Bachelard, G.
    1972 La Formation de l'Esprit Scientifique [The Formation of Scientific Spirit
       (8th ed.). Paris: Presses Universitaires de France.
    1973 Le Nouvel Esprit Scientifique [The New Scientific Spirit] (12th ed.). Paris:
       Presses Universitaires de France.

Bacon, F.
1951 Of Travel. *In* A Book of English Essays, W. Williams, ed., pp. 21–24. Harmondsworth: Penguin Books.
Baker, Ch., and P. Pasuk
2005 A History of Thailand. Cambridge: Cambridge University Press.
Baloglu, S.
2001 Image Variations of Turkey by Familiarity Index: Informational and Experiential Dimensions. Tourism Management 22:127–133.
Baran, P.
1957 The Political Economy of Growth. New York: Monthly Review Press.
Baran, P., and P. Sweezy
1966 Monopoly Capitalism. New York: Monthly Review Press.
Baranowski, S.
2004 Strength through Joy: Consumerism and Mass Tourism in the Third Reich. Cambridge: Cambridge University Press.
2005 El nacionalismo radical en un contexto Internacional: Fuerza por la Alegría y las paradojas del turismo nazi [Radical Nationalism: Strength through Joy and the paradoxes of Nazi Tourism]. Historia Social 52.
Barley, N.
1984 Adventures in a Mud Hut: An Innocent Anthropologist Abroad. New York: Vanguard Books.
1986 A Plague of Caterpillars. New York: Viking.
Barro, R.J., and X. Sala i Martín
1995 Economic Growth. New York: McGraw-Hill.
Barthes, R.
1957 Mythologies [Mythologies]. Paris: Éditions du Seuil.
Bary, W.T.de, D. Keene, G. Tanabe, and P. Varley
2002 Sources of the Japanese Tradition. Vol. 1, New York: Columbia University Press.
Barry, J.
2004 The Great Influenza: The Story of the Deadliest Pandemic in History. New York: Penguin.
Baudrillard, J.
1995 Simulacra and Simulation (The Body in Theory: Histories of Cultural Materialism). Ann Arbor, MI: The University of Michigan Press.
Bauer, Th., and B. McKercher
2003 Conceptual Framework of the Nexus between Tourism, Romance and Sex. *In* Sex and Tourism. Journeys of Romance, Love and Lust, Th. Bauer, and B. McKercher, eds., pp. 3–17. Oxford: The Haworth Hospitality Press.
Bauman, Z.
2000 Liquid Modernity. Malden: Blackwell.
2001 Community: Seeking Safety in an Insecure World. Malden: Blackwell.
2010 Liquid Times: Living in an Age of Uncertainty. Malden: Blackwell.

Beinhocker, E., D. Farrell, and A. Zainulbhai.
    2007 Tracking the Growth of India's Middle Class. MacKinsey Quarterly
        <https://www.mckinseyquarterly.com/Retail_Consumer_Goods/Tracking_the_
        growth_of_indias_middle_class_2032> (25 March 2010).
Berghoff, H.
    2002 From Privilege to Commodity? Modern Tourism and the Rise of Consumer
        Society. *In* The Making of Modern Tourism. The Cultural History of the
        British Experience 1600–2000, H. Berghoff, B. Korte, R. Scheneider, and
        Ch. Harvie, eds., pp. 159–180. New York: Palgrave.
Berlin, I.
    1990 The Crooked Timber of Humanity. Princeton: Princeton University Press.
    1997 The Proper Study of Mankind: An Anthology of Essays. New York: Farrar,
        Strauss and Giroux.
    1999 The Roots of Romanticism. Princeton: Princeton University Press.
Berry, C.
    1994 The Idea of Luxury: A Conceptual and Historical Investigation. Cambridge:
        Cambridge University Press.
Bettelheim, Ch.
    1975 Economic Calculations and Forms of Property. New York: Monthly Review.
Bhabha, H.
    1990 Nation and Narration. London: Routledge.
    1994 The Location of Culture. London: Routledge.
Bhagwati, J.
    2004 In Defense of Globalization. New York: Oxford University Press.
Bialik, C.
    2010 Suspect Estimates of Sex Trafficking at the World Cup. The Wall Street
        Journal, June 19, 2010.
Bishop, R., and L. Robinson
    1998 Night Market: Sexual Cultures and the Thai Economic Miracle. London:
        Routledge.
Black, J.
    1992 The British Abroad: The Grand Tour in the 18th Century. London:
        St. Martin's Press.
Blake, A., J. Saba Arbache, M. Sinclair, and V. Teles
    2008 Tourism and Poverty Relief. Annals of Tourism Research 35:107–126.
Blichfeldt, B.S.
    2005 Unmanageable Place Brands? Place Branding 1:388–401.
Blichfeldt, B.
    2007 Destination Branding: A Consumer Perspective, Proceedings of the 2nd
        International Conference on Destination Branding and Marketing for Regional
        Tourism Development, pp. 57–67. Macao: SAR.
Boas, F.
    1962 Anthropology and Modern Life. New York: Norton.

Bobak, L.
  1996 For sale: The innocence of Cambodia. Ottawa Sun, 24 October. OTD (Office of Tourism Development) 2010 Tourism Statistics 1998–2007. Available at http://www2.tat.or.th/stat/web/static_index.php. Accessed on April 27, 2010.
Body Miracle
  2003 Body Miracle. Porn Star Escorts <http://www.bodymiracle.com/> (29 April 2010).
Boff, L.
  1978 Jesus Christ Liberator: A Critical Christology for Our Times. Maryknoll: Orbis Books.
  1997 Cry of the Earth, Cry of the Poor. Maryknoll: Orbis Books.
Boniface, B., and C. Cooper
  2005 Worldwide Destinations: The Geography of Travel and Tourism (4th ed.). Oxford: Elsevier Butterworth-Heinemann.
Boonchalaksi, W., and P. Guest
  1998 Prostitution in Thailand. In The Sex Sector: The Economic and Social Bases of Prostitution in South East Asia, L. Lim, ed., pp. 130–169. Geneva: International Labor Office.
Boorstin, D.
  1961 The Image: A Guide to Pseudo-Events in North America. New York: Vintage.
Bourdieu, P.
  1979 La distinction: critique sociale du jugement [Distinction. A Social Critique of the Judgment of Taste]. Paris: Minuit.
  1984 Distinction. A Social Critique of the Judgement of Taste. Cambridge: Harvard University Press.
Brandon, S., J. Boakes, D. Glaser, and R. Green
  1998 Recovered Memories of Childhood Sexual Abuse. British Journal of Psychiatry 172:296–307.
Brenan, G.
  1990 The Spanish Labyrinth: An Account of the Social and Political Background of the Spanish Civil War. Cambridge: Canto.
Britton, S.
  1996 Tourism, Dependency and Development: A Mode of Analysis. In The Sociology of Tourism. Theoretical and Empirical Investigations, Y. Apostolopoulos, S. Leivadi, and A. Yiannakis, eds., pp. 155–172. London: Routledge.
Brodsky-Porges, E.
  1981 The Grand Tour Travel as an Educational Device 1600–1800. Annals of Tourism Research 8:171–186.
Brown, D.
  2003 The Da Vinci Code. New York: Doubleday.
Brown, F.
  2000 Tourism Reassessed: Blight or Blessing? London: Butterworth-Heinemann.

Brown, L.
2009 The Transformative Power of the International Sojourn: An Ethnographic Study of the International Student Experience. Annals of Tourism Research 36:502–521.
Brunner, E.
1991 Transformation of Self in Tourism. Annals of Tourism Research 18:238–250.
Brunner,, E., and B. Kirschenblatt-Gimbel,
1994 Maasai on the Lawn. Cultural Anthropology 9:435–470.
Burns, P.
2001a Brief Encounters: Culture, Tourism and the Local–Global Nexus. In Tourism in the Age of Globalization, S. Wahab, and C. Cooper, eds., pp. 290–305. London: Routledge.
2001b Interconnections, Planning and the Local–Global Nexus: A Case from Vietnam. In Interconnected Worlds: Tourism in Southeast Asia, P. Teo, T.C. Chang, and K.C. Ho, eds., pp. 282–297. Kidlington: Elsevier.
2006 Social Identities and Cultural Politics of Tourism. In Tourism and Social Identities, P. Burns, and M. Novelli, eds., pp. 13–26. Oxford: Elsevier.
Buruma, I.
2003 Inventing Japan. 1853–1964. New York: The Modern Library.
Buruma, I., and A. Margalit
2004 Occidentalism: The West in the Eyes of its Enemies. New York: The Penguin Press.
Bury, J.B.
1920 The Idea of Progress. An Inquiry into Its Origin and Growth. London: MacMillan.
Butcher, J.
2002 The Moralisation of Tourism: Sun, Sand … and Saving the World? London: Routledge.
2006 A Response to Building a Decommodified Research Paradigm in Tourism: The Contribution of NGOs by Stephen Wearing, Matthew McDonald and Jess Ponting. Journal of Sustainable Tourism 14:307–310.
2007 Ecotourism, NGOs and Development: A Critical Analysis. New York: Routledge.
Butler, R., and T. Hinch
2007 Tourism and Indigenous Peoples: Issues and Implications. London: Butterworth-Heinemann.
Byrne Swain, M., and J. Mommsen
2001a Gender/Tourism/Fun (Tourism Dynamics). New York: Cognizant.
2001b Cosmopolitan Tourism and Minority Politics in the Stone Forest. In Tourism, Anthropology, and China, C.B. Tan, S. Cheung, and Y. Ho., eds., pp. 125–146. Bangkok: White Lotus Press.
Bystrzanowski, J., and J. Aramberri
2003 The Iron Laws of Sex Tourism. Tourism Recreation Research 28:83–91.

Calzada, G., R. Merino, and J. Rallo
2009 The Effects on Employment of Public Aid to Renewable Energy Sources. Madrid: Instituto Juan de Mariana.
Cambodia Tourism Ministry
2003 Number of Visitor Arrivals <http://www.visit-mekong.com/cambodia/stats/visitor_number.htm> (27 May 2005).
Canestrelli, E., and P. Costa
1991 Tourist Carrying Capacity: A Fuzzy Approach. Annals of Tourism Research 18:295–311.
Caprioglio O'Reilly, C.
2006 From Drifter to Gap Year Tourist: Mainstreaming Backpacker Travel. Annals of Tourism Research 33:998–1017.
Caro Baroja, J.
1979a El Carnaval (Análisis Histórico-Cultural) [Carnival. A Historic-Cultural Analysis]. Madrid: Taurus.
1979b La Estación de Amor (Fiestas Populares de Mayo a San Juan) [The Season of Love. Popular Festivals from May to St. John]. Madrid: Taurus.
Carr, E.
1958 A History of Soviet Russia. Socialism in One Country: 1924–1926 (vol. 1). London: Macmillan.
Carr, N.
2010 The Shallows. What the Internet is Doing to Our Brains. New York: Norton.
Carson, R.
1962 Silent Spring. Boston: Houghton Mifflin.
CASS (Chinese Academy of Social Sciences),
2003 Dangdai Zhongguo Shehui Jieceng Yanjiu Baogao [A Report on the Study of Contemporary China's Social Strata]. Beijing: Shehui Kexue Wenxian Chubanshe (Social Sciences Literature Press).
Castro, C., Armario, and D. Ruiz
2007 The Influence of Market Heterogeneity on the Relationship between a Destination's Image and Tourists' Future Behavior. Tourism Management 28:175–187.
Cater, E., and G. Lowmann, eds.
1994 Ecotourism: A Sustainable Option? Oxford: Wiley.
Chang, J.
1991 Wild Swans: Three Daughters of China. New York: Simon & Schuster.
Chaudhary, M.
2000 India's Image as a Tourist Destination: A Perspective of Foreign Tourists. Tourism Management 21:293–297.
Chías, J.
2005 El Negocio de la Felicidad. Desarrollo y Marketing Turístico de Países, Regiones, Ciudades y Lugares [The Market of Happiness. Development and

Tourism Marketing of Countries, Regions, Cities and Places] (2nd ed.). Madrid: Pearson Education.

Chomsky, N.

1975 The Logical Structure of Linguistic Theory. New York: Plenum Press.

2002 Cartesian Linguistics: A Chapter in the History of Rationalist Thought (2nd ed.). Christchurch, New Zealand: Cybereditions Corporation.

CIA (Central Intelligence Agency)

2010 The World Factbook <https://www.cia.gov/library/publications/the-world-factbook/geos/xx.html> (23 May 2010).

Clark, G.

2007 A Farewell to Alms: A Brief Economic History of the World. Princeton: Princeton University Press.

Clarke, A.

2009 Journeys of Discovery in Volunteer Tourism. Annals of Tourism Research 36:159–160.

CNTO (China National Tourist Office)

2005 Major Statistics of China Tourism 2004 <http://www.cnto.org/chinastats.asp> (23 April 2005).

2010 China Tourism Statistics <http://www.cnto.org/chinastats.asp.> (5 July 2010).

Cohen, E.

1972 Towards a Sociology of International Tourism. Social Research 39:64–82.

1979 A Phenomenology of Tourist Experience. Sociology 13:179–201.

1980 Thai Girls and Farang Men: The Edge of Ambiguity. Annals of Tourism Research 13:18–35.

1982 Marginal Paradises: Bungalow Tourism on the Islands of Southern Thailand. Annals of Tourism Research 9:189–228.

1993 Open-ended Prostitution as a Skillful Game of Luck: Opportunity, Risk and Security among Tourist Oriented Prostitutes in a Bangkok Soi. *In* Tourism in Southeast Asia, M. Hitchcock, V. King, and M. Parnell, eds., pp. 155–177. London: Routledge.

1995 Thai Society in Comparative Perspective (Studies in Contemporary Thailand). Bangkok: White Lotus.

2000 The Commercialized Crafts of Thailand: Hill Tribes and Lowland Villages. Honolulu: University of Hawaii Press.

2001a Thai Tourism. Hill Tribes, Islands and Open-Ended Prostitution. Bangkok: White Lotus.

2001b Ethnic Tourism in South East Asia. *In* Tourism, Anthropology and China, C. Tan, S. Cheung, and Y. Hui, eds., pp. 27–54. Bangkok: White Lotus Press.

2003 Transitional Marriage in Thailand: The Dynamics of Extreme Heterogamy. *In* Sex and Tourism: Journeys of Romance, Love and Lust, Th. Bauer, and B. MacKercher, eds., pp. 57–81. New York: The Haworth Press.

2004a A Phenomenology of Tourist Experiences. *In* Contemporary Tourism. Diversity and Change, pp. 65–86. Amsterdam: Elsevier.

2004b Tourism as Play. *In* Contemporary Tourism. Diversity and Change, E. Cohen, ed. Amsterdam: Elsevier.
2007 "Authenticity" in Tourism Studies. Après la lutte. Tourism Recreation Research 32(2):75–82.
2008 Explorations in Thai Tourism. Bingley: Emerald.
Coles, T., D. Duval, and C. Hall
2005 Sobre turismo y movilidad en tiempos de movimiento y conjetura posdisciplinar [On Tourism and Mobilities in Times of Movement and Post-disciplinary Conjecture]. Política y Sociedad 42:85–99.
Comte, A.
1874 Catéchisme Positiviste [Positivist Catechism]. Paris: Leroux Editeur.
Constant, B.
1980 De l'Esprit de Conquête [On the Spirit of Conquest]. Genève: P.-M. Favre.
Côté, J.E.
1994 Adolescent Storm and Stress: An Evaluation of the Mead/Freeman Controversy. Hillsdale: L. Erlbaum Associates.
Cowlishaw, G.
1998 Rednecks, Eggheads and Blackfellas: A Study of Racial Power and Intimacy in Australia. Ann Arbor: University of Michigan Press.
Craft, L.
2003 Japan Wants You: All 10 Million of You <http://www.japaninc.net/ article.php?articleID = 1183&page = 4> (20 November 2004).
Crawford, Ch., and D. Krebs, eds.
2008 Foundations of Evolutionary Psychology. New York: Taylor & Francis.
Crick, M.
1996 Representations of International Tourism in the Social Sciences: Sun, Sex, Sights, Savings and Servility. *In* The Sociology of Tourism, Y. Apostolopoulos, S. Leivadi, and A. Yiannakis, eds., pp. 15–50. New York: Routledge.
Crow, K.
2010 Giacometti Sets Auction Record. The Wall Street Journal. February 3, p. 1.
Cwerner, S., S. Kesselring, and J. Urry, eds.
2009 Aeromobilities. Abingdon: Routledge.
Daniels, T. ed.
1999 A Doomsday Reader: Prophets, Predictors, and Hucksters of Salvation. New York: New York University Press.
Dann, G.
1996a The Language of Tourism: A Sociolinguistic Perspective. Wallingford: CABI.
1996b Tourists' Images of a Destination: An Alternative Analysis. Journal of Travel and Tourism Marketing 5:20–27.
1996c The People of Tourist Brochures. *In* The Tourist Image. Myth and Myth Making in Tourism, T. Selwyn, ed., pp. 61–81. Chichester: Wiley.
1999 Writing out the Tourist in Space and Time. Annals of Tourism Research 26:159–187.

2002 The Tourist as a Metaphor of the Social World. *In* The Tourist as a Metaphor of the Social World, G. Dann, ed., pp. 1–17. Wallingford: CABI.
2003 Noticing Notices. Tourism to Order. Annals of Tourism Research 30: 465–484.
2005a Content/Semiotics Analysis: Applications for Tourism Research. *In* Tourism Development. Issues for a Vulnerable Industry, J. Aramberri, and R. Butler, eds., pp. 27–42. Clevedon: Channel View.
2005b Remodeling the Language of Tourism: From Monologue to Dialogue and Trialogue. Paper presented to the International Academy for the Study of Tourism, Beijing.
Dann, G., and G. Parrinello
2007 Od Putopisa do "Putobloga": Redefiniranje Identiteta Turista [From Travelog to Travelblog: (Re)-negotiating Tourist Identity]. Acta Turistica 19: 7–29.
2009 Setting the Scene. *In* The Sociology of Tourism. European Origins and Developments, G. Dann, and G. Parrinello, eds., pp. 1–64. Bingley: Emerald.
Dawkins, R.
1987 The Blind Watchmaker. Why the Evidence of Evolution Reveals a Universe without Design. New York: Norton.
De Beauvoir, S.
1949 Le Deuxième Sexe [The Second Sex]. Paris: Gallimard.
De Grazia, S.
1964 Of Time, Work and Leisure. New York: Anchor Books.
De Kadt, E.
1979 Tourism – Passport to Development: Perspectives on the Social and Cultural Effects of Tourism in Developing Countries. Washington, DC: World Bank.
Deleuze, G., and F. Guattari
1977 Anti-Oedipus: Capitalism and Schizofrenia. New York: Viking Press.
1987 A Thousand Plateaus: Capitalism and Schizofrenia. Minneapolis: The University of Minnesota Press.
Deloitte & Touche, IIED, and ODI
1999 Sustainable Tourism and Poverty Elimination Study. A Report to the Department of International Development. New York: United Nations.
Derrida, J.
1994 Specters of Marx: The State of the Debt, the Work of Mourning, and the New International. New York: Routledge.
2002 Without Alibi. Stanford: Stanford University Press.
Desai, M.
2002 Marx's Revenge. The Resurgence of Capitalism and the Death of Statist Socialism. London: Verso.
Desforges, L.
2000 Travelling the World: Identity and Travel Biography. Annals of Tourism Research 27:929–945.

De Mandeville, B.
1997 The Fable of the Bees and Other Writings. Indianapolis: Hackett.
De Rougemont, D.
1983 Love in the Western World. Princeton: Princeton University Press.
De Tocqueville, A.
1886 L'Ancien Régime et la Révolution [The Ancien Régime and the Revolution]. Paris: M. Lévy.
De Unamuno, M.
1998 Tres novelas ejemplares y un prólogo [Three Exemplary Novels and a Prologue]. Madrid: Alianza Editorial.
Diamond, J.
1997 Guns, Germs and Steel. The Fates of Human Societies. New York: Norton.
2005 Collapse: How Societies Choose to Fail or Succeed. New York: Penguin.
Dos Santos, T.
1991 Democracia e Socialismo no Capitalismo Dependente [Democracy and Socialism in Dependent Capitalism]. Petropolis: Vozes.
Douglas, M.
2003 The World of Goods. *In* Mary Douglas: Collected Works (vol. VI). London: Routledge.
Dreier, P.
2004 Reagan's Legacy: Homelessness in America < http://www.nhi.org/online/ issues/135/reagan.html> (2 December 2004).
Duerr, A.
1992 Der Mythos von Zivilisationsprozeß: Nackheit und Scham (Band 1) [The Myth of the Civilizatory Process. Nakedness and Shame]. Frankfurt: Suhrkamp.
Dumazedier, J.
1962 Vers une civilization des loisirs? [Towards a Civilization of Leisure?]. Paris: Editions du Seuil.
Dumazedier, J., and A. Rippert
1966 Le Loisir et la Ville [Leisure and the City]. Paris: Éditions du Seuil.
Dumond, D.
1997 The Machete and the Cross: Campesino Rebellion in Yucatan. Lincoln: The University of Nebraska Press.
Durkheim, E.
1970 La Science Sociale et l'Action [Social Science and Action]. Paris: Presses Universitaires de France.
1997 Suicide. Glencoe: The Free Press.
Eadington, W., and V. Smith
1992 The Emergence of Alternative Forms of Tourism. *In* Tourism Alternatives: Potentials and Problems in the Development of Tourism, W. Eadington, and V. Smith, eds. Philadelphia: University of Pennsylvania Press.
Eagleton, T.
2003 After Theory. New York: Basic Books.

Easterly, W.
2007 The White Man's Burden: Why the West's Efforts to Aid the Rest Have Done So Much Ill and So Little Good. New York: Penguin.
Ebrey, P.
1999 The Cambridge Illustrated History of China. Cambridge: Cambridge University Press.
Efron, S.
2001 Me, Find a Husband? Later, Maybe. Japan's Successful, Career-Minded Women Are Savoring Single Life and Waiting Longer than Ever for Mr. Right. Los Angeles Times, June 26.
Elias, N.
1997 Über den Prozess der Zivilisation: soziogenetische und psychogenetische Untersuchungen [On the Civilizatory Process; Socio- and Psychogenetic Investigations]. In Gesammelte Schriften (Bände 3:1 und 3:2) [Works. Volumes 3:1 and 3:2] Frankfurt am Main: Suhrkamp.
Elias, N.
1998 On Civilization, Power and Knowledge: Selected Writings. Chicago: University of Chicago Press.
Elliott, J.
2006 Empires of the Atlantic World: Britain and Spain in America 1492–1830. New Haven: Yale University Press, Kindle Edition.
Elsrud, T.
2001 Risk Creation in Travelling: Backpacker Adventure Narration. Annals of Tourism Research 28:597–617.
Emmanuel, A.
1972 Unequal Exchange: A Study of the Imperialism of Trade. New York: Monthly Review Press.
Enoch, Y., and R. Grossman
2010 Blogs of Israeli and Danish Backpackers to India. Annals of Tourism Research 37:520–536.
Erickson, J.
1999 Some Babies Grow Up to be Cowboys. Denton: University of North Texas Press.
Eros Guide
2010 Eros Guide to Philadelphia <http://www.eros-philly.com/eros.htm> (3 June 2010).
Fanon, F.
1968 Les Damnés de la Terre [The Damned of the Earth]. Paris: François Maspéro.
1988 Toward the African Revolution: Political Essays. New York: Grove Press.
1991 Black Skin, White Masks. New York: Grove Press.
Faxian,
2005 A Record of Buddhistic Kingdoms. New York: Cosimo Classics.

Febas, J.

1978 Semiología del lenguaje turístico (Investigación sobre los folletos españoles de turismo) [Semiology of Tourism Language. A Study of Spanish Tourism Brochures]. Revista de Estudios Turísticos 57–58:17–203.

Fennell, D., and R. Dowling, eds.

2003 Ecotourism Policy and Planning. Wallingford: CABI.

Ferguson, N.

2003 Empire: The Rise and Demise of the British World Order and the Lessons for Global Power. New York: Basic Books.

Fernández-Armesto, F.

2001 Civilizations: Culture, Ambition, and the Transformation of Nature. New York: The Free Press.

2002 Near a Thousand Tables. A History of Food. New York: The Free Press.

Fichte, J.

1922 Addresses to the German Nation. London: The Open Court Publishing House.

Fischer, E.

1999 Cultural Logic and Maya Identity: Rethinking Constructivism and Essentialism. Current Anthropology 40:473–499.

Fleishman, A.

2002 New Class Culture: How an Emergent Class is Transforming America's Culture. Westport: Greenwood Publishing Group.

Forbes Magazine

2008 The Most Working World Countries. Forbes Magazine, September 5.

Foucault, M.

1970 The Order of Things. London: Tavistock.

1971 L'Ordre du Discours [The Order of Discourse]. Paris: Gallimard.

1972 The Archeology of Knowledge. London: Tavistock.

1973 Birth of the Clinic. New York: Pantheon Books.

1978 The History of Sexuality, vol. 1: An Introduction. New York: Pantheon Books.

1985 The History of Sexuality, vol 2: The Use of Pleasure. New York: Random House.

1986 The History of Sexuality, vol 3: The Care of the Self. New York: Random House.

1995 Discipline and Punish. New York: Vintage Books.

2001 Madness and Civilization [French Original Title: Histoire de la Folie à l'âge classique: Folie et Déraison]. Florence: Routledge.

Frank, A.

1975 Lumpenbourgeoisie; Lumpendevelopment: Dependence, Class and Politics in Latin America. New York: Monthly Review Press.

1981 Dependent Accumulation and Underdevelopment. New York: Monthly Review Press.

Freeman, D.
1983 Margaret Mead and Samoa: The Making and Unmaking of an Anthropological Myth. Cambridge: Harvard University Press.
1999 The Fateful Hoaxing of Margaret Mead: A Historical Analysis of her Samoan Research. Boulder: Westview Press.
2001 Dilthey's Dream: Essays on Human Nature and Culture. Canberra: Pandanus.
FUR (Forschungsgemeinschaft Urlaub und Reisen)
2008 Reise Analyse 2008. Erste Ergebnisse [Travel Analysis 2008. First Results]. PowerPoint document presented at ITB Berlin 2008.
Ganalh, J.
2004 Women in Asia Are Starting to Say "I Don't". San Francisco Chronicle, November 14.
Gao, X.
2002 One Man's Bible. New York: Harper Collins.
Gard McGehee, N.
2002 Alternative tourism and Social Movements. Annals of Tourism Research 29:24–143.
Gard McGehee, N., and C. Almeida Santos
2005 Social Change, Discourse and Volunteer Tourism. Annals of Tourism Research 32:760–779.
Garner, J.
1995 Once Upon a More Enlightened Time: More Politically Correct Bedtime Stories. New York: Macmillan.
Gartner, W.
1993 Image Formation Process. Journal of Travel and Tourism Marketing 2: 191–215.
1996 Tourism Development: Principles, Processes and Policies. New York: Wiley.
Gartner, W., A. Tasci, and S. So
2007 Branding Macao: An Application of Strategic Branding for Destinations. Proceedings of the 2nd International Conference on Destination Marketing and Branding: New Advances and Challenges for Practice, Macau, pp. 133–142.
Gascoigne, G.
2003 The Dynasties of China, A History. New York: Carroll & Graf.
Gaviria, M.
1975 España a Go-Go. Turismo charter y neocolonialismo del espacio [Go-Go Spain. Charter Tourism and Space Neo-Colonialism]. Madrid: Turner.
1996 La séptima potencia: España en el mundo [The Seventh Power. Spain in the World]. Barcelona: Ediciones B.
Gay, J.
1985 The "Patriotic Prostitute". The Progressive, February.
Gay, P.
2001 Weimar Culture: The Outsider as Insider. New York: Norton.

Geertz, C.
1973 The Interpretation of Cultures: Selected Essays. New York: Basic Books.
2000 Available Light: Anthropological Reflections on Philosophical Topics. Princeton: Princeton University Press.
Gellner, E.
1983 Nations and Nationalism. Ithaca: Cornell University Press.
1998 Nationalism. New York: New York University Press.
General Statistics Office (GSO).
2002 Vietnam's Statistical Yearbook 2001. Hanoi: Statistical Publishing House.
Ghosh, L.
2002 Prostitution in Thailand: Myth and Reality. New Delhi: Munshiram Manoharlal.
Gibbon, E.
1909 The History of the Decline and Fall of the Roman Empire. London: Methuen & Co.
Gmelch, G.
2003 Behind the Smile: The Working Lives of Caribbean Tourism. Bloomington: Indiana University Press.
Gnoth, J.
2002 A Country—Can it be Repositioned? Spain, the Success Story of Country Branding. Journal of Brand Management 9:262–280.
Goffman, E.
1961 Asylums. Essays on the Social Situation of Mental Patients and Other Inmates. New York: Anchor Books.
1963 Stigma: Notes on the Management of Spoiled Identity. Englewood Cliffs: Prentice-Hall.
Goodman, P., J. Pomfret, and W. Ting
2002 Sex Trade Thrives in China. The Washington Post, January 3.
Gössling, S., M. Hall, B. Lane, and D. Weaver
2008 Report: The Helsingborg Statement on Sustainable Tourism. Journal of Sustainable Tourism 16:122–124.
Gouldner, A.
1973 The Coming Crisis of Western Sociology. London: Heinemann.
Gramsci, A.
1949 Il Risorgimento [The Risorgimento]. Turin: Einaudi.
1970 Selections from the Prison Notebooks. New York: International Publishers.
Graburn, N.
1977 Tourism: The Sacred Journey. In Hosts and Guests: The Anthropology of Tourism, V. Smith, ed., pp. 132–178. Philadelphia: The University of Pennsylvania Press.
2001 Secular Ritual. A General Theory of Tourism. In Hosts and Guests Revisited: Tourism Issues of the 21st Century, V. Smith, and M. Brent, eds., pp. 42–52. New York: Cognizant.

2004 The Anthropology of Tourism. *In* Tourism. Critical Concepts in the Social Sciences, S. Williams, ed., Vol. 1, pp. 91–112. London: Routledge.

Gray, J.

2002 Straw Dogs. Thoughts on Humans and Other Animals. London: Granta Books.

2003 Al Qaeda and What it Means to be Modern. London: Faber & Faber.

Greenwood, D.

1977 Culture by the Pound: An Anthropological Perspective on Tourism as Cultural Commoditization. *In* Hosts and Guests, V. Smith, ed., pp. 129–139. Philadelphia: University of Pennsylvania Press.

Gu, H., and L. Dake

2004 The Relationship between Resident Income and Domestic Tourism in China. Tourism Recreation Research 29:25–35.

Gunn, C.

1972 Vacationscape: Designing Tourist Regions. Austin, TX: University of Texas.

Ha, J.

2004 War Trash. A Novel. New York: Pantheon Books.

Halberstam, D.

1986 The Reckoning. New York: Avon Books.

Hall, C.M.

1992 Sex Tourism in Southeast Asia. *In* Tourism and the Less Developed Nations, D. Harrison, ed., pp. 37–52. London: Bellhaven Press.

2006 The Geography of Tourism and Recreation. Environment, Place and Space (3rd ed.). London: Routledge.

2007a North–South Perspectives on Tourism. Regional Development and Peripheral Areas. *In* Tourism Peripheries. Perspectives from the Far North and South, D. Müller, and B. Jansson, eds., pp. 19–39. Wallingford: CABI.

2007b Tourism Planning: Policies, Processes and Relationships (2nd ed.). Harlow: Prentice Hall.

Hall, C.M., and S. Page

2000 Introduction: Tourism in South and Southeast Asia: Region and Context. *In* Tourism in South and Southeast Asia: Issues and Cases, C.M. Hall, and S. Page, eds., pp. 3–29. Oxford: Butterworth-Heinemann.

Hall, J.

1994 Prostitution in Thailand and Southeast Asia or How to Keep Millions of Good Women Down < http://www.links.net/vita/swat/course/prosthai.html > (7 June 2004).

Hampton, M.

1998 Backpacker Tourism and Economic Development. Annals of Tourism Research 25:639–660.

Hannam, K., and I. Atejevic, eds.

2008 Backpacker Tourism. Clevedon: Channel View.

Haralambopoulos, N., and A. Pizam
  1996 Perceived Impacts of Tourism: The Case of Samos. Annals of Tourism
    Research 23:503–526.
Harlan, J.
  1992 Crops and Man. Madison: American Society of Agronomy.
  1998 The Living Fields and Agricultural Heritage. Cambridge: Cambridge
    University Press.
Harris, M.
  1968 The Rise of Anthropological Theory: A History of Theories of Culture. New
    York: Crowell.
Harrison, D. ed.
  2001 Tourism and the Less Developed World: Issues and Case Studies.
    Wallingford: CABI.
Harrison, J.
  2002 Being a Tourist: Finding Meaning in Pleasure Travel. Vancouver: The
    University of British Columbia Press.
Hartsock, N.
  1983 Money, Sex, and Power: Toward a Feminist Historical Materialism. New
    York: Longman.
Haug, B., G. Dann, and M. Mehmetoglu
  2007 Little Norway in Spain: From Tourism to Migration. Annals of Tourism
    Research 34:202–222.
Hawkins, D., and S. Mann
  2007 The World Bank's Role in Tourism Development. Annals of Tourism
    Research 34:348–363.
Hay, D., E. Thompson, P. Linebaugh, and J. Rule, eds.
  1977 Albion's Fatal Tree: Crime and Society in Eighteenth-Century England.
    Harmondsworth: Peregrine Books.
Headland, I.
  1909 Court Life in China. New York: F. H. Revell Co.
Hegel, G.
  1970a Phänomenologie des Geistes [Phenomenology of the Spirit. Werke
    in zwanzig Bänden [Works in 20 Volumes]. Vol. 3, Frankfurt: Suhrkamp
    Verlag.
  1970b Enzyklopädie der philosophischen Wissenschaften I [Encyclopedia of the
    Philosophical Sciences I]. Werke in zwanzig Bänden [Works in 20 Volumes].
    Vol. 8, Frankfurt: Suhrkamp Verlag.
Herodotus,
  1987 The History. Chicago: University of Chicago Press.
Hershatter, G.
  1999 Dangerous Pleasures. Prostitution and Modernity in Twentieth Century
    Shanghai. Berkeley: University of California Press.

Hiebert, M.
1995 Chasing the Tigers: A Portrait of the New Vietnam. New York: Kodansha International.
Higgins-Desbiolles, F.
2007 Taming Tourism: Indigenous Rights as a Check to Unbridled Tourism. *In* P. Burns, and M. Novelli, eds., pp. 83–108. Oxford: Elsevier.
Hobson, J.
1967 Imperialism. Ann Arbor: The University of Michigan Press.
Hodgson, A.
2007 China's Middle Class Reaches 80 Million <http://www.euromonitor.com/ Chinas_middle_class_reaches_80_million.> (27 March 2010).
Hofmann, C.
2006 The White Masai. New York: Amistad.
2009 Back from Africa. London: Arcadia.
Hollinshead, K.
1992 "White" Gaze, "Red" People—Shadow Visions: The Disidentification of "Indians" in Cultural Tourism. Leisure Studies 11:43–64.
1993 Ethnocentrism in Tourism. *In* Encyclopedia of Hospitality and Tourism, M. Khan, M. Olsen, and T. Var, eds., pp. 652–662. New York: Van Nostrand Reinhold.
Honey, M.
2008 Ecotourism and Sustainable Development: Who Owns Paradise? Washington, DC: Island Press.
Horkheimer, M., and Th. Adorno
1972 Dialectic of Enlightenment. New York: Herder and Herder.
Hornblower, M.
1993 The Skin Trade. Time Magazine, June 21.
Hsu, C., and T. Powers
2001 Marketing Hospitality (3rd ed.). New York: Wiley.
Huizinga, J.
1967 Homo Ludens. A Study of the Play-Element in Culture. Boston: Beacon Press.
2005 Herffsttijd des Middeleeuwen [The Autumn of the Middle Ages]. E-Book. Project Gutenberg.
Hunter, C.
2000 The Art of Hypnotherapy. Dubuque: Kendall Hunt Publishing.
Huntington, S.
1996 The Clash of Civilizations and the Remaking of World Order. New York: Simon & Schuster.
2004 Who Are We? The Challenges to America's National Identity. New York: Simon & Schuster.
Hutnyk, J.
1996 The Rumor of Calcutta: Tourism, Charity and the Poverty of Representation. London: Zed.

Hyegyonggung, H.
1996 The Memoirs of Lady Hyegyong: The Autobiographical Writings of a Crown Princess of Eighteenth-Century Korea (translated by Ja Hyun Kim Haboush). Berkeley: The University of California Press.

Ibn Battuta,
1929 Travels in Asia and Africa, 1325–1354, translated and selected by H. Gibb. London: G. Routledge & Sons.

IMS (Internet Medieval Sourcebook)
2005 Marco Polo: The Glories of Kinsay [Hangchow] (c. 1300) <http://www.fordham.edu/halsall/source/polo-kinsay.html> (20 September 2005).

IPCC (Intergovernmental Panel on Climate Change)
2010 Organization <http://www.ipcc.ch/organization/organization.htm> (20 March 2010).

Irving, C.
1969 Fake! The Story of Elmyr de Hory, the Greatest Art Forger of our Time. New York: McGraw-Hill.

ISA (International Sociological Association)
2005 Research Committees <http://www.ucm.es/info/isa/rc.htm> (4 September 2006).

ISixSigma
2004 Dictionary: Kaizen <http://www.isixsigma.com/dictionary/> (12 November 2004).

Jafari, J.
1987 Tourism Models: The Sociocultural Aspects. Tourism Management 8:151–159.
1990 Research and Scholarship: The Basis of Tourism Education. The Journal of Tourism Studies 1:33–41.
1994 Structure of Tourism: Three Models. In Tourism Marketing and Management Handbook, S. Witt, and L. Moutinho, eds., pp. 1–7. New York: Prentice Hall.
1997 Tourism and Culture: An Inquiry into Paradoxes. In Proceedings of a UNESCO roundtable on Culture, Tourism, Development: Critical Issues for the 21st Century. Paris: UNESCO.
1998 Tourismification of the Profession: Chameleon Job Names across the Industry. Progress in Tourism and Hospitality Research 3:75–181.
2000 Encyclopedia of Tourism. London: Routledge.
2001 The Scientification of Tourism. In Hosts and Guests Revisited: Tourism Issues of the 21st Century, V. Smith, and M. Brent, eds., pp. 28–41. New York: Cognizant Communication Corporation.
2005 El Turismo como Disciplina Científica [Tourism as a Scientific Discipline]. Política y Sociología 42:39–56.

Jafari, J., and D. Aaser
1988 Tourism as the Subject of Doctoral Dissertations. Annals of Tourism Research 15:407–429.

Jafari, J., and B. Ritchie
1981 Toward a Framework for Education: Problems and Prospects. Annals of Tourism Research 8:13–34.
Jafari, J., and A. Pizam
1996 Tourism Management. *In* International Encyclopedia of Business and Management, M. Warner, ed., pp. 4903–4913. London: Routledge.
Jago, L.
2003 Sex Tourism: An Accommodation Provider's Perspective. *In* Sex and Tourism. Journeys of Romance, Love and Lust, Th. Bauer, and B. McKercher, eds., pp. 85–94. Oxford: The Haworth Hospitality Press.
Jamieson, N.
1993 Understanding Vietnam. Berkeley: University of California Press.
Jeffrey, L.
2002 Sex and Borders: Gender, National Identity and Prostitution Policy in Thailand. Honolulu: The University of Hawaii Press.
Johnston, A.
2006 Is the Sacred for Sale? Tourism and Indigenous People. London: Earthscan.
Jokinen, E., and S. Veijola
1997 The Disoriented Tourist. The Figuration of the Tourist in Contemporary Cultural Critique. *In* Touring Cultures. Transformations of Travel and Tourism, Ch. Rojek, and J. Urry, eds., pp. 23–51. London: Routledge.
JTA (Japan Tourism Agency)
2007 White Paper on Tourism in Japan 2007.
2008 White Paper on Tourism in Japan 2008.
2010a Economic Ripple Effect <http://www.mlit.go.jp/kankocho/en/siryou/toukei/kouka.html> (9 July 2010).
2010b Number of Inbound and Outbound Travelers <http://www.mlit.go.jp/kankocho/en/siryou/toukei/in_out.html> (10 July 2010).
2010c Ranking of Inbound and Outbound Tourism <http://www.mlit.go.jp/kankocho/en/siryou/toukei/ranking.html> (9 July 2010).
2010d Building a Travel Nation <http://www.mlit.go.jp/kankocho/en/siryou/archive/index.html> (18 July 2010).
Judt, T.
2006 Postwar: A History of Europe since 1945. New York: Penguin Books.
Jurdao, F.
1979 España en venta: Compra de suelos por extranjeros y colonización de campesinos en la Costa del Sol [Spain for Sale. Foreign Real-Estate Business and Peasant Colonization in Costa del Sol]. Madrid: Ayuso.
1990 España en venta: Compra de suelos por extranjeros y colonización de campesinos en la Costa del Sol Sol [Spain for Sale. Foreign Real-Estate Business and Peasant Colonization in Costa del Sol]. Madrid: Endymión.

386 Modern Mass Tourism

Kahn, J.
   2002 Lawsuits in Eden: Fury over Napa Vineyards. The New York Times, April 14.
Khanh, V., T. Thuy, K. Loan, H. Phong, and Q. Phuong
   2001 Labor and Employment. *In* Living Standards During an Economic Boom: The Case of Vietnam, D. Haughton, J. Haughton, and N. Phong, eds., pp. 43–67. Hanoi: Statistical Publishing House.
Karch, C., and G. Dann
   1981 Close Encounters of the Third World. Human Relations 34:249–268.
Keene, D.
   2002 Emperor of Japan: Meiji and His World, 1852–1912. New York: Columbia University Press.
   2004 The Tale of Genji. Broomall: Chelsea House Publishers.
Kennedy, P.
   2007 The Parliament of Man: The Past, Present and Future of the United Nations. New York: Vintage.
Kesey, K.
   1973 One Flew over the Cuckoo's Nest. New York: Viking Press.
Keynes, J.
   1936 The General Theory of Employment, Interest and Money. London: Macmillan.
Kibicho, W.
   2009 Sex Tourism in Africa. Kenya's Booming Industry. Burlington: Ashgate.
Krippendorf, J.
   1987 The Holiday Makers: Understanding the Impact of Leisure and Travel. Oxford: Heinemann.
Krugman, P.
   1994 Peddling Prosperity: Economic Sense and Nonsense in the Age of Diminished Expectations. New York: Norton.
Kuhn, Th.
   1996 The Structure of Scientific Revolutions. Chicago: University of Chicago Press.
Kuhn, T.
   2001 Objectivity, Value Judgment and Theory Choice. *In* Philosophy of Science: Contemporary Readings, Y. Balashov, ed., pp. 421–436. Florence: Routledge.
Küng, H.
   2008 On Being a Christian. New York: Bantam Books.
Lacan, J.
   1966 Ecrits [Writings]. Paris: Seuil.
Laing, R.
   1998a The Divided Self, vol. 1 of The Selected Works of R.D. Laing. London: Routledge.

1998b Reason and Violence, vol. 3 of The Selected Works of R.D. Laing. London: Routledge.

1998c Sanity and Madness in the Family, vol. 4 of the Selected Works of R.D. Laing. London: Routledge.

1998d The Politics of the Family, vol. 5 of the Selected Works of R.D. Laing. London: Routledge.

Lakatos, I.

1970 Falsification and the Methodology of Scientific Research Programmes. *In* Criticism and the Growth of Knowledge, I. Lakatos, and A. Musgrave, eds., pp. 91–196. Cambridge: Cambridge University Press.

Landes, D.

1998 The Wealth and Poverty of Nations: Why Some are so Rich and Some so Poor. New York: Norton.

Lanfant, M.F.

1981 Introduction: Tourism in the Process of Internationalization. International Social Science Journal 32:1–30.

2007 Constructing a Research Project: From Past Definite to Future Perfect. *In* The Study of Tourism: Anthropological and Sociological Beginnings, D. Nash, ed., pp. 122–135. Oxford: Elsevier.

Lanfant, M.F., J. Allcock, and E.M. Bruner, eds.

1995 International Tourism: Identity and Change. London: Sage.

Lanquar, R., and Y. Raynouard

1995 Le tourisme social et associatif [Social and Association Tourism] (5ᵗʰ ed.). Paris: Presses Universitaires de France.

Lash, S., and J. Urry

1987 The End of Organized Capitalism. Madison: The University of Wisconsin Press.

Lasswell, H.

1950 Politics: Who Gets What, When, How. New York: P. Smith.

1952 The Political Writings of Harold D. Lasswell. Glencoe: The Free Press.

Lasswell, H., N. Leites, and Associates

1968 Language of Politics: Studies in Quantitative Semantics. Cambridge: MIT Press.

Le, V. T.

No Date. Emigrants and the Problems of Development in a Large City such HCMC. Mimeograph no. VIE 95/004.

Lee, C.K., Y.K. Lee, and B. Lee

2005 Korea's Destination Image Formed by the 2002 World Cup. Annals of Tourism Research 31:839–858.

Leheny, D.

1995 A Political Economy of Asian Sex Tourism. Annals of Tourism Research 22:367–384.

Leiper, N.
  2007 Why "the tourism industry" is Misleading as a Generic Expression: The Case for the Plural Variation, "Tourism Industries". Tourism Management 29:237–251.
Lengkeek, J.
  2009 Tourism Studies in Belgium and in the Netherlands. *In* The Sociology of Tourism. European Origins and Developments, G. Dann, and G. Parrinello, eds., pp. 274–298. Bingley: Emerald.
Lenin, V.
  1965 Imperialism, the Highest Stage of Capitalism. Beijing: China Books.
Leung, P.
  2003 Sex and Tourism: The Case of Cambodia. *In* Sex and Tourism. Journeys of Romance, Love and Lust, Th. Bauer, and B. McKercher, eds., pp. 181–195. Oxford: The Haworth Hospitality Press.
Levinson, S.
  1998 Written in Stone: Public Monuments in Changing Societies. Durham: Duke University Press.
Lévi-Strauss, C.
  1948 Social Structure. *In* Anthropology, A. Krober, ed. (pp. 50–108. 2nd ed.). New York: Harcourt, Brace & Co.
  1956 Race and History. *In* The Race Question in Modern Science. Paris: UNESCO.
  1958 Anthropologie Structurale [Structural Anthropology]. Paris: Plon.
  1962 Le Totemisme aujourd'hui [Totemism]. Paris: Presses Universitaires de France.
  1964 Le cru et le cuit [The Raw and the Cooked]. Paris: Plon.
  1966a The Savage Mind. Chicago: University of Chicago Press.
  1966b Du miel aux cendres [From Honey to Ashes]. Paris: Plon.
  1968a Tristes Tropiques [Tristes Tropiques]. Paris: Plon.
  1968b L'Origine des Manières de Table [The Origin of Table Manners]. Paris: Plon.
  1969 The Elementary Structures of Kinship. London: Eyre & Spottiswood.
  1971 L'Homme Nu [The Naked Man]. Paris: Plon.
  1973 Anthropologie Structurale Deux [Structural Anthropology Volume Two]. Paris: Plon.
Lew, A.
  2000 China: A Growth Engine for Asian Tourism. *In* Tourism in South and Southeast Asia, C.M. Hall, and S. Page, eds., pp. 268–284. Oxford: Butterworth-Heinemann.
Liebscher, D.
  2005 La Obra Nacional Dopolavoro fascista y la NS-Gemeinschaft "Kraft durch Freude". Las relaciones entre las políticas sociales italiana y alemana desde 1925 a 1939 [The Fascist Institution *Dopolavoro* and the Nazi Institute *Kraft durch Freude*. Links between Italian and German social policies 1925–1939]. Historia Social 52.

Limerick, P.
  1987 The Legacy of Conquest: The Unbroken Past of the American West. New York: Norton.
Lin, C.H.
  2004 Periphery Imbalance in Tourism Development: The Case of Taiwan. Tourism Analysis 9:285–298.
Lindzen, R.
  2010 Climate Science in Denial. The Wall Street Journal, April 22.
Linebaugh, P.
  1977 The Tyburn Riot against the Surgeons. *In* Albion's Fatal Tree: Crime and Society in Eighteenth-Century England, E.P. Thompson, D. Hay, P. Linebaugh, and J. Rule, eds., pp. 82–104. Harmondsworth: Peregrine Books.
Loftus, E., and K. Ketchum
  1996 The Myth of Repressed Memory. New York: St. Martin's Press.
Loker-Murphy, L.
  1995 Young Budget Travelers: Backpackers in Australia. Annals of Tourism Research 22:819–843.
Löfgren, O.
  1999 On Holiday: A History of Vacationing. Berkeley: University of California Press.
Lomborg, B.
  2001 The Skeptical Environmentalist: Measuring the Real State of the World. Cambridge: Cambridge University Press.
  2007 Cool It: The Skeptical Environmentalist's Guide to Global Warming. New York: Viking, Kindle Edition.
  2009 Time for a Smarter Approach to Global Warming. The Wall Street Journal, December 14.
Lomborg, B. ed.
  2009 Global Crises, Global Solutions. (2nd ed.). Cambridge: Cambridge University Press.
MacCannell, D.
  1976 The Tourist: A New Theory of the Leisure Class. New York: Schocken Books.
  1984 Baltimore in the Morning... After: On the Forms of Post-Nuclear Leadership. Diacritics 14:31–46.
  1986 Keeping Symbolic Interaction Safe from Semiotics: A Response to Harman. Symbolic Interaction 9:161–168.
  1987a Marilyn Monroe was not a Man. Diacritics 17:114–127.
  1987b "Sex Sells": Comment on Gender Images and Myth in Advertising. *In* Marketing and Semiotics: New Directions in the Study of Signs for Sale, D. Umiker-Sebeok, ed., pp. 521–532. Amsterdam: Mouton de Gruyter.
  1989a Faking It; Comment on Face-Work in Pornography. American Journal of Semiotics 6:153–174.
  1989b Semiotics of Tourism. New York: Pergamon Press.

1990a The Descent of the Ego. *In* Beyond Goffman: Studies in Communication, Institutions and Social Interaction, S. Riggins, ed., pp. 19–40. New York: Mouton de Gruyter.
1990b Working in Other Fields. *In* Authors of Their Own Lives: Intellectual Autobiographies by Twenty American Sociologists, B. Berger, ed., pp. 165–189. Berkeley: University of California Press.
1992a Empty Meeting Grounds: The Tourist Papers. London: Routledge.
1992b Landscaping the Unconscious. *In* The Meaning of Gardens, M. Francis, and R.T. Hester, eds., pp. 94–102. Cambridge: The MIT Press.
1993 Democracy's Turn: On Homeless Noir. *In* Shades of Noir: A Reader, J. Copjec, ed., pp. 279–297. New York: Verso.
1999a The Tourist: A New Theory of the Leisure Class. Berkeley: University of California Press.
1999b "New Urbanism" and its Discontents. *In* Giving Ground. The Politics of Propinquity, J. Copjec, and M. Sorkin, eds., pp. 106–130. London: Routledge.
2001a Tourist Agency. Tourist Studies 1:23–37.
2001b Remarks on the Commodification of Cultures. *In* Hosts and Guests Revisited: Tourism Issues of the 21st Century, V. Smith, and M. Brent, eds., pp. 380–390. New York: Cognizant.
2002 The Ego Factor in Tourism. Journal of Consumer Research 29:146–151.
2005 Silicon Values: Miniaturization, Speed and Money. *In* Seductions of Place: Geographical Perspectives on Globalization and Touristed Landscapes, C. Cartier, and A. Lew, eds., pp. 91–102. London: Routledge.
2008 Dean MacCannell <http://lda.ucdavis.edu/people/websites/maccannell.html> (27 November 2008).
MacCannell, D., and J. MacCannell
1982 The Time of the Sign: A Semiotic Interpretatio0n of Modern Culture. Bloomington: Indiana University Press.
1993a Violence, Power and Pleasure: A Revisionist Reading of Foucault from the Victim's Perspective. *In* Up against Foucault, C. Ramazanoglu, ed., pp. 203–238. London: Routledge.
1993b Social Class in Postmodernity: Simulacrum or Return of the Real. *In* Forget Baudrillard?, C? Rojek, and B. Turner, eds., pp. 124–145. London: Routledge.
Mackay, K.
2005 Is a Picture Worth a Thousand Words? Snapshots from Tourism Destination Image Research. *In* Tourism Development: Issues for a Vulnerable Industry, J. Aramberri, and R. Butler, eds., pp. 44–65. Clevedon: Channel View.
Malia, M., and T. Emmons
2006 History's Locomotives: Revolutions and the Making of the Modern World. New Haven: Yale University Press.
Mankiw, N.
2002 Macroeconomics (3rd ed.). New York: Worth.

Mann, T.
1996 The Magic Mountain. New York: Vintage Books.
Maoz, D., and Z. Bekerman
2010 Searching for Jewish Answers in Indian Resorts: The Postmodern Traveler. Annals of Tourism Research 37:423–439.
Marcuse, H.
1955 Eros and Civilization: A Philosophical Inquiry into Freud. Boston: Beacon Press.
1966 One Dimensional Man: Studies in the Ideology of Advanced Industrial Society. Boston: Beacon Press.
Marwick, A.
1998 The Sixties. Oxford: Oxford University Press.
Marx, K.
1904 A Contribution to the Critique of Political Economy. Chicago: Charles Kerr.
1972 Das Kapital: Erster Band [Capital. Volume 1]. In Marx und Engels Gesamtausgabe (MEW), Band 23. Berlin: Dietz.
Mauss, M.
1970 The Gift: Forms and Functions of Exchange in Archaic Societies. London: Taylor & Francis.
McCabe, S.
2002 The Tourist Experience and Everyday Life. In The Tourist as a Metaphor of the Social World, G. Dann, ed., pp. 61–76. Wallingford: CABI.
McCabe, S., and E. Stokoe
2004 Place and Identity in Tourists' Accounts. Annals of Tourism Research 31:601–622.
McClain, L.
2002 Japan: A Modern History. New York: Norton.
McIver, T.
1999 The End of the World: An Annotated Bibliography. Jefferson: McFarl.
McKenna, K., and J. Barg
2000 Plan 9 From Cyberspace: The Implications of the Internet for Personality and Social Psychology. Personality and Social Psychology Review 4:57–75.
McKhann, Ch.
2001 The Good, The Bad and The Ugly: Observations and Reflections on Tourism Development in Lijiang, China. In Tourism, Anthropology and China, Ch.B. Tan, S. Cheung, and Y. Hui, eds., pp. 147–166. Bangkok: White Lotus Press.
McLeod, M., and T. Nguyen
2001 Culture and Customs of Vietnam. Westport: Greenwood Press.
Mead, M.
1928 Coming of Age in Samoa: A Psychological Study in Primitive Youth for Western Civilization. New York: Blue Ribbon Books.
Meadows, D., D. Meadows, J. Randers, and W. Behrens, III
1972 The Limits to Growth. London: Universe Books.

Mendelsohn, R.
  2006 A Critique of the Stern Report. Regulation Winter 2006–2007, pp. 42–46.
Merriam-Webster
  2002 Webster's Third New International Dictionary, Unabridged <http:// unabridged.merriam-webster.com. >.
Merrick, A., and G. Parker
  2004 Cecil McBee Makes a Name for Himself in Japan—and Sues. The Wall Street Journal, October 1.
Micklethwait, J., and A. Wooldridge
  2000 A Future Perfect. The Challenge and Hidden Promise of Globalization. New York: Crown Business.
Milman, A., and A. Pizam
  1987 Social Impacts of Tourism on Central Florida. Annals of Tourism Research 5:191–204.
Minnaert, L., R. Maitland, and G. Miller
  2009 Tourism and Social Policy: The Value of Social Tourism. Annals of Tourism Research 36:316–334.
Mitchell, J.
  1974 Psychoanalysis and Feminism. New York: Pantheon.
  1984 Women: The Longest Revolution: Essays on Feminism, Literature and Psychoanalysis. London: Virago.
More, T.
  2001 Utopia (vol. 35, Part 3). The Harvard Classics <http://www.bartleby.com/ 36/3/>.
Morgan, N., and A. Pritchard
  1998 Tourism Promotion and Power: Creating Images, Creating Identities. Chichester: Wiley.
  2000 Advertising in Tourism and Leisure. Oxford: Butterworth-Heinemann.
  2002 Contextualizing Destination Branding. In Destination Branding: Creating the Unique Destination Proposition, N. Morgan, A. Pritchard, and R. Pride, eds., pp. 59–79. Oxford: Butterworth-Heinemann.
Morris, I.
  1969 Introduction, Notes and Appendixes. In The Life of an Amorous Woman and Other Writings, I. Saikaku, ed., pp. 1–24. New York: New Directions.
  1994 The World of the Shining Prince. Court Life in Ancient Japan. Tokyo: Kodansha International.
  2004 Aspects of The Tale of Genji. Broomall: Chelsea House.
Mote, F.
  2003 Imperial China (900–1800). Cambridge: Harvard University Press.
Mowforth, M.
  1997 Tourism and Sustainability. London: Routledge.

Mowforth, M., and I. Munt
  2003 Tourism and Sustainability: Development and New Tourism in the Third World. London: Routledge.
Munt, I.
  1994 The Other Postmodern Tourism: Culture, Travel and the New Middle Classes. Theory, Culture, and Society 11:101–123.
Murasaki, Sh.
  1960 The Tale of Genji. New York: Modern Library.
Murphy, L.
  2001 Exploring Social Interactions of Backpackers. Annals of Tourism Research 28:50–67.
Murphy, P.
  1985 Tourism: A Community Approach. London: Routledge.
Nairn, T.
  1982 The Break-Up of Britain: Crisis and Neo-Nationalism (2nd ed.). London: Verso.
Nash, D.
  1996 Anthropology of Tourism. New York: Pergamon.
Nash, D., and V. Smith
  1991 Anthropology and Tourism. Annals of Tourism Research 18:12–25.
Nguyen, V.
  1997 Prostitution in a Liberalizing Vietnam. The Economy, Hierarchy and Geography of Pleasure. Paper presented at the ASPAC Conference <http://www.uri.edu/artsci/wms/hughes/vietn.htm> (12 May 2004).
Nicholson, L.
  2001 India. Washington, DC: National Geographic Traveler.
Nordhaus, W.
  2005 The *Stern Review* on the Economics of Climate Change <http://nordhaus.econ.yale.edu/SternReviewD2.pdf> (20 May 2009).
Nordhaus, W., and J. Tobin
  1972 Is Growth Obsolete? New York: Columbia University Press.
Noronha, F.
  1999 Culture Shocks. Focus (Spring):4–5.
Nozick, R.
  2001 Invariances. The Structure of the Objective World. Cambridge: Harvard University Press.
Nye, J.
  2004 Soft Power. The Means to Success in World Politics. New York: Public Affairs.
Oakes, T.S.
  1995 Tourism in Guizhou: the Legacy of Internal Colonialism. *In* Tourism in China: Geographical, Political and Economic Perspectives, A. Lew, and S. Yu, eds., pp. 203–222. Boulder: Westview Press.

1996 Tourism and Modernity in China. London: Routledge.
O'Barr, M.
1994 Culture and the Ad. Exploring Otherness in the World of Advertising. Boulder: Westview Press.
OCC (Office of Climate Change)
2010 Stern Team <http://www.occ.gov.uk/activities/stern.htm> (10 March 2010).
OECD (Organization for Economic Cooperation and Development)
2009 Society at a Glance. Chapter 2: Special Focus: Measuring Leisure in OECD Countries <http://www.oecd.org/dataoecd/36/43/42675407.pdf> (27 January 2010).
Ooi, N., and J. Laing
2010 Backpacker Tourism: Sustainable and Purposeful Investigating the Overlap between Backpacker Tourism and Volunteer Tourism Motivations. Journal of Sustainable Tourism 18:191–206.
Oppermann, M.
1998 Sex Tourism and Prostitution. Aspects of Leisure, Recreation, and Work. New York: Cognizant.
Orenstein, P.
2001 Parasites in Prêt-à-Porter are Threatening Japan's Economy. The New York Times Magazine, July 1.
Orhant, M.
News/Netherlands: Prostitution Legalized in Netherlands from October 1 <http://fpmail.friends-partners.org/pipermail/stop-traffic/2000-October/000196.html> (9 June 2004).
Ortega y Gasset, J.
1957 La rebelión de las masas [The Rebellion of the Masses] (33rd ed). Madrid: Revista de Occidente.
Overy, R.
2004 The Dictators. Hitler's Germany, Stalin's Russia. New York: Norton.
Pack, S.
2004 Tourism and Dictatorship: Europe's Peaceful Invasion of Franco's Spain. New York: Palgrave McMillan.
Page, S.
2001 Gateways, Hubs and Transport Interconnections in Southeast Asia: Implications for Tourism Development in the Twenty-First Century. *In* Interconnected Worlds: Tourism in Southeast Asia, P. Teo, T.C. Chang, and K.G. Ho, eds., pp. 84–102. Kidlington: Elsevier.
Pan, S.
2002 Three "Red Light Districts" in China. Executive Summary in English of the Book "Cun Zai Yu Huang Miu"—Zhong Guo Di Xia Xing Chan Ye Kao Cha. Shanghai: Qunyan Publishing House.

Papadopoulos, N., and L. Heslop
  2002 Country Equity and Country Branding: Problems and Prospects. Journal of
    Brand Management 9:294–314.
Papatheodorou, A.
  2001 Why People Travel to Different Places. Annals of Tourism Research 28:
    164–179.
Pareto, V.
  1935 The Mind and Society. New York: Harcourt, Brace.
Park Douglas, A.
  2004 The Japanese Fashion Experience: Morbid Outlook <http://www.
    morbidoutlook.com/fashion/articles/2000_11_japanese.html> (1 December 2004).
Parker, G.
  1997 The Thirty Years' War (2nd ed). New York: Routledge.
Parsons, T.
  1937 The Structure of Social Action: A Study in Social Theory with Special
    Reference to a Group of Recent European Writers. New York: McGraw-Hill.
  1991 The Social System (2nd ed.). London: Routledge.
Pearce, P., and F. Foster
  2007 A "University of Travel": Backpacker Learning. Tourism Management
    28:1285–1298.
Pearce, P., and U.-I. Lee
  2004 Developing the Travel Career Approach to Tourist Motivation. Journal of
    Travel Research 43:226–237.
Perrotta, C.
  2004 Consumption as an Investment: The Fear of Goods from Hesiod to Adam
    Smith. London: Routledge.
Peters, F.
  1994 The Hajj: The Muslim Pilgrimage to Mecca and the Holy Places. Princeton:
    Princeton University Press.
Pi-Sunyer, O., R. Brooke Adams, and M. Daltabuit
  2001 Tourism on the Maya Periphery. In Hosts and Guests Revisited: Tourism
    Issues of the 21st Century, V. Smith, and M. Brent, eds., pp. 122–140. New
    York: Cognizant.
Pike, S.
  2004a Destination Brand Positioning Slogans: Towards the Development of a Set
    of Accountability Criteria. Acta Turistica 16:102–124.
  2004b Destination Marketing Organisations. Oxford: Elsevier Science.
  2005 Tourism Destination Branding Complexity. Journal of Product & Brand
    Management 14:258–259.
  2007 Repeat Visitors: An Exploratory Investigation of RTO Responses. Journal
    of Travel & Tourism Research (Spring):1–13.
  2008 Destination Marketing. Burlington: Butterworth-Heinemann.

Pinker, S.
1997 How the Mind Works. New York: Norton.
Pizam, A. ed.
2005 The International Encyclopedia of Hospitality Management. London: Butterworth-Heinemann.
Pla, J.
2006 La Segunda República Española: una crónica 1931–1936 [The Second Spanish Republic. A Chronicle 1931–1936]. Barcelona: Destino.
Plog, S.
2003 Leisure Travel: A Marketing Handbook. New York: Prentice Hall.
Polanyi, K.
1957 Aristotle Discovers Economics. *In* Trade and Market in the Early Empires; Economies in History and Theory, K. Polanyi, C. Arensberg, and H. Pearson, eds., pp. 71–92. Glencoe: The Free Press.
1968 Primitive, Archaic, and Modern Economies; Essays of Karl Polanyi. New York: Anchor Books.
Popper, K.
1980 The Logic of Scientific Discovery. London: Routledge.
Postman, N.
1985 Amusing Ourselves to Death: Public Discourse in the Age of Show Business. New York: Viking.
Prendergast, M.
1996 Victims of Memory: Incest Accusations and Shattered Lives. Hinesburg: Upper Access Books.
Pretes, M.
2003 Tourism and Nationalism. Annals of Tourism Research 30:125–142.
Prideaux, B., and C. Cooper
2002 Marketing and Destination Growth: A Symbiotic Relationship or Simple Coincidence? Journal of Vacation Marketing 9:35–48.
Pro-Poor Tourism Partnership (PPT)
2010 What is PPT? <http://www.propoortourism.org.uk/what_is_ppt.html.> (25 March 2010).
Proust, M.
1982 Swan's Way. Volume 1 of Remembrance of Things Past. New York: Viking.
Pussard, H.
2005 '50 Places Rolled Into 1': The Development of Domestic Tourism at Pleasure Grounds in Inter-War England. *In* Histories of Tourism: Representation, Identity and Conflict, pp. 195–210. Clevedon: Channel View.
Rao, N.
2002 The Dark Side of Tourism and Sexuality: Trafficking of Nepali Girls for Indian Brothels. *In* Sex and Tourism. Journeys of Romance, Love and Lust, Th. Bauer, and B. McKercher, eds., pp. 155–165. Oxford: Haworth Hospitality Press.

Raguraman, K.
  1998 Troubled Passage to India. Tourism Management 24:533–544.
Rea, M.
  2000 A *Furusato* Away from Home. Annals of Tourism Research 27:638–660.
Reed, N.
  2001 The Caste War of Yucatan (2nd ed). Stanford: Stanford University Press.
Reichel, A., G. Fuchs, and N. Uriely
  2009 Israeli Backpackers: The Role of Destination Choice. Annals of Tourism Research 36:222–246.
Reisinger, Y., and C. Steiner
  2006 Reconceptualizing Object Authenticity. Annals of Tourism Research 33:65–86.
Richards, G., and J. Wilson, eds.
  2008 The Global Nomad: Backpacker Travel in Theory and Practice. Clevedon: Channel View.
Richardson, B.
  2005 Longitude and Empire. How Captain Cook's Voyages Changed the World. Vancouver: UBC Press.
Richter, L.
  1989 The Politics of Tourism in Asia. Honolulu: University of Hawaii Press.
  2007 Democracy and Tourism: Exploring the Nature of an Inconsistent Relationship. *In* Tourism and Politics: Global Frameworks and Local Realities, P. Burns, and M. Novelli, eds., pp. 17–38. Oxford: Elsevier.
Riesman, D., N. Glazer, and R. Denney
  1950 The Lonely Crowd, A Study of the Changing American Character. New Haven: Yale University Press.
Riley, P.
  1988 Road Culture of International Long-Term Budget Travelers. Annals of Tourism Research 15:313–328.
Rinschede, G.
  1992 Forms of Religious Tourism. Annals of Tourism Research 19:51–67.
Rodrik, D.
  1999 The New Global Economy and Developing Countries: Making Openness Work. Washington, DC: Overseas Development Council.
Romer, P.
  1989 What Determines the Rate of Growth and Technological Change? (Policy, Planning, and Research Working Papers). Washington, DC: The World Bank.
Rowbotham, S.
  1973 Woman's Consciousness, Man's World. Harmondsworth: Penguin.
Rowbotham, S., L. Segal, and H. Wainwright
  1981 Beyond the Fragments: Feminism and the Making of Socialism. Boston: Alyson Publications.

Rubin, P.
2010 Environmentalism as Religion. The Wall Street Journal, April 22.
Ryan, C.
2002 Stages, Gazes and Constructions of Tourism. *In* The Tourist Experience, C. Ryan, ed. (pp. 1–26. 2nd ed.). London: Continuum.
Ryan, C., and C.M. Hall
2001 Sex Tourism: Marginal People and Liminalities. London: Routledge.
Said, E.
1979 Orientalism. New York: Vintage Books.
1994 Culture and Imperialism. New York: Vintage Books.
1996 Peace and its Discontents: Essays on Palestine in the Middle East Peace Process. New York: Vintage Books.
2000 Out of Place: A Memoir. New York: Vintage Books.
Saikaku, I.
1969 The Life of an Amorous Woman and Other Writings. New York: New Directions Books.
Saint-Simon, L.
1857 The Memoirs of the Duke of Saint Simon: Abridged from the French, by B. St. John. Volume 1. London: Chapman & Hall.
2001 Mémoires. Extraits. Sous la direction de D. De Garidel [Selections from the Memoirs by D. De Garidel]. Paris: Plon.
Saint-Victor, H.
1961 Didascalion of Hugh of Saint Victor; A Medieval Guide to the Arts. New York: Columbia University Press.
Salmon, W.
1970 Bayes's Theorem and the History of Science. *In* Historical and Philosophical Perspectives of Science, R. Stuewer, ed., pp. 68–86. Minneapolis: University of Minneapolis Press.
Sansom, G.
1987 A History of Japan 1615–1867. Stanford: Stanford University Press.
1999 A History of Japan to 1334. Stanford: Stanford University Press.
Sartre, J.-P.
1964 Huis-Clos [Closed Door] (CD edition). Paris: Gallimard-Emen.
Scheyvens, R.
2002 Backpacker Tourism and Third World Development. Annals of Tourism Research 29:144–164.
Schmitt, J., and R. Ray
2008 International Comparisons of Quality-of-Life Indicators: The Right to Vacation: an International Perspective. International Journal of Health Services 38:21–45.
Schumacher, E.
1973 Small is Beautiful: A Study of Economics as if People Mattered. New York: Blond and Briggs.

Schumpeter, J.
1942 Capitalism, Socialism and Democracy. London: Harper & Brothers.
Schutz, A.
1973 Collected Papers I: The Problem of Social Reality. The Hague: Martinus Nijhoff.
Seabrook, J.
1996 Travels in the Skin Trade. London: Pluto Press.
Seidensticker, E.
1983 Low City, High City; Tokyo from Edo to The Earthquake: How the Shogun's Ancient Capital Became a Great Modern City, 1867–1923. San Francisco: Donald S. Ellis.
1990 Tokyo Rising: The City since the Great Earthquake. New York: Alfred A. Knopf.
Selänniemi, T.
2001 Pale Skin on the Playa del Anywhere: Finnish Tourists in the Liminoid South. *In* Hosts and Guests Revisited: Tourism Issues of the 21st Century, V. Smith, and M. Brent, eds., pp. 80–92. New York: Cognizant.
2003 On Holiday in the Liminoid Playground: Place, Time and Self in Tourism. *In* Sex and Tourism. Journeys of Romance, Love and Lust., Th. Bauer, and B. McKercher, eds., pp. 19–33. Oxford: Haworth Hospitality Press.
Sgrazzutti, J., and D. Beltrán
2005 Tiempo libre y disciplinamiento en las clases obreras italiana y alemana durante el período de entreguerras. Dopolavoro y Kraft durch Freude: un análisis comparativo [Free Time and Disciplining of the Italian and German Working Class in the Interwar Period. Dopolavoro and Kraft durch Freude: A Comparitive Analysis]. Historia Social 52.
Shannon, C., and W. Weaver
1949 The Mathematical Theory of Communication. Urbana: The University of Illinois at Urbana Press.
Sharpley, R.
1994 Tourism, Tourists and Society. Huntingdon: Elm.
2010 Tourism Development and the Environment: Beyond Sustainability? London: Earthscan.
Shaw, G., and A. Williams
2002 Critical Issues in Tourism: A Geographical Perspective. London: Blackwell.
Shovlin, J.
2008 Hume's Political Discourses and the French Luxury Debate. *In* David Hume's Political Economy, C. Wennerlind, and M. Schabas, eds., pp. 203–221. London: Routledge.
Shumway, N.
1991 The Invention of Argentina. Berkeley: University of California Press.

Sin, H.L.
2009 Volunteer Tourism: "Involve Me And I Will Learn"? Annals of Tourism Research 36:480–501.
Singer, P.
1979 Practical Ethics. Cambridge: Cambridge University Press.
Singh, S. ed.
2001 India. Melbourne: Lonely Planet.
Singh, S.
2004 India's Domestic Tourism: Chaos/Crisis/Challenge? Tourism Recreation Research 29:35–46.
Sitthirak, S.
1995 Prostitution in Thailand: A North South Dialogue on Neocolonialism, Militarism, and Consumerism. Thai Development Newsletter 27—28 <http://www.signposts.uts.edu.au/articles/Thailand/Tourism/353.html> (20 June 2004).
Smith, A.
2002 The Theory of Moral Sentiments. Cambridge: Cambridge University Press.
2007 An Inquiry into the Causes of the Wealth of Nations. Petersfield: Harriman House.
Smith, M.E.
1997 Hegemony and Elite Capital: The Tools of Tourism. *In* Tourism and Culture: An Applied Perspective, E. Chambers, ed., pp. 199–214. Albany: State University of New York Press.
Smith, S.
2005 The Geographical Structure of Canadian Tourism. *In* Tourism Development: Issues for a Vulnerable Industry, J. Aramberri, and R. Butler, eds., pp. 153–172. Clevedon: Channel View.
Smith, V. ed.
1977 Hosts and Guests: The Anthropology of Tourism. Philadelphia: The University of Pennsylvania Press.
1989 Hosts and Guests: The Anthropology of Tourism. (2nd ed.). Philadelphia: The University of Pennsylvania Press.
Smith, V., and M. Brent
2001 Introduction. *In* Hosts and Guests Revisited: Tourism Issues of the 21st Century, V. Smith, and M. Brent, eds., pp. 28–41. New York: Cognizant.
Snell, B.
1952 Der Aufbau der Sprache [The Construction of Language]. Hamburg: Claassen Verlag.
SNTO (Spanish National Tourist Organization)
2000a Catálogo de Carteles Oficiales de Turismo del Centro de Documentación Turística de España. Tomo I (1957 a 1979). [Catalogue of Official Posters from the Center for Tourist Documentation. Volume 1: 1957–1979]. Madrid: Servicio de Publicaciones del Ministerio de Economía y Hacienda.

2000b Catálogo de Carteles Oficiales de Turismo del Centro de Documentación Turística de España. Tomo II (1980 a 2000) [Catalogue of Official Posters from the Center for Tourist Documentation. Volume 1I: 1980–2000]. Madrid: Servicio de Publicaciones del Ministerio de Economía y Hacienda.

2005 Catálogo de Carteles Oficiales de Turismo (1929–1959) [Catalogue of Official Tourism Posters 1929–1959]. Madrid: Centro de Documentación Turística de España.

2007 Boletín Bibliográfico con Imagen de la Colección de Carteles de del Centro de Documentación Turística de España [Bibliographical Bulletin with Images from the Center for Tourism Documentation of Spain]. Madrid: Instituto de Estudios Turísticos.

Sofield, T.

2001 Sustainability and Pilgrimage Tourism in the Kathmandu Valley of Nepal. *In* Hosts and Guests Revisited: Tourism Issues of the 21st Century, V. Smith, and M. Brent, eds., pp. 257–274. New York: Cognizant.

2003 Empowerment for Sustainable Tourism Development. Oxford: Elsevier.

Sofield, T., and F. Li

1998 China: Tourism Development and Cultural Policies. Annals of Tourism Research 25:362–392.

Sokal, A.

1996a Transgressing the Boundaries: Toward a Transformative Hermeneutics of Quantum Gravity. Social Text 46/47:217–252.

1996b A Physicist Experiments with Cultural Studies. Lingua Franca May/ June:62–64.

Sombart, W.

1913 Der Bourgeois. Geistesgeschichte des modernen Wirtschaftsmenschen [The Bourgeois. Intellectual History of the Modern Entrepreneur]. Munich: Duncker & Humblot.

1967 Luxury and Capitalism (translated by W.R. Dittmar). Ann Arbor: The University of Michigan Press.

1976 Why is There No Socialism in the United States. New York: Sharpe.

1987 Der moderne Kapitalismus. Historisch-systematische Darstellung des gesamteuropäischen Wirtschaftslebens von seinen Anfängen bis zur Gegenwart [Modern Capitalism. Historical and Systematic Description of the Economic Life of European Economic Life from its Origins until the Present], 3 volumes. Munich: dtv.

2001 The Jews and Modern Capitalism. Kitchener: Batoche Books.

Sönmez, S., Y. Apostoloupoulos, C.H. Yu, S. Yang, A. Mattila, and L.C. Yu

2006 Binge Drinking and Casual Sex on Spring Break. Annals of Tourism Research 33:895–917.

Sørensen, A.

2003 Backpacker Ethnography. Annals of Tourism Research 30:847–867.

Sontag, S.
  2001a Against Interpretation and Other Essays. New York: Picador.
  2001b On Photography. New York: Picador.
Soto, H.
  2000 The Mystery of Capital. Why Capitalism Triumphs in the West and Fails Everywhere Else. New York: Basic Books.
Spillman, L.
  1997 Nation and Commemoration: Creating National Identities in the United States and Australia. Cambridge: Cambridge University Press.
Spivak, G.
  1988 In Other Worlds: Essays in Cultural Politics. London: Routledge.
  1999 A Critique of Post-Colonial Reason: Toward a History of the Vanishing Present. Cambridge: Harvard University Press.
Spode, H.
  2009 Tourism Research and Theory in German-Speaking Countries. *In* The Sociology of Tourism. European Origins and Developments, G. Dann, and G. Parrinello, eds., pp. 65–94. New York: Emerald.
Spreitzhofer, G.
  1998 Backpacking Tourism in South-East Asia. Annals of Tourism Research 25:979–983.
Statistics Bureau (Japan's Ministry of Internal Affairs and Communication)
  2004 Statistical Handbook of Japan 2004. Chapter 2: Population <http://www.stat.go.jp/english/data/handbook/> (10 December 2004).
Steele, P.
  1994 The Romans and Pompeii. London: Macmillan.
Steiner, C., and Y. Reisinger
  2006 Understanding Existential Authenticity. Annals of Tourism Research 33:299–318.
Stephens, B.
  2009 Swine Flu Hysteria. The Wall Street Journal, May 9.
Stern, N.
  2006 Stern Review on the Economics of Climate Change <http://www.occ.gov.uk/activities/stern.htm> (24 February 2010).
  2007 The Economics of Climate Change: The Stern Review. New York: Cambridge University Press.
Stiglitz, J.
  2002 Globalization and Its Discontents. New York: Norton.
Stonich, S.
  2000 The Other Side of Paradise. New York: Cognizant.
Swain, M.
  2005 Las Dimensiones de Género en la Investigación sobre Turismo: Temas Globales, Perspectivas Locales [Gender Dimensions of Tourism Research: Global Issues, Local Perceptions]. Politica y Sociologia 42:25–37.

Swarbrooke, J., and S. Horner
1999 Consumer Behavior in Tourism. Oxford, UK: Butterworth-Heinemann.
Swatos, W., and L. Tomasi, eds.
2002 From Medieval Pilgrimage to Religious Tourism: The Social and Cultural Economics of Piety. Westport: Praeger.
Takahashi, H., and J. Voss
2000 "Parasite Singles": A Unique Japanese Phenomenon? Japan Economic Institute   <http://www.jei.org/Archive/JEIR00/0031f.html#return1>   (18 December 2004).
Tasci, A., and W. Gartner
2005 A Framework for Creating Strategic Global Destination Brands. Proceedings of the International Conference on Destination Branding and Marketing for Regional Tourism Development, pp. 311–318, Macao, China SAR.
TAT (Tourist Authority of Thailand)
1994 History of Thailand's National Tourist Office <http://expo.nectec.or.th/tat/stable/history.html> (7 May 2004).
Tebbetts, C.
1987 Miracles on Demand. London: Westwood.
Teo, P., and S. Leong
2006 A Postcolonial Analysis of Backpacking. Annals of Tourism Research 33:109–131.
The Economist
2001 Find Bargain, Will Travel. The Economist, January 23.
The Smith Family/NATSEM Report
2001 Financial Disadvantage in Australia 1990 to 2000. The Persistence of Poverty in a Decade of Growth <http://www.smithfamily.com.au/documents/Fin_Disadv_Report_Nov_2001> (14 November 2004).
Tilly, C.
1978 From Mobilization to Revolution. Reading: Addison-Wesley.
2001 Durable Inequality. Berkeley: The University of California Press.
Tolbert, K.
2000 Japan's New Material Girls: "Parasite Singles" Put off Marriage for Good Life. The Washington Post, February 10.
Tönnies, F.
2001 Community and Civil Society. Cambridge: Cambridge University Press.
Towner, J.
1985 The Grand Tour: A Key Phase in the History of Tourism. Annals of Tourism Research 12:297–333.
Travel Images
2009 IATA Airlines Codes <http://www.travel-images.com/airline-codes.> (25 November 2009).
Trevelyan, G.
2000 A History of England. New York: Doubleday.

Tribe, J.
    2009 Philosophical Issues in Tourism. *In* Philosophical Issues in Tourism, J. Tribe, ed., pp. 3–24. Bristol: Channel View.
    2010 Tribes, Territories and Networks in the Tourism Academy. Annals of Tourism Research 31:7–33.
Trilling, L.
    2000 The Moral Obligation to be Intelligent. New York: Farrar, Strauss and Giroux.
    2008 The Liberal Imagination. New York: NYRB Classics.
Trotsky, L.
    1996 History of the Russian Revolution. New York: Pathfinder Press.
Truong, T.
    1990 Sex, Money and Morality: Prostitution and Tourism in South East Asia. London: Zed.
Turner, L., and J. Ash
    1975 The Golden Hordes: International Tourism and the Pleasure Periphery. London: Constable.
Turner, V.
    1969 The Ritual Process: Structure and Anti-structure. New York: Aldine de Gruyter.
    1973 The Center Out There: Pilgrim's Goal. History of Religions 12: 191–230.
    1974 Dramas, Fields and Metaphors: Symbolic Action in Human Society. Ithaca: Cornell University Press.
    1978 Comments and Conclusions. *In* The Reversible World, B.A. Babcock, ed., pp. 258–295. Ithaca: Cornell University Press.
    1982 From Ritual to Theater: The Human Seriousness of Play. New York: PAJ Publications.
UNWTO (United Nations World Tourism Organization)
    2005 Facts and Figures <http://www.world-tourism.org/facts/menu.html> (1 October 2005).
    2006a Tourism 2020 Vision <http://www.unwto.org/facts/eng/vision.htm.> (2 December 2007).
    2006b Tourism Highlights <http://www.unwto.org/facts/menu.html> (20 November 2008).
    2006c International Arrivals by Region of Origin and Regions of Destination <http://www.unwto.org/facts/menu.html> (22 November 2008).
    2006d Panorama Mundial y Actualidad del Turismo [World Panorama and Tourism Actuality]. Madrid: UNWTO.
    2010a International Tourist Arrivals <http://www.unwto.org/statistics/index.htm> (18 April 2010).
    2010b International Top Spenders <http://unwto.org/facts/menu.html> (18 July 2010).

Uriely, N., Y. Yonay, and D. Simchai
  2002 Backpacking Experiences: A Type and Form Analysis. Annals of Tourism Research 29:520–538.
Urry, J.
  1990 The Tourist Gaze: Leisure and Travel in Contemporary Societies. London: Sage.
  2000 Sociology beyond Societies: Mobilities for the Twenty First Century. London: Routledge.
  2003 Global Complexity. Cambridge: Polity Press.
  2007 Mobilities. Cambridge: Polity Press.
US Census Bureau
  2003 IDB Demographic Data for Cambodia <http://www.census.gov/cgi-bin/ipc/idbsum?cty = CB> (17 June 2004).
  2010 Domestic Travel by US Residents Households (2000–2006) <http://www.census.gov/compendia/statab/2010/tables/10s1225.pdf> (5 July 2010).
USA (United States of America)
  2003 The Declaration of Independence <http://www.archives.gov/national_archives_experience/charters/declaration.html> (27 November 2004).
Van den Berghe, P.
  1994 The Quest for the Other. Ethnic Tourism in San Cristobal, Mexico. Seattle: University of Washington Press.
Van Gennep, A.
  1961 The Rites of Passage. Chicago: The University of Chicago Press.
Varley, P.
  2000 Japanese Culture (4th ed.). Honolulu: University of Hawaii Press.
Veblen, T.
  2001 The Theory of the Leisure Class. New York: Modern Library.
Veijola, S., and E. Jokinen
  1994 The Body in Tourism: Theory. Culture & Society 11:125–151.
VNAT (Vietnam National Administration of Tourism)
  2004 Vietnam. Available at http://www.vietnamtourism.com. Accessed on January 31, 2004.
Vukonić, B.
  1996 Tourism and Religion. Oxford: Elsevier Science.
Wallerstein, I.
  1974 The Modern World-System: Capitalist Agriculture and the Origins of the European World-Economy in the Sixteenth Century. New York: Academic Press.
  1980 The Modern World-System II. Mercantilism and the Consolidation of the European World-Economy. New York: Academic Press, 1600–1750.
Walsh, E.
  2001 Living with the Myth of Matriarchy: The Mosuo and Tourism. In Tourism, Anthropology and China, C.B. Tan, S. Cheung, and Y. Hui, eds., pp. 93–124. Bangkok: White Lotus Press.

Wang, N.
2000 Tourism and Modernity: A Sociological Analysis. Amsterdam: Pergamon.
WCED (World Commission on Environment and Development)
1987 Our Common Future. Oxford: Oxford University Press.
Wearing, S.
1999 Volunteer Tourism: Experiences That Make a Difference. Wallingford: CABI.
2008 Pro-poor Tourism: Who Benefits? Perspectives on Tourism and Poverty Reduction. Annals of Tourism Research 35:616–618.
Wearing, S., M. McDonald, and J. Ponting
2005 Building a Decommodified Research Paradigm in Tourism: The Contribution of NGOs. Journal of Sustainable Tourism 13:424–439.
Wearing, S., and J. Ponting
2006 Reply to Jim Butcher's Response (vol. 14 no. 3) to "Building a Decommodified Research Paradigm in Tourism: The Contribution of NGOs" (vol. 13, no. 5). Journal of Sustainable Tourism 14:512–515.
Weaver, P.
2005 Sustainable Tourism. London: Butterworth-Heinemann.
Weaver, R.
1984 Ideas Have Consequences. Chicago: The University of Chicago Press.
Weber, M.
1971 Wirtschaft und Gesellschaft (Fünfte, Revidierte Auflage) [Economy and Society. 5th revised edition]. Tübingen: J.C.B. Mohr (Paul Siebeck).
1973 Gesammelte Aufsätze zur Wissenschaftslehre. 4 Auflage [Collected Essays on the Theory of Science]. Tübingen: J.C.B Mohr (Paul Siebeck).
1975 Max Weber: A Biography. New York: Wiley.
Wedgwood, C.
2005 The Thirty Years War. New York: New York Review of Books.
WEF (World Economic Forum)
2009. Travel & Tourism Competitiveness Report 2009 <http://www.weforum.org/documents/TTCR09/index.html> (18 July 2010).
Wikipedia
2010a. Madagascar <http://en.wikipedia.org/wiki/Madagascar> (20 January 2010).
2010b. Sustainability <http://en.wikipedia.org/wiki/Sustainability> (25 April 2010).
2010c. Climatic Research Unit email controversy <http://en.wikipedia.org/wiki/Climatic_Research_Unit_email_controversy> (15 May 2010).
Wilkinson, P.
2000 Globalization. In Encyclopedia of Tourism, J. Jafari, ed., pp. 254–256. New York: Routledge.
Williamson, O.
1975 Markets and Hierarchies—Analysis and Anti-trust Implications: A Study in the Economics of Internal Organisation. Glencoe: The Free Press.
World Tourism Organization (WTO)
2004 Facts & Figures. Available at http://www.world-tourism.org/facts/tmt.html. Accessed on December 10, 2006.

Wilson, D.
1997 Paradoxes of Tourism in Goa. Annals of Tourism Research 24:52–75.
Wilson, D., and D. Henley
1999 Prostitution in Thailand: Facing the Hard Facts. The Bangkok Post, December 25.
Wolf, M.
2006 Why Globalization Works. New Haven: Nota Bene.
Wolfe, M. ed.
2001 One Thousand Roads to Mecca. London: Grove Press.
World Bank
2003 Thailand at a Glance <http://www.worldbank.org/data/countrydata/aag/tha_aag.pdf> (7 July 2005).
2006 Data & Statistics <http://web.worldbank.org/external/default/main?menuPK = 64133165&pagePK = 64133485&piPK = 64133503&q = gdp&theSitePK = 239419> (10 September 2007).
2010 Kenya <http://web.worldbank.org/WBSITE/EXTERNAL/COUNTRIES/AFRICAEXT/KENYAEXTN/0,,menuPK:356516 ~ pagePK:141159 ~ piPK:141110 ~ theSitePK:356509,00.html> (18 April 2010).
Wright, W.
2001 The Wild West: The Mythical Cowboy & Social Theory. London: Sage.
WTTC (World Travel & Tourism Council)
2004 Thailand <http://wttc.org/measure/PDF/Thailand.pdf> (14 April 2005).
2005 Executive Summary: Travel & Tourism Sowing the Seeds of Growth. The 2005 Travel & Tourism Economic Research <http://wttc.org/2005tsa/pdf/Executive%20Summary%202005.pdf> (25 September 2005).
2006a Competitiveness Monitor <http://wttc.org/frameset3.htm.> (14 November 2006).
2006b World. The 2006 T&T Economic Research <http://wttc.org/2006TSA/pdf/World.pdf> (21 November 2006).
2010 T&T Economic Impact 2010. Executive Summary <http://www.wttc.org/bin/pdf/original_pdf_file/2010_exec_summary_final.pdf> (15 March 2010).
WTTC/OEF (Oxford Economic Forecasting)
2006 Methodology for Producing the T&T Simulated Satellite Accounts <http://wttc.org/2006TSA/2006percent20TSApercent20Methodology.pdf> (8 November 2006).
Yang, J.
2004 Qualitative Knowledge Capturing and Organizational Learning: Two Case Studies in Taiwan Hotels. Tourism Management 25:421–428.
Yamada, M.
1999 Parasaito Shinguru no Jidai [The Age of the Parasite Single]. Tokyo: Chikuma Shinsho.
Young, G.
1973 Tourism: Blessing or Blight. Harmondsworth: Pelican.

Zhang, W.
  1997 China's Domestic Tourism: Impetus, Development and Trends. Tourism
    Management 18:565–571.
Ziman, J.
  2000 Real Science. Cambridge: Cambridge University Press.